LOCAL GOVERNMENT IN ISRAEL

DANIEL ELAZAR & CHAIM KALCHHEIM
EDITORS

UNIVERSITY
PRESS OF
AMERICA

Lanham • New York • London

THE JERUSALEM CENTER FOR
PUBLIC AFFAIRS
CENTER FOR JEWISH
COMMUNITY STUDIES

Co-published by arrangement with The Jerusalem Center for Public Affairs/
Center for Jewish Community Studies

The writing and publication of this book was made possible through the
assistance of the Israel Ministry of Interior.

Managing Editor: Mark Ami-El

Typesetting: Custom Graphics and Publishing, Ltd., Jerusalem

Library of Congress Cataloging-in-Publication Data

Local government in Israel / edited by Daniel J. Elazar, Chaim Kalchheim.
p. cm.
Bibliography: p.
Includes indexes.
1. Local government—Israel. I. Elazar, Daniel Judah.
II. Kalchheim, Chaim.
JS7499.I8L63   1988
320.8'095694—dc 19   88–1601 CIP
ISBN 0–8191–6939–0 (alk. paper)
ISBN 0–8191–6940–4 (pbk. : alk. paper)

The school of democracy is in local self-government. For a worker to take a serious part in the life of his trade union, or for a peasant to take part in the life of his village, there is no need for higher education. The first test to be applied in judging an alleged democracy is the degree of self-governing attained by its local institutions...Only local government can accustom men to responsibility and independence, and enable them to take part in the wider life of the state.

Ignazio Silone, *School for Dictators* (1938)

ACKNOWLEDGEMENTS

With the completion of the work of the State Commission on Local Government, it was decided that a comprehensive book on local government in Israel was needed. The Jerusalem Center for Public Affairs was asked to undertake the task; this book is the result.

We would like to thank the Chairman of the Commission, Moshe Sanbar, and the Director-General of the Ministry of Interior at the time, Haim Kubersky, who encouraged and supported this initiative. We also want to thank the Ministry of Interior for providing the resources necessary and Arye Deri, Director-General; Arye Hecht, Head of the Local Government Department; Gershon Shafat, Legal Adviser; and Dov Kehat, Director of the Division of Management and Personnel in Local Government, for their review and useful comments on the manuscript, as well as Kallia Gelless, Assistant to the Head of the Local Government Department, for her assistance.

Daniel J. Elazar
Chaim Kalchheim

July 1987

TABLE OF CONTENTS — SUMMARY

TABLE OF CONTENTS

Table of Contents

Table of Contents

LIST OF TABLES, FIGURES AND MAPS

Local Government in Israel

List of Tables, Figures and Maps

PREFACE

Haim Kubersky

Many changes have taken place in the arena of local government in many countries in recent years, especially during the last decade — changes in function, structure, and in relations between the local and state governments. Some countries have attempted comprehensive reforms. For example, in Britain, whose tradition was the source of Israel's own basic principles of municipal organization, a new map of local government was created in 1974 which reflected a massive consolidation of local authorities and a drastic decrease in the total number of local authorities in the country.

The dissolution of the Greater London Council is another reflection of the strong-willed actions of the state government in that country to reorganize its system of local government. As a result, we are today witnessing the beginning of a general public debate over the impact of this type of local government reorganization in Britain and several other Western European countries.

These reforms which were implemented came about in response to the natural development of the governmental organization process, the growth of contiguous urban areas, and the economic burdens which resulted from an expanding level of public services. At times, partisan political power struggles between the ruling party and the opposition was a factor in the changes as well.

A decade ago, an experiment was begun in Israel as well to examine and study in depth the issue of local government and the relations between local government and state government. On 5 Tevet 5737 – November 26, 1976, the government of Israel established the State Commission on Local Government (the Sanbar Commission) to examine the division of functions between the state government and the local authorities, to study its financial and budgeting framework, to make recommendations concerning procedures of supervision and control, to review the various structures of local government and the overall map of local authorities, and to make recommendations regarding principles for a basic charter for local government and for making reforms in existing legislation.

During the period that the Commission was in operation it submitted twenty interim reports. Its final report was submitted in Sivan 5741 – June 1981. The State Commission on Local Government was no doubt one of the most comprehensive experiments ever attempted to reform the Israeli system of local government, to redivide functions, and to establish a new framework of relationships between the state and local governments — all with the full cooperation of the Ministry of Interior. It was only in 1985 that the Commission's report was approved by the government, with the exception of the Commission's recommendations regarding local government financing. The economic difficulties which the state has faced in recent years has made the implementation of reforms in this area more difficult. However this may only be a partial explanation and their lack of implementation may result in a degree of continued instability since they are part of a comprehensive package of recommendations which were designed to give a new direction to governmental organization in Israel in several areas. I think that another reason for government hesitancy in promptly adopting the full package of reforms involves the inertia of being rooted in ways of thinking and procedures of government and administration that were formed in the early days of the state which, although now a burden on the state, are difficult to remove in response to the changing demands of modern life.

During a debate in the Knesset in July 1949, the Mayor of Tel Aviv, M.K. Yisrael Rokach, emphatically stated: "At the same time that the Minister of Education is being given dictatorial powers, a burden of debt is being forced upon the local authorities." He charged that the state government had forced the law in question upon the local authorities in an undemocratic way and finished his speech by asking in a pained expression, "And what will be the powers of the local authorities?" The Minister of Education at the time, Zalman Shazar, replied, "Obviously an ultimate resolution of this issue can be made only in the framework of a discussion for a constitution." In the meantime, he suggested that the Ministry of Interior would represent the local authorities in order to enable the establishment and development of the school system.

Such a discussion could have taken place as well in every other area of joint state-local activity in those days. Moreover, after nearly forty years, the same discussions could be repeated today. A constitution governing these matters is still far away, maybe even more than it seemed during the first days of the state. In later years, Yisrael Rokach reached the Ministry of Interior and became the Minister of Interior. I had thought naively that in those years a daring experiment to change the situation had been underway, but I later found no trace of any daring or determination by the Ministry in this sphere.

Clearly there were crucial national reasons during the founding years of the state which necessitated the establishment of a strong central government with absolute control over all areas of life. Such control was also justified in the first decades as basic infrastructures had to be created in defense and economics, in education and scientific research, in the absorption and settlement of mass immigration in areas throughout the country, and in many other fields. In these first days of the state, only a strong central government could dictate the national priorities surrounding the establishment of the new state — the most crucial revolution in the history of the Jewish people. Indeed, the people accepted the authority and the custodianship of the founding fathers in all spheres of life. The very establishment and existence of Jewish self-governance in Israel expressed and represented the fulfillment of Jewish longing for a change in their national experience and existence. In addition to the uniqueness of the period which necessitated strong centralization and a comprehensive approach to governance, there were also political considerations in the background involving a jockeying for positions of power in the developing state. While the leadership of the central government in this crucial era was in the hands of parties affiliated with the Labor movement, the leadership of many local authorities was at the same time in the hands of other parties (i.e., Daniel Oster in Jerusalem, Yisrael Rokach in Tel Aviv, Shabtai Levi in Haifa, and Yosef Sapir in Petah Tikva). In the political climate of those days, no one was anxious to grant authority to a system that was led by another camp.

Although in later years there was increased political identification between the ruling circles that lead the central government and those that ruled major cities (Gershon Agron and Mordechai Ish-Shalom in Jerusalem, Yosef Namir and Yehoshua Rabinovitch in Tel Aviv, Abba Kushi in Haifa), this did not result in any greater readiness to redefine and redivide functions and powers between state and local governments. In fact, this development, in which all the circles of political power in the state, in the Zionist movement, in the Labor movement, and in the local authorities were in the hands of one central camp, served to reinforce a system of governmental patriarchy in which all the circles coordinated willingly with each other in harmony, where government decisions were made by discussion within the one supreme party authority which was common to all circles.

After the Six-Day War of 1967, internal problems began to play a more prominent role in the lives of the state's citizens and in framing their demands before governing bodies. The shock surrounding the Yom Kippur War of 1973 weakened a number of old norms including the general degree of trust in the state's institutions, and discussion and protest began to be heard concerning the exclusivity of its authority. This new trend found political expression in both the local and statewide spheres. The political leadership of local government in Israel became much more heterogeneous. Local lists were established which gained control in a number of small and medium-sized local authorities. This particular development was just one expression of a movement of citizen interest from comprehensive state problems to environmental and local problems. It is not merely coincidental that the law authorizing the direct personal election of mayors was enacted in the years following the Yom Kippur War. This personally elected mayor was also given ongoing executive authority and in the political system of Israel he is the only elected official that derives his public authority directly from the citizenry.

All of these factors brought about increasing changes in the status of local government. By the end of the 1970s and in the 1980s, local governments were better able to define their problems, to increase their own local efforts, and they also began a process of integrating local government personalities into the Knesset and the Cabinet. Local authorities began to contribute more and more in certain spheres of expertise in which they had a relative advantage. This was in contrast to a state government which is built on a rigid departmental structure with all of the problems that are characteristic to such structures, such as the need for interministerial coordination and communication which is necessary for accomplishing tasks which are beyond the jurisdiction of a single ministry. In a local authority there is now an integration of disciplines, powers and functions under the leadership of the mayor who represents this integration.

All these developments clearly necessitate a redivision of functions, jurisdictions and taxing powers, and a restructuring of the system of supervision and control which would grant greater administrative and operational autonomy to the local government, which is the basic stratum of elected government and which has the most direct contact with the citizenry.

There have been some significant beginnings in this direction with the evidence already becoming apparent in the field, although not due to any constitutional changes or on the basis of any announced national programs or plans. The Project Renewal enterprise is one expression of this trend. Other positive trends can be found in the increase in local self-reliance which leads to increasing local responsibility and an evolution from passivity to more active initiating and contributing roles. For example, in 1986 local government participation in the funding of their own budgets averaged 50 percent, while in 1979 this figure had only been 29 percent, a fact which has resulted in a marked decrease in state government participation in the budgets of local authorities. The state government is also more ready (although not yet in its day-to-day behavior and not in all areas) to bless this development.

Under the economic recovery plans of recent years, the local authorities were integrated into the comprehensive national effort and contributed their share in limiting their services and reducing their costs of administration, in addition to increasing their financial contribution to local service delivery systems. The largest service delivery organization in the state continued to deliver legally mandated services to the population while undergoing contraction, and without reaching a crisis. This phenomenon deserves special recognition in light of the many other crises which faced the state in various areas of its life.

In recent years, renewed experiments were attempted to halt the increase in centralization of authority and to try to increase the autonomy of local government. However, while speaking of decentralization, the state actually acted in centralizing ways, necessitated by the need to deal with high inflation and the economic crisis. There is a danger that the economic situation will be used beyond what is necessary in order to curb required developments in the direction of decentralization, just as at the beginning of the state the security situation was used as justification for the centralized approach and there was later little readiness to give this up willingly.

When local authorities have difficulties, some use this as an excuse to curb moves toward decentralization. We should warn against this danger, which does not serve the state and its needs.

Along with a demand to correct the defects and flaws that occur in the central government as well, the old approach of total custodianship of local government by the state government must disappear from our practice of governance. This approach, which was carried on for too many years, is part of the cause of the problems we face today. Our central government is built in a federative structure. Its parts have difficulty when trying to join together in order to accomplish major national or regional tasks (excluding security problems and situations of economic emergency). The local authority has now matured enough to be integrated into the framework of the state and to undertake more responsibility for the ongoing life and the development of new areas within its jurisdiction.

The local authority is at a special advantage in fulfilling this role, since it can act as an integrative basin into which drains all of the problems regarding the locality, headed by a major who derives his authority from the citizens who elected him directly. The state government should recognize the advantage of the special characteristics of local government and should limit itself to certain central tasks: legislation, planning, direction, control, instruction and supervision. It should concentrate on fulfilling the functions of a state headquarters and create the tools necessary for these functions. In this way we will be better able to activate the passive citizen, to utilize the contributions of each community, and to encourage the initiative, variety and self-reliance which is the lifeblood of every society.

At the eighth countrywide Conference on Local Government and Administration which took place in Jerusalem in June 1986, Professor Yehezkiel Dror devoted his lecture to "Local Government in Israel and Improving the Ability to Rule." Among other things, he stated that "almost the only area in which improvements in the ability to rule are occurring is that of local government as expressed by the successful transfer to the system of direct election of mayors, the rise of promising leadership, and a marked increase in public initiative." However, he added, "the defects in local government are many as well, but relatively it functions as a pilot to improve governance in general. Because of this, without neglecting the great need for improving the state government, we should regard the expansion of the spheres of local government activity as an important way to deal with major problems." He also regarded local government as the preferred framework within which to deal with such crucial problems as human relations, including relations between religious and non-religious and Jews and Arabs; the absorption of immigrants; culture and values; the quality of life; and the strengthening of democracy by applying it in a framework in which the individual could have real influence. Obviously, to achieve all this will necessitate "real improvements in the quality of local government — professionalization of its personnel, training for elected officials, automation, working through headquarters, and intensive, yet controlled, progress towards participatory democracy on the communal level." The Ministry of Interior decided upon the publication of this book after the State Commission on Local Government (Sanbar Commission) submitted its final report. It is co-edited by Professor Daniel J. Elazar, President of the Jerusalem Center for Public Affairs and Director of the Institute for Local Government at Bar-Ilan University, who was also a member of the Commission, and by Dr. Chaim Kalchheim, who has previously written a comprehensive work on the relationships between the local authority and the government ministries.

This is the first attempt of its kind, both in its expression and in the issues discussed, to provide the elements of the local-state government relationship to academics and others in the field, with background material that will contribute to a deeper professional and public discussion of one of the basic problems of our society.

INTRODUCTION

Daniel J. Elazar

This book describes and analyzes local government and state-local relations in contemporary Israel. While it focuses on the contemporary scene, it is written with a sense of the development of local government in the country since modern institutions were introduced in the middle of the nineteenth century and particularly since the inauguration of the Zionist enterprise in the latter years of that century.

While Israel is indivisible as a state, it is simultaneously a compound of communities, including local communities. Because of its development as a new society through the Zionist enterprise, Israel was created out of a series of local foundings which were only subsequently formed into a single countrywide community and still later, into a state. This is true whether we are speaking of:

1) the first moshavot founded by the covenanting of their first settlers in the last generation of the nineteenth century,
2) the kibbutzim and moshavim, the first of which were established by compact in the years just prior to World War I,
3) the cities, most of which were founded as separate neighborhoods even before the neighborhoods were compounded into cities, and finally
4) the regional councils which are federations of rural settlements.

In this respect, Israel is more like Switzerland and the United States, a state that has grown out of its local communities rather than one that was created to subordinate them. Moreover, as a new society, local autonomy in Israel was not a matter of vested feudal privileges which interfered with the development of democratic republicanism as was the case in most of Europe. Quite to the contrary, the localities were from the very first the principal repositories of republican government in its most democratic form. There is hardly a local authority in Israel, rural or urban, that did not have as its first form of government the general meeting, the assembly of all of its citizens (usually known as members since the

organization was that of a cooperative association) as the highest
organ of policy-making and the ultimate civil authority.

Thus, Israel has had no need to strengthen the central authority in order to promote democracy, as was the case in most of modern Europe. In fact, most of the arguments with regard to centralization or decentralization in Israel hold to the view that true
democracy is best attained by vesting more powers in the local
authorities and that it is only the necessities of governing a modern state and particularly one serving a developing country under
siege that make centralization necessary in the first place.

This is clearly in line with the political culture which the
Jewish people have carried with them since the beginning of
Jewish history and which they have successfully applied in
practice in their own commonwealths and communities insofar
as they have been able to live as Jews. For Jews, there has never
been a legitimately hierarchical state with sovereignty lodged in
one human center. Ancient Jewry developed the notion that
sovereignty can only be vested in God and that all human
authority is delegated authority. Flowing from that was the
principle enunciated clearly in the Bible that powers are to be
divided among different departments and jurisdictions — judges
and elders, kings, priests and prophets, the nation as a whole and
its various tribes — all functioning under a common law and
constitution. This approach was institutionalized in the Jewish
political tradition which continues to influence the political
behavior of Jews even if in recent centuries it has not been the only
political tradition to influence them.

With all of that, Israel is well-known as a highly centralized
state. The roots of this centralization go back to the ideologies of its
founders, drawn from European conceptions of state sovereignty
and governance. Modern conceptions of state sovereignty developed in Europe are based upon the principle that authority in the
state must be centralized and organized hierarchically. Modern
revolutions have sought to capture the state and its apparatus for
the people and to make it responsive and perhaps even responsible
to the people. But even for the revolutionaries the state remains essentially centralized and hierarchical. According to this theory,
for a state to be properly constituted, there must be a central locus of
authority and power. Local authorities, by definition, represent the
periphery, and they and their powers are derived from the center
in every respect. The center determines what the proper state-local
relationship should be, with localities simply instruments of

central authority to the extent that the center wishes to rely upon them and trust them with responsibilities, or to devolve competences upon them.

Under the conditions of the new centralized state, local communities were ipso facto made subordinate to the state apparatus. Indeed, one of the major struggles of revolutionary Europe was to eliminate local liberties or primordial local rights on behalf of central control in the name of the new ideas of liberty, equality, fraternity, or whatever. This thrust to subordinate local governance was strengthened with the introduction of managerialism which offered a plausible justification for considering local government to be merely administration. Thus, the first step in the process was to transform the primordial commune into a "local authority"; then, with the advent of managerialism, to transform its local governance role into a matter of local administration.

While the State of Israel itself borrows heavily from the kind of state structure developed in Europe to serve the reified centralized state, in practice those who operate the governmental institutions which serve the Israeli public have not found it easy to live within such a framework because it is so at odds with the people's original political culture. Consequently, they have developed various means to circumvent the formal processes of government to establish and maintain relationships that are more in line with the political tradition with which they are comfortable.

In sum, while formal centralization is hardly foreign to Israel's experience, it is quite foreign to the genius of the population of the state. This has led to an Israel which is far less centralized than would appear at first glance. Through informal processes, local officials have been able to gain a great deal of freedom of maneuver and control over local affairs. But it does not solve the very real problems of structure, powers, and jurisdiction which must be dealt with to make possible not only greater local self-government but better cooperative relationships among entities when their leaders will feel more secure in their respective competences.

In fact, the European definition of state sovereignty need not be taken at face value. There is another approach to the problem of state-building, developed for the new societies settled by Europeans who broke away from European rule, which views the democratic state as necessarily a compound of polities. This trend found its first modern expression in the United States and it has been a key element in the development of all other new societies as well. Israel is no exception.

"New societies" are those founded by covenant or contract "from scratch" as a result of migration of self-selected populations to "virgin" territories (that is, territories perceived by the migrants to be essentially uninhabited at the time of their settlement) whose settlers underwent a frontier experience as a major part of the process of settlement. Most new societies have been founded since the beginning of the modern era in the mid-seventeenth century. Thus each in its own way began as a modern society. Consequently, new societies stand out in sharp contrast to both traditional societies and those that have undergone modernization, whether from a traditional or feudal base, by virtue of that fact. The key to their birth as modern societies from the first lies in the migration of their founders to new frontier environments where they were able to create a social order with a minimum amount of hindrance from entrenched traditional or feudal ways of the past or on the part of existing populations needing to be transformed or assimilated.

Traditional or feudal societies were built upon linkages of people, communities, or estates whose origins are lost in history and, consequently are generally accepted as organic by their members. New societies, in contrast, are constructed upon conscious (and usually historically verifiable) contractual or covenantal relationships among individuals and groups, based on some sense of national vocation that bound their founders together and in some form continues to bind subsequent generations. The founders of the new societies, in creating social and political institutions anew on the frontier, were motivated by a common sense of vocation based on ideologies or commitments they brought with them, forged in the process of nation-building, a sense of vocation that continues to serve as a shared mystique (a future-oriented myth) to inspire or justify their efforts or those of their heirs at national development. The actual creation of their civil societies was almost invariably manifested through some kind of constituting act, usually one that was concretized in documentary form. Even if no single compact was involved, the social and political organization of each new society is based on many "little" compacts or covenants, necessitated by the realities of having to consciously and formally create new settlements and institutions on virgin soil, rather than allowing them to evolve slowly over time.

In new societies, then, local and national attachments are likely to go hand in hand, having developed as part of the same conscious effort to build something new. If specific local settlements preceeded the formation of national institutions, in others the reverse was the case. Under such conditions, local attachments have functioned primarily to allow for the expression of what are, in the end, nuances of differences within the overall thrust of the nation's animating mystique. While these nuances may be crucial to those who express them and may even lead to political conflict within the new society, in fact they function within the developing consensus.

More important, local attachments may well be used as a means to accommodate such differences of emphasis in such a way as to avoid head-on clashes between their proponents that might damage the overall thrust toward national integration. Thus, local attachments in new societies support political and social integration and differentiation on a new plane, where they operate in tandem to advance the overall goals of national integration while providing vital and necessary opportunities for differentiation within the overall consensus, opportunities which, if lacking, would actually jeopardize national integration itself.

Israel is a classic example of such a new society, along with countries such as the United States, Canada, Australia and New Zealand. The development of its system of local government is an equally classic manifestation of this phenomenon.

In recognition of this characteristic of Israeli society, the appropriate constitutional model for state-local relations in Israel is not hierarchical in the sense that the local authorities are to be considered administrative arms of the central government. It is not even central-peripheral in the sense that the local authorities are defined as peripheral to the central organs of the state. The State of Israel as a whole is a mosaic compounded of state and local authorities functioning together, each with its appropriate competences, powers and tasks and each deriving its authority directly or indirectly from the people. Elected officials, whether state or local, derive their authority equally from the people with their position in the overall structure essentially related to the scope of their respective constituencies.

The state provides the framework for this mosaic and its organs are responsible for its framing functions, but within that framework the local authorities and their organs are equally responsible for their respective functions. This is not to say that the state does not or should not exercise authority over local governments under the law in a wide variety of fields, including an ultimate authority under the constitution for the specific way in which local government is constituted. What it does mean, however, is that the right of local government is an inherent right guaranteed by Israel's constitutional tradition, accepted as a right in Jewish law, and reaffirmed in practice by the reality of the founding and development of modern Israel through the Zionist enterprise, part and parcel of the compact which unites the people of the land within a body politic.

The State Commission on Local Government (1976–1980) summarized this position in a resolution (adopted on March 8, 1977) setting forth the fundamental principles guiding its work in the following manner:

The State Commission on Local Government
The Subcommittee on the Structure of Local Authorities

The Status of the Local Government in the State of Israel: Outlines
(Adopted March 8, 1977)

1. The governance system of the state is constituted by both the local and state government.
2. a. The local authorities are the elected local expression of their residents.
    b. The local authorities will be elected by their residents.
3. The aim of the local authorities is to represent their residents as well as to foster their physical, cultural and spiritual welfare while making them part of the tasks of the state.
4.* The local authorities are authorized to undertake any activity that is not prohibited them by law, but must act in accordance with the law.
5. The local authorities will have at their disposal any fiscal resources needed for fulfilling their tasks.

---

* Minority opinion — Powers of the local authority should be defined on a wide range (without cancelling the U.V.) and the local authority will be authorized to carry out any activity included in this range.

Jerusalem, 20 Adar 5737
10 March 1977

This book describes, documents, and analyzes how this works in Israel in practice.

PART I — FOUNDATIONS

Chapter 1

THE LOCAL DIMENSION IN ISRAELI GOVERNMENT AND POLITICS

Daniel J. Elazar

Israel is well-known as a state in which political power is heavily concentrated in its central institutions, both government and party. The small size of the country, its development as a result of ideologically motivated effort, and the political tradition it has inherited from both Jewish and non-Jewish sources have all coalesced to make this so. At the same time, it is a mistake to think of Israeli government as "centralized" in the usual sense of the word. Power is divided among several centers within the Israeli polity but the centers are organized on cultural-ideological rather than along territorial lines. This means that local government in Israel, which is necessarily territorially based, operates at a handicap. It is often viewed as the weakest link in the state's political system. From a power perspective, local governments are indeed subordinate to governmental and party centers, not to speak of the religious and ethnic communities, in many ways. Nevertheless, it is a mistake to underestimate either the role or influence of local government in the state.

Local government plays an important role in Israeli society, particularly in connection with the following four tasks:

1) the provision and administration of governmental services;
2) the recruitment and advancement of political leadership;
3) the fostering of channels of political communication between the governors and the governed; and
4) the maintenance of necessary or desired diversity within a small country where there are heavy pressures toward homogeneity.

All four of these tasks are of great importance in the integration of what is still a very new society of immigrants or the children of immigrants. The role played by local government in meeting the challenges they pose makes it a far more vital factor on the Israeli scene than it is often given credit for.[1]

Historical Manifestations of Territorial Democracy

If ideological democracy places a premium on doctrinal faithfulness (or what passes for it) in the attainment of true citizenship and political influence, territorial democracy places a premium for their attainment on simply living some *place* by right. In one sense, the entire Zionist endeavor is a reflection of the Jewish people's movement from ideological to territorial democracy. Zionism is a recognition that every people needs a territory of its own to survive in the contemporary world. At the same time, as we have seen, the initial Zionist efforts were based upon the notion that the chosen territory would be a minor factor in determining Jewish public policy, far less important than the various ideologically-based visions of the new society in the making. Nevertheless, even these ideological movements found it necessary to develop territorially-based means of expression in order to develop bases of operations from which to influence the whole society. The two best examples of this are the kibbutz and the religious neighborhood. Both reflect that face of territorial democracy which allows people with strong common beliefs to settle together and, through the governance of the territory upon which they are settled, to assure that their beliefs will be sufficiently dominant locally to make it possible to protect a common way of life.

Kibbutzim and religious neighborhoods not only reflect this face of territorial democracy by their very existence but go beyond that. The kibbutzim are divided among several movements, each of which has its own particular vision to protect. Similarly, religious neighborhoods tend to fall into sectarian patterns, although more of a mixture may be tolerated. For both, there has been tacit recognition by the state and society of the legitimacy of their utilization of the first face of territorial democracy and they are allowed much greater leeway than other territorial units in protecting their way of life. For example, kibbutzim maintain their own schools which are nominally part of the state education system but are left fairly well to their own devices. Residents of religious neighborhoods not only maintain their own schools in one way or another but are allowed to close off their streets to vehicular traffic on the Sabbath and holidays so as to preserve their particular religious way of life, even though there are no laws to that effect.

Territorial democracy has two faces. It can be used to secure political power or influence for specific communities which occupy specific territories or it can be used in a very neutral way to secure political power or influence for any groups which happen to be resident in a particular area at a particular time. What is common to both is the role of the territorial unit as the basis for organizing power.

Whatever face is manifested, territorial democracy is not simply the same as territoriality or the areal organization of power. Both territoriality and the areal organization of power are obviously universal. In traditional or premodern political systems they are often associated with the preservation of a predemocratic status quo whereby communities claiming to be organic in origin and character *(Gemeindschaften)* are given (or at least demand) an opportunity to exercise political power to preserve their internal character within the context of the modern state.

Territorial democracy is the form of the areal division of power that is particularly associated with popular government, instituted as a means to strengthen democratic government rather than restrict it, by providing fixed bases within which public decisions can be democratically made on an appropriate scale. It may be that it is a form particularly associated with new societies since the territorial units in a new society of necessity reflect the same general goals as the society as a whole. At most, they seek to provide expression for specific facets of those goals. Thus both the towns of Puritan Massachusetts and the agricultural settlements of pre-state Israel saw themselves as communal repositories and territorial manifestations of the highest goals of the new society in the making.[2]

Both faces of territorial democracy can be found in Israel. Indeed, though they were long submerged within the framework of ideological democracy which continues to hold virtually undisputed sway at the state level, their origins lie in the origins of the modern Yishuv itself. Today, the thrust of territorial democracy has put local government in the vanguard of political development in the country.

The Local Roots of Modern Israel

Territorially-based polities of the first kind began to develop as a matter of course as the pioneers settled in and staked claims to "turfs" of their own. The moshavot, kibbutzim and moshavim came to conceive of themselves as virtually autonomous communities in the pre-state days. Their "natural" territorialism remained within and was substantially compatible with the existing system of ideological democracy as long as the territories were populated exclusively by people with professed ideological commitments who viewed the world in the appropriate ideological categories and were satisfied to function within the overall ideological structure of the society, i.e. as members of movement and party federations.

In the late 1870s and 1880s the very first colonies, beginning with Motza and Petah Tikva, were organized by pioneers who covenanted together to create territorial units which were to be as autonomous as possible under Turkish rule, protected in their autonomy to no small extent by the Sephardic rabbinical authorities responsible for governing the Jewish millet.[3] After the turn of the century, the development of collective and cooperative settlements extended the principle of territorial democracy to another sector of the rural pioneering environment. In this perspective, Degania, the first *kvutza*, was simply another form of Jewish covenant community.[4] Since it was at this point that ideological rigor began to develop on the Israeli scene, they perforce, synthesized their drive for territoriality with the incipient ideological democracy that was developing.

Israel's cities, the embodiment of the second face of territorial democracy, began their development even before the first agricultural settlements. The first of them, the new city of Jerusalem, begun in the 1860s, was founded as a synthesis of the two faces, consisting as it did of neighborhoods created as virtually autonomous communities within the city by like-minded householders contracting together to found new settlements within an urban context. The Bokharan Quarter and Meah Shearim are two of the best-known examples of this arrangement but, in fact, until the British conquest of the city, all new neighborhoods were founded as separate associations, some as mere arrangements of convenience while others were openly dedicated to preserving a very specific and concrete way of life, much as the collective settlements were.[5]

The power of the Zionist back-to-the-land movement was such that urban pioneering was ignored or denigrated until well into the first generation of statehood. At the same time, a majority of the Jews who came to settle in the land of Israel settled in cities. At its height in the 1930s, the agricultural sector did not quite reach a third of the total Jewish population in the country. Thus urban pioneering remained an important factor in the Zionist enterprise, whether recognized as such or not. It was the first pioneering sector back during the first founding, it continued to be important in the intervening years, and became the dominant pioneering sector once again after the state was declared.

The conflict between the back-to-the-land movement and the realities of urbanization led to another tension within Israeli society regarding the character of urbanization. To the extent that attention was paid to city-building at all, it was the intention of the Zionist founders to introduce rural elements into the cityscape, to build garden cities or suburbs. At the same time, the models of city-building which were known to them were almost entirely European, whether of Eastern or Western Europe, and in both cases they represented the very antithesis of this melding of rural and urban elements. This, too, is a tension which has not been resolved.[6]

The first city consciously founded as an urban settlement without an ideological base other than the general ideology of Zionism was Tel Aviv, significantly enough founded in the same year (1909) as Degania. From the first, Tel Aviv represented territorial democracy in its most neutral sense. Whoever settled within the city limits was entitled to the rights of local citizenship and could participate in political life to the extent and in the way he or she desired (within the context and opportunities offered by the political system in general) without having to subscribe to any particular ideological or religious doctrine or formula. One result was that for years Tel Aviv went counter to the nationwide trend towards socialism to become a stronghold of the General Zionists though, as the city grew larger, its population became more mixed and diversified and the city lost even the modest ideological tinge it once had.[7]

Tel Aviv became at one and the same time the paradigm and the caricature of the Israeli city as a neutral, democratic, territorial political unit. In the 1920s and 1930s and then at an accelerating rate after 1948, other cities followed its lead. As the country's Jewish population expanded, many of the original moshavot, the agricultural colonies founded in pre-ideological days, were transformed into just such neutral territorial units as they became citified. After 1948, these were supplemented by over twenty new towns, founded to absorb the new immigrants. Taken together, these cities became the major vessels for the assimilation of the waves of mass immigration which came into the country beginning in the 1930s. Today they contain two-thirds of the country's total population.[8]

Local self-government was the first vehicle for asserting the national goals of the Zionist movement. The first Zionist colonies were created as self-governing covenant communities not dissimilar in the fundaments of their political organization from the early Puritan settlements of New England. Somewhat later, the first local governments in their present forms were organized by the Jewish pioneers under the laws of the British Mandate as the precursor of the state. They were designed to give the pioneers as much autonomy as possible while the country was still under British rule.

Historical exigencies led to the development of contemporary Israel out of local roots. Given the facts of imperial control, first under the Ottomans and then under the British, the Jews could only expand their presence on a local basis, by many local efforts or national efforts expressed locally. Both rural and urban settlement patterns reflected this reality. In both, small groups of settlers came together and organized themselves locally to undertake pioneering tasks. The local role was further stimulated by the fact that the Ottoman authorities who governed the land until 1917 saw their function as essentially custodial and oriented to maintaining minimum security; all else was left to the religio-ethnic communities to develop as they saw fit. The British authorities who came after the Turks (between 1917 and 1948) did not depart from this pattern except to make it more honest and efficient. It was left to the individual religio-ethnic communities within the country to determine the kind of public infrastructure they wanted for themselves. For the ruling powers, this was a natural and highly functional way to deal with the problem of differing ethnic groups with widely differing styles of internal organization and highly divergent expectations from the public sector.

Thus the first local governments were fostered as alternatives to foreign government and were treated by the organized Jewish community in Palestine as important elements in the drive for a Jewish state. Jewish municipalities such as Tel Aviv, local councils such as Petah Tikva, regional councils (which were federations of Jewish agricultural settlements) such as Emek HaYarden (Jordan Valley) and HaGalil HaElyon (Upper Galilee), as well as the governing committees of the kibbutzim and moshavim were all encouraged by the Zionist authorities as a means of advancing the cause of Jewish self-government. In those pre-statehood days, the Jewish local governments took on many of the responsibilities that were later to become the province of the state and provided a wide range of services which they initiated and organized in the first place. In this, they were specifically encouraged by the Mandatory government which itself maintained only the minimum of governmental services for political reasons, allowing the Jews and Arabs of what was then Palestine to determine the level of services to be provided in their own sectors.

The Arabs resisted all efforts by the British to establish local government institutions in their communities on the grounds that they would interfere with the traditional patterns of local rule, where the leading family or families maintained nearly total control over their fellow villagers. This policy meant that the Arab villages remained almost unchanged until the establishment of the State of Israel. The Israeli authorities encouraged them to acquire municipal status and the services and facilities that went with such status. As a result, the Arab villages have been undergoing modernization with regard to basic municipal functions for no more than a generation.

The Jewish sector, on the other hand, wished to rapidly develop a modern, Western-style society, with all that entailed. Indeed, because of their socialist bent, the Jewish pioneers wished to provide even more services than many individualistic societies in the West. Since neither Turkish nor British mandatory authorities were interested in meeting their needs and since the Jews were not interested in having others do for them what they believed they should do for themselves, the Zionist institutions undertook the task of providing those services. Even within the framework of the federation of parties, to no small extent the execution of this task fell upon the Jewish-sponsored local authorities which served most of the Jewish population.

Local governments also served the cause of maintaining diversity within the framework of the Zionist movement. The General Zionists and other right and center parties that were excluded from positions of power in the Histadrut-dominated, countrywide organs of the Jewish "state within a state" were able to establish power bases of their own in a number of the Jewish municipalities, which gave them a share and a stake in the upbuilding of the land. Moreover, many of the future leaders of the state took their first steps on the road to political careers in the local polities, urban or rural, especially in the kibbutzim. Finally, the very nature of the

Yishuv meant that the Jewish local governments would be central factors in the enhancement of political communication among the members of the new society. The history of local government in pre-state Israel is yet to be written, but when it is, there is no doubt that the record will show that it played an important role as a training ground for the state in the making.[9]

Even local government law in the country was generally enacted by the British Mandatory regime after the fact, that is to say, after Jewish settlers had created local institutions which then had to be somehow formalized. The regional councils, a basic element in all rural local government in Israel, are good examples of this. In the late 1920s and throughout the 1930s, in those areas where there were a sufficient number of Jewish colonies to create contiguous bands of Jewish settlement, the territorial democracy of the pioneers took on an additional form. The leaders of the various kibbutzim and moshavim in the Jordan Valley, the eastern end of the Jezreel Valley and the Huleh Valley — the three areas with both the requisite concentration of settlements and the perceived need for cooperative action — found it useful and necessary to join together and cooperate with one another for the provision of common regional services. Other clusters — two on the coastal plain, two in the Jordan Valley, and two in the Jezreel Valley — began to do so in the 1930s, creating councils on a federative basis, i.e., one representative from each settlement, and possessing only such powers as were delegated to him by the constituent settlements, which retained most powers for themselves. At first they had no legal status, but in 1941 the Mandatory government took note of those councils and promulgated a law providing for their recognition as formal local government bodies and for the establishment of others. The Yishuv utilized these regional federations of settlements to create small Jewish republics (their terminology) as a form of autonomous space within the framework of the Mandate, something which could only be done from a territorial base.[10]

The regional council idea spread, particularly after 1948, to become one of Israel's major contributions to the theory and practice of local government. Appropriately, regional federations combined the principles of territorial and ideological democracy to unite settlements within the same or similar political movements.

The regional councils, particularly the older ones among them, have retained a far greater degree of local autonomy than any other governments in Israel, partly because a number of them predate the establishment of the state and had the experience of being virtually autonomous at a time when the legitimacy of the colonial government was challenged by the indigenous inhabitants of Palestine and partly because of the special place their component units (especially the kibbutzim, but agricultural settlements in general) occupy in Israeli society. As the embodiments of the Israeli mystique they have a vital place in Israeli society which tends to reinforce their position as self-governing communities.

Simultaneously, cities like Tel Aviv created statelike service systems for their residents under the permissive British rule and with the blessings of the *Vaad HaLeumi* (Jewish National Committee). Thus even the state services of the new society had local roots to no small degree and were pyramided into countrywide programs through various kinds of contractual and federal arrangements established by the parties.

The Founding of Local Government

Formally, modern local government was first introduced in Eretz Israel in the latter days of the Ottoman Empire with the enactment of the Vilayet Law of 1864 which provided for the establishment of *nahiyas* (rural districts) throughout the country. *Nahiyas* were gradually introduced between then and World War I. These *nahiyas* were under the control of *mudirs*. Under the law each was to have a local council but few such councils were actually established. Instead, *mukhtars* were installed to replace the *sheikhs* who headed the local *hamulas*. Under the law, two *mukhtars* were to have been elected in each village along with a council of village elders *(ikhtiyariyya)* but in fact most *mukhtars* were appointed, usually after consultation with the local notables. The *mukhtar* was responsible for assessing and levying taxes among the villagers, settling local disputes, and acting as an intermediary in the relationship between the provincial administration and the village.

Initially, the Jewish moshavot were outside of this system. Indeed, they resisted attempts by the provincial administration to control them. They were successful in this regard until 1904, at which time the Ottoman provincial authorities recognized the four largest moshavot as villages, recognizing their internal

11

governance structures and accepting those elected by the village councils as the *mukhtars*. By 1914 all of the moshavot had acquired a similar status.

In the interim, the moshavot themselves organized their own self-governing institutions based upon patterns of Jewish communal self-government derived from Eastern Europe and held together by local consensus rather than external legal power. The general meeting *(assefah klalit)* was the ultimate authority in each moshava. It met several times a year. It elected an executive *(hanhalah)* annually or biannually, and in some of the larger moshavot, a council *(moetzah)* as well, to which the executive was responsible. Each executive had a chairman *(yoshev rosh)* and other officers elected from among its members. In some of the moshavot all adult members were granted equal political rights from the start. In others, there were struggles between the property owners and the unpropertied, principally the workers, over the issue of political rights, but by the end of Ottoman rule equal suffrage on a universal basis had triumphed in all of them.

Municipal government was introduced at approximately the same time as rural local government and was also a product of the Ottoman reform *(tanzimat)*. Jerusalem was made a municipality by special imperial decree *(firman)* in 1863. It remained the only formally organized municipality until the enactment of the Provincial Municipalities Law in 1877 under which 22 towns and larger villages were granted municipal status in the 1880s and 1890s.

Under the law they had an impressive list of powers and responsibilities but, in fact, had very little room to maneuver under the provincial authorities. Municipal budgets were very small and the municipalities had almost no civil service. Under the law, the municipal councils *(majlis umumi)* of 6-12 members were to be elected by local taxpayers who were Ottoman subjects. In fact, genuine elections rarely took place. The general rule was that the local notables would agree upon a slate of council members. In Jerusalem, the Jewish and Christian as well as the Muslim communities were represented on the council, although the Muslims had disproportionate representation. Mayors were appointed by the government and, of course, were always Muslims.

At the outset of the British Mandate, there were 22 municipalities in western Palestine: 16 Arab and 6 mixed Arab-Jewish (Jerusalem, Jaffa, Haifa, Tiberias, Safed, and Hebron). Tel Aviv was still regarded as a suburb of Jaffa although, in fact, it was administered by a separate autonomous Jewish council. The British more or less accepted the Ottoman system until they could introduce a municipal framework of their own. In the interim, new municipalities were created by the Mandatory government through orders-in-council. The first independent step by the Mandatory government was the promulgation of a town planning ordinance in 1921, a reflection of the British interest in the aesthetics of the Holy Land. A local council ordinance promulgated in the same year established the basis for rural local government in the country for 20 years, after which it became more an expression of the government of small cities. A general municipal franchise ordinance was promulgated by the Mandatory government in 1926. It extended municipal voting rights to resident male tenants even if they held no property provided that they paid at least one Palestine pound in municipal rates annually.

It was not until 1934 that a comprehensive Municipal Corporations Ordinance was promulgated. It empowered the high commissioner to establish new municipalities or change the boundaries of existing ones on the recommendation of a public committee of inquiry, a system which continued after the establishment of the state, with the Minister of Interior inheriting the powers of the high commissioner. The Ordinance detailed the method of elections, the duties and powers of council members and the municipality, revenue sources, procedures for approving the municipal budget, methods of financial control, and regulations for filling the major administrative positions of town clerk, treasurer, and medical officer. The law also established procedures for council and committee meetings and rules for establishing committees.

Local councils were empowered to enact bylaws but only on those subjects listed in the ordinance, and subject to the high commissioner's approval. The district commissioners were given oversight and budgetary approval powers, while the high commissioner retained the right established in Ottoman days to nominate the mayors and deputy mayors. This Ordinance was carried over after 1948 and many of its provisions still apply although they continue to be modified.

The 1934 Ordinance also confirmed Tel Aviv's municipal status, broadening the local franchise to include men and women, citizens and foreign nationals who paid at least half a pound a year in municipal rates. The Tel Aviv pattern became the model for other Jewish councils established subsequently. The Ordinance also modestly changed the distribution of powers in

Jerusalem. While the city had a Jewish majority for many years and a Jewish plurality since 1860, Jews had only been entitled to 4 out of the 12 seats on the city council. After 1934, the distribution provided for 6 Jewish council members, 4 Muslims, and 2 Christians, but the high commissioner always appointed a Muslim mayor with Jewish and Christian deputies.

The 1921 Town Planning Ordinance was basically designed to safeguard the aesthetic dimensions of the country during a period of development. It was replaced in 1936 by a more modern ordinance which provided for the establishment of local town planning committees identical with the local councils and with the mayor as chairman, and district town planning commissions headed by the district commissioner in which the Mandatory government departments were represented. The latter oversaw the former and was in turn subject to general directives from the Mandatory government planning division.

The 1921 Local Council Ordinance became the formal basis for Jewish self-government under the Mandate, although the Jewish communities went beyond it in the establishment of powerful institutions of their own. Petah Tikva, the oldest of the moshavot, was the first Jewish settlement to acquire local council status in 1921. The next year Rishon le-Zion and Rehovot acquired similar status; Tel Aviv became a local council in 1923, and Ramat Gan and Afula in 1926. After that it was not until 1935, when Hadera acquired that status, that it spread to other Jewish settlements. Bat Yam, Ra'anana, and Kfar Saba followed in 1936; Bnei Brak and Herzliya in 1937.

In 1941 a new ordinance was promulgated, replacing the earlier one. It expanded the powers of the local councils, creating the anomaly that still exists that in some fields they have more powers than municipalities and, indeed, were given the power to act for the public benefit on any matter so long as it did not come in conflict with other legislation. The 1941 act provided for the establishment of regional councils as well, based on the patterns of governance developed for existing federations of Jewish settlements, which formalized the arrangements which had already been developed in the Jewish sector.

In 1945 the Local Authorities (Business Tax) Ordinance was promulgated which allowed local authorities to enact bylaws to tax businesses operating within their boundaries, subject to approval by the high commissioner. This completed the bundle of local legislation under the Mandate.

The Arab village residents regarded these ordinances as an interference with their traditional way of life and opposed their implementation. In the first five years, 21 Arab local councils were established, plus Sarona as a Christian council. Most of the Arab villages given local council status successfully fought against the transformation of their traditional organization. Instead, the Arabs secured a village administration ordinance promulgated in 1944 which provided for a more modest change in the traditional government of the villages. Twenty-four villages reorganized under that law between 1944 and 1948, but even in those cases the new structure tended to exist only on paper while the old ways were preserved. By the end of the Mandate in 1948 there were only 11 Arab local councils, while the number of Jewish local councils had increased to 26, in addition to four regional councils (Emek Hefer, Kishon, Nahalal, and Tel Ilai).

Local Government in the New State

With the establishment of the state in 1948, local government left the center of the political stage. Not unexpectedly, the new state began to assume responsibility for many public functions which had rested in local governmental hands for lack of central institutions. Political leadership gravitated toward the offices of the new state, leaving only those members of the opposition parties for whom the limited responsibilities of service in the Knesset were not sufficient and those kibbutzniks who wished to stay home, to seek local office. In the process of sorting out state and local functions, the party organizations and the Histadrut interposed themselves between the fledgling state and the local governments, further weakening the autonomy of the local leadership.

At the same time, the mass immigration to Israel in the years 1948-1953 shifted the patterns of settlement in the country in such a way that the kibbutzim and veteran moshavim, the local communities possessing the best access to the state and the most power to maintain their local autonomy, declined in importance relative to other local communities. On the other hand, the development towns and the immigrant settlements, potentially the least powerful local communities, became significant elements in the constellation of local governments. While new kibbutzim were established in this period, the kibbutz as such failed to attract many of the new immigrants.[11]

The reduction in the power of local government was not necessarily the result of calculated policy but, rather, the result of a natural transfer of powers that could only have that effect. Indeed, the new state took it upon itself to foster local government institutions from the first. Reversing the pattern established in Mandatory days, the state authorities themselves moved to establish new local authorities. The number of Jewish settlements enjoying municipal status rose from 36 in 1948 to 107 by 1968. The number of regional councils rose from 4 in 1948 to to 53 in 1985. Moreover, new rural settlements were all encouraged to develop local committees of their own for their internal self-government. Finally, and perhaps most significantly, the Arab and Druze villages were also encouraged to establish modern municipal governments of their own and did so in substantial numbers, thereby opening the door to political participation for thousands of non-Jews who had previously been caught in the embrace of a traditional society that confined political power to a tiny elite. In addition to the establishment of new local governments, existing local governments were upgraded and their structures and functions more or less regularized according to standard statewide patterns.[12]

The same standardization that was brought to governmental activities was extended to politics as well. Regularization brought with it the patterns of voting on the local plane that were becoming fixed statewide. The opposition parties lost control of most of the local governments which had been in their hands in the prestate period and were replaced by new coalitions dominated by Mapai, the Israel Labor party that was dominant in the country as a whole. If the establishment of the state strengthened the hands of central government institutions, the mass immigration strengthened the hands of the political party organizations. Whereas in the small Yishuv before statehood the party members could play significant roles in party decision-making, as the population grew and the elements which came in were for the most part politically unsophisticated, the professional party leaders took over direction of party affairs, relying upon the new voting masses who turned out for them at the polls but who were not prepared to participate actively in party government. This had the effect of increasing the role of the central organs of the political parties, enabling them to become the mediating elements between state and local governing bodies with their respective versions of coalition politics.

Local government reached its lowest point in the political system in the mid-1950s. At that point, the older local governments had lost many of their original functions and had been absorbed in the statewide party system along lines that harmonized with the patterns of rule established in Jerusalem. The most powerful local governments, those of the kibbutzim, and secondarily the older moshavim, were attracting a proportionately smaller share of the new immigrants and losing their importance in the local government constellation as a result. The new immigrant settlements that had been established after statehood were still too raw and immature to be self-governing. Even where they were given municipal status, their government offices were occupied or dominated by outsiders sent in by their respective political parties to manage local affairs until such time as "proper" (however defined) local leadership should emerge.[13]

In the late 1950s, the tide began to turn as local governments began to find their place in the framework of a state in which power was divided on other than territorial bases, first and foremost, but which also wished to encourage local governmental activity across most if not all of the four tasks or roles listed at the beginning of this chapter. The process of adjustment which began at that time has not yet been completed.

In the case of government services, after the period of mass transfer of functions to the state, the country entered a period in which shared or cooperative activity began to be stressed. With regard to functions defined as state services, the state took primary responsibility for program initiation, policy-making, and finance, while program administration — the actual delivery of services — was increasingly transferred to local government. In cases where the division was not so clear-cut, responsibility for the delivery of services was somehow divided between the state and the localities. This became true over a wide range of functions, from welfare to education to civil defense to sewage disposal.

The nature of these sharing arrangements should be made clear. They did not involve a sharing among equal partners but rather a sharing between superior and subordinate. But sharing did become the norm, which meant that, at the very least, the local governments were forced to develop cadres of civil servants with sufficient administrative skills to provide the services that the state promised all its citizens. This opened the door to the recruitment and development of a new class of participants in a

17

governmental process which out of necessity has drawn people from all segments of Israeli society.[14]

Moreover, unlike local government in countries with very heterogeneous populations like the United States, local governments in Israel undertake a range of social and cultural functions which extend beyond the ordinary police functions of local government. These range from the provision of religious services to the management of orchestras and drama groups, from the maintenance of day care centers to the awarding of literary prizes. No small share of the importance of local governments in Israel flows from its role in undertaking these functions as part of their task of fostering the social and cultural integration of the community.[15]

Forms of Local Government

Urban government in Israel legally takes two forms, cities and local councils, with the distinction between them minimal. The largest local communities are legally cities with full municipal powers, but, in the English tradition of *ultra vires,* they possess only those powers specifically granted to them. In the case of conflict with the state, city powers are interpreted narrowly. Small urban places are formally termed local councils, a status which gives them almost as much power as cities and in a few cases more, but which makes them more dependent on the Ministry of Interior for hiring personnel.[16] Both kinds of municipalities are governed by mayors elected directly and by councils elected on the basis of proportional representation. Normally, no party gains a majority in the council and a coalition is formed to govern the city, much as is the case on the state plane. Usually, even parties winning a majority will form coalitions in order to strengthen the hand of the local government or to better distribute local political rewards in consideration of statewide coalitions.[17]

While cities and local councils are the basic urban municipal units, they can confederate with one another to create larger, special-purpose municipal bodies designed to undertake specific tasks. These bodies, termed confederations of cities, can be established by two or more municipalities and can undertake one or more functions. They range from the Lod-Ramle joint high school district to the federation of cities of the Dan region, which encompasses the better part of the Tel Aviv metropolitan area and provides several services which seem to be best handled on a metropolitan-wide basis.[18]

Israel has also utilized special authorities for certain purposes. Certain of these authorities handle water drainage and sanitation problems which require adaptation to watersheds that do not follow existing municipal boundaries. In addition, there are the local religious councils in the Jewish-dominated localities, local planning committees, and the state-mandated, quasi-independent local agricultural committees established in most former agricultural colonies that have become mixed urban-rural communities.[19]

The cooperative sector is represented locally by workers' councils which are elected by the vote of all members of the Histadrut within each council's jurisdiction (which, in most cases, more or less conforms to the municipal boundaries). While formally private, many of their activities are of a quasi-governmental character, and they often wield substantial political influence, especially since cities are often dependent upon decisions taken by the cooperative sector at the higher echelons of its bureaucracy, over which they have minimal influence.[20]

The kibbutzim and moshavim, on the other hand, are elite elements in the cooperative sector. They are organized as cooperative societies and also have municipal status as a local committee *(Vaad Mekomi)* under state law. They are actually governed by two principle bodies, the general meeting (equivalent to the American town meeting), which elects the local committee on a yearly basis and which meets monthly to consider major issues, and the local executive committee, which meets as frequently as necessary, sometimes daily, to deal with current business. Most of their day-to-day business is carried on through a multitude of committees involving as many members as are capable of participating. Every kibbutz and moshav is also a member of a regional council that provides secondary local government services, in which it is represented by a delegate or delegates chosen by its own general meeting.[21]

Because of the particular character of rural settlement in Israel where even family farms are concentrated in villages with their own local institutions, the 728 rural settlements with their own local governmental autonomy have an average population of under 800.[22] In a self-selected population (which is what these settlements represent), it is possible for these small communities to provide a very high level of services. Even so, it has been increasingly necessary to broaden the scale of services as evidenced by the growing power of the regional councils. For example, all but the smallest settlements choose to maintain their own elementary school, but the provision of an adequate high school requires a somewhat larger population base. Hence, the provision of high schools is increasingly entrusted to regional councils. Yet the regional councils themselves are relatively small, ranging in population from 678 to 20,378, with only four over 10,000.[23]

There are today a total of 1,409 local authorities functioning in Israel, or approximately one local government per 2,823 inhabitants. Table 1.1 summarizes the types of local authorities functioning in Israel and the number of each type. By any standard, this is a high figure. It is particularly high given the strong formal commitment in Israel to centralized government.

Table 1.1

LOCAL AUTHORITIES IN ISRAEL

Type	Number
Cities	37
Local councils	125
Regional councils	54
Local committees	825
Federations of cities	32
Religious councils	204
Agricultural committees	26
Planning committees	84
Drainage authorities	22
TOTAL	1,409

Most local authorities serve relatively small populations. Jerusalem, the largest city in the country, has approximately 415,000 residents and is growing primarily as a result of the reunification of the city in 1967. Tel Aviv, once the largest city in the country and still the central metropolis, has a declining population, now less than 330,000, having peaked at approximately 385,000 in the mid-1970s. It is now undergoing the process of de-densification which has become common in central cities over much of the Western world, as the movement to better housing in newer parts of the metropolitan area plus urban renewal with the construction of new housing at lower densities within the city has its impact. Haifa has approximately 227,000 people and is the third largest city. There is a second cluster of five cities with popula-tions between 100,000 and 140,000. The other cities and towns range in size from 200 to 80,000. The average city size is under 18,000. Table 1.2 classifies Israel's cities by size category. While the country is highly urbanized, nearly half the population lives in villages or small cities of under 40,000 population while approximately 25 percent live in cities of over 200,000.

Table 1.2

ISRAEL'S CITIES, BY POPULATION SIZE CATEGORY

Population Size	Number of Cities
200,000+	3
80,000 – 149,000	5
40,000 – 79,000	8
20,000 – 39,000	12
8,000 – 19,000	33
4,000 – 7,900	32
2,000 – 3,900	29
Under 2,000	22

Neighborhoods have real meaning in most cities. In part, this is associated with the very formation of the cities themselves, whose modern founding was the result not only of associations of pioneers established by compact for that specific purpose, but also of a compounding of different neighborhoods, each created inde-pendently by a pioneer association and then linked through a second set of compacts to form the present city. Both large and small cities have clearly identified neighborhoods. In fact, it is fair to say that this pattern can be found in any city of over 10,000 population and in some that are even smaller because of the history of city building in Israel.[24]

Haifa, where formal neighborhood institutions are strongest and most widespread, reflects this process to the fullest. Neighborhood committees evolved, each with specific if limited responsibilities for the provision of services and for participation in the development of certain common city-wide services. Finally, taking advantage of a provision in the law, the residents of Kiryat Haim, one of the city's neighborhoods, voted to formally establish an elected neighborhood council and to assume the powers to which it was entitled.

Jerusalem was unified by the external decision of the ruling power, but because most of the older neighborhoods represented clearly distinct socio-religious communities, the city has consistently refrained from imposing itself upon them in those fields of particular concern to each. Today the city is trying to extend more formal devices for neighborhood participation to newer neighborhoods. In the early 1980s, there were successful experiments in formally institutionalized neighborhood self-government which operate today in seven neighborhoods, both old and new. As a result, Jerusalem has opted for decentralization of municipal functions throughout the city.

In Tel Aviv the merger of neighborhoods was more thorough and little, if anything, remains of the earlier framework other than names and recollections. In the past few years, however, the city has made some effort to revive consultative bodies in at least those neighborhoods which have preserved the most distinctive personalities.

The phenomenon of neighborhood committees is widespread in Israel. A recent study shows that there were approximately 385 active neighborhood committees throughout the country, characterized by intensive activities in various physical and social areas within their respective neighborhoods.[25]

Project Renewal has enhanced the already-strong neighborhood orientation of Israel's cities. This massive program of urban redevelopment undertaken by the government of Israel and diaspora Jewry, is based on targeting aid to specific neighborhoods through local steering committees which bear major responsibility for determining what should be done to improve their neighborhoods. These steering committees determine projects, set priorities, and negotiate with state and diaspora counterparts.[26]

In Israel, as in other parts of the world, there has been periodic pressure to consolidate small local units. Despite the fact that the Minister of Interior has full authority to abolish any local unit or consolidate two or more units, this authority has rarely been used and then only when such a move had sufficient political backing from local elites. In the early days of the state when political elites did not include representatives of the localities in question, more consolidations were effected. Since the early 1960s, however, even the weakest local governments have acquired political bases of their own, and any attempts at consolidation are strongly resisted. As a result, consolidation efforts have essentially ground to a halt, being replaced by efforts to create confederations of cities in order to undertake those functions which the individual communities cannot undertake by themselves.[27]

The State Commission on Local Government (Sanbar Commission), which completed its work in 1980, rejected the notion of consolidation as a basic tool of local government reform, recommending that it be considered in only one or two cases. After extensive fieldwork, the Commission concluded that the civic virtues of the smaller local authorities compensated for most of the disadvantages of their small size and that, through interlocal arrangements based on federative principles, those disadvantages could be overcome.

To date, the federation of cities device has been generally used to undertake functions of metropolitan concern and has been little used in the more rural parts of the country. This is partly because the confederation of cities idea was developed to serve cities that adjoin one another, that is to say, those in metropolitan regions. The device has not been extended to free-standing cities within a region which may be separated by no more than a few miles but which see themselves and are treated as totally separate entities. Thus, a certain amount of very real intergovernmental collaboration in planning and service delivery has been developed in the Dan region, which consists of some 20 cities whose boundaries are contiguous with one another. Yet in the Galilee, a region of several hundred thousand people with no single city of 40,000 population but with six cities of over 10,000, all within an area of less than 1,000 square miles, there are relatively few intermunicipal arrangements and little local concern with moving in that direction. This is true even though the region as a whole shares common state facilities (e.g., a large hospital in Safed, university extension courses in that city and at Tel Hai near Kiryat Shmona, district offices in Nazareth, rudimentary sewage treatment facilities near Tiberias) and has the potential of becoming a kind of multinodal metropolitan region of the kind that has developed elsewhere in the world.

State-Local Relations in a Government-Permeated Society

The fact that Israel is a government-permeated society strongly affects state-local relations. One of the major consequences of this is that local government officials must spend as much time working with outside authorities to either provide services or fund services as they do in directing their own affairs. Another is that local governments have been quite restricted in their ability to finance municipal activities. Relatively few tax resources are at their disposal, and the local share of total governmental expenditures in Israel has been on the decline for nearly twenty years.

By and large, Israeli local governments manage to maintain their freedom of movement by managing deficits, which have become the functional equivalent of grantsmanship in other polities. While there are great restrictions on local government's taxing powers, there are almost no restrictions on its borrowing powers, providing that any particular local authority can pay the high interest involved. Thus, local authorities borrow heavily from the banks in order to provide services and then turn to the state government to obtain the funds to cover the loans. As long as the services they wish to provide are in line with state policies (and there is almost universal consensus with regard to those services, so that is not generally an issue) and there is some degree of unanimity within the local ruling coalition with regard to what is being done, the state will provide the requested funds. Nevertheless, this does mean that the local authorities must spend a very large share of their time in negotiations with their state counterparts.[28]

Local leaders are also able to turn, in some matters, to the Jewish Agency and through it (or even directly, in some cases) to foreign donors to gain additional resources, mostly for capital investment, e.g., the construction of a new high school, community center, or a child-care center. Where services are provided directly by the state, local authorities will use their influence to try to negotiate more and better services or to influence those responsible for delivering those services locally, but in this they are notably less successful than they are in mobilizing funds for their own programs, partly because the Israeli political culture encourages every officeholder to act as independently as possible.[29]

Sharpening the Trend Toward Territorial Democracy[30]

At least since 1969, the local elections have been major factors in Israel's transition from ideologically-based politics to politics based on territorial subdivisions. In many respects, that is their most significant aspect. More specifically, the trend toward territorially-based politics rests upon three separate components:

1) the increasing political integration of the Israeli polity;
2) the growing localization of political action and, by extension, of political power;
3) the increasing differentiation of local political systems, as systems with distinctive patterns and orientations of their own to political action.

Israel's cities and local councils became the first frontier of political integration in the country. They provided the first opportunities for non-ideological participation in Israeli political life, which meant, in effect, opening political participation to younger people, political "amateurs," and to the new immigrants from the Afro-Asian countries or their children. As early as 1967, approximately 47 percent of the political leaders and public officials (taken together) in the local arena were drawn from those groups, in sharp contrast to the situation then prevailing in the Knesset and the ministries. Moreover, many had become mayors, giving them concomitant political and social advantages.[31] A decade later, they were in the vanguard of the Sephardic leadership in the Likud who moved into key positions in the Knesset and the government.

By any of the measures available, it appears that local government, by applying the principles of territorial democracy, is serving as a channel of recruitment of otherwise excluded groups into the political process. Even where attempts were made to send political veterans into new towns to assume positions of responsibility in the early days of their development, these people were soon overwhelmed by the rise of local leaders able to move ahead simply by virtue of their being who they were vis-a-vis their reference groups where they were. Ultimately, the parties had to accommodate them and seek to co-opt them, making necessary concessions in the process. Not the least of these concessions was an almost total ignoring of ideology in the recruitment of new local leadership so that now one finds even members of Mapam who are observant Jews and members of the Labor Party who do not have even the beginnings of a commitment to socialism. In sum, local politics has become far more pragmatic than ideological.

Significantly, split-ticket voting, a phenomenon which increased during the 1960s, continued its upward trend in the elections of the 1970s. This was widely recognized in Israel and hailed throughout the country as a sign of the growing maturity of the electorate. The increase in split-ticket voting should be understood as an indicator of greater political integration. The ability of voters to discriminate between parties and candidates on different governmental planes is a sign of the citizenry's increasing "at homeness" as members of the body politic. Since political integration, particularly in a democratic society, must necessarily involve greater rootedness within the body politic on the part of the citizenry itself, this is an important measure.

An unintegrated citizenry can be brought to the polls by party organizations to vote in overwhelming numbers. This was the case in Israel in the 1950s and early 1960s, as it was in other countries of immigration during parallel periods in their development. It is clear that the link to politics for the average voter in such circumstances exists only through the mediating force of the organization which provides certain services, frequently apolitical in character, to the new immigrants in return for the right to manipulate their votes.[32] The shift away from this in Israel, at first confined to the local elections, led in 1977 to a radical shift in voting for the Knesset and the Likud electoral victory.

Beyond the vote itself, the characters of the candidates and of the campaigns reflect this growing political integration. Increasingly, the candidates represent not only local interests and issues, but also a common statewide orientation and style. While local lists have proliferated, they rarely present themselves as "ethnic" lists, even when their internal composition reflects a particular local balance between blocs of country-of-origin subcommunities. The more successful ones present themselves as "good government" lists, designed to appeal to the voters on the basis of their ability to improve local programs and services (usually by taking a non-partisan stance vis-a-vis the national parties). In this way they emphasize what has become a common Israeli phenomenon and deny particularism as such.

The success of local lists in places like Kfar Shmaryahu, Kiryat Tivon and Ramat Hasharon (all typical upper-middle-class suburban communities) could well have been forecast by observers familiar with similar phenomena in similar suburban communities in other western countries. The residents of these communities are oriented toward the separation of local government from the larger political arena, because they perceive local government as a means for providing appropriate services administered efficiently rather than as a mechanism for political reward. The emergence of such suburban communities in Israel over the past decade has been predictably accompanied by the emergence of local non-partisan lists.

The triumph of local lists in cities like Nahariya, Kiryat Bialik and Rishon le-Zion was less predictable but not necessarily surprising. Each is a full-fledged city in its own right with a distinctive character of its own, even though the latter two have been engulfed by suburbanization in recent years. In all three cases, old elites (the children of older settlers) sought to preserve the character of their communities, and turned to local lists as a means of gaining political control. In 1973, for example, the Nahariya list was called, appropriately enough, *Ichpat Lanu* (We Care) — a slogan that has been spreading throughout Israel to symbolize a new or revived interest in civic responsibility. In Kiryat Bialik and Rishon le-Zion the lists were called *L'maan Kiryat Bialik* (For Kiryat Bialik) and *L'maan Rishon le-Zion* (For Rishon le-Zion); this is a more prosaic name, but one that also attempts to convey a sense of local concern. In the latter case, the incumbent mayor broke away from his party (Gahal-Likud) when the party's national headquarters attempted to dictate to him the other candidates on his list, and won a resounding victory.

Perhaps least expected were the triumphs of local lists in a number of development towns. In those cases, personalities who had already established themselves politically were the motivating forces behind the local lists. The campaigns themselves were based on the same "good government" orientation that had become common nationwide. Again, the names of the lists are significant. For example, in Kiryat Ono, the list was called *Hakiryah Shelanu* (Our City); in Kiryat Shmona, *Hatnua Lizechuyot*

Haezrach (Movement for Civil Rights); and in Sederot, *L'maan Sederot* (For Sederot).

The extent of these localistic tendencies is even greater than the statistics reveal. In a number of local authorities, what were actually local lists won under the banner of the national parties. The local appeal of such lists is often revealed by the difference between the vote they received and the local vote for the Knesset. Where the local branches of the national parties adapted to the new style of politics, they were successful even in defeating local lists.

The trend toward personalization of local elections has continued unabated since 1969. It intensified in 1978 after the introduction of the direct election of mayors apart from their party lists. Across the country, outstanding mayoral candidates garner votes far in excess of those cast for their tickets. They have been able to carry lists of virtual unknowns into office on their coattails, while lists not headed by attractive personalities (however defined) have suffered. In many respects, personal elections for mayor came to Israel, de facto, in the 1960s and the formal change in the law merely ratified what had already become the norm.

The Growing Localization of Political Action

The rise of personalities as a factor in local elections is also a reflection of the growing localization of politics in Israel. By the 1973 elections, local party branches were already acting in an increasingly independent fashion. At their most extreme, they rejected all efforts by the party centers to determine who should appear on their local lists and what kind of campaign should be conducted, a posture that would have failed in earlier contests.

In fact, at least until the 1983 elections, there was a steady decline in attempts by party centers to interfere in local ticket-making or campaigning. The party leaders apparently calculated that it did not pay to intervene in the case of the smaller localities; in the larger ones, they no longer had as much power to do so. Thus, in most cases, local branches could make their wishes felt on local matters without resorting to extreme measures. In those few cases where party leaders did actively try, they were sharply challenged and lost.

After the elections, local branches have insisted on the right to undertake their own coalition negotiations, rather than allowing themselves to be pawns in statewide deals by the central party leadership, as had generally been the case in the past. This has led to a number of conflicts which became quite public, but these conflicts have almost always been resolved in favor of local autonomy. On the other hand, there are many cases where local party branches may not have undertaken initiatives, not because they were told not to do so, but because they expected the party centers to be opposed and were unwilling to go against central authority.

In the 1983 municipal elections, there was an atavistic trend toward national party intervention in several localities. In every case, strong local mayoral candidates succeeded in repelling these efforts, although in some cases, the struggle cost them and their parties the elections.

Increasing Local Differentiation

The wide variety of electoral and political responses in the Tel Aviv metropolitan area is a very real indicator of the growing localization of Israeli politics. The usual statistical measures of socio-economic and demographic variables tend to portray the region as being substantially homogeneous. Most of the governmental reforms that have been proposed for the region have been based on assumptions derived from that portrayal. In fact, however, the region has relatively few suburbs in the currently accepted sense of the term. The overwhelming majority of the municipalities serve settlements founded independently, even though they may have subsequently become engulfed by suburbanization. Even the commuting patterns in the area are not simply to Tel Aviv from peripheral dormitory settlements, but are matrix-like — cutting across the metropolitan region in a variety of directions. This reflects the fact that the larger cities in the region are independent magnets in their own right. As a matter of fact, while Tel Aviv is the commercial and cultural center of the region and the country as a whole, it shares political and economic power with Jerusalem and Haifa in a manner more characteristic of large federal systems than of small unitary states.

Within the Tel Aviv region, Ramat Gan, Givatayim, and Bnei Brak — three adjoining cities — serve as major commercial and cultural foci with distinctive local characteristics. The first is a bourgeois city *par excellance* and an alternative commercial center to Tel Aviv. The second is a worker's town and the third is the seat of ultra-Orthodoxy in Israel, rivaled only by Jerusalem.

Industry is scattered throughout the region; the largest single employer, Israel Aircraft Industries, is located at the region's eastern
periphery near Ben Gurion Airport, and draws employees from
the eastern ring of towns in an arc from north to south. Each municipality has developed a politics of its own to go with its particular location, economic base and demographic composition. The
local election contests, on the other hand, demonstrate the great
diversity within the region; it is now being expressed more
clearly and forcefully through the politics of the local authorities
than at any time since the establishment of the state.

What is true of the Tel Aviv region is true of the country as a
whole. Hence, even more striking than the localization of local
politics in Israel is the increasing differentiation in the character
(political and otherwise) of the various cities, towns and regions
within the country. The two phenomena are, of course, closely
linked. Indeed, a strong case can be made that it is the growth of
local differentiation that has encouraged localization. Moreover,
local differentiation has developed hand in hand with increased
statewide political integration.

This is not the place to examine this apparently paradoxical
phenomenon, but the paradox is more apparent than real. Evidence accumulated in recent years suggests that under the conditions that sustain pluralist democracy in its various forms, increasing political integration can stimulate internal differentiation on new planes. The overwhelming majority of Israel's cities,
towns, and villages emerged within the same two-generation period as did the state, pioneered by the same elements under the
same conditions. Despite the potential for sameness that this situation offered, they have acquired quite distinct characteristics in
the course of becoming rooted communities, even as the state is becoming better integrated politically.

In part, this is a reflection of the fact that different ideological,
country-of-origin and occupational groups were settled in different localities. These differences may be the result of:

(a) ideological choices on the part of the original settlers
themselves (particularly in the case of settlements
founded before the state);
(b) the settlement of immigrant groups on the basis of when
they arrived in the country (particularly in the case of
those founded in the state's early years); or
(c) conscious planning on the part of the authorities
(particularly in more recent years), or some

combination of the three. This process alone would have produced a certain amount of differentiation, and it has. Even where the same kinds of people were settled in different places, the order of their arrival created its own patterns of differentiation. Moreover, the kinds of occupations in which the first arrivals were able to engage established status systems which are, to some extent at least, specifically local in character. In general, economic circumstances have contributed to local differentiation. When combined with location, these circumstances have played a major role in determining whether a community would be relatively stable in its population, or one with a great deal of population turnover. Migration, itself, is another factor promoting differentiation. Either initially or subsequent to their initial settlement, most individuals and families have been free to make their own choices insofar as they have the means to do so; thus, population shifts have taken place to shape the character of local communities.

Finally, history — even the brief history of communities in Israel — brings about its own differentiation. Precedents are established; certain people acquire position and power and put their own stamp on local affairs; traditions emerge; and a local pattern of doing business is forged. Even institutions mandated centrally for every settlement develop differentially on the basis of local circumstances, thus solidifying certain patterns and preventing the development of others. The result is the emergence of separate "personalities" for each community. These differential characteristics, in turn, influence future developments, attracting or repelling both people from the outside and those born locally.

For many years, the physical appearance of development towns was one of bland sameness, differentiated only by the fact that in different years the central authorities used different architectural and town planning styles. Recently, however, these towns have acquired increasingly differentiated characteristics. Netivot, Ofakim and Sederot are three development towns founded at approximately the same time along the road between Ashkelon and Beersheba, a few kilometers from one another. In Netivot, a progressive group attained power in 1973 through control of the local NRP (National Religious Party) branch, in a manner particularly appropriate to a town whose population is overwhelmingly religious. They held on for a decade and brought considerable new development to their town until ruptured by a split in the NRP. In Sederot, which voted overwhelmingly for the Labor

Alignment in Knesset and local elections until 1973, the same kind of local progressive movement achieved power through an independent local list but was unable to move the town forward to any great degree. Ofakim did not undergo the kind of political change that could make a difference in the quality of life until the introduction of Project Renewal from the outside after 1977. It remains the least politically advanced of the three towns. The differences among the three can be traced to differences in the composition of their respective populations, the economic situation created by local and statewide considerations, and the quality of their leadership. What is significant here is that such real differences have emerged in so short a period of time.

Territorial Democracy: The Minorities

Two more aspects of territorial democracy in Israel need to be considered, both of which are lineal descendents of the old millet system. While that system no longer exists in a formal way in Israel, the government has made some effort to accommodate the legitimate demands of non-Jewish minorities for local autonomy by applying its principles in the local government sphere. Thus most Arabs, Muslim or Christian; Druze, and Circassians have a substantial amount of cultural autonomy maintained through their own local councils which serve to concretize the rights secured them in Israeli basic law and also provide a basis for implementing services provided by the state through the appropriate departments in the Ministries of Religious Affairs and Education and Culture.

In 1948, there was one Arab local council in Israel and only 27 percent of all Arabs were located within municipal governments of any kind. During the years following the attainment of statehood, the Israeli authorities made a conscious and concentrated effort to give Arab and Druze villages municipal status and thereby provide them with the political basis for a substantial amount of local self-determination, particularly in the cultural and religious spheres. By 1968, there were 42 Arab and Druze local councils, one regional council composed exclusively of Druze villages and 18 villages within mixed regional councils so that some three-fourths of the non-Jewish population had its own local government.[33]

Take, for example, the Druze village of Hurfeish in the upper Galilee (present population approximately 2,200). Originally a Jewish settlement until the fourth century, after a 600 year hiatus it was resettled during the Crusades and its Druze residents claim residence from that time. From then until 1967, it was governed by traditional institutions. In 1967, the Israeli Ministry of Interior convinced the local mukhtars to accept formal municipal status.

Since the traditional Arab leadership resisted municipalization for fear that it would interfere with their traditional dominance, it came about only when a more educated generation emerged.

The first important local public service to reach the village was its connection to the state water network in 1957, freeing its residents from reliance on local wells. The first paved roads came in 1962. In 1975 the rest of the village's streets were paved and in some cases widened. The city was linked to the statewide electrical grid in 1969 and street lights were installed a year later, both as a result of the introduction of municipal government.

For the Arab and Druze, the introduction of formal local government institutions became the means for attaining an increasing amount of control over their own immediate destinies. While they are not required to do so, most Israeli Arabs and Druze remain residents of their villages even when they commute to work in Jewish cities, so that they remain members of the socio-cultural system which their village local government protects and sustains. Israeli policy in this regard has been conscious and deliberate. This is evidenced by the establishment of separate Jewish cities adjacent to principle Arab cities and villages wherever the Israeli government felt the need to do for security reasons. With two exceptions, no effort was made to create mixed municipalities. Thus Upper Nazareth was created from scratch for Jews along side of Arab Nazareth and new towns for Jews were established in the middle of western Galilee in areas with many Arab villages. In all of these cases, the municipal institutions were kept separate so that each group could preserve its local autonomy through judicious use of the first face of territorial democracy.[34] It should be noted that this strict division is now breaking down as members of the minority groups attain higher educational standards and greater prosperity.

A different kind of neo-milletization has been developed for those members of the old Jewish Yishuv and the immigrants who have joined with them to preserve an ultra-Orthodox way of life outside of the Israeli mainstream. Their territorial base tends to be confined to neighborhoods or quarters of major cities, though in at least one case they have developed municipal institutions to support their way of life. By and large, they maintain their separatism through separate government-recognized institutions, primarily schools and rabbinical courts, which receive government subsidies and are given a great deal of autonomy. These, of course, function within the "neighborhood" territories which these groups have staked out for themselves.

Territorial Democracy and Civil Community

The sum and substance of the foregoing is a strengthening of territorial democracy. Localities are increasingly finding ways to express territorially-rooted interests through political means. This is a matter of great necessity in a civil society dominated by politics, where even the economic sphere is subordinated to political concerns at almost every turn. In this respect, Israel is following a trend towards decentralization which seems to be worldwide.

The course of this pattern in Israel runs roughly as follows. From 1948 until the early 1960s, the trend was predominantly one of centralization. The state, animated by David Ben Gurion's "statist" philosophy, absorbed functions which in the pre-state Yishuv had been in the hands of local, voluntary or party bodies. At the same time, the need for local administration even in a small centralized state, combined with the democratic values of Israel's leadership, led to the quiet spread of local self-government for both Jews and Arabs. Local government law was regularized and new settlements acquired local governmental authority. From the mid-1960s onward, a trend toward decentralization has taken on greater intensity through the growth of local political power. Much of this is not visible in formal legislation, or even in the administrative orders upon which so much of the government of Israel is based. In characteristically Israeli fashion, there remains a wide gap between the formal framework, which is still pyramid-like in almost every respect, and the actual matrix of power relationships within the country.

Obviously, in neither case have all forces and factors led in the same direction. Contradictory developments abound, but overall, the pattern seems to be reasonably clear. In the earlier period of centralization, a basis was laid for local self-government. In the present period of increasing local power, new plateaus of statewide political integration are being attained.

The trend towards decentralization has been aided by two locally-linked phenomena. First, the sheer growth in size of the individual municipalities has strengthened the ability of local authorities to accept serious responsibility and make decisions with greater independence. There are approximately 20 cities of over 30,000 population in the state today, and another five are approaching that figure; these have attained sufficient critical mass to undertake the responsibilities entrusted to them by the state or by their citizens. This, in itself, makes a big difference.

Beyond that, there is an emergent local leadership able to undertake the tasks that need to be undertaken, and eager to do so, if only as a result of natural ambitions. Thus, Israel's shift from the peak of centralization into a period of greater decentralization has been assisted by the new-style politics emerging in locality after locality across the country. By 1977, a few of these new leaders began to move into the Knesset, given new opportunities by the Likud victory. They soon demonstrated their competence in the state arena. The 1981 Knesset elections brought more of them to the fore in state politics. Some gave up their local posts while others sought to combine state and local office. After 1981, 20 Knesset members also held local office, most as mayors of smaller cities. The localities may well be generating the most dynamic political leadership in Israel today. The question remains: will all this lead to structural and institutional changes that will close the gap between the formal and the informal distribution of power in the state?

A significant part of the answer to that question will have to come from the state authorities that dominate government in all areas but another part will have to come from the localities themselves. It has been suggested in this chapter that the formal local authority is not the sum total of local government in a particular jurisdiction. It certainly is not the sum total of local political or civic authority.

For one thing, power is far more diffused locally than it may appear at first glance. In addition to the municipal council and administrative departments, every locality has at least two local bodies that are essentially independent of the local council.[35] One is the religious council, a governing body appointed through a formula which involves both local and state organs and responsible for the provision of local religious services.[36] The other is the labor council which, as the local agency of the Histadrut, actually functions as the equivalent of a local chamber of commerce in the United States, a quasi-governmental body which plays a major political role locally.[37] In addition, many of the small local councils elect an agricultural committee under the terms of a state law which provides for such an elected body when a sufficient percentage of the local population is engaged in agriculture. Finally, in the large cities there are neighborhood committees, one of which, in Kiryat Haim (Haifa), is formally elected by the local residents as a kind of borough council.[38]

All of these bodies, taken together, widen the scope of local political participation considerably. More than that, they also alter the shape of Israel's republican institutions and the quality of its democratic life. On one hand, the development of a multiplicity of local decision-making bodies clearly alters the structure of bargaining in the local arena, and perhaps beyond it as well, expanding the arena in which negotiation is both necessary and possible. More than that, the dispersal of bargaining power substantially weakens the strong tendency toward centralization or monolithic control in the country, acting to diffuse power among citizens or spokesmen for groups of citizens.

At the same time, the necessary interaction among these power nodes within the local community expands the role of local government by transforming localities into "civil communities," that is to say, communities organized primarily for civic or political purposes, able to utilize a wide variety of mechanisms to shape actions affecting them as localities so as to better serve their local value system. A civil community consists of six kinds of elements:

1) The local governments that give the civil community its basic shape (the local council, the religious council).
2) The agencies of the state or the offices of the national institutions located in the community which function to serve local as well as supralocal ends (e.g., the labor exchange, the police detachment, the local office of the Jewish Agency).
3) The public nongovernmental institutions which function in the locality to supplement the governmental ones (e.g., the labor council, the various public welfare institutions, the local schools sponsored by overseas Jewish groups).

36

4) The political parties or factions which compete within the locality to organize political power.
5) The local interest groups (or powerful individuals) which effect decision-making in the community.
6) The local value system as crystallized in the constitutional documents and traditions of the various local governments within the community.

When the institutions representing these elements work together, they provide a powerful means for widespread citizen involvement, for the sharing of decisions, and for bargaining and negotiation to set policy, In addition, they offer the local community greater leverage over decisions that affect it which are made outside its boundaries.[39]

The range and level of civic activity required to transform a municipality into a civil community are just now beginning to emerge in Israel as the population settles in, develops roots, and generates the economic base necessary for an active civic life. Since voluntary effort is required to sustain so many of the components of a civil community, one can only flourish under such circumstances. Moreover, even when the objective conditions are present, civil communities are fostered only in the appropriate cultural settings. Israel's latent Jewish political culture happens to be an appropriate one, but it confronts two others — statist and subject — that are far less so, if not actually inappropriate in many ways. Thus the transformation of simple municipalities into civil communities (a trend still in its early stages in Israel) represents a major change in the political character of the country, one that is likely to have great repercussions for the country as a whole in terms of increasing its stability (since more people will have a stake in that stability), expanding the range of political recruitment, and changing the bargaining process through which statewide decisions are made.

Notes – Chapter 1

1. Weiss (1972); Freudenheim (1967), Chap. 9; Kalchheim (1976); Don-Yehiya (1987); Lazin (1979); Elazar (1977) and (1973).

2. Unfortunately, the literature on territorial democracy is very limited. Orestes Brownson was apparently the first person to use the term "territorial democracy" in *The American Republic* (1866). Kirk expanded upon it as a concept. This writer has commented on its role in American politics, see Elazar (1968). Certain aspects of the problem of the territorial organization of power have been well treated in Maas (ed.) (1959).

3. The articles of agreement of a number of the early colonies are preserved in their archives and displayed on appropriate occasions. Petah Tikva maintains its original covenant on year-round display in its municipal museum. See also Municipality of Petah Tikva (1964).

4. Buber (1950) makes a strong case for this claim; see in particular his Epilogue.

5. For a description of the development of Jerusalem in this pattern, see Vilnai (1960).

6. Cohen (1970) examines the problem of the city from the perspective of the Zionist founders and surveys the actual state of urban development in the country in those first generations. Cohen suggests that the shift away from concern with urban as well as rural settlement is also a product of the Third Aliyah revolution with its strong ideological dimensions. All told, he provides necessary corrective to the romantic view of rural Israel.

7. Tel Aviv has not been very well studied to date. For data on its development, it is necessary to go to the general histories of modern Israel. See, for example Robert Shereshevsky, et al. (1968).

8. Central Bureau of Statistics (1983). In a significant number of cities and towns, territorial neutrality has led to the development of country-of-origin neighborhoods which, however, are unable to obtain direct local representation under the present electoral system. Perhaps as a result, ethnic ticket balancing is even more pronounced in the local arena than in Knesset elections.

9. Guttman (1963) and (1958); Av-Razi (1962); Adler and Hecht (1970); and Adler (1960).

10. Gevirtz (1962a). Ben-Aryeh (1965) describes one of these "small republics."

11. Weiss (1972); Guttman (1963); Elazar (1977); and Eisenstadt (1967).

12. Alderfer (1964); Bernstein (1957); Hoven and Van der Elshout (1963); and Samuel (1957).

13. Cohen (1970); Aronoff (1973b) in Curtis and Chertoff (eds.) (1973); Spiegel (1966); and Aronoff (1973a).

14. Adler (1956); Dror and Guttman (eds.) (1961); Kalchheim (1976); Samuel (1953); and Weiss (1973).
15. Weiss (1972); Guttman (1963); Bernstein (1957); Elston (1963); and Kraines (1961).
16. Baker (1968), pp. 153-159; Gat (1976); Meljon (1966); and Rosen (1962).
17. Torgovnik and Weiss (1972).
18. Martins and Hoffman (1981) (Hebrew).
19. Amiaz (1971) and Meljon (1962).
20. Aronoff (1973a).
21. Criden and Gelb (1976) and Lanir (1978).
22. Baldwin (1972) and Brown (1974).
23. Gevirtz (1962b); Katz et al. (1982); Rosen (1973) and Sharon (1968).
24. Kramer (1970) and Rosenbloom (1979).
25. King and Hacohen (1986).
26. Elazar et al. (1980); Elazar et al. (1983). This evaluation was commissioned by the International Evaluation Committee for Project Renewal on behalf of the Jewish Agency for Israel and the Government of Israel. Carmon and Hill (eds.) (1979); Katzav (1983) and Walsh (1982).
27. Israel Institute for Urban Research and Information (1973); State Commission on Local Government (1981) and Rosen (1973).
28. Elazar (1983) and Kalchheim (1976).
29. Elazar et al. (1979).
30. Arian (1972); Elazar (1975) in Arian (1975) and Lantzman (1983).
31. Weiss (1972), Chapter 10. It should be noted that the recruitment and advancement of Sephardic and Oriental Jews is not spread evenly throughout the system of local government. The older and larger cities have disproportionately fewer while the new towns with their mainly "new immigrant" populations have disproportionately more.
32. Deshen (1970) and Weingrod (1966).
33. A good summary of the development of local self-government in the Arab towns is available in Stendel (1967). The best sources of specific data are the reports of the State Comptroller for specific towns. See also Stock (1968).
34. See Spiegel (1966). The two exceptions are Tel Aviv-Jaffa and Maalot-Tarshiha. The first was created immediately after the establishment of the state partly for security reasons and before a clear urbanization policy was established. The second represents a merger of two very weak local councils in an effort to create one viable one. In addition, Acre, Lod, Ramle and Haifa have mixed populations dating from before 1948 and Jerusalem has been a mixed city since June 1967. More recently, these "twin" communities have begun to develop cooperative activities on a variety of fronts, recognizing the regional

links that bring them together even as they seek to preserve their respective ethnic identities.
35. Ibid.; Cohen (1962); Elazar (1977); and Torgovnik and Weiss (1972).
36. Don-Yehiya (1987) and Silverstone (1973).
37. Aronoff (1973a); Bilicky (1981) and Wilner (1969).
38. Kramer (1970) and Rosenbloom (1979).
39. For an elaboration of the civil community concept, see Elazar (1970).

Chapter 2

THE DIVISION OF FUNCTIONS AND INTERRELATIONSHIPS BETWEEN LOCAL AND STATE AUTHORITIES

Chaim Kalchheim

In Israel, the state and local governments do not stand in opposition to one another, nor do they exist in a clear hierarchical relationship. The heterogeneity in local government is apparent even to the untrained eye. The local authorities are separate political and administrative units. They differ significantly in their economic, cultural and social resources, their politics and political styles and the character of their local leadership. All these influence the administration of local affairs and affect their relationships with government ministries and other important bodies.

The state government, too, is not homogeneous. It can be defined as a federation of ministries whose coordinating mechanisms are extremely loose.[1] Even if the state government were unified into one governing body, there would still be differences in the style of each ministry which would originate from differences in the tasks which they must perform. Therefore, it would be a mistake to refer to the state government as if it were a single body, which acts as one in the realm of internal policy. In many matters of importance to local government, the state is represented by different ministries, although in principle, the Ministry of Interior represents the government and local authorities vis-a-vis each other.

There is also an essential difference in the criteria which are used to assess a ministry and a local authority. Most government ministries are held accountable for planning, control and standards of quality (i.e., the Ministries of Interior, Labor and Social Welfare, and Health), while local authorities are largely accountable for the provision of services. There are ministries whose primary activity is the provision of services (such as the Ministry of Communication), but in these cases they have few points of contact with the local authorities. Therefore, problems which arise between the state and local governments do not derive from the line dividing them, but principally from the difference in their basic characteristics. The local authority is an integrative system while the state governmental system works through separate channels, not only with respect to local authorities, but in other social and economic areas as well. Moreover, even the central staff units of the government bureaucracy (such as the Civil Service Commission and the Budget Department) do not function as would be expected by their formal status and in light of the goals in whose name they were established — as a result of the subdivision which lies at the heart of the governmental system.

There are five government ministries in Israel whose activities have significant implications for the functioning of local authorities: Interior, Education and Culture, Labor and Social Welfare, Construction and Housing, and Finance. These, like other ministries, have assorted means of enforcement and varying degrees of influence on the activities of the local authority: the Ministry of Interior as responsible for its legal, administrative and financial activities; the Ministry of Education and Culture and the Ministry of Labor and Social Welfare as overseers of the most important social services in the local authorities; the Ministry of Construction and Housing as the planner and builder of housing developments and neighborhoods; and the Ministry of Finance, which is a major factor in financial policy and sometimes even intervenes on the local plane, despite the fact that it does not formally oversee any municipal activities. Although in each of these areas the principal role of the relevant ministry is clear, in many specific instances the activities and budgeting of the ministries overlap. All of these factors help create a colorful mosaic of interrelationships between the local and state governments.

Local Government and its Status in the Modern State

Many scholars and politicians have viewed the local authorities as mere weaklings, trampled upon by the government ministries. A common mistake is to view the formal status of local government as though it reflected reality, especially when focusing on the interrelationships between the state and local authorities.

In the last hundred years, many western democracies were shaped by the concept of a centralized modern sovereign state, with a reliance on theories and management practices which developed in the modern era.[2] The status of the local authority was defined as that of an administrative unit on the periphery of the national administration, as well as a unit with a distinct political identity. Yet, even in France, which represents the most radical example of a state in which the local authority is a local administrative unit *(Administration Locale)*, the local authority is managed by an elected mayor and council. Despite conspicuous differences in the structure of local government in different western democracies including Israel, nearly all of them include three basic patterns of relationships between the local authority and central government.[3]

The Central Control Model

The central control model is also known as the top down model or the principal/agent model. According to this model, the legal underpining of local authorities is legislation passed by a national parliament or, in the case of a federation, by the legislative body of a state or province. Many of these laws require the central authority to oversee the work of local governments. A sizeable portion of local government expenditures (about 70 percent in Israel) comes from grants and transfers from the state treasury. This results in a model where the state is a pyramid at whose peak stands the state government. At the base is the local authority, whose function is to execute the state government policy in accordance with relevant local conditions, but supervised by government ministries.

The Local Autonomy Model

According to this model, the local public understands local needs and how to satisfy them better than the state government. Hence every local authority is a political unit in its own right, governed by a publicly elected body. It is responsible for its actions to the public and, in many cases, is even more democratic than the state government.

The local government has the independent authority to collect taxes and is even less dependent on the national legislature for its authority than is a ministry. Therefore, the local government may act as an alternative to the government ministry for the performance of services, rather than as its subordinate.

Even the proponents of this model do not demand full autonomy for the local authority, recognizing that the state government has responsibility for matters of security and the national economy. Their intention is to reverse previous trends toward centralization and bureaucratization.

The Political System Model

The political system model is often referred to as the "marble cake" theory of relations between the federal government and local governments in the United States.[4] It posits a system in which there is no specific center of authority and power, but rather a collection of relatively independent agencies and authorities, each of which struggles to achieve its own goals in its own way. While the local governments are each separate and distinct units, there is never a single dividing line between the state and local governments. Instead, there is a multi-channeled network of communications. The fact that different local authorities allocate different proportions of their resources to the services they provide, indicates that the state government does not necessarily have the final word. The general government does not constitute a center and the local governments are not on the periphery. Local elections express only one aspect of local political life. The local authority is bound by a system of ties with associations and institutions, not all of which are political, and with local and national political parties. Ties are formed with the ruling coalition as well as with the opposition. Therefore this model is called the political system model.

According to one perspective, local government is elected by the public and hence is an independent political entity which is authorized to act as a governing authority in every field relevant to the lives of those who reside or work within its jurisdiction. A second perspective views local government as an administrative organization to supply services according to minimal national standards. Local government is formally subordinate to the state government in certain respects, and in many respects is subjected to various levels of supervision or influence by the state authorities.

In the wake of this dichotomy, many observers in academia and politics developed misperceptions which subsequently became conventional assumptions and were rarely reconsidered. The following three factors contributed to the spread of this phenomenon:[5]

1) Many scholars and political observers begin with the assumption that the legal regulations governing how matters should be executed offer accurate descriptions of how things are actually done. Most texts and studies rely on sections of the law and its regulations in their description of the authorities under discussion. Certainly the source is official and reliable, but it does not represent more than the powers which the legislature intended to grant to a particular body. The reality is likely to be quite different. For example, listing the means available to the state government for control over the local authorities without reference to whether those means are in any way applied and, if so, to the reaction of the local authority in question, adds little, if anything, to our knowledge.

2) Very little has been done to examine the influence of a local authority (or the Israel Union of Local Authorities) on legislation. Rather than seeing how the partnership works between the two planes of government, there is a widespread tendency to point out the unidirectionality of influence originating from the state government.

3) An outgrowth of the above phenomenon is the tendency to bemoan the trend toward centralization through the continuous erosion of services delivered by the local authorities. This approach ignores the trends toward strengthening the autonomy of local authorities in the fields of physical planning, building and welfare services. It is logically untenable to complain that services have been removed from the jurisdiction of the local government and at the same time claim that the state government is increasing its involvement in the affairs of the local authority in the areas or services which had already been taken away from it.

The factors which influence the degree of local autonomy can be grouped into four categories:

1) National factors — the extent of ideological pluralism in the country which allows for greater local autonomy, or the concentration of the means of production in the hands of the state government, which diminishes it.

2) Demographic and geographic factors — the size of the population in the local jurisdiction or the number of local authorities.
3) Social-cultural factors — the heterogeneity/homogeneity of the population, levels of income and education, or the composition of the income of the local authority.
4) Political factors — the stability of the local leadership, its involvement in national politics, or the activity of volunteer organizations.

The correlation between any specific factor and the extent of local autonomy is not clear, since even if a positive correlation is found between a certain factor and the extent of local dependence on the state government, the strength of the correlation is not the same in every place. The existence of a dominant factor in one country and its absence or unimportance in a different country contributes in different ways to local autonomy. In Israel, too little research has been conducted on this issue to enable us to detail the pattern of local autonomy.[6] However, we can state that discussions of the autonomy of local governments in Israel which have relied principally on the laws and formal documents have no real validity. A substantial portion of the discussion in this chapter is devoted to supporting that conclusion.

State and Local Actors and Their Functions

While the principal responsibility for state-local relations is in the hands of the government ministries, principally those ministries which oversee local authorities, three other bodies also play roles of legislation or oversight. They are: the Knesset, the State Comptroller, and the Courts.

The Knesset

The Knesset has no formal role in the establishment or supervision of local authorities, but through legislation it empowers the Minister of Interior to establish municipalities and local councils, and to organize those matters which are relevant to their operation and supervision.[7] Nevertheless, legislation passed in the Knesset establishes the jurisdiction and authority of municipalities and government ministries (principally the Ministry of

Interior) in local matters. The Local Authorities (Election and Tenure of Mayor and Deputy Mayors) Law, 5735-1975, providing for the direct election of mayors, was an important innovation in the field of local government legislation.[8]

The fact that several mayors, mostly from the two major parties — Labor and Likud, simultaneously serve as members of the Knesset creates a system of interactions which is in no way revealed by the formal documents. Very little is known about this system, or about the influence of mayors on their political parties, the state leadership, and the Knesset factions, since these issues have almost never been researched, but there is little doubt that an intensive two-way communication exists through these channels.

Another Knesset channel, its committees, provide forums for representatives of local government to express their positions on every matter relevant to municipal government. The committees take such testimony into account when making decisions, and are thus influenced by local interests.

The State Comptroller

The State Comptroller (consolidated version) Law, 5718-1958, places responsibility for the inspection and auditing of local government activities (among others) in an independent state comptroller, and specifies the formula for reporting its findings.[9] In addition to auditing, the state comptroller also serves as Ombudsman (Commissioner for Complaints from the Public).[10] Citizens or bodies who believe they have been injured by the actions of a local authority may turn to the state comptroller for relief. The findings and recommendations of the comptroller are as binding on local authorities as they are on government ministries.

The Courts

The local authority is a legal entity, and similar to any association established by law. "Its authority is defined and delimited by the law which created it, and its scope includes nothing beyond what is explicitly stated, or is required for the performance of those goals in whose name the association was formed....All that is not explicitly permitted or is thusly included is forbidden."[11] As a legal body the local authority is liable before the law, and claims against it can be made in court. The Supreme Court, in its function as the High Court of Justice, may review the legality of the activities of all governing institutions including local authorities. Any person or body who believes that their rights were violated by an act of a local authority is entitled to appeal to the Supreme Court.

Government Ministries

Ministerial supervision of local authorities is close and constant. Supervision is often required when the service provided by the local authority is one of national importance, such as education and welfare, where a minimal standard must be guaranteed which assures a measure of equality, with no radical differences between different places. Supervision of local services also assures professional standards in such areas as safety and food quality. Beyond the actual provision of services, local authorities collect revenues from local residents and spend huge amounts in their budgets. This figures prominently in the country's economy, a fact which can hardly be ignored by the state government.

Supervision by the state government is to insure that national interests are not damaged by narrower local interests. In the early years of the state it could be claimed that ministerial supervision was also justified for administrative and professional reasons. For example, many localities were comprised of new immigrants who were not able to maintain municipal services at the required level due to a lack of skilled manpower. State government involvement may also be unrelated to the supervision process, such as serving as a clearing house for useful ideas or as an arbitrator between two local authorities in conflict.

State government involvement in local affairs is necessary for a variety of reasons. We will seek to clarify below what constitutes a reasonable degree of involvement, how this can be measured, and what its practical implications are for local autonomy.

The Union of Local Authorities

The Union of Local Authorities is a voluntary organization of municipalities and local councils established in 1936 and reorganized in 1956 under its current title when the three major cities joined (Jerusalem, Tel Aviv and Haifa). The regional councils are organized separately in the Organization of Regional Councils since they have special problems which differ from other local authorities. The Union of Local Authorities does not have a statutory basis and therefore it is unable to enforce a defined policy on its members. Its goal is to further the mutual interests of the local municipalities in their relations with state organs such as government offices and the Knesset. Similarly, the Union of Local Authorities represents the local authorities in negotiations for collective wage agreements and it signs them together with the Histadrut and the government. It has many committees, both permanent and ad hoc, on assorted professional, budgetary and administrative issues. In addition, it operates various associations of key local officials such as the Association of Town Clerks and the Association of Local Treasurers.[12]

The Local Authorities

The general powers of the local authorities involve six basic areas: legislation; taxation, including obligatory payments; judgment; financial management; joint activities with other bodies; and various general powers. While not completely independent in any of these areas, a local authority is able to act on behalf of local interests within each of them according to the wishes of the elected representatives of the local constituency.

The local authority influences the physical and social environment of its residents in many and varied ways through the enactment of by-laws. These may be based on the general authority granted under the Municipal Corporations Ordinance, (new version) and the Local Councils Ordinance, (new version)[13] or by the authority of laws which relate to specific topics, such as sewage and firefighting services. These by-laws will affect the behavior, pocketbook and leisure time of local residents.[14]

The local authority has the power to assess local taxes and obligatory payments. These include the general municipal tax, levies (mostly for licensing) and participatory payments (such as for street paving). All of these payments and their levels are fixed in by-laws which require the approval of the Minister of Interior.[15]

The local authority maintains semi-judicial institutions which rule on appeals concerning local authority actions in such matters as a sewage tax,[16] welfare services,[17] and guard duty.[18]

Financial management is a central issue in the operation of the local authority and its relations with the central government and a matter which is dealt with extensively in other parts of this book as well as later in this chapter.[19]

State Services

State services, principally in the areas of education and welfare, comprise more than half the budget and an even higher proportion of the personnel employed by local authorities. They constitute the major arena of interaction between local and state authorities. In addition, in the area of physical planning and building, both the legal aspects and the dynamics of construction and development often cause local and national interests to clash. In the following sections we will briefly review the division of functions between the localities and the relevant state authorities.

Education

The Ministry of Education and Culture is the authority which sets policies and standards for most matters, while execution is undertaken by the local authority. There are instances in which the Ministry can substitute for the local authority in execution as well, if the latter does not perform according to the minimum required level. For the most part, it is the job of the local authority to provide the physical means and conditions through which the state can carry out its responsibilities in the field of education. In fulfilling this function, the local authority must act in accordance with the guidelines and norms established by the Ministry.

The law emphasizes the principle of cooperation between the two authorities, and while the exact division of functions itself is not defined by law, the Ministry is responsible for the educational program and its value content, while the local authority is responsible for the buildings and physical equipment. This division is too simplistic, however, and from the early years of the state a reality of shared responsibility developed — the local authority developed areas of educational content, while the Ministry became involved in physical development.[20] Therefore, the legal framework does not prevent the local authority from initiating educational projects and from playing a substantial role in this area.[21]

50

Welfare

In the first decade following the establishment of the state, no welfare laws were legislated. In their absence, the budgeting laws served as the basis for the participation of the state in welfare services. The Municipal Corporations Ordinance did authorize the municipality to provide certain welfare services such as housing and employment for the poor and disabled, but most welfare matters were not specified by law.[22] The Welfare Services Law, 5718-1958 obligates every local authority to maintain a welfare office for the needy, but the law does not explicitly state how these offices are to be organized and how tasks are to be divided between the Ministry of Labor and Social Welfare and the municipality. Despite this, the division between them is clear; with the exception of certain services operated directly by the Ministry, the local authority is responsible for providing most of the social work services in the community and it hires its own personnel to carry them out.

According to the regulations, services should be provided to the needy "in accordance with the instructions of the director-general of the Ministry of Labor and Social Welfare"[23] and granted legal status to the Social Work Regulations — a collection of professional and administrative guidelines prepared by the director-general. The Social Work Regulations encompass all welfare activities and set the professional, administrative and financial rules which govern the provision of welfare services. Formally, the Ministry is the authority which sets the policy and the details of execution, while the local authority acts as an agent for the execution of these instructions and is open to supervision and auditing by the state authority.

Physical Planning and Building

In the field of physical planning and building, Israeli legislation broadened the power of the local authority and its representatives in the regional and countrywide planning institutions.[24] The Planning and Building Law, 5725-1965, sets forth the principles according to which master plans are drafted and the planning institutions act in three areas — local, district and countrywide. The law grants the local planning commission considerable independence, while also broadening the regional and countrywide dimensions in planning. The local commission is comprised of members of the local council. Where it serves a planning area which includes more than one local authority, the representatives of those local authorities within the planning area form the majority.[25] The law gives the local commission responsibility for day-to-day management and on-site compliance with regulations.

The district commission is a joint state-local authority comprised of representatives of the government ministries whose field of action is relevant to the issues of planning and of representatives of local authorities in the region. The district commission approves the detailed local plans, but does not generally deal with ongoing inspection of the plans and is not certified to grant licenses for construction. It also acts as a forum for handling appeals of decisions made by local commissions.[26]

*

Even if we were to survey all of the services in which the local authority takes part, we would find it difficult to establish the extent of the independence granted it by law. It is possible to quote sections of the law which infer the subordination of the local authority to a government ministry, but this does not present a realistic picture. In broad areas such as education and welfare, there are in reality no detailed definitions of the division of authority. As far as the actual situation is concerned, it goes either way. In other services, the exact situation differs from area to area. Only in a very few instances is it possible to say anything unequivocal, such as in the case of security, where the local authority is clearly subordinate to the state authority.

The Network of Interrelationships Between the State and Local Governments

There are three major areas which reflect the network of interrelationships between the state and local governments: budgetary and operational supervision; sources of local authority income and revenue; and planning and construction. Within the format of this chapter it is impossible to deal with all aspects of these topics. Our goal will be to demonstrate the network of state-local relations in their principle fields of action.

Government Supervision of Local Municipalities

According to law, the responsibility for the supervision of local authorities in Israel rests largely with the Ministry of Interior. Education, welfare, health care and religious services, which comprise the bulk of local expenditures, are subject to different forms of state supervision. In addition to the laws themselves, there are regulations, procedures and instructions established by government ministries in every field of municipal action. However, relative to the multitude of written instructions, the extent of actual supervision is minimal. Although the term "supervision" is defined as "to oversee, have the oversight of, superintend the execution or performance of (a thing), the movements or work of (a person) (Oxford Universal Dictionary)," in a Western democracy this aspect tends to be downplayed and in its place has come the dominant type of supervision which includes professional advice and counselling, which is not always superior in its expertise to that of the local official. Sometimes we find that the supervisor also acts as an intermediary between the state government and local bodies.[27]

The direct supervisory responsibilities of the Ministry of Interior over local authorities are in the hands of its regional officials, though the regional officers, for their own reasons, actually spend only a small part of their time on matters involving the local authorities.[28] General supervision, and budgetary supervision in particular, are limited because the regional offices lack the manpower to deal with the intricacies of local authority budgets, especially for the largest ones. Lacking any objective measures for evaluating budgetary expenditures, there is no escape from setting budgets through a process of negotiation in which the local authority usually has the upper hand. The local authority invariably inflates its proposed budget prior to negotiations with the Ministry of Interior, so that even after cutbacks it is left with a budget which may be larger than strictly necessary.[29] There is reason to assume that this may be closer to the truth during years of economic well-being, and less true during leaner periods when circumstances may diminish the "negotiating margin."

The following is a typical example of the weakness of the supervisory system, despite legal and administrative improvements in the implementation of government policy in recent years. According to the budget laws of the 1980s, the Minister of Interior was authorized to determine the maximum level of manpower in each locality. If the local authority employed personnel in numbers which exceeded its allocated quota, the minister was authorized to order the local authority to stop employing those in excess of the quota and to reduce the state's grant to the local authority accordingly. The findings of the State Comptroller "point to the fact that in most local authorities that were investigated, the instructions of the Ministry of Interior concerning manpower reductions in local authorities were not implemented during fiscal year 1984."[30]

The same basic situation exists with the Ministry of Labor and Social Welfare. The supervision of local offices is nominally performed by professional supervisors from the welfare services unit of the ministry in the context of its regional offices, but in reality these supervisors are more involved with advice and counselling and less with supervision to assure that the local municipality is acting in accordance with ministry instructions. The State Comptroller has found that the ministry, which "employs tens of supervisors in its regions, has not succeeded in developing procedures for reporting and follow-up which are systematic, continuous and coordinated by the supervisory system."[31]

In a similar fashion it is not rare to find organized local interests breaking through the wall of policy set by the Ministry of Education and Culture, whether or not the matter at issue has the support of the local authority.

Generally, the lack of supervision is a clear sign of the existence of "demilitarized zones" in which the local authority can express itself without any real limitation by the rules or by ministry prescriptions. This lack of supervision has been an established phenomenon throughout all the years of the existence of the state, and is found in all of the democratic nations of the world.[32] We must then relate to this phenomenon from within a much broader context and recognize that the control of the state government over most of the other governmental bodies within the state is flimsy at best. This phenomenon is characteristic of most western democracies, despite noticeable differences among them in national and political culture.[33]

In an open society, it is difficult to maintain a close supervisory system because authoritarian tendencies, even when anchored in law, are considered foreign and unacceptable. Also, from the perspective of efficiency one should not exaggerate the power of supervision, for its mere employment is hardly a formula for the achievement of administrative or industrial efficiency. Efficiency is achieved through a combination of many factors (which cannot be detailed here) and supervision is just one of them. For our purposes, inefficiency expresses itself as the large gap between the stated goals for which the state government allocates funds for local services, and the actual local expenditures for those purposes, within reasonable limits of the declared cost. The more varied the range of social and welfare services, the more difficult it is to operate an effective supervisory system, even if the law grants the state government all the necessary tools and authority. Therefore, the weaker the supervisory system of the relevant ministry, the wider is the degree of local freedom.

In addition, the mechanisms of supervision generally remain static as compared to the dynamic developments in the social services. Not only does the supervisory system fail to achieve its goals, but it also creates two phenomena which serve to obscure the reality. On the one hand, it nurtures the illusion that its very existence is enough of a factor to prevent significant deviance, even when in reality the opposite may be true. On the other hand, the formal existence of a supervisory system, ineffective as it is, acts as a comfortable support on which the local authority can lean in order to justify inaction and to place the responsibility on the state government.

From the arguments presented above, from findings presented in detail elsewhere, and from inspection and auditing reports which have been published since the state was founded, we see a picture of local government which acts with considerable independence.[34] In many sectors there is very little, if any, control. This refutes the widespread claim that the supervisory network of the state government presents the local authorities from acting independently. These supervisory powers not only are not employed, but there are daily revelations of independent activity in almost every area of local authority — in the initiation of projects, development of services, setting of wage and pension conditions for high level officials, financial management, and more. There is then good reason to doubt the impression, widespread among scholars and political leaders, that local authority is caught in a web of state government supervision and control.

Sources of Local Authority Income

To estimate the extent of the financial autonomy of local authorities, we must first look at the composition of their income. Income can be classified according to source, while paying special attention to the strings attached to certain types of income in terms of budgetary designation. There are three principle groups, the third of which is divided into two designated types:
  a) Locally-generated income — which local authorities collect on their own (taxes, service fees, participations).
  b) Transferred income — from the state government to the municipalities according to an agreement or law (e.g. 4.828 percent of state income in lieu of the municipal property tax which was abolished in 1968, 60 percent of the Improvement Tax, and others).
  c) Direct government participation in the form of:
     1. General grant (through the Ministry of Interior).
     2. Earmarked participation — partial or complete financing by government ministries of services provided by the local authority (primarily education and welfare services).[35]
A further source of income is "loans for balancing the ordinary budget."

There are those who see the three main sources of income as representing three levels of autonomy for the local authority in the collection and use of funds. Locally-generated income, since it is collected directly by the municipality, represents local autonomy. Transferred income, though collected by the state government, is distributed by formulas which are not subject to random change, yet reflects a certain degree of dependence on the state government. Direct government participation represents local dependence on the state government.[36]

Table 2.1 shows the sources of income in the ordinary budgets of local authorities and their share of the total income for every fiscal year between 1972/73 and 1983/84.

Table 2.1

COMPOSITION OF INCOME IN THE ORDINARY
BUDGET OF LOCAL AUTHORITIES
According to Type of Source for Fiscal Years 1972/73–1983/84
(in percentages)

(1) Fiscal Year	(2) Total Income	(3) Locally- Gene- rated Income	(4) Trans- ferred Income	Government Participation		(7) Loans for Balancing Ordinary Budget
				(5) Earmarked	(6) General Grant	
1972/73	100	44	18	16	14	8
1973/74	100	36	19	19	14	12
1974/75	100	34	17	24	10	15
1975/76	100	32	16	19	23	9
1976/77	100	33	17	19	24	7
1977/78	100	33	17	19	24	7
1978/79	100	31	16	21	24	9
1979/80	100	30	12	22	31	5
1980/81	100	30	10	21	28	12
1981/82	100	36	10	23	28	4
1982/83	100	36	11	25	26	1
1983/84	100	38	11	25	23	2

Sources: For years 1972/73 and 1973/74 — *Proposed Budget for Fiscal Year 1982*, Ministry of Interior, Jerusalem, 1982, p. 185 (Hebrew).
For years 1974/75–1983/84 — *Statistical Abstract of Israel* Nos. 28–37 (1977-1986), Central Bureau of Statistics, Jerusalem.
Note: Totals do not always add up to 100 percent due to rounding.

According to the data in table 2.1, there is a clear trend show-
ing that government participation (columns 5 and 6) has grown
larger; from 30 percent of all income in 1972/73 to 50 percent and
more in the 1980s. At the same time, the portion of locally-generated income declined from 44 percent to 30 percent in 1979/80 and
1980/81, increasing again to 38 percent in 1983/84. These trends
are often interpreted as signifying a growing degree of dependence by the local authorities on the central government. Shevah
Weiss, for example, has described the situation in the following
terms:

> The local authority budget reflects more than anything else the
> relations between the center and the periphery, and is likely to
> shed light on the estimated degree of dependence of these au-
> thorities on the central government. The multi-faceted re-
> liance on government appropriations is likely to leave very
> little power in the hands of the mayor, while relatively lesser
> degrees of dependence on government appropriations is likely
> to leave the mayor with considerable power. The mayor of a
> municipality whose principle income comes from the gov-
> ernment will need to invest his greatest energies in the devel-
> opment of good relations with the government in general, and
> more specifically with the heads of the economic ministries
> and the Ministry of Interior. In contrast, the mayor of a mu-
> nicipality which is less dependent on appropriations from the
> central government is likely to have much more time to spend
> on his other communal duties. There are certainly instances
> in which the personal power of the local politician (whatever its
> sources may be) is likely to change the proportion between lo-
> cal dependence on the government, as reflected in the budget,
> and local dependence in reality. But despite this there is no
> doubt that the budget reflects with great clarity the dependence
> on the center, and can thus act as an important and reliable (if
> not exclusive) indicator for the measurement of the depen-
> dence of all local authorities on the central government, both
> separately and jointly.[37]

A more detailed analysis of the components of the principle
types of income will show that the budgetary proportions do not in
fact reflect relative degrees of dependence. As mentioned above,
government participation comes in more than one form. Also,
there is not an equal degree of dependence deriving from the different types of participation. One must first make a qualitative
distinction between a general grant and an earmarked

participation. The form of government participation which expanded at the most rapid rate is the general grant, whose receipt on the part of the local authority is not conditional on its being spent for designated purposes. It has not resulted in greater dependence because the increase does not force the local authority to use this money according to any ordering of priorities other than that which it sets for itself and because the size of this grant is influenced by the size of the population in each local authority and by other factors unique to it.

Several years ago the Ministry of Interior developed a method for dividing up the grants based on a set standard "basket of services" and "basket of income." Beginning in fiscal year 1976, the budget of each municipality was checked to see how it fit the new standards, and "the division of the grant was said to be performed on the basis of the results of the budget check according to the set standard."

Of course, as long as the system for the distribution of the grant is not carried out exactly according to formula, there is a basis for negotiation concerning its size, but even in this imperfect situation, the overwhelming share of the general grant is based on data which is specific to each place.[38] There is the same local flexibility in the use of this grant money as there is in the case of locally-generated income. When locally-generated income and the general grant are combined, we see that there has been no significant change in the total; in 1972/73 they comprised 58 percent of total local income and in the 1980s, between 58 and 64 percent, with an increase in general grants compensating for the decrease in locally-generated income.

Nor does transferred income necessarily increase local dependence on the state government; in fact, it has its advantages since most of the locally-generated income is by its very nature limited in its dynamism. Thus, in discussing locally-generated income and transferred income, we are not dealing with two levels of autonomy, despite first impressions. This problem of local government finance and in particular the diminishing portion of locally-generated income is not unique to Israel.[39] In Israel the diminishing relative proportion of locally-generated income which took place in the 1970s was primarily the result of the freezing of rates for the general municipal tax and the business tax — which make up the majority of locally-collected taxes — as well as the welfare and recreation levies; any increase in income from them has come principally from an increase in the number of apartments and businesses. Compensation for the fact that the rate of increase in locally-generated income has lagged behind the rate of increase in municipal expenditures was given through several channels, not all of which are reflected in the data in table 2.1 or even in other statistical publications.[40]

Another dynamic source balancing the slow growth of locally-generated income is transferred income. This type of income is convenient and even desirable for the local authority, which does not have to collect it and which receives this income according to its designated share of overall national receipts. In addition, the local authority does not have to commit transferred income to a defined purpose.

In fiscal year 1968/69, the collection of the property tax by local authorities was cancelled, and in exchange they receive 4.828 percent of the income of the state. This arrangement brings local authorities more income than that which they would have collected themselves. Since state income from taxes increases together with increases in wages and inflation, the amounts transferred in place of the property tax increase at a much higher rate than income from property taxes would have increased, and even more than income from property taxes when the government itself collects it.[41] To a certain extent this acts as compensation for the slower increase in municipal taxes which the local authorities collect.

Therefore, transferred income is similar to locally-generated income. If we add it to the other sources which, as we explained, do not affect independence, the portion of income whose use is open to the discretion of the local authority totaled 76 percent in 1972/73 and 72 percent in 1983/84. Except for a steep decrease in 1974/75 to 61 percent, the total of these sources throughout the 1970s and early 1980s amounted to 70 percent or more.

Moreover, the earmarked participation of the government ministries includes portions which should not be seen as reflecting dependence on the state government. In part, they cover services whose entire cost is borne by the ministry so that the provision of those services places no fiscal burden on the local authority. Even when the municipality must participate in the cost, generally it is not required to finance the entire expense. Thus, not only is the burden of local dependence on the state government not particularly heavy, but the local authority, for a minimal price, is able to supply a service whose cost is several times the portion it finances.

This is particularly important since many services defined as state services would otherwise have to be provided by local authorities, which would have to find the resources to finance them. True, not all of the municipalities would initiate all of the same activities. Still, the very fact of the participation of the state government frees funds which the local authority would otherwise have to raise in order to fund at least some of those services which it would have provided even without state government initiative.

Even if we limit ourselves to a general analysis of earmarked participation, we see that the considerable majority of these participations cannot be considered "binding income," whose receipt leads to local dependence. From the point of view of the local authority, there are two types of limitations deriving from government participation which can be viewed on two levels. The first is the designation of destination of income by the government ministry, which is defined in order to prevent the municipality from allocating the funds for a different purpose. However, the ministry's determination of its destination does not necessarily mean that the expense does not fit the needs or desires of the local population. State government involvement in a specific service does prevent a local authority from advancing services which seem to it to be of higher priority. Yet this limitation loses its rigidity in many situations, such as when the local authority would itself have allocated resources for the same purpose, when all or most of the expense is funded by the state government, or when the local authority must cover only a small sum from its other resources.

A different kind of limitation derives from the conditions under which the state participation is given, should these go against the will of the local authority which must perform the service in compliance with ministry instructions. This coercion is especially strong when a municipality must finance part of the cost of the service from its own resources which, were it not for the requirements of the ministry, would not be provided in the same form, if at all. However, it is difficult to estimate or measure the different levels of "unwillingness" of local authorities to provide money for a specific purpose. First of all, the declaration that a certain expense is not to the liking of the local authority is no measure in itself of "unwillingness," since in many cases this type of declaration is made for tactical reasons. Secondly, alternatives for financial outlays are ranked at different levels of priority. Therefore the alternative use does not fall on the entire expense, but rather means the difference between an outlay at one priority level rather than another. Since we have no way to measure degrees of unwillingness, and we do not even have techniques to measure the marginal values of the cost-benefit ratio of alternatives, the only way to prove our point is through its negation. In other words, we can survey the conditions of participation in each clause and point out that in the majority of cases the services referred to are not those that the municipality would oppose. In the case of complete or near complete financing of a certain clause, even if the municipality were to claim that it is committed to providing the service only because of the requirement of the ministry, the very fact that the municipality does not bear the burden of its maintenance undermines its claim. The difference between a service which the municipality would itself undertake and a service which it claims it would not undertake takes on significance only when government financing is partial. As we will demonstrate, the vast majority of earmarked participations do not clash with local interests.

In the 1982 budget, earmarked government participation in local authority budgets totalled 7.16 billion shekels, 4.88 billion of which came from the Ministry of Education and Culture and 2.14 billion from the Ministry of Labor and Social Welfare. The remaining 0.14 billion came from the Ministry of Health, mostly for support of mother and child services, and the Ministry of Interior for municipal fire departments.

Nearly 70 percent of the participation of the Ministry of Education and Culture was designated for three areas which have no bearing on local authority dependence: 1.12 billion shekels for wages for maintenance and secretarial staff in the elementary and junior high schools (complete coverage by the ministry); 1.47 billion shekels for graduated tuition in the high schools (since the establishment of free secondary education in 1979, the ministry pays tuition to each school in accordance with the level of services given by the school); 621 million shekels for financing pre-kindergarten day care (in these nurseries, state participation plus the payments of the parents cover 95 percent or more of the expenses).[42] Thus, at least 3.21 billion shekels out of 4.88 billion given to local authorities as earmarked government participation in education did not force them to make any outlays which ran counter to their priorities. A detailed analysis of additional clauses would show that even a higher percentage of earmarked participation does not damage a local authority's freedom of action.[43]

Approximately 30 percent of the earmarked participation of the Ministry of Labor and Social Welfare went to finance the total maintenance costs of children in boarding schools, without any required participation on the part of the local authority (about .603 billion shekels out of 2.135 billion). The remaining 1.5 billion shekels were grants to local authorities to cover between 75 and 100 percent of their recognized welfare expenses. Even if there is disagreement between the local authorities and the ministry on the definition of a recognized expense, it cannot alter the fact that most welfare expenses are covered by the ministry.

In summary, the "independence" of local authorities has not been damaged, even after significant changes which occurred in the relative division between the three sources of income: locally-generated, transferred and government participation. There is no significant correlation between an increase in the "non-independent" portions of income and an increase in dependence on the central government.

It is clear that the majority of income from participation by government ministries in the operation of state services does not force the municipality to make expenditures which it opposes. Therefore, even the increase in the levels of participation earmarked by government ministries, from 16 percent in 1972/73 to 25 percent in 1983/84, does not imply an increase in dependence on the state government because in the 1980s most of this participation covers 80-100 percent of expenses, while in the 1970s and in earlier periods it covered a lower proportion, resulting in a higher burden of local participation.

Concentrations of Power in Matters of Planning and Construction

As described earlier, Israeli legislation broadened the powers of local authorities and their representation in planning institutions at all levels. In the mid-1960s, on the eve of the implementation of the Planning and Building Law, 5725-1965, it was possible to foresee that the expansion of the legal powers of the Ministry of Interior would bring about a contradiction:

Between the broad legal authority and the very limited political power of the central physical planning unit...such that if it remains without political backing, then we can assume that it will be impossible to carry out the law, and there is likely to be an even further decline in the influence of central physical planning, as a result of the failed attempts to enforce its legal authorities in the face of a lack of the necessary power.[44]

Not only are there other state bodies involved in physical planning, but some of these have much more power to press their development objectives, a fact which severely limits the power of the Ministry of Interior. This fact should not be easily dismissed. It is a mistake to claim that these bodies also represent the state government, and that therefore it does not matter in which ministry they are located. In fact, the dispersal of these powers among several concentrations of power in the state government gives the local authority considerable freedom to promote its own initiatives or to join the initiatives of others who further its local interests in the field of physical development.

Almost every ministry is granted some authority by law in matters of planning and construction. For example, the Ministry of Health is authorized to approve planning details relating to sanitary requirements, and the Ministry of Religious Affairs has the authority to guarantee that local or district master plans protect holy sites and religious edifices. These examples and similar ones relating to almost all of the ministries concern defined and limited sectors. We should not exaggerate their influence on the general process of planning and building. However, there are three state bodies not in the hierarchy of planning institutions which have considerable influence both directly and indirectly in the field of building and construction: the Ministry of Finance; the Ministry of Construction and Housing; and the Israel Lands Authority. We will describe the general involvement of each one in planning and construction, and demonstrate the ways in which the local authority can harness these bodies (or be harnessed by them) for movement in the directions which it prefers.

Ministry of Finance — The Land Acquisition for Public Purposes Ordinance, 1943, the principal Israeli legislation concerning land expropriation, enables the Finance Minister to expropriate land for public need. The administrative handling of expropriation is in the hands of the Israel Lands Authority, but the definition of "the public need" for which the Finance Minister is authorized to expropriate, is completely at the discretion of the Minister. As long as the expropriation is carried out in good faith, even the courts do not challenge the legitimacy of the stated public need.

While this authority is granted to the Finance Minister, he, in turn, is authorized to delegate authority for the actual purchase to the local authority at whose initiative the expropriation is being performed, so that the municipality actually determines the level of compensation and payment to the original owners.[45] Since the request by the local authority to expropriate land for the public need is usually tied to its service-providing functions, the Finance Minister tends to authorize its requests without difficulty, so that in reality it is the local authority which plays a dominant role in the matter.

Aside from its role in expropriation for public need, the Finance Ministry has no formal status in the physical planning machinery. One should not exaggerate the importance of this legal authority and its potential influence on decisions concerning the use of land, since the delegation of this authority to the municipalities is quite widespread. However, the power of the Finance Ministry in the area of public financing does have a direct impact on physical planning. The ministry's policy and its involvement on various levels such as taxation (property taxes), the distribution of state funds for planning and construction, and the establishment of financing and purchasing conditions for projects or different bodies whose activities bear directly on physical planning (investments, tourism and industry), play an important role in the field of construction. The ministry's presence is also felt in other areas of social and economic development.

We do not imply that the field of planning and construction is unique in this respect. In fact, the opposite is the case. Compared to the fields of finance and business, the involvement of the Finance Ministry here is quite marginal. Some feel that a lack of formal status by the Finance Ministry in central forums or coordinating bodies in the area of physical planning results in a disconnected decision-making system in the fields of planning and finance.[46] This is not to say that there is no overlap between the formal framework and reality. Even though the Finance Ministry is the central source of financial resources in the country, many resources are dispersed among different government ministries —

Construction and Housing, Tourism, Industry and Commerce, Interior, etc. All of these have their own formal status in the planning and construction system, contributing to limit the direct influence of the Ministry of Finance in the local arena.

Still, the central role which the Ministry of Finance plays in the mobilization of Israeli and foreign capital for investments in development, places it in the center of major development projects. Every local authority is interested in the development of its tourism, commercial and industrial sectors. The Finance Ministry's control over the capital market in the country determines the direction of development in the various cities, as they are actually determined according to short-term plans in which the ministry is involved. Thus the Finance Ministry, in cooperation with the local authorities, creates facts in the field of physical planning which direct or interfere with the long-range planning for which the physical planning authorities are responsible.[47]

This strengthens the hand of the local authority when it deals with the planning authorities of the Ministry of Interior. If the local authority weighs local needs from its own perspective, and if it obtains financial resources from the Finance Ministry (or with its help) to carry out its plans, then at the same time it also strengthens its influence on the determination of land use within its jurisdiction. The process is similar when the cooperation is with other powerful economic elements in the state government. Clearly the existence of these other bodies takes away from the exclusiveness of the Finance Ministry in directing financing to development, even if all of these ministries are themselves dependent to a certain extent on the Finance Ministry.

Ministry of Construction and Housing — The Planning and Building Law grants the Ministry of Construction and Housing, and several other ministries and bodies, representation on local, regional and countrywide councils. The ministry has its own status in the context of special planning committees in development towns. As an initiator within the framework of detailed plans, it is no different from other initiators, and must act in coordination with the Israel Lands Authority, which owns the land. Although the law does not formally grant it a central role in the planning authorities, the ministry is of major importance in the field of physical planning and in different stages of planning and performance due to the tremendous scope of the planning and construction which it undertakes. Representatives of the ministry are members of the boards of directors of housing companies and financial institutions, and through them it is a partner in large construction projects. Public non-governmental construction companies are also within its sphere of influence, since the ministry allocates construction projects to them which it initiates.

From a practical perspective, the ministry has tremendous influence on the building of cities. The ministry directly controls more than two-thirds of all the residential housing in the country. From its large budget it can allocate considerable sums for planning and development and is involved in many master plans, general plans and detailed plans. Only the status of the Israel Lands Authority and its control of urban lands prevents the ministry from being a nearly exclusive ruler in the field of urban development, for, in fact, it is in no way dependent on the Ministry of Interior.

Israel Lands Authority — As the owner of more than 90 percent of the land in Israel, the Israel Lands Authority is always in the center of physical planning.[48] However, within the Lands Authority itself, significantly different ideological perspectives clash. The Lands Authority's council is made up of 12 government representatives and 11 representatives of the Jewish National Fund. The Minister of Agriculture serves as chairman of the council.

The guidelines of land policy which the government laid down in 1965, and which the Lands Authority adopted, rigidly protect agricultural land, allowing it to be transferred for leasing only. In general, urban land is also leased, though under certain conditions it can be sold. The transfer of land rights was made dependent upon the agreement of the Lands Authority and the payment of a consent fee.[49]

Such a concentration of power inevitably has tremendous implications, regardless of whether the Lands Authority has a clear policy or one which is an outgrowth of a combination of irrational and coincidental decisions. Today the Israel Lands Authority is one of the key forces in physical planning in the country, despite an essential contradiction between it and the planning and legal systems of physical planning. Theoretically, the policy of the Lands Authority should have been subordinate to physical planning policy. However, whether due to the slow crystallization of plans for physical planning, the weakness of the formal body responsible for this area (the Ministry of Interior), or the style in which the Lands Authority acts, it often dictates the lines according to which the plans are drawn. This is done through its participation in the preparation of master plans, as well as through projects which are based on the Lands Authority's willingness to respond favorably to a request for allocation of land.

The Israel Lands Authority participates together with the Ministry of Interior and the Ministry of Construction and Housing, as well as the local authorities, in the preparation of local master plans and in their financing "in all of those places in which the Lands Authority has an interest."[50] In recent years about 100 local master plans have been advanced. In 1982, only 2.2 million shekels were budgeted by the Ministry of Interior for this purpose, as opposed to 5 million shekels budgeted for the same purpose by the Lands Authority. In addition, over 10 million shekels were included in the budget of the Lands Authority for building plans. These plans are prepared at the initiative of the Lands Authority or at the initiative of other bodies with its cooperation. In accordance with an agreement with the Ministry of Construction and Housing in 1976, the preparation of plans for the establishment of residential neighborhoods is carried out by the ministry in coordination with the Lands Authority.[51]

The Israel Lands Authority has representatives on the boards of directors of 21 development and construction companies, among them Amidar (Israel National Housing Corporation for Immigrants), the Jerusalem Economic Corporation, Afridar Housing Company, Government Tourist Corporation, and the companies for the rehabilitation of poor neighborhoods in the three largest cities. This broad involvement by the Lands Authority in the planning and development of territory reflects its great interest in the advancement of planning for the purpose of establishing land values. Clearly, the more this involvement grows, the greater is the danger that the Lands Authority will invade areas in which the local authority is responsible. On the one hand, contests over physical planning usually occur in these frameworks in which the other formal bodies having an interest in the land participate, such as local authorities, the Ministry of Interior and other government ministries and units. On the other hand, many decisions are determined by the Lands Authority as the result of public pressure.

In any matter involving urban land at least three parties are involved: the local authority, the Ministry of Interior, and the initiator (many times also a representative of the public interest, such as the Ministry of Construction and Housing or a large construction company). In a complex situation such as a large-scale project, several ministries are involved — the Ministry of Construction and Housing, the Finance Ministry, the Ministry of Tourism, the Ministry of Industry and Commerce — and it is not rare to find that each has its own interests to protect. As the almost exclusive owner of state land, the Lands Authority not only provides budgets, but also subsidizes projects through its allocation of land. The Lands Authority is under constant pressure to heed the public interest and to make its lands available for use at an uneconomic, if not symbolic, price. As the public institution responsible for state land, the Lands Authority must strive to obtain the best return possible, so that its income can be put to public use. Its acceptance of less than the full price means a profit for the one who receives the land.

The various public interests represented by each of the ministries or government bodies ultimately place their stamp on the formation of a physical plan through the Israel Lands Authority, often in opposition to (or with pressure against) the legal planning authorities. It does not matter that the Lands Authority does not always intend to aid a certain public interest and to ignore the official planning institutions. The fact is that its activities and shortcomings have considerable implications for physical planning. It is enough to quote the following passage from the words of the Lands Authority itself to understand that its decision-making over the years has been faulty:

It should be noted that the data on the land which is in the Authority's possession is concentrated today in a manner which makes it inaccessible for decision-making purposes and certainly inaccessible for purposes of registration. Therefore it was decided this year to begin a multi-year project, to organize the data for the purposes of decision-making and registration.[52]

*

In summary, our discussion of the field of planning and construction has concentrated on the activities of the bodies which are not a part of the official planning hierarchy. Theoretically, each of them could have been a stumbling block in the path of a local authority, but in actuality they do not threaten the municipality's independence. The municipality's independence is threatened only to the extent that some of its ability to counterbalance forces working against it is taken away. This balance can be formed either through its own power or with the aid of another political or public body.

The Ministry of Finance, the Ministry of Construction and Housing, and the Israel Lands Authority are all intensively involved in important aspects of physical planning. However, since they each represent different interests, this paves the way for the local authority to advance those interests which it shares with any one of them, and in this way to repulse pressures activated by the others. The involvement of other ministries, (such as the Ministry of Industry and Commerce, or the Ministry of Tourism) is generally on a smaller scale, although it can reach a similar intensity in development towns. In this case, too, the local authority can find a partner to its interests from among the government ministries.[53]

Summary and Conclusions

In this section we viewed the interrelations between the local and state authorities from five different angles, and this multi-dimensional picture presents a local authority whose autonomous foundations are strong, even if they are not immediately apparent. Research in western democracies indicates more and more the existence of autonomy even if the formal legal structure or the composition of the local authority's income seem to imply that it is dependent on the state government. The degree of autonomy is an outcome of a number of factors in different areas: national factors (ideological pluralism, dispersed control of the means of production), demographic and geographic factors (size of the local population and the number of local authorities), socio-economic factors (heterogeneity of the population in terms of levels of education and income, and the composition of local income) and political factors (the local leadership and its involvement on the national political scene, and the activity of voluntary organizations).

The formal framework indeed presents a picture of dependence on the state government, but precisely in the two areas central to the activities of local authorities — education and welfare —

the law does not specify the division of authority. The rules and regulations of the two government ministries responsible for these two fields, especially in light of their high level of participation in the budgets of local authorities, are not nearly as draconic as they are often described.

Supervision of the central government is not actually activated in most sectors and therefore there is no basis for claiming that the local authority is limited in its initiatives because of state supervision. The reality proves that the local authority, large or small, is independent in nearly every field of action — initiating projects, developing services, establishing wage and pension conditions for high-ranking officials, financial management, and more. This is not meant to imply that its freedom is unlimited, but rather that it is not the network of state supervision which prevents independent action by a local authority.

The composition of income in the budgets of local authorities is often used as evidence by those who claim that the local authority is dependent on the state government for most of its income and, by implication, for its actions. However, there is no significant correlation of greater dependence on the state government due to the growth in non-locally-generated income. Most of the increase in the levels of income from government sources over the years was in non-designated income and these did not lead to increased limitations on the local authority. In addition, the growth in earmarked participation does not indicate increased dependence on the state government, but rather increased participation (up to 80-100 percent) for expenses that in the 1960s and earlier placed a much heavier financial burden on the local authority.

In the area of planning and construction, not only does the law grant the local authority considerable status in the design of its physical environs, but in reality its power extends far beyond the borders of its official realm. This power can lead to phenomena which are undesirable for local residents, such as the (purposeful or not) ignoring of building infractions which happen to enrich the local authority with value added tax or other compensation, such as the allocation of space for public use. The most extreme example of such corrupt activities are "contributions" of entrepreneurs and contractors to politicians or political parties. On another plane, the power of the local authority is expressed in joint initiatives with state authorities in the field of physical development — principally with the Ministry of Construction and

Housing and the Israel Lands Authority, but also with other ministries and institutions.

Characteristics and Criteria of Local Autonomy

Despite the differences in the social-cultural-political structure of western democratic states, they share the following characteristics:[54]

1) The existence of at least two arenas, planes or levels of government — state and local.
2) An administrative-state structure responsible for a number of activities in the local units.
3) Local political leadership elected on the basis of criteria which reflect, on the whole, local preferences.
4) The election of local and national political leadership from within regional frameworks (in Israel this characteristic is nearly nonexistent, with the exception of internal elections or other representative arrangements in party institutions).
5) Local and national party structures.
6) A national economy which allows for a certain degree of local autonomy in economic affairs.
7) A national economy in which there is public and private initiative.
8) Different levels of autonomy and of other socio-economic characteristics in the local authorities.

Generally speaking, these characteristics reflect pluralistic social systems whose political and economic power centers are scattered among the local and state arenas. In such societies, there are local political sub-units with considerable autonomy. In France, for example, the fact that two-thirds of the delegates to the National Assembly also serve in local elected positions, and that the Senate is the stronghold of local interests, indicates that even at the central government level, local politics has considerable weight.[55] In the United States, the national parties (Democratic and Republican) are neither centralized nor ideological, and therefore the local communities are quite autonomous.[56] In both cases, of course, there are additional factors which contribute to the fashioning of one or another type of local autonomy, but they share, as do all the other western democracies, the characteristics listed above. With this in mind, it is easy to understand the natural existence of fairly weak supervision and enforcement.

In western democratic cultures, the existence of local autonomy is nourished by the pluralism of the social, political and economic systems to the point that it can overcome the formal administrative structure which the country developed, often over many generations. France is the most conspicuous example of this. Among the western democracies it represents the most centralized structure, in which the local authority is a unit of the "local administration," while in the Senate, as we have noted, we find the dominant representation of local interests.

On the basis of previously-mentioned findings, we may develop a model of criteria and measurements of local autonomy. First we will classify the characteristics of the primary service, economic, and political structures according to the division of functions between state, local and other bodies as presented in figure 2.1: in separate spheres or in terms of center and periphery; in the case of mutual incursion (when both sides have activities in the field of the other); or in a mixture (when there is a wide variety of bodies and types of activities in different combinations). Figure 2.1 charts the primary characteristics and also serves as the foundation for a rating system for measuring autonomy.

We have refrained from using the term "system" (administrative system, political system, and economic system) since it is more inclusive than the concept structure used in this discussion. Structure in this context is a section of a system, whose size is liable to approach the size of a system, but does not overlap it. For example, the service structure includes only services provided by the state and local authorities, either directly or indirectly, through cooperation or consensus, and does not include business and commercial services which are exclusively private. In order to understand and study the characteristics of a service structure in a specific country, we must first list the services provided by the state administration and then, opposite them, those provided by the local administration. These two types will be separately included in section A1 of the chart. At this level we get only a general and in many cases mistaken impression of the scope of functions in the hands of local government. In order to reach more significant conclusions we must complete the classification and make comparisons between the formal definitions and the actual division of functions. In section A2 we will include

Figure 2.1

CHARACTERISTICS IN ADMINISTRATIVE, POLITICAL
AND ECONOMIC STRUCTURES

Division of Functions	A Service Structure	B Political Structure	C Economic Structure
1. Separate spheres	national and local administration	elections of local and national political leadership	national economy permitting local autonomy
2. Mutual incursion	state administrative structure responsible for a number of local units	involvement of national political bodies and people in local issues	initiatives of national bodies (or of industries with their encouragement) which have an impact on the character of local authority
	local administrative units which provide state services not provided by state	representation of local interests in national bodies	local socio-economic initiatives with an impact beyond local needs

3. Mixture and Pluralism	services provided by state, local, public, private in different combinations (central-local, public-private) separately, in competition, or overlapping	parties and national and local unions for achieving identical, similar or opposing purposes	private, public, state, local, outside, joint initiatives; different motives from competitive-economic to non-profit public interest

the "exceptional" functions on each level; in other words, the "state" functions performed by local authorities and vise versa — performance or intervention of a government ministry in local functioning. In this section we achieve a higher ranking than in its predecessor since it gives a clearer indication of local autonomy. For instance, to the extent that we find more cases of incursion from one direction, it is easier to infer the degree of autonomy of the local authority. In section A3 are listed the types of services which are not included in A1 and A2 because they are provided by bodies other than the two governments or in different cooperative combinations. Their classification is according to whether their belonging or attraction is stronger in the central or the local direction.

The listing of services according to sections as described above makes it possible to diagnose major trends in the degree of autonomy, all without having developed the relative weights of all the services. With the formation of a scale which has several levels for ranking services according to their belonging to local government, it will be possible to measure autonomy by the values which we give to the different variables. The preparation of such measurement instruments must be based on detailed analyses of the formal frameworks — legislation, administrative regulations, and agreements — as opposed to actual activity in the various fields.

Only in the last few years have Israeli researchers begun to systematically locate and identify the goals and functions of the local authority.[57] However, even before collecting such basic detailed information to establish criteria and values with a reasonable level of precision, we may be assisted by looking at the horizontal direction of the chart, in the indicators of the division of functions in other structures in the country. For example, classification of the characteristics of the political structure with relation to the election of local or national leadership, or the involvement of national leaders and political bodies in the local arena, or the representation of local interests in national institutions (sections B1 and B2 in figure 2.1), can help us form a clearer picture of the autonomy reflected in the parallel sections (A1 and A2). The listings in the other sections can be used in the same way. Likewise, it is possible to expand the chart and include sociological characteristics, in an additional column, or in a combination of columns B and C which would give a listing of characteristics of the socio-political or socio-economic structures.

The operational scheme sketched above is based on the view that an open society runs or is run from centers of power scattered among the state and local arenas which draw their power not only from the resources identified as belonging to their arena. In addition, the power centers are not lined up in coalitions of local interests which go out for a joint struggle to achieve mutual goals in opposition to the coalition of national or state interests. Indeed the starting point for government policy derives, on the one hand, from the principle that the government must see the overall national picture and act according to principles which will guarantee a balanced approach to the local authorities (and similarly to other groups which demand their share of national resources). On the other hand, the local authority (and similarly every group with a shared interest) strives to mobilize as much help as possible for its own purposes from the government or other resources.

As it turns out, it is impossible to generalize that the goals of state government stand in opposition to those of local government. Quite to the contrary, the objective of each is to assure the physical and spiritual welfare and security of their common citizenry. There are certain areas, such as defense or economic policy, about which everyone agrees that the state government is responsible. The rest of the topics, including certain economic and security functions, are divided between the state and its localities at different levels of responsibility, each country according to its own system.

In a democratic country, even if the formal relations between the different arenas of government are ordered primarily according to hierarchical principles, in fact the two arenas maintain interactions of various direction and kind among themselves and with other bodies. The more varied the pluralism of each structure, the greater will be the pluralism of the relations between them. Therefore, the less a country is developed, the more centralized it will be in its service administration, political and economic structures, and the like. There is not complete symmetry in the levels of pluralism of the different structures, just as there is no perfect consistency in the economic and social indicators which characterize the levels of economic development of a country — those developed, developing, and undeveloped.

However, as the existence of extreme asymmetry of the economic structure typifies the undeveloped country (for example, when there is only a single export commodity, or when there is only one highly developed technological industry), there is also radical asymmetry in the political structure which typifies a narrower democratic base. The service structure is influenced by the political and economic structures, as well as other structures which comprise the basis for a comparative analysis, but it also influences them. Therefore, indicators of pluralism in one structure underscore the significance of pluralism found in another structure.

* * *

The phenomena which we have discussed in this chapter divide into two types: those which contradict the accepted assumption that there is a one-way connection between the increase in government participation and the increase in the state government's control of local services vis-a-vis the local authority; and those which point to pluralism in the functions of the two levels of government. Both present a picture of a local authority with considerable room for autonomous activity or independent decision-making. Like decision-making in any other system, decisions here also take into consideration other factors and pressures from outside the local system.

77

This does not mean that chaos dominates government administration in democratic countries in general, and in Israel specifically. Just as the difference between democracy and anarchy in political theory is clear, so we can distinguish between pluralism and chaos in government administration. Without entering into a philosophical discussion of the meaning of the elements in the definition of democracy — nation, government, equality and freedom — it is clear that what distinguishes a democracy is its constitutional system which allows all of the mature population of a specific territory to manage its affairs through its representatives and to replace them every so often. In every democratic regime there is deviance from the norms established in law and practice, but as long as the regime proceeds peacefully without breaking the basic rules, the regime turns neither totalitarian or anarchic. Similarly the administration of the state is grounded in the formal frameworks according to which the functions of different bodies are divided. Even if the frameworks are breached, as long as the administration has not turned into a rigid hierarchical structure which leaves no discretion to the periphery, or does not crumble and approach a situation of chaos, it acts according to the pluralistic forces which exist within it.

In summary, the findings concerning the laxity of state supervision of the activities of local government prove that state authority over local government does not, as is often portrayed, reflect the limitations written in law and other formal documents. Therefore the local authority has the power to initiate and act well beyond formal definitions which seem at first glance to limit its independence to make its own decisions. The economic power and authority available to the state government, though not fully utilized by monolithic policy and administration, do not allow local and other bodies to do away with boundaries, since their existence is nourished by the various kinds of government funding. The pluralistic relations enable the local government to integrate into the welfare and education service systems, which are primarily funded from state resources, without having to pay in return through a loss of actual independence.

Notes–Chapter 2

1. See also Chapters 6 and 7.
2. The State Commission on Local Government (1981), p. 9.
3. See Dunshire (1981), upon whom the description of the models is based, and also Thrasher (1981).
4. Even in a federal system like the United States, contrary to the legalistic view of the division of powers, intergovernmental relations have been this way since the beginning. See Elazar (1962), and Grodzins (1960), p. 265.
5. See the first chapter of Dearlove (1973).
6. In addition to the discussions in Chapter 1 and later in this chapter, see the following for trends of strengthened local communal political expression: Elazar (1975); Gaziel-Berabi (1981); Doron-Mevorach (1982a) and (1982b); Torgovnik (1972) and Torgovnik-Weiss (1971).

Weiss (1973), in the chapter, "Arrangements and Styles in the Relationships Between Government Ministries and Local Government — Formal and Informal Aspects," portrays the central government as dictating its will to the local government through its statutory and financial powers. Similarly, he says elsewhere (ibid., p. 52) that one can clearly discern from the budgets of the local authorities their estimated dependence on the central government. Nevertheless (ibid., p. 54), he later contradicts this, saying that one should not exaggerate the power of the central government over the local authorities in assisting them to cover their deficits. He stresses the superiority of the central government on one hand (ibid., p. 77, 92, 94) and on the other hand notes important areas of local independence: taxation (ibid., p. 71); licensing (ibid., p. 32), and expropriation (ibid., p. 75), all without explaining why certain tendancies and not others are more characteristic of local government.

7. Municipal Corporations Ordinance (new version), section 3; Local Councils Ordinance (new version), section 1.
8. On this topic see: Shafat (1984).
9. See the State Comptroller (consolidated version) Law, 5718-1958, section 5.
10. Ibid., section 31.
11. Supreme Court (S.C.) 36/51 Chet vs. Haifa Municipality, 1553.
12. Meljon (1966).
13. Section 250 and section 22 accordingly.
14. Ibid., section 258a and section 22 accordingly.
15. The general municipal tax comprises most of the locally-generated income of the local authorities. In a forecast for the year 1986, it was expected to total 509 million new shekels (about $340 million), while income from local services, levies, service taxes and owner

participation were expected to total 304 million new shekels (about $203 million). See Treasury-Interior (1986), p. 82.

16. Local Authorities (sewage) Law, 5722-1962, sections 29-31.
17. Welfare Services Law, 5718-1958, section 2.
18. Local Authorities (guarding arrangements) Law, 5721-1961, sections 12-14.
19. See Chapters 6 and 7. Naor et. al. (1978) reviews the functions of the local authorities in Israel on the basis of the legal sources only, and is a concentrated source of information on matters of local government as they are reflected in legislation until 1977.
20. Kubersky (1965), p. 46.
21. Naor et al. (1978), p. 61.
22. In the area of welfare, the Municipal Corporations Ordinance states that the municipality has the authority to provide housing for the poor, and to build shelter for the disabled, and places of work for the employment of the poor — section 249(5) and (6). In general the municipality is authorized to establish and manage services in any area which the council declares is for the public good — section 249(2).
23. Regulations for the Organization of Welfare Offices (the Role of the Manager and Welfare Bureau), 5723-1963, section 4.
24. Silverstone (1965), pp. 28-29. Also see Goldman (1973), pp. 21-25 and Levy (1980). For court opinion and commentary, see Revital (1984).
25. Planning and Building Law, 5725-1965, section 19.
26. Ibid., section 18(c).
27. See, for example, Hartley (1972), pp. 447-453, and Harris (1965), pp. 3-15. In a comparative study of 13 major cities in different countries around the world, it was determined that "extensive detailed controls do not add up to effective power over the major directions of local policy and the quality of local projects. Where supervising authorities are overwhelmed with giving pro forma approvals, they often miss the forest for the trees." See Walsh (1969), p. 144.
28. State Comptroller (1969), p. 448; ibid., (1976), p. 646. A special report by the State Comptroller on local government refers to many aspects of the relationship with the Ministry of Interior as well as with the "freedom of action" of the local authorities; see State Comptroller (1986).
29. Barzel (1982), pp. 8-9.
30. State Comptroller (1986), p. 65.
31. State Comptroller (1976), p. 646.
32. For a detailed discussion of government supervision of local authorities, see Kalchheim (1980).
33. See Sharkansky (1979)
34. See note 32.
35. In the documents of the state budget, this income is called "earmarked ministry participation." For an explanation of the

different types of income in the budgets of the local authorities, see Treasury-Interior (1986), p. 82 ff. For a more detailed explanation, see Chapter 7.

36. Barzel (1976). For additional points not discussed in this chapter, see Kalchheim (1979).

37. Weiss (1973), pp. 53-43. The Ministry of Interior, relying on the increase in government participation in the municipality budgets, also has stated that "the dependence of the local authorities on the central government for financing their activities has been increasing in recent years." See Ministry of Interior (1973), p. 12.

38. The State Comptroller points out that in the fiscal years 1977 and 1978, the Ministry of Interior continued to distribute "a significant amount of the grant money for the municipalities, not according to the method of distribution based on the standard services and income which it calculated." The Ministry of Interior explained that this was due to the need to introduce the new system gradually and with consideration for decisions taken before the introduction of the method. See State Comptroller (1979), pp. 118-119. See also Chapter 7.

39. Iula (1955)

40. Hecht (1972), p. 66.

41. Barlev and Levy (1974), p. 10. See also Chapter 7.

42. The budget data are based on Treasury-Interior (1982), pp. 156-160; on the issue of free secondary education, see State Comptroller (1980), p. 289 ff. In accordance with the data of the Ministry of Education and Culture, the participation of parents covered about 54 percent of the cost of the operation of nurseries, the Ministry about 41 percent, and the owners about 5 percent. Most of the nurseries (5,237 out of 6,749) are public and under the ownership of the municipality or of public organizations. See State Comptroller (1981), pp. 338-340. In a control sample taken from five municipalities for the year 1979, it became apparent that in each one of them extra payment was made to the municipalities since the number of children who learned was lower than the number reported (see ibid., p. 343.) Deviations ranged from 5 percent to about 25 percent. In other words, the municipalities covered their portion and even received extra income.

43. Another aspect which deserves testing is the influence of government participation on the degree of satisfaction of the residents. Gaziel points out the paradox according to which the residents who receive a higher budget allocation per resident are less satisfied, and it is even possible to identify lower educational outcomes, a high dropout rate and a high crime rate in these municipalities. See Gaziel (1982).

44. Akzin and Dror (1965), p. 111.

45. The ombudsman dealt with this matter at length, especially on the question of the delicate division between the public interest and the right of the individual to his property. See Commissioner for Complaints from the Public (1973), pp. 12-22.

46. Baruch (1971), p. 39.
47. Ibid., pp. 39-40.
48. Treasury-Israel Lands Authority (1982), p. 25.
49. Treasury-Israel Lands Authority (1973), p. 19.
50. Treasury-Israel Lands Authority (1982), p. 84.
51. Ibid., and Treasury-Interior (1982), p. 75.
52. Treasury-Israel Lands Authority (1973), p. 21.
53. For a case study reflecting the system of relations between the Ministry of Construction and Housing, the Israel Lands Authority and the municipality, see Kalchheim (1976), Chapter 11.
54. These characteristics were classified by Clark. Of course, most of them could characterize other regimes, but some of them (3,4,6,7) are unique to Western democratic regimes. See Clark (1974), p. 22.
55. Kesselman (1974), pp. 25-26. Concerning decentralization tendencies and reforms in the 1980s in local government in France, see Gremion (1987).
56. Clark (1974), pp. 111-112.
57. See Naor et al. (1978) which covers surveys of the formal division of authorities between the central and local governments. The next and principal stage should be a detailed comparative test of the actual activities of the municipality versus its formal authority.

Chapter 3

URBAN POLICY

Efraim Torgovnik

A countrywide urban policy can be analyzed from a variety of perspectives. J. Blair and D. Nachmias discuss urban policy in relation to the expanding role of government in programs that relate to urban affairs, to rising needs, and to declining resources.[1] J. T. Dois and M. Danielson speak of urban growth as an independent variable relating to "policies, programs and other action of government officials."[2] J. Kasarda speaks of "federal policies which mitigate the social and economic problems that redistribution has engendered for many core cities and their inhabitants." It is possible to find narrower service delivery program approaches than these or, on the other hand, broader ones. For example, the statement that national urban policy must take an entirely new view of functions of cities and of the triadic relationship among deconcentration, private sector development and urban economic welfare is not only broad in scope, but also reflects a clear stand about a limited regulative role of government in a market economy.[3] Urban policy in Israel relates to decisions regarding national spatial activity, and the strategies and programs it entails for regions and settlements. The role of government in urban policy means strong, deliberate and direct interventive action. This was especially the case in the formative years of the state, thus any such discussion must look to the formative years, when urban activities were set in motion. Current programs will be dealt with here only indirectly.

Urban policy involves deciding on specific strategies to pursue societal goals. An urban strategy suggests definable domains of action that can be translated to specific programs. In the United States, for example, the urban policy of the 1960s related to equity. It involved measures against poverty and support for weak regions, and thus related policy and strategy to identifiable normative structures. A key question posed here is: which spatial strategies in Israel are related to identifiable normative features and how are these strategies translated to the means to implement societal goals?

An urban policy is identified when it is accompanied by controls and support systems that involve resource allocation. An urban policy can be said to exist when a difference is ascertainable regarding the extent that the government intervenes in urban matters, or alternatively leaves such matters to the operation of the market place. For example, a spatial policy involving locational questions of population, such as reducing centralization and population dispersal, can be a result of marketplace choices of individuals or it can be a deliberate, systemically controlled policy of incentives, support and subsidies. Urban policy and strategy should not be confused with developmental policies which political systems such as Israel are likely to adopt. Development policies are broad in scope and are likely to overlap with countrywide economic, social and spatial policies.

Policy, strategy and programs are means that relate to a higher order of societal goals. In Israel these goals are: (1) national security, (2) development, (3) absorbing immigrants, (4) controlling allotted and disputed space, and (5) commitment to a high measure of personal equity. Regional equity in Israel may be regarded as a secondary consideration, salient to goals three and four. There is, in general, a hierarchy of concepts from societal goals to policy, to strategy, and lastly to the program level. Each element of the hierarchy is likely to have its own goals, but in the final analysis these goals are but a link between the hierarchical elements. According to H.W. Richardson, spatial goals "are not ends but means, i.e. ways of using spatial reorganization as a means of achieving the higher level societal goals."[4]

The framework of themes that will dominate this discussion of urban policy in Israel relates to an infrastructure of various policy elements that are required in order to facilitate and achieve the realization of goals. These policy elements are political commitment, ordered planning and implementation procedures, identifiable procedures of control, and ordered resource allocation (which includes incentives and subsidies). These elements are universal and can be applied to systems other than Israel; they thus have comparative implications, although no comparisons with other systems are attempted here.

Political commitment in the form of political support within the administrative structure is the first necessity. The other three policy elements are really implementation instruments.

Instruments of implementation vary and no single theory can help determine the appropriateness of particular instruments. Each national setting is likely to vary in the selection of instruments. Moreover, implementation strategies differ depending on what societal goals are to be served.

Control and support of a policy follows a political decision. The policy may involve: (1) new modes of implementation and administrative structures, (2) the use of extensive planning, (3) a differential incentive support and subsidy system. Control of a policy is identified when the implementation structure possesses mechanisms of correction.[5]

General Features of State Urban Policy

Active Zionism dates back to the last decade of the 19th century. It has always been involved with the movement of populations, establishment of settlements and development. These activities reflected identifiable normative features and were directed by national political and administrative centers.

In 1922, 83,000 Jews resided in what was then called Palestine. A third lived in the Tel Aviv district and vicinity.[6] The Jewish population doubled between 1922 and 1931, and tripled between 1931 and 1944.[7] In 1948 the population reached 717,000; in 1951, 1,404,000; in 1957, 1,763,000; and in 1985, 3,517,000. Between 1948 and 1951 the population doubled. It doubled again between 1951 and 1973. Since then, a number equivalent to the 1948 population has been added to the total.

Urban strategy in Israel involves intervention decisions; Israel has rarely opted for the market option. The exception is the policy toward the big cities up to 1948, when the state was established. Up to that time the ruling institutions took these urban centers for granted. Hence, the cities were left to market development. They emerged in sharp contrast to the rural section, which was planned, directed and enjoyed high status. After 1948, however, a new towns development policy received much state attention and resources.

The establishment of the state in 1948 did not diminish the dominant rural ideology, but the nature of settlement patterns and planning changed. The doubling of the population through mass immigration and the continued plans to absorb immigrants posed new and unexpected pressures on the governing bodies. Israel

85

willingly absorbed survivors of the Holocaust and others who left the Islamic countries in the wake of the Arab-Israel conflict. This influx of people dictated events and the result was a new urban orientation and strategy. The masses of new immigrants were not directed to existing cities, but to new towns.

Israel was concerned with the security and control of newly acquired and then still disputed territories, hence the strategy of population dispersal. The existing kibbutzim (collective settlements) and moshavim (semi-private settlements) were closed socioeconomic units that chose not to expand or change their ideologically homogeneous character, despite demands that they absorb new immigrants. Being an important part of the ruling Labor party, they were able to resist pressure for change. Given their own outstanding example, they argued for dispersal — pioneering in remote places — as they themselves had done in the past. Moreover, it is doubtful whether the bulk of the new immigrants were inclined toward collectivist living. The majority were from a traditional background which emphasized the family and familial authority. They rejected socialism, the dominant ideology in the formative years. Since most came from urban centers, they were largely alien to rural living.

The new towns signified a major change in Israel's urban policy and planning outlook. Their establishment made inroads into the agrarian emphasis and polar model of planning. The polar model was supported by those whose political allegiance was to the ideological, rural framework which did not provide for intermediate size towns in the hinterland.

The new hierarchical spatial planning model was a familiar concept to those versed in European planning. The hierarchical model decentralized activities to the regions in the form of rural village settlements, rural centers (population up to 1,000), rural-urban centers (population up to 12,000), medium-sized towns as regional centers for the lesser settlements (population up to 70,000) and large urban centers.

The new towns policy was followed by a major institutional planning reform, the Planning and Building Law, 5725-1965. Agrarianism was also entrenched formally by clauses in this law relating to the preservation of agricultural lands, which became the major tool for regulating open land use (see chapters 2 and 5).

The compound structure of ideology and new national goals contributed to the acceptance of the new towns policy among the political leadership. With the establishment of the state there was the need to control disputed areas, coupled with the belief in the lasting political effects of a Jewish physical presence in the newly acquired land. Concomitant with this was a psychological factor; the waves of immigration in the early 1950s, and the potential Jewish immigrants from Russia and western countries created rising expectations, which in turn created political support for bold, new policies. What attracted the political elite to the planners' hierarchical new towns structure was the possibilities it offered for population dispersal of the mass of immigrants.

E. Brutzkus, who had a key role in planning in the early years, has reported that Prime Minister Ben Gurion personally ordered the acceptance of the hierarchical model, which became the basis for the new towns policy of rural-urban centers and middle size towns.[8] The state budget gave expression to the new towns and dispersal policies. Planners in the government, the Jewish Agency and in various settlement research centers became geared to the new planning concept. One administrative intervention technique was the formation of settlement teams to implement the overall plan for specific new towns. M. Aronoff has studied how this was done in the new Negev town of Arad. The implementation team had to negotiate constantly for resources with the fractionalized governmental system of competing ministries. That they, and eventually the local government established in the new town, were able to do this with some measure of success is indicative of the measure of success of the whole process of settlement politics. Despite out-migration because of their unattractiveness, remoteness, and the stigma attached to some of them, the new towns took root.[9]

Rural and Urban Policy

Prior to the establishment of Israel, the Jewish governing institutions in Palestine produced an impressive array of planned settlement programs. Applying planning skills to the rural sector produced a network of rural settlements and a thriving agriculture, but it was at the expense of the city. After 1948 these programs were linked to the effort of development and nation building. A similar linkage took place in urban policy. Common to both development and urban policy is the deliberate character of resource allocation and the controls used to implement it. An important distinguishing factor between the two activities and periods lies in

Local Government in Israel

their underlying planning concept. Before the establishment of
the state, the idealized rural sector received preference in budget
allocations (table 3.1).

Table 3.1

PARTIAL EXPENDITURE OF JEWISH INSTITUTIONS
BY SECTOR: 1921-1937

Purpose	Pounds Sterling (thousands)	%
Agricultural Settlement	2,055	34
Immigration	716	12
Urban Settlement	481	8

Source: World Zionist Organization Executive and Jewish
Agency Executive, Report for the 20th World Zionist
Congress, p. 234.
Note: Expenditures for housing and culture not included. Figures
relate only to the expenditure of Keren Hayesod, the
building organ of the Jewish Agency.

At the 13th World Zionist Congress held in Karlsbad in 1923, it
was decided that 30 percent of the budget would be allocated to
agriculture. This preference was of long standing. Some of the
American and European delegations to the Congress raised the
question of the importance of urban expenditures and succeeded in
passing a resolution that recommended, in vague terms, that the
Jewish National Fund allocate land not only to agriculture but
also to housing for new immigrants. However, the Labor section,
representing those who actually lived in Palestine, determined
the activities which were focused on the rural sector.[10]
The early preference for the rural sector was an outcome of the
Zionist ideological framework that viewed the return to the land
as the core of national revival. The Jewish governing institutions
were guided by this ideology. There were also more prosaic
reasons for ruralism. Zionism was concerned with acquiring

88

legitimacy over the land; a physical presence was thus an important element of nationalism. A. Rupin, who was in charge of channelling the resources of world Jewry to Palestine, made this point clear by noting that "agriculture helped colonization," by which he meant the legal acquisition of land.[11]

The result was the relative neglect of urban areas by the state governing institutions. The example of the city of Tel Aviv is a case in point. Tel Aviv grew through market forces, neighborhood by neighborhood, but it lacked an urban concept. By 1933 it had grown to a population of nearly 80,000 against the background of an anti-city ideology and an elite bent on not supporting city life. Paradoxically, at a time when rural pioneering was a national ideology, it was the urban center of Tel Aviv that was the focus for all economic activity, trade and industry. Political institutions, newspapers and leaders were all located in the city. The mass of middle class immigrant absorption took place in the city. Between 1922 and 1924, for example, immigrants were largely Polish Jewish merchants and craftsmen with some capital. They were not inclined to rural living. Their enterprise gave Tel Aviv its economic thrust. The socialization of some part of the new immigrants to the very notion of rural pioneering also took place in the city.

The political power acquired by the Labor elite at this time resulted from their ability to present themselves as the spokesmen of the Jewish population in Palestine, both rural and urban.[12] Skillfully controlling national and world Jewry resources, the Labor party mobilized masses of immigrants with non-rural inclinations to the rural ideology.[13] The Labor elite forged the Histadrut (General Federation of Labor), which was instituted along collectivist lines. The idea was to embrace the masses of immigrants, mobilize them and deliver them from the evils of city life. The Histadrut was not a mere trade union, but an organization deeply involved in members' lives. Collective resources were used to accommodate individual needs, with the federation providing work, indoctrination into socialist ideals, housing, education and health care.

The lack of urban planning which characterized the pre-state period had a negative effect on the achievement of the societal goals of the new state. Israel's new towns could not answer the needs of the waves of immigrants and only about 20 percent settled in them. Far more were accommodated in the temporary dwellings of the camps established to receive them on their arrival in the country, located close to the cities. These temporary dwellings later turned into centers of poverty and slums. Now municipalities in their own right, most are still looking for solutions to the social problems which developed in those early transient camps. These realities strengthen Cohen's argument that the neglect of the city was detrimental to the declared labor goals of national development, as it is inconceivable to think of modernization without cities.[14]

Ruralism as Personal Redemption

The discussion of urban and rural planning must be put into a broader perspective. It was no surprise that Zionism viewed the return to the land as a redeeming process. In the European diaspora, Jews were not as a rule allowed to own land. Their concentration in ghettos made for a closed economy. According to Sloski, in the mid and late 19th century, the occupation structure of Jews in Europe was about a third in inn-keeping and housing, another third in trade, over a sixth in artisanship, and only one percent in farming. Sloski's categorization leaves out the "camouflage" professions, known in Yiddish folklore as *luftgeschiften,* meaning literally trading in air and implying an unstable ephemeral type of trading. By comparison, 24 percent of the Jews in Palestine in 1944 were engaged in agriculture.[15] Dreams of change were linked to land ownership. Jewish movements in Eastern Europe, such as BILU (1890-1900), formed the moshavot — semi-agricultural towns based on private entrepreneurship. The land as a source of livelihood and personal redemption had very early roots.

Borochov, a socialist writer and intellectual who adopted Marxian and Tolstoyan ideas, spoke about the lopsided pyramid of the Jewish occupational structure. He argued for the creation of a pyramid whose broad base is the land. Providing impressive statistics that showed the low percentage of Jews in agriculture at the turn of the century (Germany, 1.3 percent; the U.S., 1.0 percent; Russia, about 4 percent), Borochov concluded that the more a profession is removed from nature, the greater the number of Jews. The ideas advocated by Borochov and his contemporaries became the ideological foundation for collective corporative ownership of economic enterprises and settlements.[16]

The glorification of land and work is identified in Israel with A.D. Gordon.[17] According to Gordon, man actualizes himself through working on the land. Gordon's example, in the form of the first *kvutza,* Degania, was much emulated. B. Katznelson, the much admired labor leader and ideologue, argued that land has a rehabilitating capacity. Although he settled himself in a kibbutz, he also helped to build the Histadrut complex in the city.[18]

It was only during the fourth major wave of Zionist immigration to Eretz Israel (1924-29) that labor leaders began to realize the importance of city needs. Over 60,000 persons arrived, mainly from Poland, escaping the anti-Jewish policies of the Polish government. These immigrants differed from the earlier pioneers in that they were mostly tradesmen and craftsmen and possessed some capital. Many of these immigrants could have emigrated elsewhere, but the U.S. was blocked by restrictions. Palestine was viewed as a place to live in but Zionist pioneering was not necessarily viewed as a national mission. Indeed, when hardships and a recession occurred, 25,000 persons left. Non-socialist leaders such as M. Dizengoff lamented their absence because the capital they had brought with them was no longer available for investment in the city. Those who remained stayed mainly in the cities and were greatly influenced by the rural collectivist ideology. According to D. Giladi, they perceived their stay in the city as a deviation from the idealized rural image.[19]

Despite a reduction in the percentage of the population in the rural sector from 25 percent in 1945 to about 9 percent in 1980,[20] the high status of the rural sector did not diminish in terms of its political strength within the Labor party and the Histadrut. By the 1980s the kibbutzim and moshavim had adjusted to technological change; the kibbutzim in particular have capitalized on their organization as collectives to achieve economic might through the fostering of industrial enterprises and modernized agriculture. In 1984 the value of production in the kibbutzim rose by 10 percent over the previous year to around one billion dollars.[21]

The historic momentum of Jews seeking to settle the land continued in the 1980s, but through center-right political movements far more than Labor. That effort has become part of the internal debate over Israel's right to settle in the controversial areas of Judea, Samaria and Gaza. Whether settlement activity is as appropriate now as it was in the past is open to question. Whatever the answers to these questions, continuity in policy-making can be discerned including central decision-making, resource allocation by the state, and various features of bureaucratic control.

The Role of State Authorities

The brief historical note above, and the sections below that deal with urban policies in the post-state period, hold the matter of national urban policy as an important undertaking of the Zionist revolution. In both periods state authorities played a key role. Their current role is briefly considered before analyzing specific policies.

In the pre-state period up to the late 1920s, the authorities in the form of world Jewish organizations played a major role in settlement policies. Since the early 1930s, however, an indigenous central authority emerged in Palestine. This authority enjoyed wide support from world Jewish organizations, but the latter were clearly subservient to it. The center's capacity to determine policy became dominant when the State of Israel was established and when processes of development, urbanization and modernization received further momentum.

Local government in Israel since 1948 has increased in scope and intensity, but has had to deal with a steadily weakening capacity to finance itself. In the early 1950s, local government in Israel financed about 65 percent of the education budget; in the 1980s its share is about 35 percent. The government evolved a network of administrative, financial and policy links to each locality, either through its regional offices or directly. At the same time, strong political parties made further links with state and local authorities. The major policies of settlement and absorption of immigrants were determined by the state government and the mobilization of resources and taxation remained in the hands of state authorities. Implementation, however, must involve the local plane. Disagreement and conflict is worked out through negotiation and bargaining between the single local community and a government ministry. The results of negotiations are not always predictable. Clearly in a unitary system such as Israel's, there is strong potential for state intervention, especially through rule making. Yet, the democratic nature of government allows for various avenues of expression at the local level. A fruitful way to view the state-local relationship is to see that both levels of government act on different policy issues with different motivations and varied aspirations of control of the issue at hand.[22]

The pattern of state-local relations resulted in policy-making capacity increases at both state and local levels, continuous interaction between state and local governments with varied degrees of institutionalization, and constant change in roles and scope of activities. The role of state government is rarely purely hierarchical in relation to local government. The role of state versus local government in urban matters is dominant in some policy areas, but often it is minor and one can almost always view the relationship as a shared responsibility (see also chapter 2).

Political developments influenced both state and local governments and their relationships. Growing political self-rule for local governments emerged at a time when national parties became weaker. A major example is the continuing phenomena of split-ticket voting (see chapters 2 and 4). This change persisted in spite of the financial weakening of local governments. State tutelage over local governments is on the wane due to the universalization of procedures and removal of political considerations in resource allocation, the institutionalization of allocation rules, and the emergence of indigenous assertive local leadership. The only major democratic structural reform to take place in Israel at the local level was the direct election of mayors in 1978 (see also chapters 1 and 4).

The state-local partnership that emerged was the setting for at least three major policy proposals which were placed on the public agenda:

1) *metropolitan reforms,* which would include the streamlining of services and government structure in the major urban regions of Israel;

2) the *level of government financial support* for local governments, which was placed at a universal ceiling of 75 percent of the cost of state-sponsored or approved services, thus removing politics and bargaining from resource allocation and providing for a policy of redistribution;

3) the effort to *redefine state-local relations* constitutionally and financially through the State Commission on Local Government (Sanbar Commission).[23]

Of these three policies, only the second was implemented. Efforts at structural reform are still on the public agenda, although many features of the proposed reforms have been implemented in a piecemeal manner. For example, the Sanbar Commission argued for clear standards and criteria for the allocation of government funds to local communities. Progressively, each local unit receives welfare and education resources on the basis of clear allocation factors (per capita, community wealth). The Ministry of Interior now provides for a redistributive balancing grant to achieve a minimum service level to all.

In the early years of the state, its role was more dominant in the policies of population dispersal, new towns policies and other activities. These are discussed in the following sections.

Population Dispersal

Dispersal policy has a positive ring to it. It hints at the notion of deliberately dispersing population from the central region. Dispersal, when actualized, can take different forms, such as the fostering of secondary cities, regional subsystems, a development axis, new towns, and numerous other options. Population dispersal in Israel has a number of major features.

First, centralization was viewed as negative, and with good reason. Up to 1948, the Jewish population was unevenly distributed. In 1936, 36.35 percent of the population resided in Tel Aviv and over 42 percent in its vicinity. By 1947 the latter figure had grown to 55 percent.[24] Second, there was a dominant notion that it was possible for the government to disperse populations using planning tools and implementation measures. Third, the fact that Israel was a willing host and ready to absorb waves of immigrants made it almost self-evident that population dispersal was possible. Fourth, considerations of market forces that regulate matters of location were excluded from the decision-making arena. Lastly, dispersal was viewed as contributing to the widely agreed upon notion of state security, safe borders, and control of space and territory.

The instruments to implement dispersal were readily available. There was a will to settle and develop the newly established state. The notion of Israel as a melting pot for Jews from different countries created an excitement. A sense of legitimacy for state intervention in peoples' lives was built up during the pre-state years of socialist leadership. Consequently, the early years of nationhood gave the leadership much freedom. The relative poverty of most of the immigrants who arrived in Israel in the first decade and a half of its existence contributed to the emergence of various tools of managing people. When the government established the famous *maabarot* transit camps and settlements, it could locate them with relative freedom in remote places, near the agriculturally developed settlements or near the big cities where some employment was available. By the time programs for new towns were undertaken, dispersal policy was a widely accepted societal goal that encompassed control of the territories and guided economic development (even today, new towns are called "development towns").

Slowing down centralization through population dispersal may be viewed as both an urban policy and a normative stand against city life, whose evils allegedly plagued the Jewish people in the diaspora.[25] The targets set by plans for the dispersal of the country's population provide a basis of measurement for the success or failure of the policy. This is true for the aggregate measures of people per region, or for people per city. (The relative effectiveness of the various dispersal tools will not be measured here, however.)

The implementation process of the population dispersal policy involved: (1) planning, (2) a system of incentives, used to persuade people to relocate to the more distant places, and (3) the deliberate and controlled relocation of poor immigrants to specific locations. The combination of outright intervention and subsidization is in itself interesting, but was it successful? Were the goals of dispersal achieved? This is of particular importance because behind the deliberate intervention efforts was an open locational market where private choices could be made, especially during periods of economic prosperity.

The dynamics involved in the first and third instruments, the planning process and the direction of people away from centralization, are considered here. The second instrument, the system of incentives, is considered in the following section on new towns. A word of caution is necessary, however. In a work of this scope it is not possible to refine aggregate data on population location and to ascertain who went where and why. The most that can be achieved is the explication of a pattern, and in this vein migration balances will be indicated. The variables contributing to individual choice to move away from nationally preferred locations is discussed in the section on new towns.

Plans of Dispersal

The deliberate efforts to disperse population are attested to by the fact that since 1949, seven plans for population dispersal have been prepared by the Ministry of Interior on behalf of the government. The 1949 plan was targeted for 2 million people, the 1951-52 plan for 2.7 million, the 1954 plan for 3.3 million, the 1957-58 plan for 4 million, and the same in 1963 and 1967. In 1972 the plan foresaw 5 million people in the various regions by the year 1992. An interim report of the 1972 plan foresaw 4 million people in 1981.[26] A new plan for the year 2010 forsees 7 million people in Israel.

All plans prior to and including the 1972 plan were similar in a number of respects: (1) Although the plans had no legal status, they were prepared and implemented by professional planners within the Ministry of Interior; the planners had access to planning and regulating organs such as the district planning commissions, and in this way were able to influence population dispersal decisions; (2) dispersal plans were only formally adopted after a period of trial and error; (3) the prevalence of the normative features previously elaborated, and the high legitimacy of intervention, helped to create a high degree of integration in the actual implementation.

Dispersal policies were aided by two major factors — first, the availability of abandoned Arab neighborhoods and towns in various locations provided places for settlers; second, deliberate planning efforts, such as took place in the Lachish region. These two factors, aided by a huge national commitment of resources, contributed to slowing down centralization. The development of the Lachish region was a concrete planning effort. It was not only a secondary growth center, but was also juxtaposed to the regional development program of Beersheba, a former Arab town and colonial regional capital. The plans prior to 1972 helped to create a network of settlements that, by 1972, were existent and which the 1972 plan took into account and projected into the 1990s. Stated differently, the 1972 plan can be said to have taken into account past deeds as given constraints and hence projected growth using a given growth setting.

Effectiveness of Dispersal

Population dispersal is a formally adopted program that meets the criteria of an effective policy instrument. It involves state allocation of resources, a high degree of control, and correcting mechanisms in the statutory implementation tools at the local, regional and national levels, together with relative freedom to use incentives and subsidies. The actual effectiveness of population dispersal may be defined as the net movement of actual populations in the various preferred regions, notwithstanding market forces and private choices. In measuring the effectiveness there is a hidden assumption that some regions were less attractive than others when measured against private choices.

Of the immigrants (excluding prior populations) that arrived in Israel between 1961 and 1972, 28 percent went initially to the southern region, 20 percent to the north, and 19.5 percent to the central region. The Tel Aviv region received 12.9 percent of the immigrants, Haifa received 15.2 percent, and Jerusalem 6.8 percent.[27] The data indicate that, at least initially, the settlement of people met some criteria of effective distribution.

The most dramatic change of population was in the relatively arid southern region. Between 1948 and 1961 the relative percentage share (in terms of population) of this region grew from 0.9 percent to 8 percent. The central region grew from 15.2 percent in 1948 to 19.7 percent in 1972. The preferred Tel Aviv region had 43.2 percent in 1948; in 1972 it held only 33.5 percent (table 3.2).

Since 1972 it has been possible to make more specific comparisons in relation to approved statutory plans. Table 3.3 enables a comparison of the actual population distribution in the districts for 1972 and 1981 against the 1972 population dispersal plan (approved in 1975), which is the long range plan for 1992. Comparison will enable us to ascertain the net effectiveness of the dispersal policy. The most striking difference is found in the central district. The 1972 plan foresaw an 18.8 percent share. By 1981 the share was 22.4 percent at the expense of the Tel Aviv district. The plan has not achieved its aim of decreasing the relative share of the central district, which is attractive as a private individual choice.

Local Government in Israel

Table 3.2

JEWISH POPULATION DISTRIBUTION BY DISTRICT:
1948-1981

Region	1948 (000)	(%)	1961 (000)	(%)	1972 (000)	(%)	1981 (000)	(%)
Jerusalem	84.2	12.0	187.7	9.7	261.1	9.7	335.3	10.1
North	53.4	7.6	194.3	10.0	255.7	9.5	322.0	9.7
Haifa	147.7	21.1	322.3	16.7	408.8	15.2	464.8	14.0
Center	106.2	15.2	380.1	19.7	535.3	19.9	743.7	22.4
Tel Aviv	302.1	43.2	692.6	35.9	899.9	33.5	552.7	29.9
South	6.0	.9	155.3	8.0	323.8	12.1	434.9	13.1
Judea, Samaria, Gaza and Golan	—	—	—	—	2.1	.1	23.2	.7
Total	716.7	100	1,932.3	100	2,686.7	100	3,320.3	100

Source: Central Bureau of Statistics, *Statistical Abstract of Israel 1983*, Jerusalem, p. 33.

In Jerusalem, the 1.4 percent difference between the projected and actual means that the target of increasing the Jewish population as compared with the Arab population has not been met. In Tel Aviv, the aim of decreasing the scope of centralization was moderately accomplished, mainly because of the high cost of living in the central location and various urban problems. Suburbanization reduced the population of the center of the city which spread out into the surrounding towns of Bat Yam, Holon and Ramat Hasharon.

The dispersal of population involves complex factors such as development, housing, education, individual choice, and deliberate government action. Although the government was successful in settling the southern region, it was less able to control individual choice and growth in the central region. Measuring the success of population dispersal thus requires a broader perspective than sheer statistical data. Another factor lies in the projections themselves. S. Reichman rightly notes that population projections

Urban Policy

Table 3.3

COMPARISON OF POPULATION DISTRIBUTION
BY DISTRICT: 1972 PROJECTION COMPARED
WITH ACTUAL 1981 POPULATION

District	1972 Population Projection		Actual 1981 Population	
	Total (%)	Jewish Population (%)	Total (%)	Jewish Population (%)
Jerusalem	12.6	11.5	11.5	10.1
North	15.7	10.1	15.8	9.7
Haifa	15.2	14.6	14.3	14.0
Center	17.4	18.8	20.3	22.4
Tel Aviv	26.9	31.1	25.2	29.9
South	12.2	13.2	12.2	13.1
Judea and Samaria	—	.7	—	.7
Population (in thousands):	3,970.5	3,378.0	3,977.9	3,320.3

Source: *Five Million Distribution Plan,* Planning Division,
Central Bureau of Statistics, Jerusalem, July 1972. See
also *City and Region* (Jerusalem: 1972-3).

were not always in tune with economic growth projections and
hence there was little coordination between different government
ministries.[28]
Another important factor behind the projections is the assumption that the government acts in concert and with coordination.
This assumption is highly questionable given the relatively high
level of independence of the various ministries in their respective
areas within the Israeli government and their experience prior to
the 1972 plan. Although the government does have plans of dispersal, its control of individual choice and economic activity is too
weak to effect meaningful population dispersal according to the
plans. For example, a firm's decision on location involves factors

99

such as the availability of skilled manpower, proximity to technology and research, etc. These factors counteract the government's efforts to draw firms to remote places through tax incentives and subsidies. Furthermore, the plans were expected to guide planning and government action, but since there was never any coherent and comprehensive government policy on their implementation, it was only to be expected that deviations would occur. For example, because of the strength of economic activity in the central regions, it is not likely that these regions will lose their preeminence. The government attempted to offset the high cost to firms in the central regions by giving subsidies to firms in other regions, but this can only be partially successful. Government control in a mixed economy can be expected to be effective on a project level, or on a single town level, but it is much less successful within the context of a comprehensive national policy.

New Towns Policy: Stability and Change

Since the inception of the new towns policy in Israel, research has been concerned with the outcome of this planning effort. Beyond professional questions such as site location, the social profile of the population, the economic base, and center vs. periphery, research has focused on the question of the success of the development towns.[29] Success was measured around in- and out-migration and its net effect in terms of the number of people in a given town (a measurement concept much favored by geographers). The in- and out-population measure suffers from certain shortcomings. For example, the measure takes no account of the types of populations and the socioeconomic forces that affect group cohesion. It is not surprising, therefore, that the success of the new towns policy has been discussed indirectly in terms of population dispersal. This was done, for example, by A. Shachar and S. Reichman.[30] Measuring the success of a specific town is, of course, beyond the scope of a paper on national urban policy. Needless to say it involves complex procedures. My concern here is with the new towns policy as a reflection of a deliberate national activity that involves resource allocation and control. Let us therefore relate the in-out migration issue to the government's ability to control.

In the democratic milieu of Israel, the control of people and their place of settlement can only be indirect, through incentives and subsidies. Beyond these tools, Israel was and remains an open market for individual choice. True, some of the incentives for people to remain in development towns are highly attractive: low rent, individual tax concessions, low cost loans to individuals and businesses, etc. However, the direct control of people's location (toward new towns) existed only initially, at a time when the masses of immigrants arrived with no capital or familiarity with the system. These people were indeed directed and physically delivered to the more remote settlements. Their towns were often run by government-appointed officials, and the inhabitants' livelihood often depended on government-sponsored work projects.

The new towns policy aimed at changing the settlement mosaic in Israel. The southern region, for example, was sparsely populated with agricultural settlements. By 1955, 13 new towns had been established there. Between 1950 and 1951 alone, the government allocated resources for 5 new towns. The peak of the effort was in 1964 when 27 new towns could be counted, as well as an additional 8 as a result of abandoned Arab towns.[31]

This deliberate effort emerged against a background of long-standing experience with the planning and establishment of agricultural settlements and the urgent need to settle newly arrived immigrants. The development towns emerged as either rural centers or regional towns. From the outset the planning conception designated them as service locations, and trade and small industry centers. This planning conception implicitly assumed continued governmental tutelage, support and control until an assumed take-off would occur. The new towns were innovative not so much in the planning conception they represented, but in their deviation from the dominant rural ideology and practice that had previously dominated planning.

Another novel feature was that the new towns policy, along with the agricultural settlements, dispersed population and broke down the basic polarized structure of the pre-state period in which nearly 60 percent of the Jewish population lived in the urban centers of Tel Aviv, Haifa and Jerusalem. The new towns were the first major effort at countrywide urbanization (apart from the traditional centers of the three major cities which, to a large extent, had evolved by market mechanisms). This deliberate urbanization effort is clearly identifiable by the fact that by 1980, new towns accounted for nearly 20 percent of the population.[32]

Ongoing evaluation of the new towns policy resulted in a variety of correcting programs involving housing for the young, the moving of public institutions to new towns and continuous assessment of their economic and social performance. Some results of this evaluation were: (1) the establishment of a special office to encourage professionals from central areas to move to new towns, by providing many incentives; (2) designations of the new towns on a scale of need and providing corresponding subsidies to the local government, individuals, and entrepreneurs; (3) organization of a subsidized service delivery system that assured a minimum level of services to the development town; (4) preference for new towns as regards special community services and educational programs. The housing element, within the subsidized service delivery system, is the most costly. The centralized programs of housing enabled a measure of equity to take place within the context of different costs of construction.[33]

State policies do not imply concerted action. Ministries in Israel represent a political coalition mosaic. They often act as if the government were no more than a confederation of ministries. Administrative coordination of field activities is weak. This affects the ability to act from the center and directs policy decisions of the government as a whole. For example, in three development towns, calculations showed that creating a communication axis between the towns and the regional centers would improve the towns' social networks. However, the Ministry of Construction and Housing expected the funding to come from the Ministry of Transportation, which had its own priorities in different towns.[34] These types of problems, however, pose a difficulty for all settlements in Israel, not merely the new towns.

State control is also facilitated by political development in the new towns. Places that were managed by state political agents in the early 1950s are managed in the 1980s by highly politicized local leaderships. In contrast with Israeli politics generally, the political leadership in the new towns is young. These highly socialized leaders use the system to deliver resources to their towns that might have been lost in the state administrative bureaucratic maze. A prime example of this is the mayor of the town of Yavneh who, through sheer skill and political acumen, succeeded in rapidly mobilizing the resources due his town for neighborhood renewal. His political skills and activities rationalized government action.[35]

Control Through Subsidies and Incentives

Subsidies and incentives are key instruments in implementing a national urban policy. The most recent example of such implementation is in Judea and Samaria, where scores of new towns and cities were established between 1977 and 1984, and previously from 1968. The government assured the growth of these regions by direct full financing, comprehensive planning and implementation, by providing an elaborate infrastructure and communications network, and financial incentives and subsidies to individuals and firms. The pattern was not new. Setting aside unique features such as ideology, political factors and involvement of the military, it was similar in the implementation of urban policy in new towns inside the pre-1967 Israel borders.

Some examples will illustrate the scope of the system of supports. In the Ministry of Construction and Housing publication that lists the various loans and subsidies available for housing, a word of caution appears: "In no case shall the overall loans exceed 95 percent of the cost of the apartment."[36] A second example is even more illuminating. Each town has a list of subsidies and supports that are available. In one set of supports for residents of 24 "development settlements," as the ministry refers to them, 20 percent of the personal loan is not linked to a cost-of-living index — and this at a time when the annual inflation rate was more than 500 percent (November 1983). The result is that about 8 percent of the cost of the apartments is practically a direct additional subsidy. In Judea and Samaria, the subsidy was even higher when at one time the cost of infrastructure was not included in the price of housing.

State control of policy through incentives and subsidies takes other forms. A variety of government corporations provide low-cost financing to entrepreneurs. Tourism projects, for example, can be undertaken in selected new towns as well as in other places. A more direct system of incentives and grants encouraging investment in development towns is made through the Encouragement of Capital Investments Law, 5719-1959. The preamble to the law says that its purpose is to attract capital to Israel, encourage economic initiatives and investments in order to absorb immigration, promote proper dispersal of the population over the entire area of the state, and create new places of work.³⁷ This broad description addresses itself to population dispersal and new towns policies. The law provides for a long list of subsidies, tax incentives and grants to investors.

One outcome of this law has been a system of classifying the development towns on a scale of privileges. The government defines weak and strong towns, and supports those which it wishes to "prefer." This indeed is an awesome tool of development control. In assessing this law a call should be made for its evaluation in terms of its effectiveness in mobilizing capital and less in terms of what supports it provides. The fact remains that in one town an investor will receive more incentives and in another less. This situation has created a "politics of classification." Towns fight hard for the coveted A+, which is the highest level of support. For example, Upper Nazareth and Migdal Ha'emek, two development towns in the Galilee, were recently reclassified by the budget division of the Treasury as development region B. In previous years, they were classified as A, and each year the Ministry of Industry and Trade would appeal for their reclassification. In 1984 they were refused the A classification.

The case demonstrates inter-ministerial conflict over the right to determine policy. The director of the Ministry of Industry and Trade reacted to the changed classification by arguing that: "the new classification may force a number of investors in these towns to reconsider and move elsewhere. It may stop the development of these towns following the change of classification. Enterprises are interested in the A classification. If they do not enjoy the terms given to other development regions they will most likely move to Judea and Samaria in areas near the coast (the central region) and thus enjoy all the benefits denied to them in the Galilee."³⁸

The head of the development towns department in the Ministry of Industry and Trade is also, by title, coordinator of the government of Israel in the Galilee. It appears then that there is a commitment to assure the economic viability of the development towns, but that control remains divided within the confederated structure of the Israeli government. An illustrative example is the town of Yeruham. One government commission classified it as an A town and another commission classified it as B on the list of subsidies.³⁹ The Ministry of Construction and Housing gives Yeruham an A rating in one version and a lower rating in an other. The Ministry of Industry and Trade gives the town an A rating. These classifications are based on each ministry's emphasis. For example, the Ministry of Construction and Housing considers population dispersal as a criterion; the Ministry of Industry and Trade uses instead a broad criterion of advancing settlements with a population of less than 10,000, which is the minimum required for an independently supported unit.[40]

The scope of this chapter does not permit complete discussion of all incentives. Mention should be made, however, of one additional program. In the 1980s the Ministry of Labor and Social Welfare ran a program to direct people to development regions. It advertised incentives including rent support and professional allowances on national television and in the press. Over a period of five years, the ministry supported the transfer of 2,821 people to development towns.

Viability of New Towns

Measures of in-and out-migration give a final outcome. Below are some basic data (tables 3.4 and 3.5) for a sample of 16 development towns and a discussion of factors contributing to the viability of the towns. Obviously, the relative weight of the factors varies; the causes for in- and out-migration can be pinpointed only in a more precise, causal type of analysis.

Table 3.4 shows the number of people in 16 development towns and the year of their establishment. In two points of time over ten years, table 3.5 indicates a negative balance of migration. It shows a dynamic process of individual choice. In Beersheba, for example, over 3 percent of the population are in a state of flux. The government, as a matter of policy, is much concerned with the success of the development towns; consequently, it views negative balances of migration with some alarm. However, this pattern of change is a phenomenon common to developments in other countries.

Table 3.6 shows the extent of government support for the regular service budget of these communities. On a per capita calculation we find that the state government share in the development towns is up to four times the capital share in the major cities. Some of these towns can hardly be said to be viable when they are unable to mobilize resources from local sources. However, the important

Table 3.4

NUMBER OF INHABITANTS IN 16 DEVELOPMENT TOWNS
AND THE YEAR OF THEIR ESTABLISHMENT

	Year Founded	1955	1961	1972	1985
		(Population in thousands)			
Beersheba	1948	20.5	43.5	85.3	115.0
Beit She'an	1948	6.4	9.7	11.3	13.1
Beit Shemesh	1950	3.0	7.0	10.1	13.8
Dimona	1955	0.3	5.0	23.7	26.5
Eilat	1951	0.5	5.3	13.1	20.4
Hatzor Haglilit	1953	2.0	4.6	5.3	6.6
Kiryat Gat	1954	–	10.1	19.1	27.1
Kiryat Malachi	1951	2.7	4.6	8.9	13.2
Kiryat Shmona	1949	6.3	11.8	15.1	15.5
Ma'alot-Tarshiha		1.3	3.3	5.0	8.7
Thereof: Jews	1957	–	1.7	3.2	5.0
Migdal Ha'emek	1952	2.7	4.0	10.0	14.3
Netivot	1956	–	2.9	5.8	8.7
Ofakim	1955	0.6	4.6	9.3	13.4
Or Akiva	1951	1.7	3.2	6.4	8.2
Sederot	1951	1.0	3.5	7.6	9.3
Yeruham	1951	0.5	1.6	5.9	6.0

Sources: Central Bureau of Statistics, *Statistical Abstract of Israel
1986,* Table II/14; D. Rosen, "Municipal Survey, 1973,"
Jerusalem: Ministry of Interior (Hebrew).

Urban Policy

Table 3.5

INTERNAL MIGRATION BALANCE IN
16 DEVELOPMENT TOWNS

	(1971-72)			(1981-82)		
	Arriving	Leaving	Total	Arriving	Leaving	Total
Beersheba	4,833	3,034	1,799	3,910	4,602	-692
Beit She'an	426	498	-72	275	539	-264
Beit Shemesh	466	350	116	465	603	-138
Dimona	1,274	1,313	-39	729	1,507	-778
Eilat	2,869	2,014	855	2,594	2,725	-131
Hatzor Haglilit	84	219	-135	281	326	-45
Kiryat Gat	923	486	437	407	375	32
Kiryat Malachi	529	608	-79	1,005	1,175	-170
Kiryat Shmona	382	631	-249	624	1,275	-651
Ma'alot-Tarshiha (Jewish only)	219	156	63	592	389	203
Migdal Ha'emek	837	315	522	427	592	-165
Netivot	180	159	21	401	343	58
Ofakim	364	509	-145	531	746	-215
Or Akiva	212	271	-59	276	466	-190
Sederot	692	583	109	307	348	-41
Yeruham	259	204	55	300	337	-37

Sources: Internal Migration Balance in Municipalities and Local Councils, *Local Authorities in Israel 1971/72: Physical Data*, No. 419, Jerusalem 1973, Table 6, pp. 16-17; Internal Migration Between Localities and Settling of Immigration by Local Authority, *Local Authorities in Israel 1981/82: Physical Data*, No. 719, Jerusalem, 1983, Table 9, pp. 45-46.

Local Government in Israel

Table 3.6

PERCENT OF GOVERNMENT PARTICIPATION IN
REGULAR BUDGET OF 16 DEVELOPMENT TOWNS
IN THE YEARS 1971/72 AND 1980/81

	1971/72 %	1980/81 %
Beersheba	35.4	63.7
Beit She'an	77.9	81.9
Beit Shemesh	73.1	86.3
Dimona	59.5	81.4
Eilat	17.7	69.1
Hatzor Haglilit	77.2	No data
Kiryat Malachi	65.4	81.1
Kiryat Gat	45.3	76.1
Kiryat Shmona	64.1	83.5
Ma'alot-Tarshiha	78.4	86.5
Migdal Ha'emek	67.2	83.0
Netivot	57.7	83.8
Ofakim	40.7	89.1
Or Akiva	58.4	83.8
Sederot	42.0	86.3
Yeruham	66.0	84.2

Sources: *Local Authorities in Israel 1971/72, Financial Data.*
Income in ordinary budget by source of income, Table
10, pp. 32-42, Jerusalem, 1973, No. 425; *Local Authorities
in Israel 1980/81, Financial Data.* Income in ordinary
budget by source of income, Tables 19, 20, pp. 25-26, 32-
33, Jerusalem, 1983, No. 709.

factor for our discussion is the government's policy of support and
commitment to these towns. The high share of government support
also suggests a potentially high level of interventive capacity. It
should be noted, however, that often high government support
indicates commitment but not necessarily interventive power.
Through politics and links with national parties, a town is likely

108

to receive resources with less than the necessarily interventive power. The government also acts as an equalizer of opportunities. It provides what J. Dye called a minimum service level.[41] A previous study has shown how government intervention is able to improve a town's position as regards per-capita expenditure for major services.[42]

Factors Affecting Individual Choice

The reason why people chose to leave a place of residence in metropolitan or rural areas has been the subject of much research.[43] A variety of factors are involved in the decision of a person to move. For example, one might consider the relative weight of the economic situation of the domicile in comparison with the forces of attraction of the target area. An important variable with regard to development towns in Israel is the initial act of population mix by government action. This is likely to be critical to the new town's viability. A. Berler noted the importance of having differential economic levels and differential levels of professional status.[44]

Because concern here is with urban policy, discussion of the major factors that contribute to in-out migration must take into account the following question. Can government policy undermine the negative effect of the elements that contribute to a decision to leave a town? Relative weights of the various factors are not provided here. They are referred to as evidence of what the government must undertake in order to retain viability, avoid abandonment, and actually encourage people to stay in the remoter places.

A study of a development town located near a security border that was the object of shelling from across the border shows that, contrary to expectations, out-migration was low in spite of the security danger and high unemployment.[45] This highlights an important notion: not only are internal town factors to be considered, but the potential of outside economic attraction is a key factor.

The cultural background of those who chose to leave is another contributing factor. The number of people of European-American origin who chose to leave population dispersal areas is higher than those of the lower socioeconomic strata of Afro-Asian origin. Europeans are generally more able to move because they have relatives in the central areas and their possibly higher socialization level. Recent revisionist writings claim that a greater number of Jews of European origin left the more remote settlements for the prime cities much earlier than the Jews from the Arab countries and North Africa. This literature often discusses these issues more as a challenge to alleged discriminatory practices of population absorption rather than as an urban issue.[46]

Another finding concerns the security situation in the new towns. Following security tension (shelling, etc.), there was often increased government support in the form of an input of resources and incentives. However, the additional support rendered by the government often had a potential boomerang effect in that it reinforced peoples' decisions to leave.[47]

The very smallness of Israel is another factor in moving out of development towns. As early as 1969, Amiram and Shachar noted the attractiveness of the larger central areas and how this endangers the government's dispersal policy.[48] This rather common sense type of finding becomes more significant in relation to a recent study that points not to problems such as unemployment, but to the stigma with which some development towns are plagued and the socioeconomic status of the residents.[49] Studies have repeatedly shown that the new towns have many features that do not contribute to their attraction to those who freely choose a place to live.

This brief outline of factors contributing to migration can also be taken in reverse, i.e., that improved economic conditions, housing, education, security, ethnic mix, type of employment, etc., can contribute to the retention of population and promote in-migration. The following conclusion can be made: government incentives and economic policy are key factors in contributing to regional and town viability. The effect of government incentive policies on spatial distribution in manufacturing, for example, has been rated by Gradus and Krakover.[50]

One can question continued government support for selected towns on economic or urban grounds, but there is little room to question government policy when it reflects generally agreed upon societal goals. The new towns policy is a case in point. In such a case one can deal with outcomes, some of which are unanticipated. For example, some new towns would not have been located where they are, were it not for the government's desire to show Jewish presence in the area.

Government policies are likely to reverse the negative effects of factors contributing to the abandonment of towns. In Israel, the government controls the level of unemployment, subsidies and incentives. This was identified in the past history of the new towns. The government can direct industry to the new towns either by subsidies or by channelling production orders, but the will to do this is primarily political. In terms of state policy there seems to be a continuous government role. The government has to correct what it created by acting against the forces of the market or by complimenting them. In sum, government policy cannot but help contribute to social and economic problems; over time the government obviously has to counteract these problems.

Proposal for Reforms

A variety of factors led to a clear need for reform and change in the government's attitude, goals and the organization of its relations with the development towns. Foremost was the basic reality that emerged in the past thirty years. Some of the towns remained economically highly dependent on central support. Others passed a take-off stage. Old towns were added to the list of development towns by political pressure in order to become eligible for government support and incentives (e.g. Kfar Tavor and Ramat Ishai and the many settlements in Judea and Samaria).

The renewed commitment of the government to the development towns took a variety of forms:

1) Mayors of development towns have established a forum for negotiation with the government.
2) The political debate over the national settlement effort in Judea and Samaria made salient the relative neglect of the development towns in Israel proper.
3) In 1985, key national unity government ministers Ariel Sharon, David Levy, Moshe Katzav and Gad Yacobi, have competed for the reactivated post of chairman of the Interministerial Government Committee for Development Towns.
4) Then Prime Minister Peres restated the government's commitment to support new industries in the development towns even at the expense of investments in Judea and Samaria.

111

5) Economics Minister Yacobi submitted proposed legislation for capital investment and incentives to entrepreneurs in development towns. Labor and Social Welfare Minister Katzav surveyed all industries in the towns and proposed ways to foster their capital and technological base, and Deputy Prime Minister Levy outlined a housing expansion program for these towns.

6) The stringent efforts of the Minister of Labor and Social Welfare, who is himself a mayor of a development town, to place the issue on the public agenda, which resulted in the establishment of a commission whose task it was to outline the major lines of national government policy regarding the new towns. The major proposals of the commission include a new classification of settlements entitled to be called development towns and hence eligible for various incentives (map 3.1).

The new classification is based on distance from the central region and economic and social viability. Based on these criteria, 21 development towns emerge and 13 old towns were removed from the list. An additional proposal argues for a separate transitional, two-level incentive system: 11 additional towns will be high incentive towns and 10 towns low incentive ones. Urban settlements will be eligible for inclusion in the development town category. The community settlement category, with a population of higher economic potential, will be subsidized only in land purchase and personal loans. Another major proposal by the commission relates to policy coordination and control. The commission proposed the reestablishment of the dormant Interministerial Government Committee for Development Towns. Up to the present time, development towns policy was handled by a government welfare committee which did not deal exclusively with development towns.[51]

The "New" New Towns

Had the settlement pattern in the areas of Judea, Samaria and the Gaza Strip since the ascent of the Likud party to power in 1977 been undertaken under more hospitable international political conditions, the thrust of the effort would have been considered exemplary national planning policy and control. Perhaps,

Map 3.1
Proposed Revised List of Development Towns

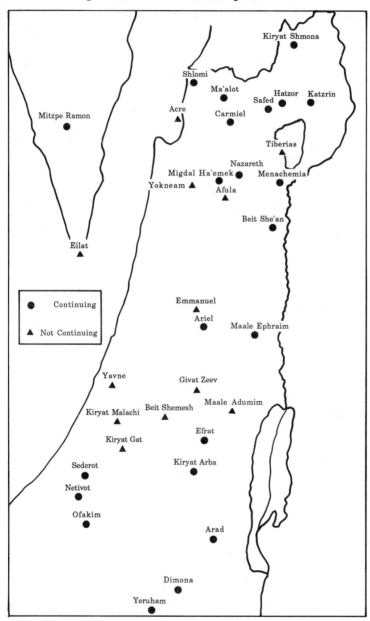

Source: Ministry of Labor and Social Welfare, Center for Direction to Development Towns, Proposal of the Center for Government Policy in Development Towns (Jerusalem,October 1984).

113

ironically, it is probable that only under high pressure can policies (which include not only settlements but also major regional cities) of this scope be undertaken.

The settlement pattern was initially influenced by national security considerations, as defined by successive Israeli governments. The Jordan River is viewed as Israel's eastern security line. It is a natural barrier. The area of Judea and Samaria has about 800,000 Arab inhabitants. The Palestinians view it as an area where the state they aspire to might emerge; Jordan and Israel are in dispute over the area. The relative status quo and growing Arab threats dictate old and familiar conceptions. One acquires legitimacy over disputed territory by establishing a physical presence in the form of settlements, especially where projected future borders are likely to be negotiated.

When the Labor party was in power it asserted a historic right to Judea and Samaria, but argued that settlements were to reflect security conceptions as outlined in the Allon Plan. When the Likud came to power in 1977, they took these security considerations for granted and underlined the ideological element. A look at the settlement map of Labor shows a preponderance of settlements along the Jordan River, but few within the mountainous heartland. The Likud's map is more dispersed throughout. It reflects more strongly an ideology of control and presence based on historic rights.

A clear Likud government policy directed massive resources to the development of infrastructure and settlements in Judea and Samaria. The Ministry of Defense was a major decision-maker in the policy process, and this assured a high level of control and execution. The settlers in Judea and Samaria are mostly strong supporters of the ideology of a territorially complete Israel. This only facilitated government policy. The willing settlers were a far cry from the reluctant newcomers to Israel's development towns.

Settlement patterns in Judea and Samaria are also influenced by Gush Emunim, a highly effective political pressure group, and more recently by a new political party, Tehiya, which until the 1984 elections controlled the government's settlement committee. When government action was viewed as too slow, Gush Emunim simply occupied open public land or purchased land from Arabs and staked a claim. The government allowed itself to follow where it feared to lead. One famous case was Sebastia, near the major Arab city of Nablus, where between 1974 and 1976, the Labor government gave in to pressure and allowed a settlement that transcended security considerations. Later, during the Likud government, the city of Ariel was built. There emerged around it lesser cities, rural towns, and a privately sponsored and financed city.

Israel's settlement effort has increased the urban industrial base in Judea, Samaria and Gaza which were previously mostly rural regions. Table 3.7 details the number of settlements Israel established in the areas it controlled after the Six Day War in 1967. Israelis who have settled in Judea, Samaria and Gaza now total 60,000.

Table 3.7

JEWISH SETTLEMENTS IN JUDEA, SAMARIA, GAZA
AND GOLAN REGIONS, 1983

Region	Number of Settlements by Type	
	Urban	Rural
Judea	4	51
Samaria	1	62
Gaza	–	10
Golan	1	29

Source: E. Efrat, *Geography and Politics in Israel* (Tel Aviv: Ahiasaf 1983), pp. 91-95, 123, 134, 153, (Hebrew).

Land Regulation Policy and Population Movement

A concrete element of rural ideology found its way into the Planning and Building Law, 1965 via the regulative Committee for the Preservation of Agricultural Land (CPAL). The CPAL regulates the activities of urban planning institutions and plans conformity as far as agriculturally designated lands are concerned. Through its veto power, it also determines the scope of land development.

Its regulative role is outlined in article 49 of the law. Item I prescribes that agricultural lands be preserved and the CPAL oversee national, regional and local plans regarding their compliance with the preservation of agricultural land (the committee also has regulative power over forests and open spaces). Although its administrative structure is meager, CPAL exerts a dominant influence on urban policy through piecemeal, allocative intervention during the various planning stages. The CPAL has the statutory power to declare land as agricultural land.

Up to the present time, the members of the committee have represented the agricultural sector and almost by definition have been sensitive to agricultural interest groups. The CPAL is faced with constant appeals by cities and towns to change land designation and thus enable urban growth. A forthcoming study of the CPAL found that it is able to block or expand urban development by rulings regarding the appropriateness of land for agriculture.[52] In one case, a decision of the CPAL to release twenty acres of agriculturally designated land adjacent to a suburban town near Tel Aviv for the purpose of building a low-cost housing project for young couples and the poor was negated by the Supreme Court of Israel. The court referred to item II of the law, which states that the CPAL shall not use its authority except in relation to agricultural land and its generic use.

In the specific case above, its decision was challenged and revoked, but not all of the CPAL's decisions are challenged. The CPAL can remove land from agricultural use, thereby opening the way for redesignation for urban use. In later cases the role in urban development of the CPAL was more readily recognized. In one case it involved redesignation of urban land to agricultural land. The decision was upheld by the court, thus recognizing the role of the CPAL beyond just preservation.[53]

The government in Israel has a key role in urban development. It is estimated that some 90 percent of the land is owned or controlled by the government. When the government stands neutral vis-a-vis decisions of the CPAL, urban development of agriculturally designated land can be halted. The CPAL can also influence development in towns and rural settlements. The scarcity with which agricultural lands are released for use for housing or development determines the cost of housing and people's life style. The more land that is released, the faster urban revitalization can take place in deteriorating towns and in decaying areas. In semi-urban towns it is often difficult to find the proper balance between conflicting urban and rural needs. The policy of restricting land use is government policy, albeit influenced by the previously dominant rural interests, but it is debatable whether this is the proper policy for urban growth or city revitalization.

The policy of preserving agricultural land emerged as one of the outcomes of the previously dominant ruralism. But it also stands in line with other policies such as population dispersal and open land policy. It is not likely that in the initiation of the policy of the preservation of agricultural land, the current metropolitan growth in the major urban areas was foreseen. Despite this misgiving, the CPAL does perform a useful function in eliminating the speculative value of agricultural land. Through the CPAL, agricultural land in urban centers becomes open space. For example, the city of Tel Aviv has about 800 acres of agricultural land, and its adjacent suburb, Ramat Hasharon, some 3,000 acres. According to the city's master plan, the population of Tel Aviv is expected to be about 460,000, compared with 320,000 today. The agricultural lands will not, of course, provide the space for such growth.

Controlled Increase of Regional Population

The government makes deliberate efforts to increase the share of the Jewish population in some cities and in those regions of Israel that have a large non-Jewish population. The policy is accompanied by special administrative structures and resource allocations. Cases in point are the northern region of the Galilee and Jerusalem. Judea and Samaria may be included, although there one can speak in terms of settlement and urban policy.

Uneven regional development has been the object of much research in many political systems; it has also become a recognized academic specialization. Attempts have been made to characterize Israel in terms of regional-territorial political behavior.[54] It is open to debate, however, whether Israel possesses features of regionalism, given its 4,500,000 people and a travel distance from north to south of 537 kilometers. Two conditions for the identification of a regional will is the emergence of a regional interest and a means to express it. Regional interests have emerged, but it has been harder to find ways to express them. In the Galilee region, for example, the kibbutzim and moshavim are the most powerful elements but they are affiliated with their own countrywide organizations; they do not easily separate themselves from the powerful countrywide organizations to which they are affiliated. This aspect was overlooked by Gradus when he more than hinted at the emergence of regional interests.[55]

Israeli regional governmental policies are better discussed in terms of their effective and coordinated field administration.[56] Regional interests are channelled through the countrywide organizations, which in turn deal with the state government. From the state government perspective, a stronger and more coherent national urban policy and service delivery systems in the regions would be achieved through tighter coordination of the implementing agencies. However, this is difficult to achieve given the politically confederated structure of government departments. The fact that the regions operate under a long tradition of direct relations between single settlements and central agencies, and only in a lesser measure with governmental field offices, hinders the introduction of concerted government action.

Any discussion of regionalism must also involve issues of decentralization and area participation. This seems especially the case as the state government oversees urban and other development. The effort of the state government is best seen in relation to Judea and Samaria, where the bulk of the settlements were planned by the government as industrial villages, towns and cities. Notwithstanding regional voting patterns or behavior, the effort remains a state government undertaking. In Judea and Samaria, the old emphasis on working the land is given much lip service; but government subsidies dominate the scene. Another example of the government's role can be seen in the specific programs to increase the Jewish population in the Galilee. State plans resulted in the establishment of a network of 28 mini-settlements, which are actually housing neighborhoods located in strategic locations to demonstrate Jewish presence and potential.

Jerusalem is an example of deliberate urban development. In the Six Day War in 1967, Israel gained control over the entire city and its environs. Between 1967 and 1984, the population of the city doubled. The reclamation and rebuilding of the Jewish Quarter in the Old City, and the construction of six new Jewish neighborhoods around the city, was jointly undertaken and executed by the city, under the leadership of Mayor Kollek, and the Israeli government. This deliberate urban policy was executed at great speed, and very substantial resources were applied. The Ministry of Construction and Housing and its planning staffs were often removed from the regular authority of the relatively slow-moving planning organizations into special organizations, which had the authority to bypass the normal decision-making processes.

The government commitment to the increased growth of Jerusalem was such that the city planners and administration became dedicated to restoring planning authority to the city. They came into conflict with the government regarding a potential negative aesthetic impact on the city resulting from forceful government development and construction efforts. In Jerusalem, as elsewhere in Israel, the old proven notion was at work that where Jews settle, there is little disagreement about their right to the areas. The planning conflict between the city and the government was misread as meaning the mayor's opposition to the creation of Jewish preponderance, which he hastened to deny.[57]

Prime Minister Golda Meir often took on the role of arbitrator between the various actors involved in order to achieve quick settlements. She emulated the early precedent of Ben Gurion's direct involvement in new towns and dispersal policies.

Neighborhood Renewal

Project Renewal, a major neighborhood renewal and rehabilitation program, was initiated following the ascent to power of the Likud party in June 1977. The projects under this program were aimed to assist populations in distressed neighborhoods. The government intended a new approach to community renewal that would include social and community rehabilitation through citizen participation. To give the program the broadest possible commitment it was decided that it would be a joint undertaking of the Israeli government and world Jewry.

Project Renewal meets the criteria set out here of a national urban policy. Its various programs are accompanied by a political commitment, an elaborate administrative structure, procedures of resource allocation, and controls that include identifiable self-correcting mechanisms. Project Renewal has an inter-organizational decision-making structure and a degree of institutionalized citizen participation.

Project Renewal superseded slum clearance programs that were previously carried out by the Ministry of Construction and Housing under a specially designated 1965 law that limited the programs to clearance and redevelopment, but with hardly any provision for physical improvements. In 1972, $2 million was budgeted for eight neighborhoods; in 1977, at the beginning of Project Renewal, nearly $14 million was allocated to about fifteen neighborhoods.

The government of Israel provided administrative instruments for the implementation of Project Renewal by establishing an inter-ministerial committee headed by the deputy prime minister. In order to emphasize the individual and community rehabilitation features of the program, the committee was named the social and welfare ministerial committee. A state policy steering committee outlined strategies of implementation, and the partnership with world Jewry through the Jewish Agency added to the formalization of the Renewal policy. The result was a formal control system with mutual prodding for action. By 1979, 25 neighborhoods were included, 39 were added in 1980, and by 1982 there were 80 neighborhoods.[58]

By 1984, the cumulative allocation for Project Renewal was about $400 million, of which the government of Israel provided $250 million and world Jewry about $150 million.[59] The year-by-year increase since 1978 reflects the incorporation of new neighborhoods and the extension of the scope of the programs. Early activities focused on physical improvement in living conditions; later, neighborhood environment programs such as parks and gardens were implemented, and more recently much emphasis was placed on social development programs that included enrichment and head-start activities.

The residents themselves took part in the planning of the social programs through forums that gave the locality a large measure of control over the type of programs to be instituted. A study of one of the neighborhoods in Tel Aviv revealed that the residents defined their needs in terms of education. Local government officials and Project Renewal administrators agreed that the program was more than just an urban renewal undertaking. Consequently, resources were applied toward a variety of educational, psychological and enrichment programs for adults and children. Control of these activities was twofold: (1) the actors (residents) and the actual activities became a part of the bureaucratic implementation process, and (2) the residents became persistent defenders of the programs. This type of control is not possible in a standard hierarchical arrangement. In the case of Project Renewal, state, national (world Jewry) and local structures had a share in influencing decisions concerning the program. One advantage of such a complex structure is that it creates a mutual watchdog system. It is, in other words, a tool to control the implementation process.

The desired emphasis on people, social features and the community was, at first, unsuccessful. Emphasis was placed on physical housing and environmental renewal. This occurred for a number of reasons. Project Renewal had raised high expectations. It was necessary to begin with projects that produced immediate results. The complex organizational structure was such that quick feedback was necessary in order to mobilize further resources. Jewish communities from countries around the world required concrete evidence when they visited their adopted towns and neighborhoods. Physical renewal gave the whole policy, including the social community aspects, its necessary momentum. There were additional reasons for the early emphasis on the physical features. Bad housing conditions were the catalyst for local steering committees. They supported the early emphasis on reconstruction. Once this was achieved there occurred a shift in emphasis to the social and educational aspects of the programs. Within the context of the rehabilitation of deteriorating neighborhoods in the cities and in previously established new towns, Project Renewal involves many of the policy elements outlined earlier. It can be said to reflect a national urban policy.[60]

Conclusion

The various policy elements outlined at the beginning of this chapter are essential determinants of a national urban policy and were used as a background for our discussion of urban policy in Israel. These elements are universal and can be applied comparatively to systems other than Israel.

Political Commitment

New towns and dispersal policies require a political commitment, which was evident in the high consensus among the ruling elite regarding these policies. Conflict over the new towns policy was generated by the planners of the rural sector. New towns development represented a planning concept of a hierarchical, spatial distribution of settlements that would negate the former polar model, which had historical roots and did not provide for intermediate size towns in the hinterland. The hierarchical planning concept was an innovation that required new political support, notwithstanding the inclination of the Labor elite toward the rural development features of the polar model. Political support was forthcoming in the context of new national goals that arose after the establishment of the state. The pattern was repeated in Judea and Samaria, where political commitment followed the acquisition of territory and was then strengthened by the ideology of the ruling groups. The political commitment to the new towns policy, the non-polar planning concept, and settlement of Judea and Samaria, offered a variety of rewards for the ruling parties. It contributed to Israel's presence and control of relatively vast areas. These policies thus helped popularize the issues around national goals.

Ordered Planning and Implementation

With the adoption of the new hierarchical planning approach, urban policy became a formalized viable domain. Indeed, the actual establishment of towns was an ordered process in concept and administration. It penetrated the ideologized milieu of agrarianism and operated in parallel and interactively with the huge rural planning sector and its aims. For example, the Lachish region settlement plan launched by Prime Minister Ben Gurion was an attractive combination where professional planning gave expression to normative features involving control of territory and nation-building. The element of planning and ordered implementation was a salient factor in the national policies in Judea and Samaria and in the policy of neighborhood renewal. In both domains there was an overt political commitment that aided the ordered implementation. It appears that ruling groups that have the capacity to initiate state urban policies and generate the framework for implementation strategy are likely to reap varied political benefits.

Identifiable Procedures of Control

The very deliberateness with which the implementation of urban policy strategies were followed suggests a certain level of control. The elaborate administrative structure surrounding the effort assured a variety of correction mechanisms. Control was aided by political commitment, administration, planning, and the continuity of projects. Other contributing factors were that the success of the development towns was a major national concern. Not surprisingly, new towns drew resources in their direction. Research and evaluation accompanied the process. For example, the ideal ethnic combination of a new town constantly occupied the implementers and researchers. The ongoing evaluation of the new towns policy resulted in a variety of corrective programs, which involved housing for the young and the moving of public institutions to new towns. Control was facilitated by the institutionalization of procedures concerning the allocation of state resources, which included a well-defined system of incentives and subsidies.

Control over the overall governmental commitment to a policy such as new towns does not, of course, assure success in specific instances. The strong governmental interventive role was often mitigated by a free market, which modified the government's ability to control the policy. High government commitment often meant control over resource allocation to failing enterprises. The continuity of government support to failing towns, for example, required a new support policy that was an outcome of the original commitment to the new towns policy. Lastly, it should be noted that the Israeli commitment to the new towns policy often negated the ability to truly intervene and correct. A town's leader could rely on the state's commitment and urge only a minimum of local effort.

Ordered Allocations: Incentives and Subsidies

State direction of urban policy is facilitated through incentives and subsidies. It can take a variety of forms. In Judea and Samaria, for example, the government provides financing of infrastructure in the context of direct incentives and subsidies to individuals and firms. The pattern is not new; it was used in the implementation of urban policy in new towns in Israel proper. A variety of government corporations provide subsidies, tax incentives and grants to investors. New towns receive different classifications relating to the subsidies and incentives to which they are entitled.

In summary, to achieve a high level of control of a national urban policy, one would expect intensive coordination efforts to be apparent. This is difficult to introduce given systemic features such as exist in Israel. Notwithstanding this difficulty, urban policy in Israel shows identifiable administrative features worthy of attention. For example, budgetary powers are apparent, but the level of coordination and control is not the same for all programs and all agencies. In the initiation stage there is great saliency to the policies and hence there are likely to be more coherent activities than in later stages when correction mechanisms are set in motion. Hierarchical coordinators and controls are not likely to be found over time in a system such as Israel's with its federation of government ministries and coalition governments.

The elements of state policy introduced here were identified to various degrees in the policy domains considered. It is possible to identify a national urban policy and its implementation processes even though much of what is seen in implementation over time is correction of unexpected spatial and other outcomes. Indeed, it is important in future studies to view correction mechanisms as a sine qua non of national urban policy.

Notes – Chapter 3

1. Blair and Nachmias (1979).
2. Dois and Danielson (1980), pp. 852-61.
3. Kasarada (1980), pp. 373-400.
4. Richardson (1981), p. 270.
5. Landau (1969), pp. 346-58.
6. Gurewitz and Geretz (1940).
7. Schachar et al. (1973), pp. 41-42, 70-119.
8. Brutzkus (1964), pp. 39-55 and Richardson (1980), pp. 67-85.
9. Aronoff (1973a).
10. Ruppin (1925).
11. Ibid.
12. Gorni (1973).
13. Shapira (1975) and Giladi (1973).
14. Cohen (1971).
15. Slosky (1973).
16. Borochov (1944), pp. 210-211.
17. Shechter (1957).
18. Shapira (1975).
19. Giladi (1973), pp. 36-40, 176.
20. Data based on regional division. See Sikron and Lesman (1976), pp. 3-25.
21. *Haaretz*, 25 September 1984.
22. This pattern was noted in the issue of location of power stations; see Torgovnik (1972), pp. 469-90.
23. Commission for Improving Local Authority Financing (1975); State Commission on Local Government (1981); Israel Urban Information Institute (1973), (Ben Shahar Commission).
24. Central Bureau of Statistics (1980).
25. Cohen (1970b) and Shahar et al. (1973).
26. Brutzkus (1973), pp. 3-25 and Gil (1979), pp. 19-30.
27. Sikron and Lesman (1976), p. 7.
28. Reichman (1973), pp. 26-43.
29. Soen (1983), pp. 22-27.
30. Shachar et al. (1973) and Reichman (1973), pp. 26-43.
31. Aronoff (1973a).
32. Berler (1970); Lichfield (1971); Spiegel (1966) and Efrat (1976).
33. Efrat (1976).
34. Borochov and Werczberger (1980).
35. For more information on the growth of political leadership, see Torgovnik and Weiss (1972).
36. See also Center for Direction to Development Towns (1984a).
37. See Chapter 1 of the Law (sections 1-3).
38. Green (1984), pp. 4-5.

39. Kochav (1969) and Naor (1972a).
40. Naor (1972b).
41. Dye (1978).
42. Torgovnik (1978), pp. 211-39.
43. Kirschenbaum (1972 and Hansen (1973).
44. Cohen (1966), pp. 117-31 and Berler (1970).
45. Zuckerman-Bareli (1978), p. 192.
46. Segev (1984) and Svirsky (1981).
47. Zuckerman-Bareli (1978), p. 198.
48. Amiran and Shachar (1969).
49. Cohen (1966), pp. 123-34.
50. Gradus and Krakover (1977), pp. 393-409.
51. Center for Direction to Development Towns (1984b).
52. Torgovnik (forthcoming).
53. S.C. 324/71; 445/71; 601/75.
54. Elazar (1974).
55. Gradus (1983), pp. 388-403.
56. Partial efforts in this direction have been undertaken by N. Menuhin and Ludmor (1982).
57. Interview with Mayor Teddy Kollek and City Planner, Meron Benvenisti.
58. Alexander (1980).
59. International Committee for the Evaluation of Project Renewal (1984).
60. Degani (1980). For a comprehensive discussion of Project Renewal, see King et al. (1987).

PART II — AUTHORITIES AND FUNCTIONS

Chapter 4

LOCAL ELECTIONS

Giora Goldberg

Local politics is the grassroots of the state's political system. In a state such as Israel, which lacks a formal federal structure, an understanding of local politics is particularly important. The importance of local politics is manifested both in the local arena and in the interactions between it and the statewide arena.

Local elections are the height of the local political process. A detailed analysis of the various aspects of the electoral process, including the constitutional arrangements, nomination of candidates, political competition, voting turnout, and electoral results, all put in clear perspective the essence of the transformations in the character of the local political culture which have taken place over the years. Those changes are reflected in the development of local lists, the phenomenon of split-ticket voting and a general "changing of the guard" on the local plane.

Local Elections Laws

In the days of the pre-independence Yishuv, the local election laws were not uniform. This lack of uniformity actually encouraged deep local attachments. Thus, for example, the leaders of Tel Aviv took pride in the fact that their city was more democratic than others in that it granted voting rights to a broad range of groups, as will be seen later. In addition, the fact that local elections were not generally held on fixed dates or at the same time in all municipalities contributed to this localistic feeling.

The question of voting rights was a political issue which aroused fierce differences of opinion in the Yishuv. Community committees *(vaadei kehillot)*, whose main tasks were charity and religious services, were usually chosen according to prior agreements which prevented the holding of elections. Giladi notes that "the division into groups occurred on a family or ethnic basis and did not reflect ideological positions."[1] In settlements numbering up to 200 members, the committee was chosen by the general assembly. In larger settlements there were supposed to be elections for membership on the committees, but in the moshavot the veteran and well-to-do farmers tried to protect themselves from the increasing power of other groups such as craftsmen, clerks and laborers by making enfranchisement conditional upon payment of a property tax and residence of at least two years in the moshava. Conflicts among these groups erupted in several places including Kfar Saba (1927) and Ramat Gan (1926). One of the veteran leaders in Kfar Saba presented the approach of the farmers quite bluntly: "If the workers influence our moshava, it will cease developing, for new owners of capital who might want to invest their capital in our moshava will fear their influence and withdraw."[2] It has been found that "in all the moshavot, the owners of agricultural property had complete control of the local committees. They took advantage of the fact of their earlier arrival and through undemocratic regulations they withheld from the new population (workers and residents) their rightful share, in accordance with their numbers, in the administration of local affairs."[3]

The two principal documents which regularized the method of elections for municipalities and local councils were the Municipal Corporations Ordinance of 1934 and the Local Councils Ordinance of 1941. The Municipal Corporations Ordinance authorized the High Commissioner to appoint or dismiss mayors, thereby limiting the influence of the residents on the election of the mayor. Officially the authorities could ignore the decision of the electorate, but in fact they never exercised this authority. The Municipal Corporations Ordinance enfranchised only men 25 and older who paid property taxes of at least 500 mils per year or municipal taxes of at least one lira per year. While the Municipal Corporations Ordinance did not grant voting rights to all city residents, it did grant them to those who were non-residents but paid taxes on property located within city limits. Thus a voter who lived in city "A," owned an apartment in city "B," and owned a business in city "C," could participate in local elections in all three cities.

The third addition to the Municipal Corporations Ordinance related specifically to Tel Aviv. It established that the minimum voting age there would be 21, that a municipal tax payment of 500 mils per year was sufficient for voting rights, and that the wives of those who were enfranchised could themselves vote. In addition, Tel Aviv residents who were not citizens of Palestine could receive voting rights. The leaders of the city took great pride in this liberal stance.[4] During this period, Tel Aviv was a widely imitated model for the entire Yishuv as a stronghold of powerful local attachments and a workshop in participatory-representative democracy.

Leftist circles protested to the British about the establishment of the 500 mil requirement, but their claims went unheeded. In fact, this limitation was practically insignificant and the suspicions of the left of its negative impact were unwarranted.[5]

The Local Councils Ordinance of 1941 did not explicitly determine how the local councils would be elected. In fact, it depended on the ability of the leaders in each place to reach agreement and receive authorization from the British authorities.

Politically, members of the civil camp, particularly the General Zionist Party, dominated the municipal arena. In Tel Aviv they were eclipsed by the Labor Movement for only two years, from 1925 to 1927. In the other cities and moshavot, the General Zionists ruled. Only in the 1940s did the Labor Movement win long term control of its first local council — in Holon.[6] There is no doubt that the civil camp was aided by election rules that assured their control. However, this factor should not be seen as an exclusive explanation of their power in the local arena, but rather as a secondary factor.

In December 1948, the Provisional State Council amended the Municipal Corporations Ordinance. Financial limitations on enfranchisement were eliminated and voting rights were extended to women and to residents who were not citizens. The minimum voting age was set at 21.[7] In July 1949, the minimum voting age was reduced to 18 for all Israeli elections, even though the government had initially recommended age 20.[8] The first municipal elections were held separately from the first state elections, since the latter were to choose a constituent assembly.

In determining the method for conducting the first local elections after the establishment of the state, substantive disagreements surfaced between the parties as to the place of local government within Israel's governmental system. A bloc which included the religious parties and two of the civil camp — the General Zionists and the Progressives — supported the interests of local government over those of the state government; however, Mapai (the ruling party), Mapam (which included Ahdut Ha'avoda) and Herut supported the opposite approach. The religious parties, the General Zionists and the Progressives proposed that local elections not be held on one day, but should take place over an extended period. The reasons given by their representatives left no room for doubt, as in the following quote from Yosef Sapir: "It is my opinion that for the benefit of the interests of the municipal sector, the general debate now raging in the state between two or more approaches or outlooks should not be introduced at the local level."[9] In the words of Zerach Warhaftig, the holding of simultaneous municipal elections "denies the municipal elections their local character and turns them into general state elections."[10] An unsuccessful attempt was made after the first elections in 1950 to change the method of elections. It was claimed that the "elections did not revolve around local problems; the elections did not revolve around the personal qualities of those who were to be chosen to administer local affairs; the elections revolved around political and state issues, both internal and external."[11]

The approach which won out was expressed by the opposite viewpoint: "Whoever believes that it is possible to hold elections in Tel Aviv or Jerusalem on a local basis only is certainly mistaken. This whole description of 'localism' is a search for a more convenient basis in other elections for all elections in the country will be to a large extent [party] political."[12] A representative of Mapai claimed that local government deals with political problems and that "it is a matter for political parties, who generally express public opinion."[13] The parliamentary debate concerning the method of local elections clearly revealed the foundations of the statist political culture within Mapai: "I do not think that local patriotism in its various forms is a becoming trait which we should cultivate. In general it is expressed in a particularly unbecoming form. We should cultivate the broader perspective of the state."[14]

Even the proposal to transfer the authority for delaying local elections from the government to the Knesset was rejected. The General Zionists made a futile attempt to make changes in the proposal which had been accepted. Thus, for instance, they requested that the mayor be personally elected by the voters and not by the council, and that one-third of the seats of the council come up for election every two years.[15] One of the few proposals that expressed a clear locally-oriented stance which was accepted was the granting to voters of the right to cross out the names of candidates from their ballots, so that a candidate whose name was crossed out on more than half of the valid ballots could not serve on the council. This referred to the crossing out of names from a list which the voter supported. However, before elections were held, this section was withdrawn at the initiative of Mapai, Mapam and a representative of Poalei Agudat Israel in the United Religious Front, despite the vigorous opposition of the General Zionists.[16] Thus a change in the law in August 1950, three months before the elections, prevented the voters from expressing any opinion concerning specific candidates.

The proposal by the General Zionists that taxpayers who were not local residents should also be allowed to vote, as had existed during the period of the Yishuv, was also rejected.[17] The section which regularized the division of mandates did not arouse any disagreement. Any list which received at least 75 percent of a minimum quota participated in the allotment of the mandates. The quota was calculated by dividing the number of valid votes by the number of members of the council. Afterwards, a second calculation took place which divided the number of valid votes received by the lists eligible to participate in the division of mandates by the number of members of the council. The number of votes which each list received was then divided by this second measurement in order to determine each list's number of mandates. The remaining mandates were allocated according to the method of the highest surplus. The significance of this system is that the electoral threshold in local elections was considerably higher than the electoral threshold for the Knesset, which is 1 percent.

The following example may help to clarify this matter. In a municipality with up to 5,000 residents, the number of council members was determined by law to be 9. If there were 1,800 valid votes, the initial quota would be 200, and any list receiving 75 percent — 150 votes — could participate in the allotment of mandates. The electoral threshold is therefore 7.5 percent. Obviously as the number of council members increases, the electoral threshold decreases.

The new election law established that the next municipal elections would be held after three years, and then would be held every four years. The second municipal elections were supposed to be held in 1953, but were postponed to 1955. When the General Zionists joined the government, they made an agreement with Mapai to delay the local elections. The entire spectrum of the opposition opposed this vigorously. In the law which was adopted, not only were elections delayed, but it was established that they would be held on the day of elections to the Third Knesset and from then on would be linked to Knesset elections. The Hapoel Hamizrachi faction requested that elections be held at the end of four years; in other words, in autumn 1954. Herut proposed that elections be held in December 1953 and from then on every four years in the last week of December. The intention of the two parties was to prevent the linkage of the municipal elections to the Knesset elections. The new stand of the General Zionists meant their abandonment of the cause of localism which they had championed in the past. It was also a sign of the victory of a state-centered political culture.[18]

Prior to the elections to the Fourth Knesset, the problem of linkage of municipal and state elections was once again placed on the agenda. With the passage of the Basic Law by the Knesset in 1958, which established that elections for the Knesset would be held during the month of Heshvan, a situation was created in which municipal elections were supposed to be held several months before the general elections. The Progressives and the General Zionists requested that the elections not be linked and proposed a private law on this matter. Yisrael Rokach from the opposition, who had served as Minister of Interior when the General Zionists had supported the delay of municipal elections in 1953, admitted that he had then made a mistake when he supported linking the two elections.[19]

The government decided to hold municipal elections on the same day as elections for the Fourth Knesset, while in the future municipal elections would be held every five years, thereby separating local and state election dates. Under pressure from the Minister of Interior, Yisrael Bar Yehuda (Ahdut Ha'avoda), the law that was passed left out the section which would have required that municipal elections be held every five years.

On the eve of the 1959 elections the government presented a renewed proposal for holding municipal elections every five years. The most important part of this proposal was the introduction of direct, personal elections for the office of mayor. Under this proposal the mayor would have to receive more than half of the valid votes to be elected. If no candidate received an absolute majority, then a second round of voting would be held the following week between the two candidates who received the largest number of votes. Mapai, the General Zionists and the Progressives supported the proposal, while the rest of the parties adamantly opposed it.[20] Opponents of the change claimed that Mapai's initiative was rooted in its ambition to take over the local authorities, since the law granted a clear advantage to large parties. The proposed law was accepted at its initial reading by a majority of 55 to 34, but legislative work was not completed before the end of the Fourth Knesset.

The early elections for the Fifth Knesset in 1961 created a situation in which the municipal elections were supposed to be held separately in 1963. The coalition factions — Mapai, Ahdut Ha'avoda, the National Religious Party and Poalei Agudat Israel — presented a private proposal to postpone the elections and link them to the elections to the Sixth Knesset in 1965. All of the opposition factions opposed the proposal, but to no avail.[21] The local councils which had been elected in 1959 served for six years until 1965.

The Fifth Knesset also had the issue of the direct election of mayors on its agenda. The General Zionists and the Progressives, now together in the Liberal party, presented a private proposal in the spirit of the government proposal of 1959. The government requested that this proposal be removed from the agenda, not because of any opposition in principle, but because the Ministry of Interior was working on an overall proposal for local government reform. In contrast to 1959, the parliamentary discussion was brief and lacking in polemics and the proposal was defeated.[22]

In 1966 two private proposals were advanced regarding the direct election of mayors. Pinchas Rosen (Independent Liberals) once again advanced the proposal which he had presented as Justice Minister in 1959, but this time the initiative was private rather than governmental. Mordechai Ben Porat (Rafi), from the opposition, advanced a more radical proposal. He proposed that elections for mayor and council be held at different times; that a mayor be chosen for a period of five years, which would overlap the tenure of two councils; and that one-third of the valid votes would be sufficient to elect a mayor if more than two candidates were involved. The government did not interfere in the initial legislative stages of the proposals.

On the eve of elections for the Seventh Knesset, the two proposals, now unified into a single proposal, were brought for a first reading. The separation of election dates for the mayor and the council was withdrawn. Two formulas were proposed concerning the method of elections: 1) to require a majority of more than half of the valid votes and the holding of a second round of elections if such a majority was not achieved; 2) the holding of one round of elections only, the winner becoming mayor. The proposed law passed its first reading but was then buried. The two large blocs —

the Labor Alignment and Gahal — were unable to reach unified positions in their own ranks. Herut, Ahdut Ha'avoda and the older leadership of Mapai did not want the amendment, while the Liberals, Rafi and the younger generation of Mapai favored the proposal.[23] The National Religious Party proposed that municipal elections be postponed from 1969 to 1970 in order to separate them from Knesset elections, but their proposal was removed from the agenda.[24]

In 1969, for the first time since the establishment of the state, the Knesset passed an election financing law. This law made no distinction between elections for the Knesset and for the local authorities. Financing arrangements were determined without any consideration of the results of municipal elections and completely ignored the existence of local lists. Elections for the local authorities were funded like the elections for the Knesset, according to the results of the Knesset elections.

Nearly a year after the elections for the Seventh Knesset, in June 1970, the Knesset approved the government's proposal to apply the Continuity Law to the proposed law dealing with changes in the method of local elections. This meant that consideration of the proposed law would not be interrupted by the election of a new Knesset, but rather would continue from the stage at which the previous Knesset had arrived.[25] The version formulated by the Constitution, Law and Justice Committee set a minimum threshold of 40 percent of the valid votes and if no candidate reached this, the mayor would be chosen by the council. However, at the second reading in the beginning of 1973, the Knesset rejected this and instead accepted two different and even contradictory versions.

The version proposed by the Mapam faction in the Labor Alignment, Agudat Israel and Maki established a threshold of 50 percent and the choice of the mayor by the council if this threshold was not reached; the version presented by Gahal and the National Religious Party also set the threshold at 50 percent, but required a second round of elections if this was not attained. Acceptance of both conflicting versions was made possible because of cooperation between the parties which proposed them, together with the fact that the Independent Liberals changed their position and did not vote with the Labor Alignment, the State List and the Arab lists, despite their commitment to do so. When the proposal was brought up for the third reading, it failed to gain a majority since the Labor Alignment did not support it.[26]

In June 1973, supporters of the proposal made another attempt with a version which set a threshold of 40 percent and required the election of the mayor by the council if this was not attained. Knesset members from the Labor Alignment, the State List and the Independent Liberals, as well as Meir Avizohar and Uri Avneri, were the initiators of the proposal. Yet once again the proposal failed to be enacted into law.[27]

The issue of election financing came up again in 1972. A private legislative proposal presented by representatives of the Labor Alignment, Gahal, the National Religious Party and the Independent Liberals dealt with the financing of Knesset elections and the timing of local elections. As in the past, the proposed financing arrangements ignored the local lists and the results of local elections. During the legislative process the proposal was changed from the financing of elections to the financing of political parties. Therefore the version which was accepted contained no mention of the local dimension.[28] The municipal elections of 1973 were postponed for two months, together with the elections for the Eighth Knesset, due to the outbreak of the Yom Kippur War.

In May 1974, a private legislative proposal was once again presented concerning a change in the method of local elections. The sponsor of the proposal was again Ben Porat (Labor), who was supported by members of the Knesset from his own faction, the State List and the Free Center in the Likud, the Independent Liberals, the Citizens' Rights Movement and Moked. This latest version was similar to that which had failed in the previous Knesset, with a threshold of 40 percent which, if not attained, would allow selection of the mayor by the local council. Three members of the National Religious Party proposed a version which included a 50 percent threshold and choice by the local council if not attained. Both proposals easily passed the pre-reading stage.[29] Ben Porat's proposal reached the first reading without a final formula for the method of elections, but rather with three versions: 40 percent and choice by the local council if not attained, 50 percent and choice by the council if not attained, and 50 percent and a second round of elections if not attained. In December 1974 the proposal passed the first reading.[30] In July 1975 it reached the stages of the second and third readings.[31] The proposal for 50 percent and a second round of elections which was presented by the Likud and Moked, was supported by the National Religious Party, Agudat Israel, Poalei Agudat Israel and Rakah, who opposed the change in the method of elections, but supported this version in order to try to soften the impact of the change as much as possible. Yigal Allon (Labor) and Shulamit Aloni (Citizens' Rights Movement) also voted in favor of the Likud's proposal, which was accepted by a vote of 55 to 50. Boaz Moav (Citizens' Rights Movement) proposed a threshold of 40 percent and a second round of elections, but his proposal was rejected by a vote of 52 to 47.

The change in the method of local elections was thus completed in July 1975. The party machines could no longer hold back the strong localist trend which was expressed in the 1973 elections and which was represented by a group of Knesset members from various parties who had come from the local arena. The following year the Likud agreed to lower the threshold from 50 to 40 percent and in 1976 the law was thus changed, over the opposition of the religious parties and Rakah.[32]

After the elections for the Ninth Knesset were advanced to May 1977, a proposal was presented by representatives from the Labor Alignment, the National Religious Party, Agudat Israel, the Independent Liberals and Moked which would delay the municipal elections for a year to November 1978. The Likud, then in the opposition, opposed the proposal, but it was supported by a majority of the Knesset.[33] Another proposal by Moav to explicitly establish that local elections would always be held one year after elections for the Knesset passed the pre-reading stage, but was later buried.[34]

The municipal elections which were to be held in the autumn of 1982 were once again delayed for a year, this time in the wake of Operation Peace for Galilee which began in the summer of 1982. The Knesset thus has made rather frequent use of its authority to reschedule municipal elections. The considerations guiding the decision-makers were not at all related to local affairs.

Despite the difficulties on the long road which characterized the change in the method of local elections, it should be emphasized that this has been the only important constitutional change made in Israel. All of the legal reforms proposed during the years since the founding of the state have been rejected and the arrangements established at that time have remained unchanged. Only in the area of local election reform has there been an essential constitutional change — a change which reflects a move from a parliamentary system to a presidential system.

Nomination of Candidates

In the 1950s and 1960s the procedures for nominating local candidates were dominated by the state party machines. The pattern was similar to that for nomination of candidates for the Knesset. The nominating committee was controlled by the leaders of the state party machine and especially by the heads of the municipal departments in the state party headquarters. Party branches were only partially involved in the nomination process, primarily in consulting roles, and rarely played a substantive part in decision-making. Only a few members of the local party branches, primarily the branch leaders, participated in the process, while the party masses were left without influence.

During the 1970s and 1980s some changes took place in the nominating process for both the Knesset and for the local authorities, making it more democratic. On the local plane there was a conspicuous growth in the role of the local party branches in the nominating process and a corresponding shrinkage in the role of the state party headquarters. Within the branches themselves, groups which had not been previously involved now penetrated the inner circles. Primary elections were not held, but the local party institutions, whose membership was relatively large, became the focal point of decision-making.

The change in the method of local elections contributed to democratization at the local level and to the loosening of state party bonds. This process had already begun in earlier elections when local lists succeeded in attaining the mayoralty, but the new format was at least a catalyst. In order to become mayor, a candidate now had to be popular and accepted in the local community. The party label could not longer guarantee electoral success. Therefore the phenomenon of candidates brought in from outside almost completely disappeared.

A candidate without deep local roots could no longer be nominated for mayor with any chance of success. A mayor elected directly by local voters becomes relatively independent of state party headquarters. The state party leaders could not even attempt to nominate a different candidate for the upcoming elections if a current mayor was not to their liking, since electoral success is ultimately their most important objective. Dependency relationships are thus reversed; it is now the party headquarters which needs the victorious local leader. The state party leadership now hopes that a successful local leader will be able to swing votes to the party in the state elections as well. This point is particularly significant in the Israeli electoral system where the method of state elections lacks any regional component.

Occasionally, the local branch may choose a new candidate over the incumbent. This rarely occurs, but when it does the change usually results in defeat at the polls. This is what happened in the 1983 elections to the Labor branch in Netanya and the Herut branch in Ashdod. The two rejected mayors ran on independent lists, but the victory in both cases went to the rival party — the Likud in Netanya and Labor in Ashdod. On the other hand, even a veteran mayor may be replaced by the voters, as happened in the 1983 elections in Ramat Gan, where the Likud mayor was replaced by the Labor candidate, and in Herzliya which went from Labor to Likud.

Local intervention by the state headquarters has occasionally been requested in the two large party blocs — Labor and Likud — stemming from the background of internal rivalries among the parties which make up the blocs. When the blocs were established in the 1960s, the state leaders decided that existing power relationships would be frozen. Each party would continue to choose its own candidates, but the order of the candidates on the local list would be determined by the power relationships which existed in the municipal elections which preceded the establishment of the bloc. The candidate for mayor was similarly determined. In Labor there are fewer local rivalries than in Likud, since in all of the local authorities the advantage of Labor over Mapam was considerable and there was therefore little disagreement as to mayoral candidates. In the Likud (Gahal until 1973), however, the power between Herut and the Liberals was more balanced. When Gahal was established before the 1965 elections, the arrangements between the parties were determined by the results of the previous municipal election, which had taken place in 1959. The party which in 1959 had received more votes than the other gained the right to head the local list and since the change in the method of elections, its local leader has been the Likud's mayoral candidate.

Over time, it has become more and more problematic to maintain that formula. The changes occurring in the various municipalities cannot find expression at the crucial stage of party list compilation. Thus, for instance, fierce differences of opinion have broken out in Herzliya, Holon, Netanya and Haifa, as well as in other cities. The internal dispute in Haifa in the 1978

140

elections was particularly intense. According to the 1959 election results, the Liberals had the right to place their leader as the Likud's candidate for mayor of Haifa. In anticipation of the 1978 elections the Liberals chose Zvi Zimmerman as their candidate. Opposing him was Amnon Linn, from the third component of Likud, La'am, who sought the nomination on the basis of his relatively high popularity in Haifa. The Liberals were not prepared to yield and after extended discussions, the dispute was brought before then Prime Minister Menahem Begin, who decided in favor of the Liberal party. Linn then established a local list (Haifans for Haifa) which essentially split the Likud in the city. Linn received 23,060 votes (25.1 percent), while Zimmerman received only 15,771 votes (17.2 percent). The split in the Likud enabled the Labor candidate, Arye Gurel, to easily win the mayoralty.

In a few cases the state party leadership has agreed to local switches; in localities in which Herut was entitled to nominate the mayoral candidate it was transferred to the Liberals, and vice versa. In other instances the two parties ran on separate lists. Attempts to intervene in the composition of the lists of the other party have failed. This was the case, for instance, when prior to the 1983 elections in Tel Aviv, Shlomo Lahat, the Liberal mayor, attempted to interfere in the selection of Herut candidates for the city council.

The national nominating committee in Herut is primarily made up of members of the party executive. The committee which acted prior to the 1965 elections was comprised of seven members; five held high-level party executive positions, such as the head of the organization department, the treasurer, the head of the financial department, etc.[35] The nominating committee prior to the 1973 elections consisted of nine members, seven of whom were members of the executive and two — Yitzhak Shamir and Yoram Aridor — who had no municipal background whatsoever.[36] The decisions of the nominating committee were authorized in two of the executive meetings. The party branches also had their own nominating committees. In the past the branches had no need for their own nominating committees. Each branch would compile its list and pass it on to the party headquarters, which had the authority to change it, but generally authorized it without change. The use of local nominating committees was an intermediate stage between a procedure which included nomination by the branch committee and confirmation by the national nominating committee, and one

141

in which there was broad local participation in the nomination, including the branch council, and in which the national nominating committee served only as a formal rubber stamp.

In the 1950s, when the influence of state party headquarters on the nominating process was dominant, there was no tendency to interfere as long as the branch committee was able to compile a list without creating shock waves which deviated from the local framework. The case of Magdiel in the 1955 elections illustrates this point. The representative of Herut on the local council was rejected by the branch committee as a candidate for the 1955 elections. He sent an angry letter to party headquarters, claiming that "they have conspired in order to depose me from my position," and that the committee which deposed him had never been elected. He demanded that headquarters change the decision of the branch committee, threatening that otherwise the party would lose in the upcoming elections.[37] The response of the party executive, A. Drori, was quite instructive: "The party headquarters, which makes the final decisions as to the composition of the list, is not generally eager to overturn the opinion of local members....In addition, you must agree that there are times when it is proper to introduce changes, to replace representatives, and to give an opportunity to the younger generation to enter public life."[38]

Control by headquarters over the branches, though not necessarily in the matter of nominations, was more in the voting for council representatives, relations with representatives of other parties, and the arranging of surplus vote agreements before elections and coalition agreements afterwards. Relatively strong branches such as in Petah Tikva and Netanya, where there was a nucleus of party veterans, mostly members of the Histadrut-General Labor Federation, guarded a certain degree of independence and tended not to accept the authority of headquarters. In contrast, the influence of headquarters was greater in the newer municipalities.

A similar pattern of central control over the nomination process and other aspects of center-periphery relations existed in Mapai. The overall interests of the party were perceived as superseding local interests. As the ruling party, the Mapai headquarters had a conspicuous advantage in terms of the amount of resources at its disposal. The branches served as tools of the headquarters for the transfer of various resources to party members and loyalists. A typical example of this is seen in a letter from party headquarters to the Ramat Gan branch committee which

142

expressed astonishment at the fact that a party activist "had still not been given a job. He is one of our party's activists in the diaspora and it is essential that a suitable arrangement be found for him."[39] Another aspect of the dependence of the branches on headquarters was related to the party's control over government ministries. An example of this was the appeal of the mayor of Lod to the national party secretary in 1950 to request assistance in expediting the transfer of money from the Ministry of Interior to the Lod municipality. The municipality had received only 9,000 out of the 20,000 Israeli pounds which it had been allocated for the period from July 1948 until March 1950. The mayor urged the party secretary: "I hereby turn to you with a request to help expedite the transfer of the grant money to our authority."[40]

In later years, the state party headquarters would show particular interest in the selection of the head of the list and the order of its candidates. For example, in the nominating process to select a Labor candidate for mayor of Haifa prior to the 1973 elections, the state party feared that it might lose one of its most important strongholds and turned to the Minister of Labor, Yosef Almogi, to stand at the head of the list. But Almogi hesitated:

> Sapir said to me that if I would not be the mayoral candidate we were likely to lose Haifa and this at the same time that we faced a similar danger in Tel Aviv. Golda invited me to a discussion and told me that she had received many letters requesting that the administration of the city be handed over to me....Golda noted that I was one of the best ministers in her government and it was a pleasure for her to work with me, but that the matter of Haifa worried the party and a proper solution had to be found. She commented that once the party had asked her to stand at the head of the list of candidates for the Tel Aviv municipality and she had not refused. I tried to defend myself by saying that I had never been attracted to dealing with municipal problems.[41]

In the end the decision was transferred to a joint meeting of "Haverenu," an informal party forum, and members of the party executive, which was held in the office of the prime minister:

> With a heavy heart and with great hesitation I agreed to head the list of Labor candidates for the municipality. Sapir rode with me to the Knesset after the meeting and in order to

encourage me he promised that I would serve for only four years in the municipality, train a proper replacement, and afterwards return to the government."[42]

Almogi left his position as mayor of Haifa after only two years to serve as chairman of the executive of the Jewish Agency and the World Zionist Organization. The prime minister at the time, Yitzhak Rabin, had requested that Almogi accept the position, which had become vacant in 1975 after the death of Pinhas Sapir. This episode demonstrates the secondary nature of the local dimension in the priorities of state party leaders and the marginal role played by the party branch in this matter.

Nominating procedures for local lists are generally not so democratic. Often a small group of individuals will decide on the composition of a list and the selection of its leader. Sometimes local lists have an entirely personal character, in which the founder of the party heads the list, chooses the candidates and places them on his list. An example of this can be seen in Abie Nathan's list, "Sapan," which competed in Tel Aviv in the 1983 elections. In the older parties, by contrast, the nominating procedures are generally more open and democratic than in local lists.

Election Results

There are two components in local election results: the success of the different party lists and their control over the mayoralty. Prior to the 1975 change in the election method, it was possible for a list to achieve first place at the polls, yet remain in opposition due to the formation of a coalition by smaller parties. Thus, for instance, Mapai came in first in the 1955 elections in Tel Aviv with 30.6 percent of the vote; yet the General Zionists, who received only 23.6 percent, gained the mayoralty due to a coalition with Herut and the religious parties. Similar losses occurred in the 1950 elections to Mapai in Jerusalem and to the General Zionists in Petah Tikva. Since 1975, the mayor is always the winner of the direct personal elections for the position, even though his party's list for the council may not win.

The following is an analysis of the results of local elections from the founding of the state through 1983 according to major blocs: the Labor bloc, the Likud bloc, the religious bloc, the local lists and others. Table 4.1 describes the voting strength of these blocs. For 1978 and 1983, data is presented for both mayor and council elections.

Table 4.1

RESULTS OF LOCAL ELECTIONS IN JEWISH
AND MIXED MUNICIPALITIES:
1950–1983
(in percentages)

			Political Bloc		
Year	Labor	Likud	Religious	Local	Other
1950	38.5	34.8	12.9	4.4	9.4
1955	44.8	27.7	14.4	2.6	10.5
1959	48.7	24.0	15.9	4.4	7.0
1965	49.8	23.0	14.1	4.5	7.1
1969	40.8	25.2	15.2	6.9	11.9
1973	39.3	28.6	15.3	8.9	7.9
1978 (Council)	34.9	26.3	16.5	17.6	4.7
(Mayor)	39.1	31.3	12.0	15.9	1.7
1983 (Council)	36.9	23.5	19.5	16.5	3.6
(Mayor)	40.4	28.6	11.1	17.7	2.2

Sources: Publications of the Central Bureau of Statistics, Special Series of Publications, No. 51, 111, 216, 309, 461; *Results of Elections for the Local Authorities — 1978,* Ministry of Interior, 1978; *Official Gazette,* 1983.

The Labor bloc won overall in all of the local elections in Israel. The Likud bloc has come in second and the religious bloc third. Since 1973 the local lists have received many more votes than the other small parties. In the 1950 elections the General Zionists won nearly a quarter of the votes and were perceived as the victors, but afterwards there was a consistent rise for the Labor bloc and a decline for the Likud parties (the General Zionists and Herut). While the gap between the two blocs stood at only 3.7 percent in 1950, it grew to 26.8 percent by 1965. Overall, the election results for the two major blocs show a general stability, with a slight decline for Labor and a stronger decline for the Likud.

The decline of the two major blocs was linked to the rise of the religious parties and the local lists. The last time the religious parties lost ground was in 1965. Since then they have demonstrated a clear upward trend. The religious issues are especially meaningful in the local arena. The decline of the religious bloc in elections for the Knesset (primarily in the 1981 elections) was not paralleled in local elections. In the 1983 elections the religious bloc received only 4 percent less than the Likud, although the difference between them in the state arena was much larger — 21.9 percent.

The most conspicuous improvement occurred in the position of the local lists. With the exception of the 1955 and 1983 elections, their improvement has been consistent. Their sharpest gains occurred in 1978 — 8.9 percent — nearly doubling their strength. This change happened precisely at the first time in which elections were held by the new method. Contrary to expectations, it was not the large blocs which gained from the change, but rather the local lists. The other parties, whose strengths peaked in 1969, have drastically declined since then and their impact on election results has been minimal.

During this time there have been important changes in the composition of the voting population. The outstanding achievement of the General Zionists in 1950 was due, among other things, to the fact that most of the voters came from the large cities and the moshavot, which were the strongholds of the General Zionists. A large portion of the immigrants who still lived in transit camps did not yet vote in municipal elections. In addition, the massive aliya had still not been completed at the time the elections were held. The decline of the Likud bloc until the mid-1960s primarily reflected the decline of the General Zionists, while the rise of the Likud since 1969 is basically the result of a strengthening of Herut.

The electoral success of the two large blocs is more evident on the mayoral level. This is not true of the religious parties, however, due to the fact that they did not participate in mayoral elections in about one-third of the localities. Sometimes pre-election agreements were reached between one of the main blocs and the religious parties, whereby the religious voters would support a candidate of the large bloc in exchange for participation by the religious parties in the ruling coalition, which would bring them yet additional rewards. Among the local lists there was no significant difference in results for mayor and council elections, although in 1983 their success in the mayoral elections was slightly higher.

Table 4.2 describes the voting strength of the blocs in local mayoral elections during the years 1950–1983. The Labor bloc is also the strongest in terms of controlling the local municipalities. During the 1950s the increase in the proportion of Labor mayors was even greater than the increase in the total number of mayors. However the 1960s saw the beginning of a decline, which accelerated in the 1978 and 1983 elections. After the introduction of the new method of elections, the Labor bloc lost the absolute majority among the mayors which it had long enjoyed. The Likud and the local lists benefitted from the change, while the religious parties declined. By 1983 the number of mayors belonging to local lists nearly matched the number of Likud mayors.

Table 4.2

MAYORS IN JEWISH AND MIXED MUNICIPALITIES
ACCORDING TO POLITICAL BLOCS: 1950–1983

	Political Bloc					
Year	Labor	Likud	Religious	Local	Other	Total
1950	26	6	4	5	1	42
1955	52	7	2	7	3	71
1959	67	4	3	8	2	84
1965	64	6	11	8	2	91
1969	55	15	10	10	1	91
1973	58	14	8	12	0	92
1978	39	25	11	18	1	94
1983	39	27	5	25	0	96

Sources: See Table 4.1; D. Rosen, *Six Elections for Jewish Municipalities and Local Councils during the Thirty Years of the State,* Ministry of Interior, 1978, (Hebrew).

Election results from 1983 were also analyzed according to type of municipality. The local authorities were divided into three types: development towns (33 municipalities); metropolitan areas; and other municipalities. Table 4.3 describes the results of elections for councils (party lists) and mayors according to type of municipality.

On both the council and mayoral levels, Labor appears weaker outside of the metropolitan centers. Although Labor's advantage over the Likud is conspicuous on both levels across all three types, this advantage is smaller in the development towns and is at its peak in the metropolitan areas. Despite the Likud's gains in Knesset elections in development towns since the 1970s, on both levels of local elections the Likud is slightly weaker in development towns than in other types of municipalities. The differences between the three types are smaller for Likud than for Labor. The religious parties and especially the local lists had conspicuous success in the development towns, as opposed to the other types of areas. The success of the local lists in the development towns was greater than that of the Likud on both levels. The other parties, from their perspective, achieved their best results in the metropolitan areas.

The most important conclusion from table 4.3 is that there was a strong movement of votes from the Likud to the local lists in the development towns in 1983.

Voter Turnout

The voter turnout for local elections is high, as it is in Knesset elections. Table 4.4 describes voter turnout in all of the local elections and also in those Knesset elections which occurred at the same time. Over the years there has been a noticeable decline in voter turnout for local elections. This trend began in 1969 and accelerated in the 1978 and 1983 elections which were held separately from Knesset elections. It is intriguing to note the high voter turnout — nearly 80 percent — in the local elections of 1950 which also were held separately from Knesset elections.

There has been a clear decline in voter turnout for local elections. The change in the method of elections seems to have accelerated the trend. In the five times during which elections were held for the Knesset and the local authorities at the same time,

148

Table 4.3

LOCAL ELECTION RESULTS IN 1983 IN JEWISH AND MIXED
MUNICIPALITIES ACCORDING TO TYPE OF MUNICIPALITY
(in Percentages)

| | Type of Municipality | | | | | |
| Political Bloc | Development Towns | | Metropolitan Areas | | Other Municipalities | |
	Council	Mayor	Council	Mayor	Council	Mayor
Labor	27.7	30.7	40.8	44.8	32.1	33.5
Likud	22.1	26.9	23.8	28.8	24.7	30.8
Religious	21.5	12.6	18.7	10.3	19.7	13.2
Local	26.6	29.0	12.0	13.1	23.3	22.2
Other	2.1	0.8	4.7	3.0	0.2	0.3
Total	100.0	100.0	100.0	100.0	100.0	100.0

Source: G. Goldberg, "The Local Elections in Israel — 1983,"
Electoral Studies, Vol. 3, No. 2 (August 1984).

voter turnout was higher for the Knesset elections. The difference
was most pronounced in 1973 — 5.6 percent; in other words, 7 percent of those who voted for the Knesset did not bother to vote in the
local elections.

Voter turnout in the Arab sector is higher than in the Jewish
sector. In 1978, for example, 88.6 percent of the voting population
participated in elections for Arab local councils, as compared with
68.1 percent in the Jewish and mixed local councils. In the towns
and cities, almost all of which were Jewish, only 53.9 percent
voted. This may reflect the fact that local elections are the only
elections available to the Arab population to express strictly Arab
political preferences.

Another interesting finding concerns the second round of
elections in Jewish and Arab authorities in those cases in which

Local Government in Israel

Table 4.4

VOTER TURNOUT IN LOCAL ELECTIONS: 1950–1983

Year	Local Elections	Knesset Elections
1950	79.6	
1955	78.6	82.8
1959	79.0	81.6
1965	82.7	83.0
1969	79.0	81.7
1973	73.0	78.6
1978	57.3	
1983	58.0	

Sources: See Table 4.1; Data for 1983 is based on *Ha'aretz*, 26 October 1983, p. 1, based on a report from the Interior Minister.

no candidate for mayor received 40 percent of the valid votes. The voter turnout in the first round in these 31 municipalities was 59.3 percent, while in the second round, where the competition intensified with the participation of only the two strongest candidates, voter turnout fell to 51.6 percent.

There is a strong correlation between the size of a municipality and voter turnout. As the number of residents increases, voter turnout tends to decline. This correlation may to a certain extent explain the difference between Jewish and Arab voter participation. In a small municipality the resident feels more strongly that his vote may make a difference; internal solidarity and social pressures are also more often factors. Table 4.5 clearly demonstrates the correlation between size of municipality and degree of political participation.

There are substantial differences in voter turnout between the very small municipalities and the larger cities — 49 percent in the large cities versus 75 percent in the small municipalities. Among the three large cities, Jerusalem has a particularly low voter turnout — 41 percent — which may reflect the combination of East Jerusalem Arab abstentions and the abstention of the extreme ultra-Orthodox, two groups which do not recognize the legitimacy of the state. The rate for Tel Aviv stood at 49.7 percent, while in Haifa it was 54.5 percent.[43] Safed, the Jewish city with the highest voter turnout — 69.3 percent — is also the city with the fewest voters. In two small councils the voter turnout exceeded 90 percent: in Metulla, 278 out of 300 eligible voters participated (92.7 percent) and in Menachemia, 428 out of 473 (90.5 percent). Metulla is, however, the Jewish local council with the fewest eligible voters.

Table 4.5

VOTER TURNOUT IN 1978 LOCAL AUTHORITY ELECTIONS
IN JEWISH AND MIXED MUNICIPALITIES
According to Number of Eligible Voters

Number of Eligible Voters	Voter Turnout
Up to 5,000	75.3
5,001 – 10,000	68.8
10,001 – 20,000	60.3
20,001 – 50,000	59.8
50,001 – 100,000	53.2
100,000 and more	49.0
Total	55.4

Source: Calculated from statistics in *Results of Elections to the Local Authorities – 1978*, Jerusalem, Ministry of Interior, 1978.

Multi-Party Structure

How many lists and mayoral candidates compete in local elections? Is the multi-party structure of the state system duplicated in the local system as well? To what degree is the local system divided and fragmented among the different parties? Table 4.6 describes the average number of lists which participated in local elections from 1950 onward.

Local Government in Israel

Table 4.6

AVERAGE NUMBER OF LISTS PARTICIPATING IN LOCAL ELECTIONS IN JEWISH AND MIXED MUNICIPALITIES: 1950–1983

Year	Average Number of Lists
1950	5.8
1955	7.2
1959	6.7
1965	7.1
1969	6.0
1973	5.7
1978	4.8
1983	5.8

Sources: See Table 4.1.

Despite fluctuations occurring over the years, the average in 1950 is identical to that of 1983. In 1955 and 1965 the average exceeded seven lists. The election reform was not accompanied by any changes in the number of competing lists; in 1978 there was indeed a decrease, but in 1983 the situation returned to what it had been previously. The average in the Arab municipalities was higher than in the Jewish ones; in 1978 the average in the Arab municipalities was 6.5 versus 4.8 in the Jewish and mixed municipalities, while in 1983 the average was 7.5 versus 5.8. In contrast, the average number of candidates for mayor was slightly higher among the Jews than among the Arabs: 3.3 versus 3.2 in 1978 and 4.0 versus 3.2 in 1983. When considering all municipalities — Jewish, mixed and Arab — the average number of candidates per municipality was 3.3 in 1978 and 3.7 in 1983.

The overall picture is one of fragmentation which views an average of six lists competing alongside four candidates. The 1978 elections in Kiryat Ono can serve as an example of this pattern. Four candidates competed for the mayoral position from the lists of Labor, Likud, the religious parties and a local list. In the election for municipal council two additional lists participated; one local and the second from the Democratic Movement.

Degree of Competitiveness

The degree of competitiveness between the mayoral candidates can be inferred in two ways: the proportion of municipalities in which the elections were not decided in the first round and the gap between the two leading competitors. In 1978 the elections were not decided in the first round in 22 out of 94 Jewish and mixed municipalities (23.4 percent). In 1983 a second round was held in 27 out of 96 municipalities (28.1 percent). There was no substantive difference in the level of competitiveness between the two elections. Still, in 1983 the competition went to a second round in one of the large cities — Ramat Gan. In eleven Jewish municipalities a second round was held in both 1978 and 1983: Even Yehuda, Beit Dagan, Dimona, Hazor, Tirat Hacarmel, Yavniel, Yeruham, Mevasseret Zion, Netanya, Ramle and Sederot. In each of these the ruling party and mayor were replaced in the 1983 elections.

When competitiveness is measured according to the difference between the votes received by the two leading candidates, it becomes clear that no great change occurred in the depth of competitiveness in the 1983 elections. The average degree of competitiveness according to this measure in Jewish and mixed municipalities was 28.9 percent in 1978 and 29.1 percent in 1983. In the Arab municipalities the competitiveness was twice as strong — 14 percent in 1978 and 14.6 percent in 1983. In both sectors the competitiveness decreased slightly in 1983. The average for all of the municipalities was 23.8 percent in 1978 and 24.6 percent in 1983.

Analysis of the relation between competitiveness and municipal size offers some interesting findings. The lowest degree of competitiveness in the 1978 elections in the Jewish municipalities was found in the smallest ones (up to 5,000 eligible voters) — 35.8 percent on the average and in the large cities (over 100,000 eligible voters) — 34.1 percent on the average. A high degree of competitiveness was found in cities with 20,000–100,000 voters — 19.4 percent — and in municipalities in which the number of eligible voters ranged from 10,000–20,000 — 19.9 percent. In the municipalities numbering between 5,000–10,000 eligible voters, competitiveness was moderate — 26 percent on the average. Competitiveness tended to intensify as the size of the municipality increased. However, in the largest cities there was a decline in competitiveness. Menachemia can serve as an example of a very small settlement in which competitiveness is low: only one candidate ran for mayor — Benny Shalita. Jerusalem can serve as an example of a large city in which competitiveness is low — 49.5 percent — with Teddy Kollek dominating the local electoral scene.

Change in Government

While changes in government have been rare on the state plane, they occur quite frequently in the localities. Among the 99 Jewish and mixed municipalities in 1983, only in 24 had there never been changes in the party — or parties which belong to a specific political bloc — heading the authority; one political bloc maintained rule of the municipality during the entire period of its post-state existence. Bnei Brak is the only municipality which has always been controlled by the religious parties, although it is true that different religious parties — National Religious Party and Agudat Israel — controlled during different periods. In nine settlements, the most conspicuous of which is Kiryat Bialik, local lists have always ruled. Fourteen settlements have always been controlled by Labor including Haifa, Givatayim, Holon, Kfar Saba, Carmiel, Nahariya, Upper Nazareth and Acre. The Likud has not succeeded in maintaining unbroken rule in any municipality. Its last stronghold in Ramat Gan fell in 1983. In Menachemia, Benny Shalita from the Liberals has led the local council since its first elections in 1957, but up until 1965 he ran on a local list ("Lema'an Menachemia.")

Thus 24 municipalities have demonstrated unbroken rule by a single bloc, compared to 75 municipalities in which there have been changes in government. The two major blocs were in control in 39 (including Tel Aviv, for example, where Labor and Likud have both ruled); in 27 municipalities there have been three different blocs in power (including Beit She'an, for example, where the religious parties sometimes ruled as well as the two major blocs); in 9 municipalities there have been four blocs in control (including Dimona, for example, where a local list was sometimes victorious.)

Out of the 99 Jewish and mixed municipalities in 1983, the Labor bloc had been in power in 87 during one period or another, the

Likud in 51, local lists in 43, the religious parties in 30, and other parties in 8. These data reveal an extremely dynamic local political system. In the 1983 elections, for instance, changes in government occurred in nearly one-third of the municipalities — 31 in number. This turnover was high in relation to earlier elections. In addition, in 1983 there were personnel changes in 11 local authorities as a result of the nomination process. However, these were internal party changes, in which the mayoralty changed hands, but the party whose representative had held the position remained in power.

Split-Ticket Voting

Split-ticket voting refers to voting for two separate parties in simultaneous elections. In the five election campaigns of 1955, 1959, 1965, 1969, and 1973, the voters voted for the Knesset and the local authority on the same day. Whoever voted for a certain list in the Knesset elections and a different list in the local election is considered to have split their vote. The local election reform made another type of split possible in the 1978 and 1983 local elections, supporting a certain party list while at the same time supporting a mayoral candidate from a different list.

Measurement of split-ticket voting runs into several difficulties. When using aggregate data of election results, there is no escape from the necessity of ignoring some of the splitting. This is the case because some of the data may cancel each other out, leaving some of the splitting undetected. For example, if a certain party in city "A" gains 20 percent of the votes for its mayoral candidate and 15 percent of the votes for the local council, one could assume that those same 15 percent also voted for that party's candidate for mayor. However, it is definitely possible that the splitting was larger, that only 10 percent of these voted for this candidate while the other 5 percent split their vote, voting for a different party's candidate for mayor and for the first party for local council.

Split-ticket voting is measured while taking into account the four major blocs: Labor, Likud, the religious and local parties (the latter include the "other" parties as well).[44] Almost certainly there is also splitting within the blocs themselves, such that once again the measurement cannot reflect the whole scope of the phenomenon.[45] The picture is of an increase in the phenomenon of split-ticket voting over time. In 1955 the standardized countrywide average was 6 percent; in 1959 it grew to 7.6 percent; in 1965 it climbed to 9 percent; in 1969 it grew to 10.9 percent; and in 1973 it took off to 15.8 percent. In light of the within-bloc split and the mutual cancellation — two factors not taken into account in the measurement — more than 15.8 percent of the voters split their vote in 1973.

Split-ticket voting in 1978 and 1983 was different in character — only 11.7 percent in 1978 and 14.1 percent in 1983. These data at first seem to express a decline in the scope of the phenomenon as opposed to the 1973 elections, but it must be remembered that split-ticket voting is a learned political behavior. A new procedure requires learning and experience on the part of the voters and until the procedure is institutionalized, the scope of the split-ticket voting will not be as extensive. In addition, the fact that in the past there were two types of ballots on different planes (state and local), which represented different institutions (the Knesset and the local authority), made split-ticket voting easier, while since 1978 this distinction between planes and institutions has no longer existed, thus making split-ticket voting more difficult.

Until 1973 split-ticket voting also increased because every vote for a local list was considered split. Since 1978, however, it has been possible to vote for a local list and its candidate without splitting the vote. Still, the ideological character of the elections until 1973, being part of the struggle for control of the state government, made split-ticket voting more difficult, while the separation of the local and Knesset elections in 1978 and 1983 and the lack of ideological overtones of the local elections should have strengthened the scope of split-ticket voting.

A very high level of split-ticket voting is likely to create a situation in which the mayor does not have a majority in the council. This is a reasonable possibility in a presidential system and, despite its limitations, it does not necessarily mean a paralysis of the local authority's activities. Cases such as these occurred in a few municipalities, prominent among which were Ramat Hasharon in 1978 and Beit Shemesh in 1983.

Local Lists

As noted earlier, the nominating process in the local lists is even less open and democratic than in the state parties. In addition, many of the local lists lack a firm political base, meaning that local lists that fail to gain or participate in electoral power are likely to disappear from the local scene. By contrast, the state parties are typically more stable. Electoral failure does not mean the end of the party's activities between elections, since state party headquarters assures continuity by sparking local branch activities.

Sometimes the state parties hide behind the labels of local parties. An extreme example of this was in the 1978 elections in Yeruham. In addition to the religious parties, four different local lists competed, while Likud and Labor did not present their own lists. Popular mayors may sometimes act similarly as in Jerusalem, where Mayor Teddy Kollek stands at the head of the local "One Jerusalem-Teddy's List," when, in fact, the Labor branch stands behind the list. Avraham Krinizy of the General Zionists did the same thing in 1950 when he lead the list "Lema'an Ramat Gan." In these two cases it is problematic to view these lists as purely local, since in actuality the state party machines backed them. In contrast, the list of Hanania Gibstein in Rishon le-Zion can be legitimately viewed as a local list. In 1969 he was elected on the Gahal list (predecessor of Likud) as mayor, but since then he has competed at the head of a local list, "Lema'an Rishon le-Zion," while the Likud competed with its own list.

Some of the local lists resulted from splits in party branches. In the 1983 elections, the lists at whose head stood Zvi Zilker of Ashdod and Maxim Levy of Lod are examples of local lists which came to life out of splits in Herut branches, while the lists of Reuven Kligler of Netanya and Eliyahu Nawi of Beersheba represent the same phenomenon in Labor. There are few local lists with extensive longevity. An outstanding exception is the list, "Lema'an Kiryat Bialik," headed by Zvi Karliner, which has won in every election since the founding of the state. The "Public List for Ramat Hasharon," in existence since 1969, is another survivor among the local lists. Many local lists, however, quickly disappear from the political arena.

Some of the local lists were established in the name of neighborhood interests. In Rehovot, for example, several neighborhood lists have participated in the elections: "The Unified Independent List for Shaaraim and the Neighborhoods" (1965), "The United List for Marmorek and Shaaraim" (1950, 1955, 1960), "The Independent List for Shaaraim (1955) and others. In Bnei Brak in 1973, "The Independent List for Pardes Katz" competed, and in

Jerusalem in the same year "The List for Kiryat Hayovel and its Environs" participated. This type of list usually does not achieve electoral success, although its authentic local basis generally exceeds that of local lists built on party fragmentation, ethnic awakening or personal motivation.

In general it can be said that the local lists succeed more in the smaller than in the larger municipalities. One can assume that the reason for this is the stronger local feelings which prevail in the smaller municipalities. In the 1978 elections, local lists in the Jewish sector attained 27.7 percent of the vote in municipalities in which the number of eligible voters was below 5,000, and only 8.8 percent in the large cities in which the number of eligible voters exceeded 100,000. The greatest success of the local lists was in the small settlements numbering 10,000 to 20,000 eligible voters — 29.6 percent. The group of municipalities with 5,000 to 10,000 eligible voters deviates from the pattern — only 11.4 percent, as opposed to 17.3 percent in the group of 20,000 to 50,000 eligible voters, and 18.9 percent in the group of 50,000 to 100,000 eligible voters. The relation between the size of the municipality and the degree of success of local lists exists, but it is not very strong. Success is largely dependent on the particular candidate and the degree of stability of the local branches of the larger parties.

In small established municipalities, local lists are particularly successful. Examples include Kfar Shmaryahu, Omer, Even Yehuda, Metulla and Yesod Hamaala. Some of the small established municipalities do not even hold elections, since the residents agree ahead of time on a single list (Kfar Tavor, Kineret, Ramot Hashavim, Shavei Zion). The success of local lists can also sometimes be explained against the background of a local crisis, as in the success of the list of "Zeirei Yavneh" in the 1969 elections and the success of local lists in the 1978 elections in Haifa. On the other hand, local lists have not had much success against a popular mayor in a town on the move. Thus, Abie Nathan and his "Sapan" list failed in the 1983 elections in Tel Aviv. It is difficult to predict whether the decline of the local lists in the 1983 elections represents the beginning of a trend in local politics or a one-time phenomenon.

The Ethnic Factor

Voting patterns are particularly instructive in demonstrating the separation of local and state politics. While on the state plane the ethnic factor has recently become dominant in explanations of political preference, it is much less important on the local plane. Under-representation from which the Sephardim suffered on the state plane is almost nonexistent on the local plane; half of the mayors of Jewish and mixed municipalities elected in 1983 are of Sephardi origin, as opposed to only one-quarter of the members of the Knesset.

The relative unimportance of the ethnic factor is revealed in an analysis of election results in the different neighborhoods of Tel Aviv and Jerusalem. In the Knesset elections the proportion of Likud votes in Tel Aviv was highest in the southern neighborhoods of the city, while Labor was strongest in the northern neighborhoods. This quite clearly reflects the ethnic distribution in the city's neighborhoods. Thus, for instance, in 1981, subquarter 12, which includes Ramat Aviv, Neve Avivim and Afeka, was the area in which the Likud achieved its poorest results — 26.3 percent. By contrast, this was the area of Tel Aviv in which Labor achieved its best results — 52.8 percent.

In the local elections of 1978, on the other hand, the influence of the ethnic factor was nowhere to be found. Labor's candidate, Asher Ben-Natan, received only 32.8 percent of the vote as opposed to 61 percent for Shlomo Lahat of the Likud. Even in the council balloting the Likud won handily — 44 percent to 35.7 percent. In subquarter 93, which includes the Hatikva and Ezra quarters, the Likud attained its best results in Tel Aviv in the 1981 elections — 66.7 percent against 13 percent for Labor. In the local elections in 1978, however, the Likud was weaker — 52.6 percent in the council (party) balloting and 57.4 percent in the mayoral (personal) balloting, while Labor was stronger than in the Knesset elections — 18.9 percent for council and 19.6 percent for mayor. The achievements of the Likud candidate were better in Ramat Aviv and Neve Avivim than in the Hatikva quarter, in complete contrast to the Knesset election results. The strong support for the Likud and its candidate was particularly conspicuous in Ramat Aviv.

Analysis of the Jerusalem data reveals the opposite trend, since the victorious mayoral candidate was from Labor as opposed to the Likud in Tel Aviv, and also points to the weakness of the ethnic factor in local elections. In subquarter 41, which includes the Katamon neighborhoods, the Likud received 57.4 percent of the votes in the 1981 Knesset elections, but only 18.5 percent in the 1978 local elections (17.2 percent for mayor). Labor received only 22.1 percent in the 1981 Knesset elections in Katamon, but 51.9 percent in the local elections in 1978 (66.5 percent for mayor). In subquarter 15 (Rehavia and Kiryat Shmuel), Labor won in the 1981 Knesset elections with 40.4 percent versus 25.2 percent for Likud. In the local elections in 1978, Labor was victorious here as well with 57.5 percent (78.3 percent for mayor) versus only 9 percent for the Likud (6.9 percent for mayor).

It is instructive that the great gap between the two areas in the Knesset elections all but disappears in the local elections. In Beersheba, for example, in the 1978 local elections the two Likud lists received 12.3 percent (10 percent for mayor), as opposed to 47.5 percent in the Knesset elections of 1981. The factor of party identification thereby plays a secondary role in the determination of voter preference.

Conclusion

In the past two decades local politics in Israel has progressively distinguished itself from state politics. Originally a mere accessory to state politics, local politics has developed into an independent force in its own right. This development has occurred simultaneously on different levels — on the structural-constitutional level with the election reforms and the expansion of mayoral authorities, and on the behavioral level where local elections progressively differed from state elections in their voting patterns, with more rapid changes in government, considerable split-ticket voting, and the success of local lists. In addition, nominating procedures for local elections have become more open and democratic than they were in the past.

The contribution of the change in the method of local elections to the process of localization or territorialization of local politics has been limited thus far. Even before the reform, voters were largely motivated by considerations at whose foundations stood the personality of the candidates who headed the lists. This phenomenon was especially conspicuous in 1969 and 1973. The reform has not brought about any significant change in the quality of those elected, including the mayors. It could be that the time has come to hold a comprehensive and extensive public discussion of additional electoral reforms which would strengthen the local-ization or territorialization process, and at whose foundation would be the holding of neighborhood-based regional elections for local councils.

Notes – Chapter 4

1. Giladi (1973), p. 132.
2. ibid., p. 134.
3. ibid., pp. 134-35.
4. Tel Aviv Municipality (1945), p. 9. Concerning the conflicts on the issue of voting rights in the 1920s, see Giladi, ibid., pp. 140-42, and Horowitz-Lissak (1977), p. 396, note 137.
5. Giladi, ibid., p. 245.
6. Horowitz-Lissak, ibid., p. 145.
7. Provisional Council of State, pp. 20-23.
8. *Divrei Haknesset*, 2, pp. 1173-76.
9. ibid., 3, p. 547.
10. ibid., 7, p. 689.
11. Words of I. Cohen, ibid., p. 686.
12. Words of H. Rubin, ibid., p. 687.
13. Words of Y. Guri, ibid., 3, p. 548.
14. ibid., p. 549.
15. ibid., pp. 551-85.
16. ibid., 6, pp. 2362-64, 2407-14, 2609-15.
17. ibid., 2, pp. 1175-76.
18. ibid., 13, pp. 583-86, 905-10, 923-32; ibid., 14, pp. 2501-04.
19. ibid., 55, pp. 587-88.
20. ibid., 27, pp. 2559-61, 2595-612, 2614-38.
21. ibid., 37, pp. 2405-08.
22. ibid., 39, pp. 1075-78.
23. ibid., 55, pp. 3607-16, 3628-51.
24. ibid., 54, pp. 1556-59.
25. ibid., 58, p. 2252.
26. ibid., 66, pp. 2016-47.
27. ibid., 67, pp. 3439-43.
28. ibid., 65, p. 180; ibid., 66, p. 1394.
29. ibid., 70, pp. 1404-08, 1414-22.
30. ibid., 72, p. 913.
31. ibid., 74, pp. 3761-85, 3966-67.
32. ibid., 76, pp. 2406-08.
33. ibid., 79, pp. 1283-84, 1361-62, 1605-06.
34. ibid., p. 1283.
35. Herut Movement (1966), p. 24.
36. Herut Movement (1975), p. 86.
37. D. Anzilevitz to the Central Election Committee of the Herut Movement, 6.12.55. File 63 of the Municipal Department, Jabotinsky Institute, the Historic Archives.
38. A. Drori to D. Anzilevitz, 6.27.55, ibid.
39. H.R. to P.Z., 10.5.50 (File of branch committees in the cities, 1950, Beit Berl Archives).

40. Pesah Lev to Zalman Aharonovitz, 1.2.50, (ibid.).
41. Almogi (1980), p. 298.
42. ibid., p. 299.
43. Analysis of the voter turnout in Tel Aviv according to neighborhoods reveals that in the south of the city, populated primarily by Sephardim, the voter turnout was lower than in the north of the city. In 1978, for example, 59.9 percent of the residents of Neighborhood "L" voted, 58 percent in the area of Ichilov Hospital, Neve David and Beeri Street, and 57.8 percent in the area of State Square. In contrast only 37.8 percent voted in Menashia, Neve Shalom and Neve Zedek, 39.5 percent in Kerem Hatemanim and Carmel Market, and 39 percent in central Jaffa and Shderot Jerusalem.
44. The fourth category which includes the local lists and other parties does not constitute a natural political bloc. While the Labor, the Likud and the religious blocs each represent an historic political camp, the use of the fourth bloc is for analytical needs and is based on methodological considerations.
45. The measurement is made by calculating the gap in absolute numbers and percentages between the two types of ballots for the four blocs in each municipality. The gaps were summed and divided by two in order to prevent artificial doubling of the splitting. In other words, voters who preferred party "A" in one type and party "B" in another type could have split their vote in such a way that it is impossible to calculate the actual split made with respect to each party. In order to give a picture of the elections in a certain year, the split-ticket voting scores for each municipality were standardized according to the number of voters in it.

Chapter 5

LEGAL STRUCTURE OF THE LOCAL AUTHORITY

Israel Peled

Introduction

The structure of the legislative system in Israel today resembles the legislative system originally established during the British Mandate. The fundamental difference between the two is that the Mandatory system was not democratic; the laws were enacted not by an elected parliament, but rather by the British Crown. They were handed down as "ordinances."

In the State of Israel the Knesset is the legislative body, its members elected by the people in democratic elections; its legislative acts are called "laws."

The ministry responsible for enforcing a law is usually given the authority to issue regulations — supplementary published laws which detail the primary law. Each specific law prescribes this authority for the relevant ministry or ministries.

In municipal matters the Ministry of Interior usually has the authority to issue regulations, but there are some areas which concern several government ministries. Matters concerning traffic and transportation within municipal boundaries involve both the Ministry of Interior and the Ministry of Transportation; public health laws involve the Ministries of Interior and Health, etc. In such instances the regulations are signed by the two relevant ministers.

The laws and regulations become effective when they are formally published in the Book of Statutes or the Compilation of Regulations, unless the law explicitly states a different effective date. The law also allows a minister to wield certain powers through his implementation of orders. An order is given by the minister to the person or group of people to whom it is designated. Local authorities may execute their responsibilities with the help of by-laws or ordinances enacted by the local council and with the approval of the Ministry of Interior.

The decisions of the courts and their interpretations of the law become a part of the law itself; precedents established by the courts, and especially by the Supreme Court, guide later applications and enforcement.

Until the British conquest in 1917, the Land of Israel was a part of the Ottoman Empire. For the first few years the British maintained those legal arrangements which had existed prior to their entry. As they gradually established local government frameworks, they were guided by the administrative principles applied in other British colonies and protectorates which were adjusted to local conditions. These included the needs of the Jewish Yishuv who wished to cultivate self-government.

In 1934, the Mandatory authorities issued the Municipal Corporations Ordinance, 1934, which essentially established the legal basis for the present system of local government. It served as the foundation for the Municipal Corporations Ordinance (new version) under which municipalities in the State of Israel operate today.

At the time of the publication of the Municipal Corporations Ordinance, 1934, Tel Aviv was the only Jewish city in Palestine, while there were about twelve cities with Arab or mixed populations. Only in Tel Aviv did the electoral system meet the requirements of a democratic public. Its method of election later became the model according to which other Jewish cities and towns, such as Petah Tikva, Rehovot, Rishon le-Zion and Ramat Gan, were to operate. While these local authorities operated with a certain degree of autonomy, the Mandatory authorities retained considerable power vis-a-vis the Jewish local authorities. For example, the power to appoint the mayor and his deputy from among those elected to the local council remained in the hands of the district commissioner. By-laws and budgets required the approval of the High Commissioner. Appointment of statutory clerks, the upper levels of the local bureaucracy which included the town clerk and treasurer, required the approval of the district commissioner. To this day some of these powers remain in the hands of the Ministry of Interior and its district representatives.

The Local Councils Ordinance, 1941 set forth the formal legal framework for the operation of local councils. This legal framework has remained as the basis for the operation of local councils in Israel.

In 1936 the Town Planning Ordinance, 1936 was published. It was to be replaced by the Planning and Building Law, 5725–1965 enacted by the Knesset.

The transition from the British Mandate to independent Israeli rule necessitated legal arrangements which would maintain the legal continuity of frameworks and authorities. Therefore, at the time of the proclamation of the establishment of the State of Israel, the Law and Administration Ordinance, 5708–1948 was enacted. It established that the "municipalities, local councils and other local authorities will continue to act within their areas of jurisdiction and in the framework of their authorities" (section 4), and that the powers granted by the Municipal Corporations Ordinance, 1934, the Local Councils Ordinance, 1941, and the remaining Mandatory laws of the High Commissioner relating to issues of local government were transferred to the Minister of Interior.[1]

The Definition of a Local Authority

In the Interpretation Ordinance (new version) (section 1), a local authority is defined as follows: "A local authority is a municipality, local council or some similar authority, which was established by the power of a law in effect at the time, which prescribes instructions concerning the establishment of authorities of local government."

This short definition is intended for use in legal terminology and does not describe the structure, competences and methods of administration of a local authority. The following definition includes these more functional aspects: a local authority is a statutory corporation whose competences and areas of jurisdiction were established by ministerial orders by authority of the law and whose goal is the determination of procedures and rules for the local government of the residents of that same area.

After combining the elements of the two definitions with the addition of a description of the principal functions, we can arrive at the following extended definition:

1. Local authorities include municipalities, local councils and similar authorities.

2. The local authority is a legal personality — a corporation,

established in accordance with the desires of the residents of the area through ministerial orders derived from the relevant law — to have a local jurisdiction over the area. In its status as a legal personality, the local authority has the right to prosecute and be prosecuted in its corporate name.

3. The boundaries of the area within which the legal jurisdiction of the local authority applies are determined by the Minister of Interior, by virtue of the powers granted him in the Municipal Corporations Ordinance.

4. The local authority is responsible for planning, licensing and supervising buildings within its area, as well as for the development and provision of services to the population living within its jurisdiction. For this purpose, the local authority is entitled to enact by-laws and to collect property taxes and other levies.

Establishing a Local Authority

How is a local authority established? There are two types of local authorities: municipalities and local councils. While not mentioned explicitly in the law, it is the criterion of size which distinguishes between a municipality and a local council and guides the Minister of Interior in making distinctions between the two. The general rule is that a local council whose population exceeds 20,000 is granted the status of a municipality. There are exceptions to this rule — for instance, when the government wished to encourage problematic border settlements such as Eilat and Kiryat Shmona, it granted them municipal status even though they contained fewer than 20,000 residents. On the other hand, the local council of Ramat Hasharon, whose population exceeds 20,000, has refused to change its status to that of a municipality.

Municipalities

Section 3 of the Municipal Corporations Ordinance (new version) sets forth the procedure for the Minister of Interior to follow when announcing the establishment of a new municipality. From the time that it seems desirable to establish a new municipality in a certain area, and that this is indeed the desire of the residents of this same area, the minister is permitted to appoint a board of inquiry to study the matter. After reviewing the findings of the board of inquiry, the minister may exercise his own judgement and announce that the residents of the area in question will comprise a municipality. The minister is not required to accept the recommendations of the board of inquiry, but he must appoint it and read its memoranda. Only after he has done so may he announce a decision.

In his order announcing the establishment of a municipality, the minister must define the area under its jurisdiction and issue instructions concerning the procedures and dates of elections for the municipal council, performance of local functions prior to the election of the first council, and any other details required for the activation of a municipality.

A change in the area of jurisdiction of an existing municipality is usually carried out according to a similar procedure (Municipal Corporations Ordinance, section 8 and 8a). In such a case, however, the minister may announce an extension of the area of jurisdiction of a municipality and order that residents from the annexed territory be included in the municipal council, even without having first established a board of inquiry.

The minister has the authority to change the status of a local council to that of a municipality or to unify a number of local authorities into one municipality (Municipal Corporations Ordinance, section 5 and 6). In such a case the minister must take the necessary steps to assure a proper transition from the now defunct local councils to the newly established municipality. Thus, in his announcement of the change, he must include all of the conditions and instructions for the transition period so that the continuity of rights and obligations are protected.

In 1987 there were 39 cities:

Acre	Haifa	Lod	Shfar'am
Afula	Herzliya	Nahariya	Tel Aviv-Jaffa
Ashdod	Holon	Nazareth	Tiberias
Ashkelon	Jerusalem	Netanya	Umm al Fahm
Bat Yam	Kfar Saba	Petah Tikva	Upper Nazareth
Beersheba	Kiryat Ata	Ra'anana	Yavne
Bnei Brak	Kiryat Bialik	Ramat Gan	
Dimona	Kiryat Gat	Ramle	
Eilat	Kiryat Motzkin	Rehovot	
Givatayim	Kiryat Shmona	Rishon le-Zion	
Hadera	Kiryat Yam	Safed	

The law also considers the highly unlikely possibility of the abolition of a municipality (Municipal Corporations Ordinance, section 11). This possibility is most realistically seen in the context of annexation to a different municipality or a theoretical change in status from that of a municipality to that of a local council.

Procedures for abolishing a municipality are identical to the procedures cited earlier for establishing one, involving the appointment of a board of inquiry followed by an announcement of the procedures and conditions of abolition, including the appropriation of municipal property. In the economic sector the abolition of a corporate body is accomplished by dismantling the failed business and appointing a receiver. In a municipality, as noted later, there is an option of appointing a special committee.

Municipal Quarters: — The law leaves room for the establishment of statutory frameworks for neighborhoods within the context of the municipality, called "Municipal Quarters" (Municipal Corporations Ordinance, sections 12-16). If residents of a neighborhood or quarter in a city are interested in special development or the provision of special services which the city does not grant its residents and the Minister of Interior is made aware of such interest, he may declare the neighborhood to be a municipal quarter. The quarter committee, elected by its residents, may decide about special services or special development projects within the neighborhood. In order to carry out such projects, the committee must submit its proposal and budget to the municipal council and the district authority. Following their approval the committee may implement the plan, collecting the required funds from neighborhood residents by increasing their general municipal taxes, as is done, for example, in Kiryat Haim in Haifa.

Local Councils

The law which governs the establishment and activities of local councils is the Local Councils Ordinance (new version). This law grants the Minister of Interior the authority to establish a local council according to the recommendation of the district authority; in this case there is no need for a board of inquiry.

Prior to 1959 the Minister of Interior issued separate establishment orders to each local council, but with the publication of the Local Councils Ordinance (a), 1950, the order was applied to all of the councils established between the years 1936 and 1950, according to the list included in the appendix of the order. The order applied to most of the local authorities and defined their areas of jurisdiction and methods of administration. The Local Councils Ordinance (b), 1950 was issued concerning smaller councils. There are no significant differences between local councils described in the two separate orders. The Minister of Interior, in establishing the two types, was apparently guided by the criterion of size.

Regional Councils

The procedures for establishing a regional council established in the Local Councils Ordinance (Regional Council), 5718–1958, are similar to the procedures for setting up a local council. The first council is established by the decree of the Minister of Interior, who both fixes the number of members of the council and appoints them, after consultation with local residents. This council functions until the election of a new council, or until some other time fixed by the Minister of Interior.

The Institutions of the Local Authority and Election Laws

The local authority is run by institutions whose members are democratically elected. The election laws and the authority structures of local institutions are complex. The council and the mayor are elected separately. The mayor is simultaneously responsible to the voting public from whom he derives his power and to the council which was elected parallel to him. In addition, the council and mayor are subordinate, according to the law, to the instructions of the Ministry of Interior and other central organs, to such an extent that their independence is often denied them. Prior to the passage of the Local Authorities (Election and Tenure of Mayor and Deputy Mayor) Law, 5735–1975, under which the mayors are directly elected by the voters, there had been one unified election procedure for both the members of the council and the mayor. The voters would elect all of the members of the local authority council in elections which were general, direct, equal, secret and proportional. The elected council members then chose the mayor and his deputies from among themselves.

The change introduced in 1975 is much more revolutionary and extensive than it appears at first glance. It is in fact a switch to a presidential system in miniature which grants the mayor considerable powers, as he derives most of his power directly from the voters. In fact his status during his four year term is one of such independence that during debates in the Knesset concerning the change in the law, Knesset members who opposed the change claimed that it would create small dictatorships.

To effect the change, the State Commission on Local Government (the Sanbar Commission), in its first interim report following the implementation of direct mayoral elections, proposed a reorganization of the relations between the mayor of the local authority and its council. The Municipalities Ordinance (Amendment No. 24) Law, 5739–1978, which originated in a private legislative proposal of several members of the Knesset, was enacted approximately one week before the local elections were held. This amendment was similar to a memorandum presented to the government containing a legislative proposal in the spirit of the Sanbar Commission recommendations. The private proposal, however, reflecting the interests of the parties which supported it, left to the council some of the powers granted to the mayor in the legislative proposal presented by the Commission. In parallel to this amendment to the Municipalities Ordinance, the Minister of Interior amended the Local Councils Ordinance.[2] However, as noted later, the amendment did not solve all of the difficulties and it will be necessary to find further solutions.

On the one hand, the new law made it possible for a mayor to find himself in a minority position facing an adversary council on a series of issues on his agenda. This situation could bring the work of the municipality to a near halt, leading to a significant decline in both the level of services provided and in the quality of life for local residents. On the other hand, we have been witness to a tendency in Israeli society to follow the strong, which would lead in this case to doing away altogether with the opposition and creating broad coalitions in which every faction or council member seeks a position of power. In such a case, the mayor may gather too much power and, lacking any effective opposition, may indeed be able to act as a minor dictator.

The Electoral Process

Elections for local authority councils and mayors are held simultaneously throughout the country every four years on the third Tuesday in the month of Heshvan. The Minister of Interior has the power to postpone the elections in a specific local authority if there are special justifying circumstances.

Local council elections are general, direct, equal, secret and proportional. The elections for mayor are similar, except that the mayoral elections are personal, while the elections for the council are proportional.

In both cases, the right to vote is granted to every resident of an authority who is listed in the population registry and who has reached 18 years of age by the beginning of the relevant year. No further criteria must be met (such as Israeli citizenship, for example) for the resident to receive local voting rights. The right to serve on the council is granted to anyone whose name is listed in the voter registry, who is 21 years of age or older on the day of registration of candidates, and whose place of residence is within that authority.

A candidate may not be a civil servant serving in a position which influences any issues related to that same local authority. This rule applies also to employees in certain public institutions as detailed in the Local Authorities (Restriction on Right to be Elected) Law, 5724–1963.

In addition to the limitation on the right to be elected due to position or influence, the law specifically disqualifies those who within the five years prior to candidate registration were convicted of a crime. A candidate may also be disqualified according to the Capacity and Guardianship Law, 5722-1962, as can someone who has declared bankruptcy within the period of his declaration of candidacy and two years after receiving a final exemption order or an order cancelling the original declaration (Bankruptcy Ordinance, 1936).

Anyone who can be a candidate for council elections may also be a mayoral candidate, with two additional conditions — he must be an Israeli citizen and he must head his list of candidates for the council. A list of candidates must contain at least one-third of the number of the members of the council. The list of candidates must be presented with the signature of at least 200 potential voters or 2 percent of the number of potential voters, whichever is lower. A mayoral candidate must gather 750 signatures or 3 percent of the number of voters, whichever is lower. A list from the incumbent council may submit a mayoral candidate without any signatures. The number of votes required for a council seat, called the quota, is calculated after the election by dividing the number of valid ballots cast by the number of seats on the council. Thus, each list of candidates will receive the number of seats calculated by dividing its total votes by the quota.

If a mayoral candidate is approved and he is from a list of candidates which was authorized, according to the Election Law, as the only list in the council elections, the election clerk is to declare the candidate as mayor. If there were two or more candidates, the candidate who received the largest number of valid votes will be elected, on the condition that he received at least 40 percent of the overall total. If no candidate received 40 percent, or if two candidates received an equal number of votes, a runoff election between the two candidates will be held within 14 days. If there was only one candidate, he will be elected, but on condition that he received at least 40 percent of the total valid votes in the council elections. If the candidate did not receive 40 percent, the council may appoint a mayor from among its members.

The mayor has one deputy who acts as his replacement when necessary, who is chosen from among the members of the council. The council of a local authority with less than 250,000 residents may choose one or two deputies, while a local authority which exceeds 250,000 residents may choose three deputies.

Mayor-Council Relations

In general, the council acts as the legislative, policy-making, guiding and controlling authority, while the mayor and his deputies act as the executive authority. The principal power of the council is in its budget approval function, both for the municipality's ordinary budget and its development (or non-ordinary) budgets. Approval of the budgets is usually the testing ground for relations between the mayor and the council, since once the budget is approved, the mayor can manage the authority within the framework of the budget almost independently of the council. The main test then is once a year at the time of the budget proposal.

The lawmakers took into consideration the possibility of serious conflict between the mayor and the council, which could be expressed in the council's refusal to approve the budget, an outcome which could bring about a freeze in the work of the local authority and considerable suffering to its residents. In order to cope with such an eventuality or at least to minimize the damage inflicted upon municipal services, the law established a mechanism for activating a temporary budget which could be tapped until an arrangement between the two sides could be worked out. Section 206 of the Municipal Corporations Ordinance states that as long as the council has not approved the budget, the mayor may continue to implement municipal services by utilizing 1/12 of the previous year's budget per month, with an addition for special expenses as approved by the Minister of Interior. A contrary council can, of course, place additional roadblocks in the path of the mayor by refusing to approve by-laws he recommends, for example.

Additional means are granted to the council by law for overseeing and influencing the administration of the local authority including an auditing committee which, while lacking executive powers, can publicize its findings and criticisms. Various other council committees, enumerated below, may act in an advisory capacity.

A mayor may attempt to amend a council decision which was accepted despite his opposition by exercising his right to request a second round of deliberations and to delay the implementation of the decision until such deliberations are held, under the Local Authorities (Election and Tenure of Mayor and Deputy Mayors) Law, 5735-1975.

If a mayor resigns during his period of office, his resignation will take effect 48 hours after his letter of resignation reaches the Minister of Interior, after which the council is to choose a new mayor from among its members. Therefore, the new law does not make an absolute division between direct mayoral elections and election by the council. Under certain conditions the choice is given back to the council, as it had been under the old law.

At times it may be necessary to remove a mayor from office. In such a case the question arises as to who has the power and what is the procedure. The law recognizes three cases in which a mayor may be deposed from office — criminal conduct, ill health and inappropriate behavior. In each of these cases the power to depose the mayor is given to a different authority.

Deposing a mayor for criminal conduct is carried out by the courts. If a mayor is convicted and the court, in response to a request made before the delivery of the verdict by the government's attorney or his representative, decides that the offense is a serious crime, the court will oust the mayor from office. It can be assumed that a traffic violation will not be considered a serious transgression, while crimes such as bribery, fraud and the like would be included in this category (ibid., section 20).

Deposing a mayor for reasons of ill health is within the jurisdiction of the Minister of Interior. If the minister believes that the mayor is unable to carry out his responsibilities due to a permanently incapacitating illness, he may remove him from office. In order to do this the minister must be convinced that the mayor is permanently incapacitated and not suffering from a temporary illness (ibid., section 21).

Deposing a mayor for inappropriate behavior is the responsibility of the council. If the council believes that the mayor is behaving in a manner which is inappropriate to his position and feels therefore that he is not worthy of his office, it may, after having given him a chance to defend himself, depose him from office (ibid., section 22).

The decision to depose a mayor from office must be well explained and accepted in a special, closed session of the council by at least three-fourths of the council members. Such a decision also requires the approval of the Minister of Interior.

The lawmakers foresaw the possibility that a mayor would refrain from calling a meeting of the council which would discuss his deposition due to inappropriate behavior. The law thus states that if the mayor has not called such a meeting within 14 days of the day that a majority of the council requested that he do so, the council itself may call such a meeting and determine who will chair it.

This section of the law was recently tested in an incident in the municipality of Kiryat Shmona. The members of the council, who wanted to oust the mayor, thought that this section made it possible for them to do so. The mayor for his part believed that, by virtue of his personal election, he had the power to govern the municipality even without the council's cooperation. The members of the council thought that they could interpret this behavior as inappropriate and thus legally remove him from office. Here, however, they were mistaken. Disagreement between the mayor and council on matters of substance cannot be defined as inappropriate behavior for the purpose of implementing section 22 for the removal of a mayor from office. Inappropriate behavior must be shown to be damaging to the respect and status due the office of mayor, such as public drunkenness.

If a confrontation arises which neither side is able to bridge and municipal services are thereby affected, causing undue suffering to local residents, then the Minister of Interior may use his authority to disperse the council and appoint a mandated committee in accordance with section 143 of the Municipal Corporations Ordinance. Thus one of the problematic aspects of the new law is that it does not provide a mechanism for internal resolution of a situation in which the mayor and council are deadlocked.

An additional problem in the relations between a mayor and council has to do with the constitutional aspects of the new structure. If we assume that the structure is one of division of authority between the legislative and controlling authority — the council — on the one hand and the executive authority — the mayor — on the other, then it is inappropriate that the mayor should also serve as chairman of the council during council meetings. This, however, is what the law requires. In the first supplement to the Municipal Corporations Ordinance it is explicitly stated that "the mayor will determine the agenda of the meeting" and in a different section "the mayor will be chairman in meetings of the council" (sections 23a and 34a).

The State Commission on Local Government (Sanbar Commission) discussed this question, but did not recommend amending the law. It sufficed with a recommendation that the following experiment should be conducted in one of the large cities: the council should choose a council chairman from among its members and this chairman would then set the agenda and run the meetings of the council, while the mayor would report and respond to inquiries.[3]

The Local Authority: General Powers and Functions

The council is the highest body in the local authority in the areas of policy-making, budget approval, legislation of by-laws, and overseeing the functioning of the executive authority, i.e., the mayor and his administration.

Section 13 of the Municipal Corporations Ordinance sets the number of council members in accordance with the size of the local authority as follows:

Number of Residents	Number of Council Members
Below 5,000	9
5,000 to 25,000	9 to 15
25,000 to 100,000	15 to 21
Above 100,000	21 to 31

The exact determination of the number of council members within the above framework is the responsibility of the Minister of Interior. The law requires that the council meet formally, in routine meetings, at least once a month. The procedure for non-routine meetings is fixed in the second supplement to the Municipal Corporations Ordinance. In its meetings the council approves budgets, by-laws, tax levies, contracts, etc.

To insure the moral integrity of the members of the council, the law specified a series of limitations and prohibitions. For example, members of the council are forbidden to participate in deliberations in which they have a personal interest (sections 122-123 in the Municipal Corporations Ordinance).

The law lists a variety of committees through which the council operates. Obligatory committees are those which the council is obligated by law to sustain. Optional committees are established according to the council's wishes. There are committees in which only council members participate, while some also contain representatives of the public.

Obligatory Committees

a. A Tenders Committee is comprised only of council members. Its role is to examine cost proposals presented to the municipality in response to publication of a tender for work required by the municipality and to recommend to the mayor the proposal which the committee believes is worthy of approval. The mayor cannot be a member of the Tenders Committee.[4]
b. A Finance Committee is appointed by the council from among its members, whose role is to advise the council on all of the municipality's financial affairs.

c. The Emergency Committee is concerned with the preparation of public facilities for emergency conditions. This committee includes public representatives who are not members of the council.
d. The Security Committee exists in any municipality in which a civil guard has been established. It is composed of representatives of the council, a representative of the security services and others.
e. The Auditing Committee is composed only of members of the council, whose number may not exceed seven. The chairman of the committee must be from a faction other than that of the mayor. Members of the municipality's administration may not participate in the Auditing Committee. The composition of the committee should, to the extent possible, match the factional composition of the municipal council.

In addition to these obligatory committees, the council may choose to establish other permanent or temporary committees, whose function it is to advise the council in various matters and circumstances.

Optional Committees

Most of the local authorities maintain optional committees such as an Education Committee, and Youth and Sport Committee. There are also more specific committees such as a Committee for the Encouragement of Tourism (in tourist cities), or a Committee for the Improvement of the Beach (in coastal cities). These committees are composed partly of members of the council and partly of public representatives. Section 162 of the Municipal Corporations Ordinance states that at least 25 percent of the members of the committees should be council members, while the rest must be eligible to serve on the council, with the additional condition that the overall factional composition of all committees matches the factional composition of the council.

These optional committees are advisory bodies only. While their powers are thus severely limited, the inclusion of representatives of the public who are not council members serves the important function of keeping the council members, who are chosen only once every four years, in close touch with the public pulse and with the changing wants and needs of the local residents.

An important optional committee, composed of council members only, is the Executive Committee, whose function it is to advise the mayor in all matters relevant to the performance of his job. The Executive Committee also serves as the committee forum for all issues which are not within the mandate of any other permanent or temporary existing committee. The number of members of the Executive Committee is set by the council and its members include the mayor, his deputies, and other council members selected by the council.

By-Laws

One of the important powers granted by law to the local authority is the power to adopt by-laws. A by-law enacted by a local authority requires the approval of the Minister of Interior, or the Minister of Interior plus the minister responsible for the specific issue. The enactment of by-laws makes it possible for an authority to carry out the powers and functions which it is permitted by law to execute. They empower a local authority to require a property owner or holder to perform work on his property which is required for the achievement of the authority's objectives (Municipal Corporations Ordinance, section 250). The Sanbar Commission proposed to cancel the requirement for Minister of Interior approval of local by-laws.[5]

At first glance, it would seem that the ability to establish and enforce by-laws places a great amount of power in the hands of the local authority — the powers of legislation, execution and enforcement all together. However, there are many limitations placed on these powers. First of all, the authority may legislate by-laws only for matters which state law permits. Secondly, all by-laws require the approval of the Minister of Interior. Thirdly, these by-laws are open to review by the Supreme Court in its role as the High Court of Justice. The court may invalidate any by-law on the grounds that it is unreasonable, discriminatory, or an offense against the natural laws of justice.[6]

The powers of the municipality to enact by-laws extend over a very broad field. Their importance is considerable in areas relating to the quality of life, public health, sanitation, recreation, paving roads and installation of water and sewage lines, as well as in a large variety of other areas of municipal life. Through its use of by-laws the municipality collects various forms of taxes in order to finance its activities. The means available to the municipality for the enforcement of its by-laws include fines and even imprisonment in certain instances, or performance of the work at the expense of the objecting citizen and the collection of the expenses from him (linked to the Consumer Price Index).[7]

Obligations and Powers in Light of Court Decisions

The obligations and powers of the local authority are defined in section 223 of the Municipal Corporations Ordinance as those of a statutory corporation whose roles, as defined in the law, are the only roles which the authority is permitted to perform. The following passage from the High Court of Justice states this explicitly:[8]

> The municipality is a legal body created by law and it has no existence other than according to the law. The scope of its authorities is defined by the law and any deviation from it is null and void *(ultra vires)*....The general rule for weighing whether a certain act deviates from the authority of the council or not is not whether the Municipal Corporations Ordinance forbids the act explicitly, but rather whether it is explicitly permitted. It is not enough that an act is not forbidden; it must be permitted in order for it to be proper in the eyes of the law. It is not as though the law leaves an empty space which it is permissible to fill at will.

Justice Zilberg makes the distinction between those roles which the municipality must perform and those which it may:[9]

> Section 96 (233 in the new version of the Municipal Corporations Ordinance) discusses the principal necessary functions which every municipality *must* fill, for if they do not, there will not be regular life for the town's residents; section 95 (249 in the new version) deals with other matters, not necessarily essential, which the municipality *may* perform, if it sees a need for it and if it has the required means.

The municipality may not act in areas which are not included in their powers and obligations. The powers of the local council were fixed in sections 146–152 of the Local Councils Law (a), 5710–1950. These are formulated more generally than for the municipalities and here also there is no clear distinction between obligations and powers. Still, it is possible to infer from the fact that in some of the sections the lawmakers used the term "the council may," that these refer to powers, in contrast to those sections which speak of the functions of the council, which refer to obligations.

In the context of a discussion of the obligations of the local authority the question arises as to whether a citizen may compel the municipality to perform one of its functions in which he is particularly interested such as, for example, the obligation of the municipality to install drainage systems in flood-prone areas. While it would seem that it is the right of the citizen to make this demand and the obligation of the municipality to prevent property damage to its citizens, the courts in fact concluded that in matters requiring a setting of priorities and budgetary allocations, the municipality may use its own discretion.[10]

While the court recognizes the discretion of the municipality, the lawmakers also granted powers to the district authority. The elected officials must carry out his requests and instructions "so long as they do not conflict with the by-laws which were approved and with the ongoing budget" (section 234 of the Municipal Corporations Ordinance).

In order to clarify the difference between obligations and powers we will now specify some of the obligations as they are described in the law in sections 235-248. The local authority is an administrative governing authority and a citizen who sees himself injured by its decisions or actions has the right to request aid from the Supreme Court. The Supreme Court will not interfere when a different court has the authority to discuss the contended issue, but when no other court has the authority, the Supreme Court will use its authority under section 7 of the Courts Law, 5717–1957. The first condition is that the local authority do only what it has been mandated by the law to do and any activity which is not within its mandate *(ultra vires)* does not hold. At the same time, with regard to those activities which are within its mandate, the law grants the local authority its own discretion. As long as it is "reasonable," the Supreme Court does not place its own discretion above that of the local authority.[11]

In the following cases the Supreme Court will not interfere in the decision-making of the administrative authority in whose hands the decision lies:
a) where there was no breach of authority;
b) where judgement was not passed using invalid or inappropriate considerations;
c) where the decision was not arbitrary;
d) where the decision did not oppose the natural laws of justice.[12]

In other words, the local authority has broad powers to use its own discretion as long as it acts within its mandate and does not transgress any of the above listed rules. Several examples which involved the Supreme Court will clarify these rules:

1) A member of the local council of Ramat Hasharon appealed to the Supreme Court against the mayor who delegated some of his authority to three council members. According to the law the mayor is permitted to delegate authority to his deputy, to a member of the Executive Committee, or to an authorized employee, but not to a member of the council. The conditional order became decisive and the Supreme Court determined that there had been a deviation from proper authority.[13]

2) The Jerusalem municipality refused to give a license to a business which displayed and sold sexually-oriented products. The owners of the business appealed to the Supreme Court, whose decision stated: "When the issue is one of limiting the freedom of business the court will be strict with the licensing authority and will insist that the authority may refuse to license a business only if it was explicitly given that authority by the law, and that the decision of the authority is anchored in factual material which justifies the use of the decision." The court then stated definitively that the law does not grant the local authority the role of guardian of the public's sensitivities.[14]

3) The Herzliya municipality made the use of a sidewalk for the erection of an awning for a taxi company office conditional on several things, among them that the taxi company operate a special Herzliya-Tel Aviv line. The Supreme Court invalidated this decision because the authority's considerations were beyond the issue at hand.[15]

4) A man requested a license to open a delicatessen in Bat Yam, but the council refused the request without specifying its reasons. The Supreme Court decided that such a decision on the part of the local authority was arbitrary and invalid and commanded it to reconsider the request while weighing all of the relevant circumstances.[16]

The Supreme Court will also interfere with decisions of the local authority if they are deemed to oppose the natural laws of justice, such as if an injured party is prevented from exercising his right of public appeal, or if a public official participates in a decision in which he has a personal interest.

In the local council of Taiba, the Tenders Committee, on which sat the mayor's brother-in-law, decided on the appointment of a school principal. Due to his close family relationship, the Supreme Court saw this as a case of a man who had a private interest in the decision and therefore invalidated the decision.[17]

When the local authority employs reasonable discretion, the court supports its decisions. For instance, the municipality of Ramat Gan refused to permit the opening of a gambling house on the grounds that it endangered the public peace and the court decided that, considering the circumstances of the case, the municipality's concerns were valid.[18]

An analysis of court decisions reveals that despite the broad powers and considerable discretion granted to the local authority, it remains open to the oversight and criticism of the Supreme Court. Therefore, a local authority must keep in mind that if it wants its actions upheld, it must stay within the bounds of the various court decisions.

Local Authority Powers in Land Use Planning and Building

The Local Commission

The local authority, in its role as the local planning and building commission, is responsible for planning, licensing and overseeing construction.[19] This is one of the municipality's most important functions. Through this institution the character and color of the locality are determined: will it be an industrial city or a vacation center, a city with important commercial centers or a residential city dependent upon nearby commercial centers, a city with a dense or sparse population? Such primary issues are supplemented by a long list of secondary land use questions (park land, sports facilities, and the like).

The Planning and Building Law, 5725–1965, establishes the rules for dealing with such decisions. The law discusses three levels in the physical planning hierarchy: state, district and local. In this chapter we will discuss only the work and functions of the local commissions.

From a formal legal point of view the local planning and building commission is separate from the municipal council. It is a statutory body whose powers and functions are derived from the Planning and Building Law. At the same time, the members of the city council are also the members of the local planning and building commission. Whether or not the two bodies are identical depends upon the area declared as a "local planning area" by the Minister of Interior. If the Minister of Interior declares the municipality to be a local planning area, then the municipal council will constitute the local planning and building commission. However, if the minister includes several local authorities within a single local planning area, he is responsible for specifying the membership of the local commission in his planning order.

Representatives of the Ministries of Interior, Health, Construction and Housing, and Police are always invited to deliberations of the local commission in an advisory capacity. Two of these ministry representatives acting together have the right to appeal any decision of the local commission. Every decision of the commission is conditional upon the approval of the district planning and building commission.

A local commission which is identical to the municipal council must establish a subcommittee for planning and building. The following functions are retained by the full commission:

a. The decision to change, cancel or propose a local master plan;
b. Use of the right of appeal, when granted to the local commission via-a-vis decisions of the district commission;
c. Expropriation of land and the performance of any act necessary for expropriation according to this law;
d. Discussion and decision-making concerning claims and compensation following damage to land resulting from an approved plan;
e. All other functions and powers not granted the subcommittee.

The subcommittee has the following functions and powers:

a. Preparation of detailed plans and decision-making concerning them;
b. Division and unification of land;
c. Discussion and decision-making concerning requests for approval of exceptions and concessions;
d. Consideration of demolition orders and their execution;
e. Discussion and decision-making concerning requests for building permits;

f. Presentation of civil claims for collection of profits from illegal building.

Where a planning area is regional and includes more than one local authority, the regional building and planning commission will then include the following members: the district commissioner or his representative; seven members who will be appointed by the Minister of Interior from a list of people recommended by the regional authorities; a representative of the Ministries of Interior, Construction and Housing, and Police; and a representative of the district commission. Once again, the representatives of the ministries serve in an advisory capacity only.

Special Planning Area

The term "special planning area" refers to unsettled territories which are earmarked for new settlement, or to an area in which the Ministry of Construction and Housing builds a neighborhood in which 75 percent of the constructed units are government funded. An order declaring a special planning area remains valid for the period specified in the order up to a maximum of five years. This time period may be extended by an additional order, however.

The objective of this planning device is to free the Ministry of Construction and Housing, in its establishment of a new settlement or neighborhood, from the limitations and pressures of local authorities, thus enabling the rapid development required to meet the needs posed by immigration, absorption and housing shortages.

Joint Commission

There are certain instances in which the Minister of Interior establishes by order a joint planning commission, after consultation with the national planning council and other relevant planning institutions. A joint commission will have the powers and functions of a district or local commission in its area of jurisdiction, depending on the matter at hand. An example of such a joint commission is the one set up to plan the use of the land upon which

Bar Ilan University was built. The university land is situated within the jurisdictions of two local authorities — Ramat Gan and Givat Shmuel. The land also belonged to two separate state administrative districts — the Tel Aviv district and the Central district. When the university presented development plans that extended across the territories of two local authorities and two administrative districts, there was no choice but to establish a joint commission which could study the plans and issue the requested building permits.

Master plans must fit into their hierarchical level. The local plans must fit into district plans, which in turn must be integrated into the countrywide master plan.

Within the context of a local master plan, the local commission may at any time prepare a detailed plan. The district commission may also request that the local commission prepare a detailed plan for the land within the local planning area. Such a detailed plan determines the division of building lots, the shape and length of building fronts, designation of areas for public facilities, parking space, the location of buildings, and their capacity, height, shape and external appearance. Construction permits are then issued within the framework of this plan. The detailed plan is then presented to the district commission to consider for a fixed period which may not exceed two year. During this period anyone who feels injured by the plan may express his opposition. If his claim is rejected, he may appeal to the district commission within thirty days of receiving notice of rejection.

Whoever receives a building permit must build in accordance with the permit. If the builder deviates illegally from its terms, he can be brought to trial and the local commission may request a demolition order. In the case of a deviation, the court must issue a demolition order in addition to any other penalty which it assigns according to the law. In cases where the construction cannot be demolished, the offender will be charged two or three times its worth, in addition to any other penalty fixed by law. In other words, if a local commission brings such a claim to court, the court may fine the offender for a sum equalling two or three times the benefits which he earned by deviating from the permit, in addition to any other penalty. This assures that the violator does not ultimately benefit.

Appreciation Tax

If the value of a property increases due to a change in planning or zoning, the owner of the property must pay 50 percent of its increased value to the local authority in the form of an "appreciation tax." The idea behind this law is that a property owner may not receive exclusive benefits from the increased value of his property which comes as a result of a public planning activity. There is also a practical angle; the appreciation tax revenues help the local authority to cover the additional expenses resulting from changes in the plan.

For example, if a local authority increases the permitted density in a certain neighborhood from one living unit per dunam of land to four units per dunam, this will result in a considerable increase in the value of the land. At the same time, the expenses of the local authority in this neighborhood will also increase, since an increase in population density will result in an increased need for nurseries, schools, libraries and other public services. It would not be just if the property owner were to make a tremendous profit as a result of the local authority's change in the plan, while the burden resulting from the plan fell completely on the public. Thus the appreciation tax is intended to balance the social injustice created by the change in the plan.

As noted earlier, in the field of planning and building the local authority acts in three spheres: planning, approval of building permits, and oversight of construction. However, some claim that the composition of the commission is not suitable for the proper fulfillment of its functions; since the commission is comprised of politicians (council members) lacking professional knowledge, it is claimed that its members are particularly prone to the influences of interested parties who oppose planning values. These same critics claim that the fields of planning and building should be entrusted to professionals only. However, experience has shown that professionals are not totally pure in such matters and that they, too, are influenced by special interests and professional ties.

Some claim that those sectors of the public most affected by the plan, both those who are injured and those who benefit, do not participate enough in the decision-making which could have a significant impact on their lifestyle and the quality of their environment. Indeed there are countries in which the public is given a greater opportunity to participate more actively in the planning process of the authority in which they live than is the case in Israel.

Licensing Businesses

One of the most important and controversial laws concerns the licensing of businesses. Local authorities have tried to interpret the law broadly, to consider both the economic regulation of businesses and the maintenance of public morality. This could result in a decision to grant or withhold a license based on such economic considerations as the fact that there are already enough businesses of a similar kind in the same area. Similarly, local authorities have forbidden the opening of gambling houses or other businesses which may have a negative impact upon public morality.

The courts have limited the discretion of local authorities in this area, stating that the lawmakers did not intend to give the local authority the right to interfere with a citizen's right to open a business. Thus the courts determined that as long as the legislature has not appointed the local authority to oversee public morality, it may not take such considerations into account when deciding whether to grant a license to businesses such as gambling houses.

However, with regard to the economic considerations there is a difference between municipalities and local councils — the latter may also consider economic factors. It is difficult to understand why this difference between municipalities and local councils exists. Some explain it by referring to the fact that because a local council is a smaller authority, economic considerations also have social implications, thereby justifying their additional area of discretion.

After extended public discussion of the issue of licensing businesses which may damage public morality, the law was amended in 1983 to restrict the power of local authorities in this area. Local authorities used to have an additional power with which to regulate businesses — the requirement to renew business licenses annually. However, following criticism by the courts, the law was amended and most businesses (with the exception of restaurants and other food businesses) now receive a permanent license. In addition, the local authority may not delay the approval of a license as a means of pressuring the owner of a business. An analysis of the law and the court decisions show that the intent of this law is to enable the local authority to maintain public health, order and security.

The Licensing of Businesses Law, 5728-1968, replaced three Mandatory ordinances — the Workshop and Industry Ordinance, the Intoxicating Drinks Ordinance of 1935, and the Public Entertainment Ordinance of 1935.

The objectives of the Licensing of Businesses Law were defined as follows:

a. Guaranteeing an appropriate level of environmental quality including proper sanitation, prevention of public nuisances, and the upholding of planning and building regulations;
b. Prevention of public disturbances;
c. Assuring the safety of those within the place of business and its immediate surroundings;
d. Prevention of dangers to the public health from animal-borne diseases or contamination of water resources.

Licensing is performed by the mayor or whomever he delegates. Licensing requests must be considered according to a system which employs proper and efficient work methods in order to prevent unjustifiable delays.[20]

The issuance of a license to a business located on rented property is not conditional upon the agreement of the property owner unless this is in opposition to the master plan. In such a case, approval for a business will be given only after prior approval by the relevant minister or his delegated representative. If an additional law applies in this case, then the license will require approval according to that law as well. The Chief Rabbinate, Worker's Council, or employment services may not interfere with the granting of licenses. The licensing authority may approve the license with the addition of special conditions, but the licensee may demand justification for the placing of these conditions and he may appeal them before a court.

The municipality may not withhold a license because of its obligations towards a third party. There are several court opinions on this matter. For example, the Supreme Court ruled invalid the refusal of a municipality to grant a license on the grounds that it had given a guarantee to one company that it would not grant a license to a competitor:

The local government has only those powers granted it by the law and it may not take upon itself whatever powers it likes outside of the framework of the law. If so, the local government may use its discretion to refuse to grant a license only in those cases where the granting of the license impacts on those areas and interests which the law mandates it to protect.[21]

Similarly, rationalizations such as "an offense to good taste" or "consideration of public sensitivities" are unacceptable, as is a refusal to grant a license because the licensee is expected to sustain a financial loss. Such considerations are not among those which fall within the domain of the local authority considering a license request. In general, approval will be given when the request is in line with the city's master plans.

In the wake of court rulings the Knesset published amendment No. 5 to the Licensing of Businesses Law (section 2b), which stated that a licensing authority may use its powers while considering the requirements of public order, public peace or public education.

The lawmakers also granted the local authority the power to issue an administrative order closing a business which has opened without a license or which has violated the conditions of its license. The purpose of the order, which is valid for 30 days, is to prevent any injury to the public until the legal status of the business is clarified. A person who feels unjustly injured by the order may appeal to the courts to request its cancellation. The local authority has the right to extend the order for an additional 30 days.

The Regional Council

The regional council is a federation of settlements through which a number of small settlements work together to provide governmental services and initiate joint projects. The regional council comprises one of the important forms of local government in Israel and it serves as the municipal framework for small settlements whose residents number anywhere from several tens to several hundred.

In 1980 there were 51 regional councils, whose members included 255 kibbutzim, 400 moshavim, 35 cooperative moshavim, as well as a number of Arab settlements and villages — altogether including about 300,000 people. Since then this figure has grown as new regional councils have been established in Judea, Samaria and Gaza.

In the Regional Councils Ordinance of 1941, the High Commissioner was authorized to establish councils which would include a number of settlements; he did not make use of this authority, however, until 1945. The small Jewish settlements which had common problems in the areas of services, education, security and the like, organized themselves into voluntary frameworks called "bloc committees." These committees taxed their member settlements in order to cover expenses.

In 1945 the first formal order was issued, establishing a regional council in the Kishon region. While the order did not explicitly use the term "regional council," it did refer to the local councils and the other local authorities in the region. By the end of the British Mandate there were five regional councils within the territory that was to become part of the new State of Israel. In 1949 the Jordan Valley regional council became the first to be officially established by the State of Israel and in its wake tens of regional councils arose, most of them in the 1950s. In 1958 the Regional Council Ordinance was issued, institutionalizing current practices and delineating clear and obligatory rules for the establishment of a regional council.

A regional council may include a number of different types of rural settlements:

1) *Cooperative settlements,* as defined in section 1 of the Ordinance, include the kibbutz, kvutza, moshav, cooperative moshav, and any other settlement in which at least 80 percent of the adults are members of the Cooperative Association for Settlement, which is recognized by the regional council.
2) *Undefined settlements* are those settlements not considered cooperative settlements as defined above, as well as community settlements. Among the latter are most of the new settlements in Judea and Samaria which act in accordance with the orders of the military governor, which were adjusted to the requirements of the region.
3) *The Arab village* — There are many Arab villages which are too small to have local councils, which have been integrated into mostly mixed, Arab-Jewish councils.

The unique character of the regional councils is especially evident in their election procedure: representatives are elected by the settlements or by local committees from a list of candidates, rather than directly by the residents. Any individual who is 18 years of age by election day and who is a permanent resident of a settlement may be a candidate for election as a representative of that settlement. The number of representatives from each settlement is determined by the regional council. Official notice of this determination must be given to all of the settlements of the council and any resident may file objections to this decision within 14 days of its publication. The council must forward these objections, along with its own comments, to the Minister of Interior who will make the final decision.

One of the conspicuous limitations of the election procedure is the denial of voting rights to certain residents of kibbutzim and moshavim who are not members of the cooperative association.

Section 10 of the Ordinance states that each settlement included in a regional council should be managed by a local committee. The composition of the local committee and the procedures through which it is elected are different in cooperative and noncooperative settlements. In a cooperative settlement, the members of the local committee must be individuals who are currently serving as members of the administration of the cooperative association.

Since it is the local committees who actually elect the regional council, those residents who are not members of the cooperative association and therefore do not have the right to vote for the local committee are also not represented in the elections for the regional council. In kibbutzim this problem is negligible, since it affects only a very small number of residents who do not seek membership by choice. The problem, however, becomes more severe in the moshavim. The moshav is based upon a fixed number of plots of land. Each unit is an economic unit which must sustain a family. When a plot is passed on as an inheritance (or in some other way), it can be passed on to only one family. If the family has several grown children with families who continue to live on the moshav, most of them are left without land, thus also leaving them without voting rights, even though they were born and grew up in the settlement. This presents a direct clash between a specific ideologically-based lifestyle and the elementary principles of democracy.

This issue has reached the Supreme Court in three cases, but in all three the court did not deal with the problem in depth, since in no case was it emphasized by the parties involved.

In addition to the problems of voting rights, there has been a lack of clarity in some settlements concerning the division of functions between the local committees and the regional council.[22] Following an appeal to the Supreme Court (641/78), a compromise was arranged that the Ministries of Interior, Labor and Social Welfare, and Justice would appoint a commission to study representation on regional councils. The commission was appointed on 5 December 1979 under the chairmanship of Yoram Bar Sela, deputy legal counsel to the government. The commission submitted its report on 21 June 1983. In its report, the commission expressed the need to assure a clear definition of authority to the regional council, on the one hand, and to the local committee, on the other.[23] The Local Councils Ordinance (Regional Councils) (Amendment No. 2), 5746-1986, reflects the recommendations of the commission.

Cooperation Between Local Authorities

The regional council is an example of cooperation between small local authorities. There is also a need for cooperative solutions to problems between neighboring municipalities. The need for such cooperation derives primarily from the following three requirements:

a) the need to coordinate activities in adjacent territories such as regional planning, regional transportation, joint sewage projects and educational projects;
b) the prevention of duplication and waste of public funds;
c) the undertaking of projects or services which are complex, costly or have advantages of scale when serving a population larger than that of one municipality.

The need for inter-municipal cooperation has become particularly important in two metropolitan areas: the Dan region (Tel Aviv and its neighbors — Ramat Gan, Givatayim, Bnei Brak, Holon, Bat Yam) and in the Haifa-Krayot region.

Attempts to establish comprehensive supra-municipal frameworks for cooperation between local authorities in Israel have not been successful even though the Ministry of Interior has set up commissions for both of the above regions which have recommended the establishment of appropriate frameworks for cooperation. There has been no real movement in this direction because of a lack of cooperation between the relevant authorities, lack of serious public concern, and a de facto lack of power to coerce change on the part of the Ministry of Interior.

There exists a legal framework for limited cooperation between local authorities under the Municipal Corporations Law, 5715-1955. A municipal federation is a statutory body established by order of the Minister of Interior with the status of a local authority. The federation is organized as a legal entity separate from those local authorities which comprise it, with its own chairman and administration. It provides a framework for several local authorities to meet their joint needs such as, for example, the Federation of the Cities of the Dan Region for Veterinary and Slaughterhouse Services, which includes the municipalities of Ramat Gan, Givatayim and Bnei Brak.

A municipal federation is usually established when the service which must be provided is beyond the power or financial resources of a single authority and there is a need to enlist the cooperation of several authorities. There are about 40 such federations currently operating in Israel.

The federation may sign contracts, undertake obligations, own property, employ workers, legislate by-laws and levy taxes. It has a separate budgetary framework and, as with local authorities, its budget must be approved by the Ministry of Interior. The institution of municipal federations does sometimes bring individual authorities together for specific purposes, but it does not reach the level of comprehensive cooperation.[24] In fact, a local authority may participate in one municipal federation with certain neighboring authorities for one specific purpose and in a different one with other neighboring authorities for a different purpose.

Notes – Chapter 5

1. Supreme Court 3/58. Berman et al. vs. Minister of Interior. Verdict 12(3)1493.
2. See Shefat (1984).
3. As far as is known to the author, an attempt was made only in the municipality of Ramat Gan. Since this attempt was not anchored in law and there was no explicit definition of the functions and powers of the chairman of the council, his role as a legislative authority and as a control and counterweight to the mayor as an executive authority was limited.
4. In 1986 legislation was proposed to enable the participation of municipal employees on the Tenders Committee.
5. State Commission on Local Government (1981), p. 133 cf.
6. Supreme Court 428/72. Boneh et al. vs. Tel Aviv-Jaffa Municipality, Verdict 27(1)398.
7. Local councils and regional councils are authorized to enact by-laws according to section 22 of the Local Councils Ordinance. Municipal federations are authorized to establish by-laws according to section 14 of the Municipal Union Law, 5715-1955. A court will not invalidate a by-law except: "in the case of discrimination or arbitrariness or if the by-law seems to it to be fundamentally invalid for any other important reason." See S.C. 384/58 Zebner and Co. vs. Mayor, Council and Citizens of Tel Aviv-Jaffa et al. Verdict 14(1)419.
8. S.C. 36/51. Tat vs. Municipality of Haifa. Verdict 5,1553.
9. S.C. 40/49 Nachmias vs. Legal Counsel. Verdict 3,127.
10. The law in this matter was established in S.C. 247/55. Sereg Adin Ltd. vs. Municipality of Tel Aviv et al., Verdict 11,1110, which appeals a request from the court to charge the municipality for damages caused to a factory during a flood which allegedly occurred because of improper drainage. Although the installation of drainage systems is among the obligations of the municipality, the court held that: "the municipality has discretion in determining the order of priorities according to which it performs its duties."
11. S.C. 292/80. Levi vs. Minister of Transportation, Verdict 35,57.
12. Ibid.
13. S.C. 702/79. Goldberg vs. Sherman (Ramat Hasharon Council Chairman) and five others, Verdict 34(4)85.
14. S.C. 230/73. S.Z.M. vs. Mayor of Jerusalem, Verdict 28(2)113.
15. S.C. 279/69. Miller vs. Mayor of Herzliya, Verdict 24(1)37.
16. S.C. 159/57. Efrati vs. Bat Yam Local Council, Verdict 11,1322.
17. S.C. 333/74. Yehiya vs. Taibe Council Chairman, Verdict 29(1)457.
18. S.C. 287/71. Da'abul vs. Mayor of Ramat Gan et al., Verdict 26(2)821.

19. A description of the roles and powers of the local committee is based upon the relevant sections in the Planning and Building Law, 5725-1965, (primarily chapter 2, sections c, d, and e, and the third addendum).
20. The Supreme Court admonished the local authorities several times regarding their manner of license approval.
21. S.C. 161/52. Refinery Co. vs. Mayor of Rishon le-Zion, Verdict 7(1)113.
22. S.C. 255/69. Balat vs. Minister of Interior and Regional Council of Mateh Yehuda, Verdict 23(2)389; S.C. 270/78, 96/79. Shaham et al. vs. Minister of Interior; S.C. 641/78. Cohen vs. Minister of Interior et al.
23. See the Commission on Representation in Regional Councils (1983).
24. In Haifa an attempt was made in 1978 to establish an encompassing municipal federation, but the project did not succeed.

Chapter 6

ADMINISTRATIVE ISSUES IN LOCAL GOVERNMENT

Jacob Reuveny

Israel has a very complex system of local administration. It originated in the pre-independence era and in the early years of statehood. In this chapter we will analyze several key aspects of this system: the structure of municipal organization, the role of the mayor and council members, the internal organizational structure of the local authority, the service delivery system, personnel management, and certain aspects of financial management, a topic discussed at length elsewhere in this book.

We will also look at the religious councils, which are a semi-autonomous part of the local service system, responsible for providing religious services for Jewish residents. Due to the unique characteristics of the Arab local authorities, we will devote a separate section to them. In our concluding section we will attempt to single out several key characteristics of the administration of the municipal system, as well as to focus on differences between the main groupings of local authorities.

Introduction: The Organizational Context of the Local Authority

A broad question which can serve as a starting point for an analysis of the local government system relates to the character of its relations with the state government. There are multiple aspects to local-state government relations — legal, financial, political and administrative. The first three are discussed in different chapters of this book, while in this chapter we will relate to the last — the administrative aspect, defined as the administrative context of the local authority. Relations between the two planes of government depend largely on the organizational points of contact between them. To a large extent a point of contact is an outcome of the organizational characteristics of each one of the systems involved in the contact, and especially of those among them who are responsible for contact with the second system.

The State Government: A Multiplicity of Uncoordinated Organs

Israel is formally a unitary state in which local government fulfills functions in a wide range of fields. As a result of the scope of the services provided by local authorities, and due to the small physical dimensions of the state, the state and local governments maintain close contact. Since the type of services provided by the local authority creates an attachment to many of the branches of the state government, the question arises whether, and to what extent, the state government appears as a united and coordinated body in its relations with the local government, or in contrast, a many-branched octopus, whose structure makes coordination between the branches difficult to achieve. This question arises at two levels — at the level of the state government in Jerusalem and at the level of field administration, i.e., the peripheral extensions of the ministries.

It can be established that Israel is characterized by weak interministerial coordination, a weakness which is part and parcel of her political and administrative structure.[1] The state system is tied to the local government through a multitude of loosely coordinated channels, as will be illustrated later. However, on the political level there are factors which balance the fragmentation of the state administrative structure.

The Israeli political system was classified until the 1977 elections as a "dominant party system." At its center stood the major party, which never achieved an absolute majority, and therefore always needed junior coalition partners. Many such regimes typically develop patronage systems, based on an exchange between political support and economic benefits based on preferential allocation of resources.[2] The municipal system, being less structured and less prone than the state government to the supervision of the state controlling mechanisms, was a natural framework for this kind of politics. Therefore, the political dimension of local-state relations had an integrative impact and helped to mitigate some of the consequences of administrative fragmentation of the state government in its relations with local authorities.

On the level of field administration, the Israeli government structure can be categorized as an "unintegrated prefectorial system." During the period of the British Mandate local control was in the hands of district commissioners who coordinated field administration (as portrayed in figures 6.1 and 6.2).[3] Through this institution as well as the overall coordination of the chief secretariat, a unified and coordinated government policy on municipal issues was carried out.

The source of the present model of an unintegrated prefectorial system can be traced to the period of the establishment of the state. With the establishment of the state, the system of district administration was never formally abolished. Even the position of district commissioner remained in place. In contrast to the field administration before the establishment of the state, however, the new government ministries formed direct hierarchical ties between the state and localities without retaining the previous coordinating role of the district administration. The reason for this is inherent in the character of the state government, in the tendency of the ministers to develop maximal autonomy, and in the fact that the field administration of the various ministries crystallized before that of the district administrations. In addition, some of the government ministries which were founded in Israel after the establishment of the state were not a part of the Mandate government machinery, but rather part of the national Jewish institutional framework. The Ministry of Interior, rather than inheriting its authorities from the Mandate in the area of field administration, inherited only some coordinating functions. The administrative division of the state by the Ministry of Interior into districts and sub-districts did not bind the other government ministries, most of whom formed their own autonomous administrative divisions. The ministry was thus left with the functions which had been in the hands of the Mandatory government vis-a-vis the local authorities, the most important of which was supervision of local finance.

Various divisions of the state government deal with local government, with only limited coordination among them. Steps have been taken since the establishment of the state to try to cope with this problem. One of the accepted frameworks was the establishment of permanent or ad hoc coordinating structures. These include ministerial committees and committees of directors-general and lower level functionaries. The effectiveness of these

Figure 6.1
Integrative Prefectorial Structure

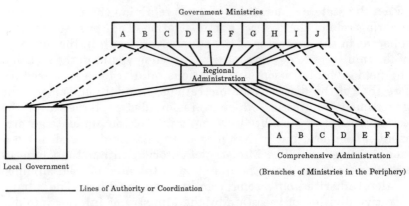

Government Ministries

| A | B | C | D | E | F | G | H | I | J |

Regional Administration

Local Government

| A | B | C | D | E | F |

Comprehensive Administration

(Branches of Ministries in the Periphery)

———————— Lines of Authority or Coordination

− − − − − − − − Exchange of information, consultation & professional contact

Figure 6.2
Non-Integrative Prefectorial Structure

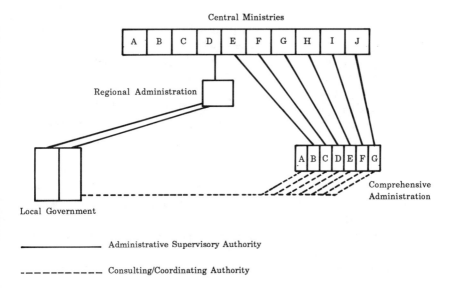

Central Ministries

| A | B | C | D | E | F | G | H | I | J |

Regional Administration

A B C D E F G

Comprehensive
Administration

Local Government

————————— Administrative Supervisory Authority

— — — — — — — — Consulting/Coordinating Authority

coordinating bodies has been limited, as they can act only on issues which are not under political or administrative dispute.

The absence of a unified and coordinated mechanism by the state government for coping with local government is a basic fact in the network of relations between the state and local planes and influences different internal aspects of the administration of the local authority.

Municipal Organization: Autonomy, Fragmentation and the Formation of a United Front vis-a-vis the State Government

Each local authority in Israel is an autonomous administrative unit. There are, however, a number of frameworks for cooperation between municipalities. The most outstanding among these is the institution of the municipal federation, established by the Municipal Corporations Law, 1955,[4] which provides a framework for coordinating physical or social services between different cities. Other examples of joint frameworks include: the Company for Automation, founded jointly in 1968 by the government and the Union of Local Authorities for the purpose of providing local government with central automation services; the Bank of Local Government, founded in 1953, which serves as a central financial institution of the local authorities through which they are given development loans; as well as the National Lottery, which supports local services.

The administrative autonomy of local authorities has reached a crisis point in the last several years. In Israel, as a result of growing urbanization, there are many local authorities which are geographically continuous with one another. In contrast to many European countries in which there has been a decline in the number of local government units and an increase in the territory and population of each local authority,[5] parallel reforms have been rejected in Israel. The different authorities have largely protected their local autonomous area from incursion of adjoining units. The number of unifications, border adjustments and other changes of significance has been negligible.

There are several motivations for inter-municipal cooperation. These include coordinating positions on financial claims vis-a-vis the state government, labor relations and collective bargaining, and representing municipal interests vis-a-vis other authorities. Local government is a part of Israel's public sector. In recent years the state government has participated in over half of its expenditures. Since the first years of the state, municipal policy has been influenced by macro-economic considerations which enjoyed primacy. A noticeable effort has been devoted to halting the growth of local budgets, but these have been met in turn by techniques and strategies developed by the local authorities for increasing their share of the public budget and obtaining greater support from the state government.

The main framework for cooperation between local authorities is the Union of Local Authorities in Israel. This voluntary organization was first established as the Union of Local Government in 1936, and was reorganized in 1952. It serves as a roof organization for cities and local councils. Its purpose is the formation of joint policy and the joint presentation of that policy before the forums which influence local government: the Knesset, the government, the Ministry of Finance and other ministries. The Union of Local Authorities provides its members with joint services, especially in the fields of personnel administration, labor relations, tenders and other types of administrative guidance. It has no statutory powers over its members, hence is not able to enforce any definite policy on its members. It also represents the Arab municipal sector, even though a separate organization was founded for Arab local councils in 1974.

There is a considerable degree of asymmetry in relations between the state and local governments. The state government acts dividedly in its formal relations with the local authorities. Its very nature makes it difficult to cope with matters which demand an integrative and a unified position vis-a-vis local government. In contrast, local government has achieved substantial coordination and an ability to present a unified front, especially on financial matters.

Management by the Council and Council Members Holding Executive Positions

City administration in Israel inherited the British concept of management by council, i.e., that executive power is exercised by the council as a corporate body. Council members are unpaid local citizens. This conception is inherent in the Municipal Corporations Ordinance, 1934, which reflects to a great degree the principles underlying the English municipal system which prevailed in the mid-thirties (with the exception of the extensive supervision of the high commissioner and the district administration.) This ordinance was not formally repealed, however, the process today largely deviates from its spirit.[6]

The council members are convened after an election. The first post-election act is the formation of a local coalition and approval of an executive which combines policy-making and management functions, headed by the directly-elected mayor and reflecting the coalition. Other statutory committees of the local authority are appointed, some of these are obligatory and some optional. Some are comprised only of elected officials and some include officials and other individuals who are not among the authority's employees or elected council members.[7] In a city council, all council members serve on the town planning committee.

This process to a great extent parallels the formation of a government in a parliamentary regime; the council resembles the parliament and the committees resemble parliamentary committees. The next stage is a division of control over administrative departments among members of the coalition (council members appointed as deputy mayors and as members of the executive board). This process resembles that of cabinet formation. According to the Municipal Corporations Ordinance, 1934, authority is vested in the council, as noted, and not in a cabinet-type management.

A number of factors should be considered in understanding the background of the present system. On the political level, municipal politics quickly turned into a reflection of state politics.[8] On the other hand, there has been a trend to minimize the executive role of the council in favor of active council members of the local coalition. This trend can be traced in the development of the functions of the head of the local authority and of the other elected officials filling executive functions, as well as the role of the council and its committees.

In Israel, as in England, the head of the authority (defined as either mayor or chairman) is the chairman of the local council. But, unlike England, his is not a ceremonial role.[9] The mayor is responsible for the execution of council decisions and remains in office for a fixed term. Over the years, the mayor has gained influential status in the areas of decision-making as well as execution. To a great degree, the introduction of direct personal elections for the post of mayor in 1975 represented a kind of legal recognition of the existing situation in which the mayor was not only the chairman of the council, but also the head of its executive branch.

A second institution which is not fully covered by law is the council member who fills an executive position. This can take two forms; either the council member who usually fills the position of deputy mayor (covered by the 1934 Ordinance), or the non-salaried council member, most often a member of the executive board. In 1984 there were about 200 salaried elected local government officials in Israel, not including the mayors. The phenomenon is especially common in cities and large local councils.[10] The council member who serves in an executive position usually has responsibility for an administrative department or a number of departments in the local authority (a "portfolio"), or a part of an administrative unit, as sometimes major units are divided between two council members.

There are no guidelines determining the scope of the functions of deputy mayors[11] or the nature of their involvement in areas of day-to-day management. There are only statutory limitations concerning their number. England has recently begun to provide nominal financial compensation for its elected officials.[12] The phenomenon is often part of the political process of coalition formation, in which the senior coalition partner grants a representative of a junior partner an active role in local government. In many cases this takes the form of a salaried deputy mayor with responsibility for a certain portfolio. (The education and welfare portfolios are often given to the representatives of the National Religious Party.) The position of deputy mayor is not only a means of influencing the management of the authority, but is also a personal favor to the person who fills it, as it entails relative permanence as well as pension rights, which accumulate at a rate similar to the pension of a member of the Knesset.[13] There are deputy mayors in the local authorities who have held this position for an extended period and who have taken on a bureaucratic attitude towards their position over the years.

Only a small number of local council members are regularly active. The primary difference in activity level is between council members who serve on the executive board and those who do not.[14] Only the important committees met with any frequency — the executive board, the tenders committee, the finance committee and the planning and construction committee. Some of the committees never met at all.[15]

207

The process of forming the committees is part of the political bargaining process. In many cases the committees are unworkable or have no practical role due to an overlap between committees, or due to the fact that they are responsible for areas under the jurisdiction of administrative departments operating under detailed instructions. This latter group includes, for example, welfare committees which act alongside welfare departments, or committees for water, sewage or lighting. The institution of the municipal committee, therefore, to a great extent reflects the weakness of the council and the greater power of council members who hold executive positions over members of the council who do not hold such positions.

The introduction of personal elections for mayor constituted a turning point in the direction of strengthening the mayor's executive base. It is true that even after the change in the law, most mayors prefer a wide coalition base.[16] However, the power and weight of the council member, even if he is a coalition member, has declined, especially if he belongs to a party which was in the past a junior coalition partner and did not compete for the position of mayor.

The change in the status of the mayor gave birth to proposals in the State Commission on Local Government (Sanbar Commission) for a separation between the executive branch, headed by the mayor, and the council. Definite authority would be granted to the council in certain areas and the possibility of appointing a council chairman other than the mayor was to be considered for a number of local authorities.[17] These proposals were enacted into law but have not yet been implemented locally where habit has led to a continuation of the coalition approach.

Beyond the formal factors, there are also informal factors which influence the degree of power of different elected officials and their relative influence on decision-making in the municipality. The power of the mayor is largely contingent on a set of informal factors: personality, local public standing, effectiveness in attainment of resources and in contacts with influential political functionaries as well as his position within his political party. All of these factors are equally valid in determining the weight and power of each council member. Non-coalition members of the council may gain influence as "tribunes" dealing with complaints by particular groups.

In summary, the Municipal Corporations Ordinance, 1934 introduced the management conception, accepted at the time in local government in England, which was based on corporate management by a council. In Israel, a different pattern evolved favoring council members who perform executive roles within a quasi-cabinet system. This tendency was reinforced by the position of the mayor as chief executive, by the phenomenon of council members, some of whom are salaried, who fill executive roles, and by the limited influence of most of the council members. This development reflects the characteristics of the Israeli administrative culture, among which is the weak dividing line between the policy-making and the executive function.

The Internal Organizational Structure

Background

The foregoing system of governance has widespread implications for the management of municipal affairs. In contrast to municipal systems of management based on pyramidal organization, in which there is coordination between the different administrative functions and a clear dividing line between the administrative and the elected strata, the British system of local management is anchored in the assumption that the council and its committees are themselves the governing body. According to this system, the administrative network was built according to departments, each with a "Chief Executive Clerk" as department head.[18] There was no general manager with interdepartmental managerial authorities in this structure (such as the City Manager or Chief Executive Officer in the United States). The English system did, however, include the office of Town Clerk (or Clerk of the Council), whose authority differed from place to place, and who sometimes filled the role of a director-general.[19] The Municipal Corporations Ordinance, 1934, required a similar organizational structure.

Since 1934, the English system has undergone some changes. The British Reform Committees which dealt with the structural aspects of English local administration found that this structure is problematic due to the inevitable lack of coordination, the overlap of roles and authority between the elected and administrative echelons, and especially, the tendency of committees to take on executive functions. The penetration of national political considerations at the level of the local authority aroused suspicion of the politicization of decisions.[20] The gist of the recom-mendations on this issue is a policy of increasing the distinction between "decision," "policy" and "execution," while simultaneously narrowing the executive functions of the elected echelon. On the elected level, a recommendation was made to establish a central directing committee, the Policy and Resources Committee, to be paralleled by a coordinating team of department heads from the municipal bureaucracy.[21] There has been some progress, though uneven, to implement these recommendations.

These changes symbolize the crisis of the classical English municipal management system, and its inability to meet the demands of modern management.[22] These issues seem relevant for Israel as well. As in England, so in Israel, the managerial conception anchored in Mandatory legislation has reached a point of crisis and there has been a growing demand for reform, towards some form of "corporate management."

The Present Israeli Model

In Israel, the principal administrative office is that of the town clerk, known in Hebrew as the secretary of the local authority.[23] The roles of the town clerk were similar to those of the town clerk in the old English model — coordination of the work of the local council and its committees and acting as a bridge between the council and the bureaucracy.

Changes in municipal administration in Israel since independence have affected the administrative structure of the local authority. The authorities grew and their functions expanded. There were changes in the administrative culture which lowered the status of generalists in the organization and enhanced specialization and differentiation. The weight of integrative factors in the structure lessened, while the weight of divisive factors increased. This trend had a negative effect on the status of the town clerk. The office still retains coordinative power in small and medium-sized local authorities.

A major trait of organizational structures is their lack of uniformity. Figures 6.3-6.6 present the organizational structures of four local authorities: a large city, medium-large, medium and small.[24]

An analysis of these structures reveals the following attributes:

a. The structures contain elements which reflect the coalitional history of the local authority. Sometimes the division of functions or the establishment, abolition or unification of departments were made according to the requirements of coalition formation, and sometimes even according to the personal areas of interest of council members.

b. Besides organizational divisions made to fit the needs of coalition formation, there are those which with time become permanent. One example is the distinction between the Department of Education, which is often in the hands of the National Religious Party, and the Department of Culture, Youth and Sport, that has responsibility for activities conducted on the Sabbath, which is in the hands of a secular party.

An analysis of the organizational structure of the large municipality (figure 6.3) according to the principles of organizational theory reveals the following attributes: the lack of separation between staff and line; diffusion of similar or complementary functions in different departments; lack of distinction between planning and executive functions; and dysfunctional placement of administrative sub-units. In the large municipality, many instances were found in which sub-units of one department were divided among different council members.

c. There is still no comprehensive typology for classifying patterns of relations between the elected echelon and the bureaucrats in Israel's municipal system. An initial analysis suggests that the size of the authority partially affects the relations between the political and administrative strata.[25]

In the smaller authorities, the range of positions is narrow, the level of specialization low, and organizational room for maneuvering is limited. Hence, the degree of interference by council members in issues of personnel management and other executive issues is relatively limited. In contrast, the relations between echelons become more problematic in medium-sized local authorities. The lack of "organizational distance" between the

211

Figure 6.3
**Administrative Structure of Municipality of Tel Aviv 1975
(Not including elected officials)**

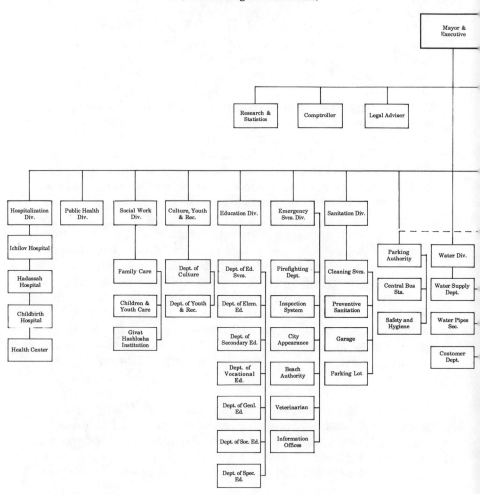

Administrative Issues in Local Government

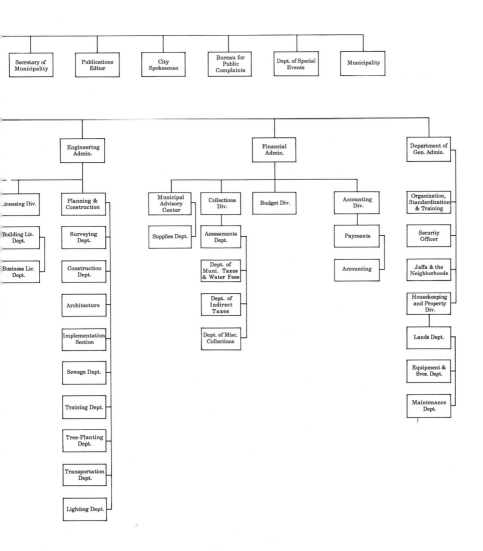

Figure 6.4
Administrative Structure of a Medium-Large Municipality

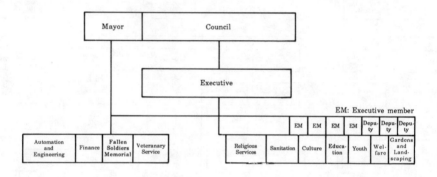

Figure 6.5
Administrative Structure of a Medium-Sized Municipality

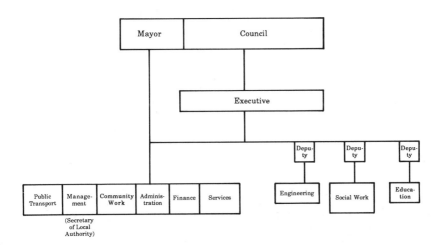

Figure 6.6
Administrative Structure of a Small Municipality

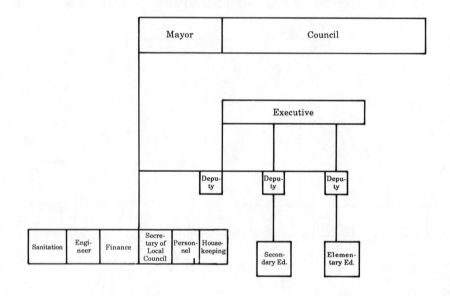

bureaucrat and the council member, the possibility of organizational maneuvering, and a low level of professionalism encourage politicians to interfere in administrative processes. In the large local authority there is greater organizational distance between the political and administrative levels, a factor which lowers the probability that politicians will interfere in daily administration. On the other hand, the mere size of the organization and the greater autonomy of the larger authority in finance and personnel management increase the motivation of politicians to create organizational structures in line with their political aspirations. In large cities there is a tension between two factors which tend to contradict one another. On the one hand, members of the top level of the bureaucracy are more professional than their counterparts in the smaller authorities and in terms of professionalism they may be similar to the staff of state government departments. On the other hand, there is a tendency among politicians to cherish ambitions for a career in state government, such as top level positions in the state bureaucracy, Knesset membership or even ministerial positions. These ambitions lead to steps in the municipal field aimed at image building. There develops then a tension between ambitious politicians, on the one hand, and bureaucrats who have a higher professional orientation than is usual in the smaller local authorities, on the other.

Proposals for Organizational Reform

The problems in the internal structure of the Israeli municipal system have been recognized on various occasions in the past. They were noticed partly in light of the question of inter-departmental coordination and other organizational problems, such as the need to secure unity of command and professionalism of municipal decision-making. Proposals for reform could be classified into two groups:

a. Proposals for the creation of a post of Chief Administrator according to the model of the American City Manager;
b. Proposals favoring the amalgamation of administrative departments into broader frameworks of "Divisions."

The first method implies a pyramidal structure whereby all administrative functions would be subordinated to the Chief

Administrator who is supervised by the head of the authority, or by the local council, or both.[26]

Such positions have been introduced in a number of municipalities, among them Jerusalem, Herzliya, Givatayim and Holon. Despite the title of "city manager" which was attached to the position, the individual involved was not in fact given the opportunity to control the operative functions of the local authority, such as planning and construction and education. He acted instead as a kind of city secretary with extensive authority in the areas of personnel management, the secretariat and public relations.

The second proposal is aimed at forming a standard municipal organization comprised of a few major divisions: a general administrative division, financial division, engineering division, welfare division, and in the larger authorities even a supervision and control division. Whereas it was intended that these divisions be directly subordinate to the head of the local authority, council members who act as deputy mayors are intended to chair the committees of the authority related to the different divisions. According to this proposal the central role is given to the town clerk of the local authority to act as chairman of the general administration, i.e., a division in charge of secretariat, personnel management and various residual functions.[27]

These two proposals raise the question of the willingness of politicians, particularly those who belong to the smaller parties in the coalition, to accept an arrangement which is likely to reduce their power. Opposition may derive from two principal causes:

a. The council members tend to regard executive roles as a means for enhancing their political power. Both reforms are likely, then, to be interpreted as a reinforcement of the mayor's position at the expense of the other council members, an issue whose sensitivity increased with the introduction of direct elections for mayor.

b. The principal injured parties from such internal reforms are likely to be the representatives of the smaller parties, who generally never achieve mayoral positions. The second method, that of divisions, is the more practical of the two proposals. This method does not rule out the possibility of political interference in management. By grouping activities together into defined divisions, it takes into consideration organizational needs and prevents recurring organizational changes aimed at satisfying requirements of coalition formation. It thus represents a reasonable compromise between administrative regularity and political necessity.

The problems of internal municipal organization in Israel are not qualitatively different from those which typify a number of important municipal systems in the West; the difference is principally a matter of degree. The Israeli model is characterized by a relatively low degree of separation between politics and administration, between "decision," "policy" and "execution." Any appropriate structure has to take this factor into account.

The Organization of Municipal Services

The local authority in Israel is responsible for delivering a large number of services. The organization of these services is complex, either in terms of relations of municipal departments with external agencies, or from the point of view of their inner structure and function. Most of the services of the local authority are obligatory, i.e., prescribed by laws, regulations or precedents. There are other services which are non-obligatory. The scope of these services varies from one municipal unit to another. They may include hospitals, music schools or community centers.

The obligatory services are primarily local services and state services (that is, services mandated by the Knesset for the entire state but executed by local government under state supervision). The main instructions concerning local services are contained in the Municipal Corporations Ordinance, 1934 and in subsequent legislation. These include the paving, repairing, cleaning, lighting and drainage of roads, licensing and control of construction, drainage and sewage, construction and maintenance of water works, supervision of markets and slaughterhouses, sanitation, public health, disposal of sanitary nuisances, licensing of businesses and maintaining a firefighting service. The local authority also provides state services, either alone or in cooperation with state agencies. The main state services are education, welfare, health and religion (primarily through participation in the budget of the religious councils).

Local Government in Israel

The relative proportions of local services (including water works) and state services in the local authority can be inferred from the distribution of personnel presented in table 6.1.

Table 6.1

EMPLOYEES IN MUNICIPALITIES AND
LARGE LOCAL COUNCILS
According to Type of Service: 1981–82

Destination	Municipalities No. of Employees	in %	Large Local Councils No. of Employees	in %
General Management	5,522	8.5	1,086	9.0
Local Services	12,708	18.5	1,766	14.8
State Services	39,211	60.0	8,132	68.0
Projects	8,372	13.0	985	8.2
Total	65,813	100.0	11,969	100.0

Source: Central Bureau of Statistics, *The Local Authorities in Israel 1981/82, Physical Data,* Jerusalem, 1984.

More than half of the employees in the local authority are assigned to the provision of state services. (See also table 7.3 in Chapter 7.) Since the "projects" category includes functions partly related to state services, the proportion of state services in the activities of the local authority is even higher. There are, however, differences in the proportions of local and state services. The greatest variety is found in the proportion of local services, a variety which testifies primarily to the differences in the levels of needs and demands of different populations.

Local Services

In the category of local services, the most prominent functions are engineering and urban construction, sewage and drainage, sanitation and water. Another major function in this category, though legally subordinate to the state government, is firefighting.

Engineering and Urban Construction — This field is one of the oldest and most important activities of local government. In Israel, the scope of this function and the degree of specialization in it depend mostly on the size of the authority. In a large municipality there is specialization in sub-fields such as planning, construction, execution, roads, landscaping, traffic, licensing, building permits, sewage and drainage. In the smaller authorities several of these functions are carried out within the framework of one division, or a division and several departments. Since this service is on the border between state and local services, it is often a key issue in contacts between the state and local governments, and is discussed in greater detail elsewhere in this book.

The field of planning and construction necessarily requires countrywide planning and a great deal of integration between the different arenas. Yet it is one of the fields with the greatest local autonomy. This can be explained by the organizational problems that were discussed previously; the lack of proper interministerial coordination, on both the state and district levels, leading to inadequate information, consensus and organizational power in the state planning bodies.[28]

Sewage — The sewage function is tied to the engineering division, although its organizational position varies from one authority to another. According to the Local Authorities (Sewage) Law, 5722-1962, it is the function of the local authority to install a sewage system in its territory and to maintain it in proper working order. The sewage installations are the property of the local authority. Some authorities also install purification plants which, in a number of cases, are within the jurisdiction of the city unions. The local authorities are responsible for connecting buildings to the network. They must also monitor the quality of the waste reaching the regional network and verify that dangerous or poisonous wastes do not flow into it. Residents of the authority must pay a sewage tax which is linked to the water tax.

In light of defects in the state sewage treatment situation, a statewide sewage plan was formulated with the help of the World Bank and is now close to full implementation. To implement it, an interministerial forum was established, consisting of directors-general of the Interior, Health, and Agriculture ministries, and the Water Commission, chaired by the director-general of the Ministry of Interior, the ministry in charge of the plan. It has been one of the more successful examples of interministerial cooperation in providing the resources, authorizing the plan and voluntarily promoting the issue in the local authorities, usually to their satisfaction.

Water — The local authority is obliged to establish and manage water works. Water management is regulated by various laws, particularly the by-laws of each local authority, which regulate the distribution of water to the residents and the collection of user fees.

The water works maintain a water storage and delivery system to local residents, industry, institutions and farmers within the authority's jurisdiction. For this purpose they employ control installations, pumps and water towers, as well as collection pools for use in times of peak consumption or emergency. The local authority is responsible for the installation and maintenance of water pipes within its jurisdiction and for supervising the connection of buildings to the central system. Financing the installation is done through a pipe-laying levy collected from property owners.

A few authorities have water sources within their jurisdiction. However, most of the water delivered to local authorities is purchased from Mekorot, the national water company. The price of the water usually reflects cost, but is subject to the authorization of the Water Commission, in line with the policy of the Ministry of Interior which strives to make the price uniform. In the past, user fees covered the cost of service and even allowed some development funds to be put aside. In 1980, through the initiative of the Ministry of Interior and the Water Commission, a Water Administration for local authorities was established to act as a coordinating body.[29]

Sanitation — The local authority is responsible for removal of refuse, street cleaning and maintaining a proper level of sanitation. In recent years the growing sensitivity to ecological problems has influenced the policies of local authorities and led to the creation of municipal frameworks for environmental protection. The Sanitation Division is one of the largest in most local authorities. In a large authority it includes an administrative staff, an accounting department, a veterinarian (in large municipalities there is a separately organized veterinary service), supervisors and drivers. More than two-thirds of the personnel in these units are sanitation workers. In many authorities, this work is performed with the help of contractors. These functions include street-sweeping, refuse collection and burning, operation and maintenance of public toilets, veterinary services and preventive sanitation. Sanitation is one of the areas in which there is inter-municipal cooperation.

Firefighting — The firefighting service is controlled by the Ministry of Interior and requires inter-municipal coordination. The Firefighting Services Law, 5719-1959 obligates the formation of regional city federations for matters pertaining to firefighting. The law grants the local authority executive functions, whereas authority on issues of policy are formally entrusted to the chief firefighting supervisor in the Ministry of Interior. However, this field has become one of the most autonomous activities of local authorities. This autonomy persists despite financial dependence on the state government and the obligation of the state to support the firefighting services at a fixed rate. In contrast to education and welfare, this field is not characterized by joint execution and interference in the daily administration of the service. There is no state government machinery for matters of firefighting, except for the post of chief firefighting supervisor and the role of the Ministry of Interior in authorizing personnel, providing professional training and other supervisory and directing functions.[30] This autonomy is due to the lateral cooperation between different firefighting services, as well as the nature of the function itself, which does not attract political attention.

State Services

In terms of their scope, the major state services within a local authority are education and welfare. Much of the interaction between the state and local governments takes place in these areas, a subject discussed elsewhere in this book. Here we will only briefly outline the division of principal functions in these two areas.

The state's education functions are divided between the Ministry of Education and Culture and the local authorities. The ministry is in charge of determining the curriculum, endorsing textbooks, maintaining a system of discipline, training teachers, authorizing the opening of schools and paying teachers' salaries. The local authority is responsible for student registration, auxiliary services (secretarial and janitorial), meals, health services and a number of other designated services. The local authority has its own education department whose head is locally appointed. The department has responsibility for hiring principals for local schools and providing supplementary programs beyond the minimum required by the ministry which often can be substantial additions to the school program. The department and the principals of the individual schools are responsible for hiring teachers from the ministry's approved lists. The provision and maintenance of school buildings is a local responsibility, although authorization and funding come from the ministry and in the case of high schools and pre-schools from the Israel Education Fund of the Jewish Agency. According to this arrangement, the local authority has very little influence on the educational content and process in the schools. A slight change in these relations was made with the implementation of the Inspection of Schools Law, 5729–1969.[31]

In contrast to the field of education, the staff of the local welfare office are local authority employees, though officials of the Ministry of Labor and Social Welfare have influence in the appointment of the local welfare office manager.[32] The local office takes care of social and administrative casework, subject to the supervision of the district office of the ministry. The ministry itself provides certain services to the needy through its institutions, especially hospitalization. In the field of welfare, as in education, there is a certain amount of dual subordination. However, in contrast to education, the fact that local welfare office employees receive their salary from the local authority contributes to the greater influence of the local authority on this function.

Welfare, more than education, is connected to the activities of several other ministries in addition to the Ministry of Labor and Social Welfare. Municipal welfare departments often form contacts with different government ministries, often taking advantage of the lack of coordination between them in order to obtain financial support. According to an arrangement in force since the mid-1970s, the local authorities receive state government compensation for at least 75 percent of recognized welfare expenditures. Yet this did not lead to uniformity in the scope of welfare services in the different local authorities.

The municipal public service delivery system in Israel is among the most complex in the world. It is, however, characterized by a remarkable difference between local and state services. Whereas the organization of local services is relatively simple, the organization of state services is complex and is viewed as cumbersome by many students of public administration. In some functions, it is difficult to find a clear distinction between state supervision and local execution. Instead, in the absence of a clear definition of authority in laws and regulations, deviations from existing definitions lead to a degree of "joint action," overlap, friction and conflict between the local and state planes.[33] Proposals for reform are of two kinds: one favoring centralizing the function in the government ministry, and the other relegating the function to the local authority and minimizing state government involvement.

Internal Auditing

The local authority is subject to auditing from several directions: the State Comptroller, accountants hired by the Ministry of Interior, the Municipal Auditing Committee and internal auditors.

Since the establishment of the office of State Comptroller, the municipal sector has been a principal object of scrutiny. Yet due to limitations in resources and manpower, it has been impossible to carry out frequent audits of any particular local authority. The normal lapse between audits in large local authorities is five to seven years. It is even greater in small ones. The State Comptroller's office has relative advantages due to its independence and high professional standards. However, as a result of the low frequency of its audits and the fact that it is an external body, there is usually a large time gap between the events which triggered the call for an audit and the presentation of the report, a fact which greatly impedes its effectiveness.[34]

The use of accountants is anchored in section 216 of the Municipal Order, which authorizes the Minister of Interior to appoint accountants for the purpose of financial auditing of local authorities. The auditing reports are presented to the Ministry of Interior.

Local authorities have Municipal Auditing Committees. In the past these were optional committees, but since 1979 the committee has been mandatory. This committee is comprised of up to seven local council members. The chairman must be a representative of a party other than that of the mayor, if such a party exists. The mayor or deputy mayor is not permitted to be a member of the committee.

By the end of the 1960s, there was a growing trend towards institutionalizing the function of internal auditing within public administration and public corporations in Israel, a trend which affected local government as well. In some of the large local authorities, especially in Tel Aviv and Jerusalem, offices of internal auditing were established, although their role was not uniform and clearly defined. In 1971 a law was enacted requiring any municipality of more than 30,000 residents, or where the Minister of Interior otherwise ordered, to appoint a municipal auditor. The auditor carries out audits of the activities of the municipality's employees, manages its accounts, maintains the quality of municipal finances and property and reviews the qualitative dimensions in the actions of the local authority such as ethical standards, economy and efficiency. All bodies under the control of the municipality (e.g., municipal companies) are open to auditing, including the religious councils.

The internal auditor has discretion as to the choice of topics and the timing of audits, but he must comply with the requests of department heads and of the Auditing Committee. Council members and employees must make available to the auditor any document or information which is necessary for the completion of his work. Once a year the auditor presents a report to the mayor; in special cases reports may be presented more often. Within three months of the receipt of the report, the mayor must submit his comments to the Auditing Committee. The public discussion of the findings of the internal auditor in the Auditing Committee serves to direct public attention to the results of the audit, which is one of the means for increasing its effectiveness.

The advantages of internal auditing include expertise and familiarity with the work of the audited body, as well as the relative speed with which the auditor can respond to defects. The mere existence of the institution may act as a preventive factor. In more than a few instances, it has been the internal auditor who detected criminal infractions carried out in the local authorities. It is part of the role of the internal auditor to act as a link with the State Comptroller, as well as to verify the carrying out of recommendations of the State Comptroller.

There are several difficulties, however, which hamper the effective functioning of the internal auditor. Control is an extremely sensitive personal and political issue. Despite the official trend to grant the auditor relative autonomy, he is nonetheless a municipality employee and dependent on its administration for his status, working conditions and staff. The organizational structure of the local authority makes the status of the auditor problematic due to the lack of a pyramidal-hierarchical framework, and especially the absence of a clear cut separation between the political and the administrative spheres. He is dependent for his effectiveness on the informal cooperation of the mayor, the council members and the division heads.

The status of the auditor differs from one local authority to another. His status is relatively firm in the three major cities as well as in Petah Tikva, Holon and Bat Yam. There are some local authorities in which the auditor does not carry out the full range of functions assigned to his position or acts as an auditor only on a part-time basis. The level of results of auditing is, therefore, dependent on several factors such as the backing of the local administration and public alertness.

Handling Complaints Against Local Government

The local authority has powers and duties whose execution may infringe upon individual rights. Besides judicial control, administrative frameworks have been designed to cope with grievances. The handling of complaints has a double significance. First, it concerns an elementary obligation of the authority towards its residents. Second, it implies a potential feedback mechanism. However, the issue is not specific to local government. It has concerned Israeli public administration since the late 1960s. Over time, the role of the ombudsman in state organizations has become increasingly institutionalized. In Israel, the State Comptroller is also the Commissioner for Complaints from the Public as part of his official role.[35]

Handling complaints in local authorities is carried out on several levels. In many local authorities the citizen turns directly to the head of the relevant department. One alternate channel is the public relations officer. Often some council members, especially those elected on local lists, act as a permanent address for public appeals. In the larger cities such as Tel Aviv, there are local ombudsmen as well as alternative institutionalized channels for complaints in specific areas such as in matters of sewage or sanitation. In some authorities, the function of handling public complaints is integrated into the functions of the internal auditing unit. There is a distinct advantage gained by the institutionalization of the public complaint offices and the existence of an address for individual appeals. The main function which the institution fills is the handling of private claims of individuals who are not a part of any pressure group and who do not have access to organized support or financial resources. A significant percentage of complaints were found to have indeed been justified. Although public complaint offices have not yet been established in the majority of local authorities, in the larger authorities such offices have gained social recognition and esteem.

Personnel Administration

Local governments employed over 80,000 persons in fiscal year 1981–82.[36] This bureaucracy is second in size only to that of the state government. The large share of wages in overall local government expenditures is a focus of much public and government attention. Beyond its economic implications, the nature of personnel administration is significant from a wide range of administrative perspectives, including the quality of personnel, the nature of the senior administrative staff, the degree to which the municipal bureaucracy represents the local population, and its integrity and professional orientation.

Basic Characteristics

Some patterns of personnel administration in local government were influenced by the administrative traditions inherited from before the establishment of the state; however they were largely molded during its first years of independence. The basic elements of the system — the wage scales, recruitment and promotion patterns, pension plans and collective bargaining — were deliberately modeled on the state government pattern. This transfer was part of a policy of standardization of administration in the public sector initiated by the state government. It was partly in line with the interests of local authorities, as it relieved them of the necessity of repeated confrontations with local employee unions. The standardization of personnel management practices and service conditions made it easier for the local authorities to present demands for financial aid to the state government to cover expenditures incurred by government personnel policies.

However, there was only a partial similarity between service conditions in the municipal sector and parallel conditions in the state government. The reasons for these differences were largely the result of three factors. First, the state government was unable to impose effective control over local personnel policies and practices. This difficulty was identical to the difficulties of supervision in the budget and other operative areas in which the state government tried to enforce a unified policy in the municipal sector. A second factor was the administrative autonomy of each local authority. Whereas in the state government, the function of personnel management is directed by the state civil service administration and there is the official status of a "state employee," each local authority is an independent employing agency and its employees are not related to the entire municipal sector.[37] The fact that each local authority is a separate employing agency makes uniform methods of management less applicable. A third factor is the character of the municipal administration, its proximity to the population and the variety of its functions. The variety in local government organizations make it difficult to apply uniform management formulas.

The transfer of conditions of service from the state service to local government without the possibility of their effective and complete application, as well as the obligation of the state government to finance part of local government expenditures, led to a series of attempts to increase state government supervision of personnel administration in the local sector, including attempts to establish a state personnel authority for local government.[38] Yet these attempts to control personnel administration in the municipalities were unsuccessful. The intensity of state government control of personnel management in the local sector is inversely related to the size and municipal status of the authority. As opposed to cities where the scope of control is limited, control of local personnel management was more effective in local councils. Administrative orders by the Ministry of Interior in 1961 and 1962 established in the ministry an Administration for Employees of Local Councils, which had centralized jurisdiction over major areas of personnel administration, and especially job designation (the grading of positions according to their duties and responsibilities.)[39]

The multiple channels of contact between the local authority and various government ministries affect the administration of personnel in state services, since the relevant ministries — the Ministry of Labor and Social Welfare, the Ministry of Education and Culture, and the Ministry of Health — are authorized to establish or cancel positions in the fields for which they are responsible. The Union of Local Authorities acts as a coordinating, advising and directing body on issues of wages and labor relations. Affiliation with the Union is voluntary and differs from one authority to another; it is relatively weaker in the larger authorities and especially in the three largest municipalities.

The Basis of Labor Relations

Labor relations between an authority and its employees are essentially contractual. The main document which regulates these relations is a 1959 contract, signed by representatives of the employees (the Clerks Union) and the Union of Local Authorities as a representative of management (with the exclusion of the three largest cities). On the basis of this contract, a set of regulations on service conditions was accepted in 1960. Most of the provisions in these regulations have been changed over the years, but as of yet there is no substitute for the agreement as the basic framework for labor relations. Employees hired by a local authority accept the contractual obligations which derive from this document and other regulations which apply to their class and grade. The municipalities accepted several of the statutory arrangements which apply to state employees, among them the Civil Service Regulations and the State Service (Benefits) Law, 1955. While the Benefits Law is obligatory in character, being accepted as part of a collective agreement, the Civil Service Regulations, which concern both rights and obligations, are applied only selectively, mostly in residual cases.

Control of Staff Positions

In light of the economic implications of the scope of municipal employment, the question of the establishment of staff positions is a central issue in local personnel administration. The Hebrew term, *teken*, has several meanings: the authorized number of posts of a ministry, the grade of the post according to its duties and responsibilities, job descriptions and their hierarchical order. The number of government-funded positions is subject to parliamentary supervision. There have been attempts to apply a similar method in local government, but with limited success. Due to the lack of this tool, the state government imposed personnel ceilings for local authorities as a way to limit growth in the bureaucracy. There are also instructions on levels of grading in local authorities according to a scale which takes into consideration the size of the authority, as well as rules concerning promotion and minimal periods of service at each grade. In the past, the lack of a comprehensive designation for staff positions contributed both to the lack of uniformity among local authorities in employment and to the rapid growth of the number of employees relative to the population.[40]

The question of the optimum level of municipal employment is difficult to answer; it depends on the range of services and on the level of enforcement of laws and regulations.[41] The data in table 6.2 portray the growth of municipal employment beyond the rate of population growth.

Table 6.2

EMPLOYMENT IN JEWISH LOCAL AUTHORITIES AS A
PERCENTAGE OF LOCAL POPULATION: 1971/72-1981/82

Type of Authority	% of Municipal Employees in the Population	
	1971/72	1981/82
Municipalities	1.8	2.1
Large Local Councils	2.4	2.5

Source: Calculated on the basis of *The Local Authorities in Israel — Physical Data,* from 1971/72 and 1981/82.

A detailed analysis of the changes in local government employment between the years 1969 and 1978 reveals a disproportional rate of personnel growth relative to the general population. In certain local authorities, especially in development towns, the growth rate was particularly high — 60 percent in Dimona, 145 percent in Kiryat Shmona and 89 percent in Beit Shemesh. In contrast, the rate of growth was more moderate in older, medium-sized local authorities and in some there was even a relative contraction in the bureaucracy. It seems probable that the change from the status of a local council to that of a municipality entails a rapid growth of the bureaucracy.[42] If we analyze the ratio of employees to residents in the local authority, in 1981/82 we find it to be 1.57 percent in Jerusalem, 3.19 percent in Tel Aviv, 1.56 percent in Givatayim, 2.75 percent in Dimona, 1.28 percent in Kiryat Yam and 4.48 percent in Kiryat Shmona.[43] Different explanations have been given for these disparities.[44] In addition to the expansion of services, there are also social considerations such as the provision of employment in border areas, political considerations and the characteristics of the administrative system.

Tel Aviv is above average in local government employment, most probably reflecting the characteristics of a main metropolitan center and the disproportional character of the services which it provides. In contrast, the relatively low figure in Givatayim or Kiryat Yam reflects, at least partly, their proximity to a large city. Of course, the disparity may derive from other sources as well, such as political considerations, including the political power of the authority. The disparities could also be partly attributed to inadequate criteria for employment in the local sector and to weakness in the mechanisms of staff control. Comparisons between scope of municipal employment and state government funding infer that the rapid increase in municipal personnel was largely financed by the state government.[45]

Recruitment and Career Patterns

In the 1950s and 1960s, political factors were most obvious in local hiring decisions.[46] However in the 1970s and 1980s, this phenomenon was on the decline. This change occurred not because of a radical turn towards professionalism and a decline in partisanship, but rather due to other trends such as full employment, greater security of tenure, and especially the interest of municipal employees in filling vacant positions at the middle to upper levels from within the service. In the large and medium-sized local authorities, unions often exerted pressure against political appointments.

Local authority recruitment is formally similar to entrance into the state service. For low-level clerical and blue-collar positions, employees are hired through the state employment service, while higher level positions require a comprehensive examination, although in practice this is rarely done. Under the Municipal Corporations Ordinance, 1934, the appointment to some positions requires authorization by the council.

Whereas the state service has a mechanism of examinations and selection committees, the relatively small scale of the local authority, and especially the small local authority, as well as the lack of public interest, have led to different and less formal recruitment procedures.

Professional positions are filled through personal acquaintance — the family, professional or political ties of currently serving employees. Large authorities are assisted by the services of personnel agencies. Retired army officers are often recruited for managerial positions. As in the state service, there is a policy of preference for promotion from within and most middle and upper level positions are filled in this manner. Hence, relatively few positions in the higher echelons are filled from outside. Therefore, the main channel for entry into municipal employment is the low and low-middle ranking grades. Union resistance to outside recruitment for higher positions largely limits the recruitment of professionals and new university graduates to municipal careers and often leads to the promotion of veteran employees who lack the adequate knowledge and skills for executive positions. Union insistence on promotion from within departments limits interdepartmental mobility and career planning.

While union power curbed political appointments, it equally limited the scope of maneuverability of the local authority in matters of personnel management.[47] A local authority must often resort to reorganization and even the creation of a new department in order to undertake new higher level appointments, either on political or professional grounds. Career patterns in municipal service differ from one authority to another, influenced by factors of size and level of specialization. In large local authorities the career pattern is closed. It is more open in small and medium-sized local authorities.[48]

Another factor which affects municipal career patterns concerns pensions. The State Service (Benefits) Law (consolidated version), 5730–1970, grants pension rights to an employee with 10 years of service if dismissed at age 40 or above. The right to an early pension leads to excessive security of tenure and low mobility, and puts severe strains on the personnel policy of the local authority.

The Conduct of Labor Relations

Labor relations in local government are handled in part locally, where relations revolve around issues specific to each authority, and in part statewide, where decisions apply to the entire sector. Local authorities are represented by the Union of Local Authorities which signs collective agreements on their behalf with the Clerks Union of the Histadrut-General Federation of Labor. The Union of Local Authorities, acting more as a mediator than as an employer, does not take on full responsibility for the obligations entailed in the agreements. Rather, it passes on the demands of the municipalities to the government, which occasionally helps the local authorities to meet their obligations.

Collective agreements in the municipal sector are not rigidly and explicitly worded. Instead, they tend to be general and flexible, so that each local authority may negotiate separately and adjust the interpretation of the agreements to its unique conditions. Still, there is a certain degree of "linkage" between authorities. Employees demand and receive the preferable conditions which their counterparts in another authority have managed to receive. More than in the state government bureaucracy, local authorities allow flexibility in working conditions and special benefits and salaries for senior employees. One of the results of this flexibility is evident in strikes. Municipal government has the lowest frequency of strikes in the public sector.[49] However, the relative industrial peace in local government is achieved at considerable economic cost.

Retirement Benefits

The State Service (Benefits) Law (consolidated version), 1970 grants civil servants extensive non-contributory pension rights.

This law, which allows much discretion in determining individual rights, was originally prepared for application in a centralized system such as the state government or the state police force, where discretion was applied by a central body such as the Civil Service Commission. The transfer of these provisions to the municipal system soon created many anomalies. The lack of supervisory frameworks and central guidance essentially grants each municipality, large or small, an authority similar to that of the Civil Service Commission or the inspector general of the police. It has been found that the municipalities do not uniformly apply the law even within the same authority.[50]

This problem is especially acute when the decisions being made entail a considerable public expense, such as cases of forced early retirement, or the increase of pensions for employees whose service has been relatively short. It turns out that local authorities have acted very liberally in these areas, thereby building up a heavy debt for future budgets. One of the outcomes of these arrangements is the obscuring of differences between employees who have served for extended periods and those whose service was relatively short. In the absence of a statutory arrangement specially designed for local government, decisions are reached according to the different precedents in each authority. Local government employees may therefore enjoy retirement conditions which are superior to those of the state bureaucracy. Local government employees are also entitled to the benefits of a provident fund, a right denied to employees of the state civil service.

A related question concerns the financial burden involved in the institution of pensions in the local authorities. There were 11,350 pensioners in municipal service in 1981/82. The number of pensioners relative to employees varies from one authority to another (see table 6.3). The differences derive in part from the age of the settlement (it is relatively low in new development towns), the rate of turnover, and differences in retirement policies. In the future there may be a need for a common framework aimed at balancing the burden of pension expenses among the local authorities.[51]

Standards of Conduct

In local government, the social and political ties between the politicians, civil service and citizens can generate situations in

Table 6.3

EMPLOYEES AND PENSIONERS IN 9 MUNICIPALITIES:
1981/82

1 City	2 Number of Employees (not including pensioners)	3 Number of pensioners	3:2 % of pensioners
Tel Aviv	10,450	3,455	32
Haifa	4,854	2,052	42
Netanya	2,035	454	22
Petah Tikva	2,228	497	22
Ramat Gan	2,289	574	27
Nazareth	402	81	20
Lod	709	169	29
Beit She'an	449	43	9
Eilat	521	53	9

Source: Central Bureau of Statistics, *The Local Authorities in Israel, Physical Data, 1981/82*, Jerusalem, 1984.

which basic principles of right public conduct may be violated. Israeli municipal administration and politics have had their share of problems of personal or political integrity since the first years of the state. Several areas of activity were particularly problematic, such as town planning, tenders and contracts. Regulations concerning the obligations and prohibitions binding council members and employees are scattered throughout a multitude of laws, regulations and precedents. Besides the general statutory provisions in the Criminal Code and the Municipal Corporations Ordinance, there has been an increasing trend towards establishing a network of disciplinary courts. In the past, only a few authorities maintained their own disciplinary courts. Only in 1978 did the Knesset approve a law dealing with discipline and disciplinary courts in local government, a law based on the parallel model of the law for state employees passed in 1963.[52]

After the passage of the law, existing disciplinary courts in the large local authorities were granted statutory standing. Regional courts were established for the other authorities. The courts have considerable disciplinary powers, the harshest of which is dismissal without retirement benefits. Yet the scope of the courts remains limited. The local authority has discretion as to whether or not to transfer an issue to the court. There are many considerations which might prevent the authority from taking such action, including its own public image as well as union resistance. One issue which has gained recent attention is the need to formulate rules of ethics and conduct for council members and officials of the local authority.[53]

Aspects of Financial Management

Financial administration is a major aspect of local government. It reflects the totality of the relations between the local authority and the state government and widely affects internal administrative processes. Financial administration is characterized by three main traits: the long-term trend toward expansion of the role of the state government in financing the local authority (and the parallel decline of the proportion of revenue from local sources); the variance in the size of municipal budgets and in the composition of income; and the impact on local government finance of soaring inflation between 1978 and 1985.

Since the end of the 1960s there has been a continuous decline in the share of revenue derived from local sources (taxes and service charges), and a complementary increase in the share provided by government grants. This increase did not necessarily create increased dependence or subordination of the local to the state government, as discussed in Chapters 2 and 7.[54]

The decline in autonomous financing and the growing dependence on state government support has both administrative causes and consequences. It was probably made possible, in part, by the flexibility of the government allocation mechanism and the existence of a multitude of financial channels between different government ministries and the local authorities, along with the overall lack of adequate interministerial coordination on issues of local government finance. Local government has improved techniques designed to extract resources from the state government. From the point of view of the local authority, increased government grants carry a higher marginal effectiveness than attempts to either increase internal efficiency or increase revenue from internal resources, most probably a politically unpopular activity. On the other hand, the high level of state government participation in municipal budgets, especially in development towns, is a disincentive for administrative efficiency.

The increase in state government participation coincided with a growth, in real terms, of local government budgets over the last fifteen years. One of the potential results of the high level of government participation in local authority budgets is the possibility granted to the state government to assist in standardizing the public services provided by local authorities and in reducing the disparities in local revenue. To what extent did government support really contribute towards this objective?

Variance in Size and Composition of Municipal Revenue

Table 6.4 presents the per capita revenue in shekels in the ordinary budgets of 181 local authorities of various types, as well as the mean and standard deviation in each category.[55] The level of variance is extremely high in comparison with other municipal systems with high levels of government participation.[56] Even if we ignore the differences between the Jewish and Arab sectors, an issue which we will discuss later in this chapter, it is possible to point out considerable variance within the Jewish sector itself. This variance reflects not only differences between categories, but also differences within each category as expressed by a high standard deviation. In the Jewish cities, the share of revenue from local sources is above the overall average. Government participation is slightly higher than 50 percent. A similar trend exists in the large, established Jewish local councils. In contrast, the share of revenue from local sources in the new, large Jewish local councils is about half the level of the older authorities; transferred revenue is also about half. The level of government participation (general and designated) in these authorities is higher — approximately three-quarters of the income in the ordinary budget.

In absolute terms, the per capita income in the large Jewish local councils and the regional councils is considerably higher than in the older cities and local councils. The variance of revenue can also be explained by the difference between metropolitan and satellite cities.

238

Table 6.4

PER CAPITA REVENUE IN THE ORDINARY BUDGETS
OF LOCAL AUTHORITIES
According to Types: 1981/82
(mean and standard deviation in parentheses)

Type of authority	Number of local authorities	Per Capita Revenue	% of local sources	% of Trans- ferred Revenue	% of Government Participation
Overall Average	181	3,941 (2,320)	27.7 (13.3)	7.1 (5.5)	64.7 (16.2)
Jewish Municipalities	34	4,153 (1,365)	34.2 (11.9)	10.3 (4.4)	55.2 (15.1)
Arab Municipalities	2	1,753	26.6	7.1	66.2
Old, Large Jewish Local Councils	11	4,640 (788)	33.7 (10.2)	9.8 (4.7)	56.4 (14.4)
New, Large Jewish Local Councils	21	5,277 (1,384)	19.6 (9.6)	5.3 (1.4)	74.9 (10.0)
Large Arab Local Councils	25	1,355 (497)	24.2 (10.8)	5.4 (2.8)	68.2 (17.0)
Old, Small Jewish Councils	24	4,826 (2,046)	25.0 (13.8)	9.5 (11.3)	64.4 (20.1)
New, Small Jewish Councils	8	4,824 (1,903)	28.0 (14.5)	7.4 (4.1)	64.4 (15.4)
Small Arab Councils	8	1,418 (641)	20.9 (8.3)	6.0 (2.8)	73.0 (8.9)
Regional Councils	38	5,610 (2,525)	33.2 (15.1)	5.0 (3.1)	61.7 (14.8)

Source: Based on Central Bureau of Statistics, *The Local Authorities: Financial Data 1981/82,* Jerusalem, 1984.

An additional explanation is inherent in the flexible system of allocation of government financial support and the inability to impose rigid standards. Various authorities reach certain levels of expenditure and the government allocation system tends to adapt to them. One of the manifestations of the flexibility of the municipal financial system is the issue of timing. A municipal business cycle can be detected in the rapid growth in local authority budgets before and during election periods, and their subsequent decline afterwards. This growth is primarily comprised of an expansion in the non-ordinary budget. The size of the gap between authorized budgets and de-facto budgets in local authorities is particularly large on the eve of elections.[57] The existence of a municipal business cycle parallels a similar phenomenon at the national level.[58] The level of real growth in local authority budgets on the eve of elections — nearly 50 percent in the 1965 elections, over 20 percent in the 1973 elections, and over 10 percent in the 1978 elections — is testimony to the considerable degree of flexibility and maneuverability in the municipal financial system.

A final question is whether government participation in local authority budgets is, by its nature, progressive. Do less prosperous areas enjoy levels of government assistance larger than the national average? On the basis of available data, there is a trend towards progressive participation which is achieved primarily through the general grant.[59] However, the transferred revenue acts partially in the opposite direction, as it tends to favor the more prosperous authorities.

Financial Management Under Three-Digit Inflation

Inflation in Israel has increased since 1978, and in 1979 it entered three-digit levels. The acceleration of inflation posed difficulties for financial management in both the private and public sectors.[60] The impact of the inflationary process on the municipal sector is unique due to its special position. On the one hand, the municipal financial system is tied to the government sector. On the other hand, the authority acts as a self-contained entity; it levies taxes, collects payment for services, purchases equipment and makes commitments to suppliers and contractors. One difficulty arises from the nature of the authority's revenue. Whereas in the private sector there is a certain flexibility gained by the possibility of raising prices, the authority is bound by political, administrative and legal constraints.

Until the end of 1983, there were signs of adaptation to the inflationary process. The acceleration of inflation towards the end of 1983 brought additional difficulties for financial management. At the same time, the supervisory tools of the Ministry of Interior were weakened, along with financial management within the local authority itself. All of the usual internal financial management tools, and especially the management of cash flow, lost their significance. By the summer of 1985, the accepted time-span for financial planning was only one month. At the same time there was increasing pressure on the Ministry of Interior to cover urgent expenses.

Under three-digit inflation, the timing of receipts, as well as their size, influences the financial situation of the local authority. The guarantee of a fixed income at regular intervals, such as through the payment of property taxes by a standing order at the bank, for example, is worthwhile to the authority despite discounts given to residents who pay in this way. The sharp drop in inflation by the end of 1985 and during 1986 had a positive impact on the finances of the relatively established local authorities which in some cases accumulated surpluses.

In summary, the three basic traits of financial management in local government in Israel in recent years were the growth of government participation, the variance in size and composition of municipal revenues, and the impact of accelerating inflation. These phenomena created a vicious circle. The major role of the state government did not contribute towards standardizing municipal budgets. Inflation impeded attempts to apply fixed criteria for government support of local authorities. The soaring inflation led to growing financial dependence on the state government to cover the urgent debts of local authorities and to their continuing dependence.

A certain advantage inherent in the current municipal financial process may be found precisely in its flexibility. A local authority which is interested in developing projects and has a degree of local initiative can raise the funds necessary to carry out the projects.

The key issue for the financial management of local authorities is how to increase revenue from local sources. Growth of local revenue is a necessary condition for proper management of the authority's finances, for inculcating awareness of the connection between income and expenditures and for a responsible approach on the part of residents of the authority. Above all, it is the key to the future political autonomy of local authorities.

The Religious Council

The religious council is a statutory body linked to the local authority and responsible for providing religious services to the local Jewish population. There is no parallel institution for non-Jewish residents. Government support for non-Jewish religious services is handled by the Ministry of Religious Affairs, which supports religious services primarily through the voluntary organizations of the respective religious and communal bodies.[61]

Religious councils exist in about 200 Jewish localities. Some of these councils are in settlements which do not enjoy the status of a city, local council or regional council, such as religious moshavim or kibbutzim.[62]

The principal statutory basis for the activities of the religious council is the Jewish Religious Services Law (consolidated version), 5731–1971 and the regulations enacted on its basis.[63] A religious council is established by the Minister for Religious Affairs. The law does not state the number of council members, but it does state in section 2 that their number must not exceed the number of council members in the local authority of the same settlement. Ten percent of the council members are chosen upon the recommendation of the local rabbinate, 45 percent on the recommendation of the Ministry of Religious Affairs, and 45 percent on the recommendation of the local authority. Appointment of members of religious councils is for four years.

The revenue of the council derives from independent sources (levies and payments for services); income covering the rest of the expenditures is from the Ministry of Religious Affairs (one-third), and from the local authority (two-thirds). Since revenues from independent sources are limited, especially in small and medium-sized local authorities,[64] most of the financial burden falls upon the other two sources.

The religious council is responsible for the performance of weddings, maintenance of synagogues and ritual baths, supervision of Kashrut (dietary laws) and ritual slaughtering, performance of burials and maintenance of cemeteries. These last services may border on the responsibilities of the local burial societies; responsibility varies from place to place. In several settlements the burial societies have been integrated into the local religious council.[65] In addition to these clearly defined areas, the religious councils provide religious information, sponsor religious events, and aid in the building of religious buildings such as synagogues and libraries for religious texts.

The religious council is a sort of local authority for religious matters. Its functioning reflects the administrative problems also characteristic of other parts of the municipal sector, and in several areas there are parallel administrative solutions. Similar to the Union of Local Authorities, there is a body which represents the religious councils — the Union of Religious Councils. This organization fills several functions, among which are the representation of religious councils vis-a-vis other public bodies on issues of finance and labor relations, and the provision of professional and administrative guidance to the various councils.

In contrast to the local authorities, the religious councils are administratively subordinate to the Ministry of Religious Affairs. However, the considerable allegiance of religious councils to their respective local authorities diminishes the influence of this ministry. The principal factor influencing allegiance is the budget. Since the Ministry of Religious Affairs contributes only 40 percent of the support, whereas the local authority contributes 60 percent, the influence of the local authority on the religious council is greater. Moreover, the budget estimates of the religious council are presented, in principle, simultaneously to the Ministry of Religious Affairs and to the local authority, but if the local authority allocates beyond the allocation of the ministry, this obligates the ministry to increase its portion accordingly. Attempts to coordinate between the institutions which finance the religious councils have not yet achieved any significant success.[66]

Most of the internal procedures in a religious council are not specified by law or regulation. In the regulations concerning the management of religious councils, a procedure was established for the selection of a chairman. If the council wishes it can appoint one or more deputy chairmen, subject to approval by the Ministry of Religious Affairs.[67] The regulations do not establish the wages paid to the chairman and the other religious council members. They state only that the wages should not exceed the salary of the deputy mayors of the local authority in whose jurisdiction the religious council acts. Sometimes the post of chairman of the religious council is full-time, and sometimes it is taken on in addition to other roles; sometimes it is professional, but in many cases it is more political in character. The central administrative position in the religious council is that of the secretary, which is similar to the role of the town clerk.

The councils differ in size and in administrative patterns. Religious councils have over 3,000 employees.[68] Attempts have been made to classify religious councils into six categories. Only in 1975 was a set of regulations governing working conditions adopted for the religious councils, parallel to the regulations in the local authorities. This was the result of a contract signed by the Union of Religious Councils, the Clerks Union, and representatives of the government.

As is the case with local authorities, an outstanding feature of religious councils is the variance in terms of the scope of activities and per capita expenditures in different local authorities. There is some justification for this variance. In the activities of religious councils it is difficult to define a standard list of services since the need for religious services differs from place to place in accordance with the differences in religiosity of the populations involved. For instance, the support for religious services of the municipality of Bnei Brak, a town with a predominantly Orthodox population, totalled 133 shekels per person in the budget year 1981/82, while the support of the municipality of Haifa, with a predominantly secular population, totalled only 79 shekels per person in the same year.[69]

In addition to these differences, there is a considerable degree of variance which differences in religiosity cannot explain. For instance, in 1981/82 in Kiryat Bialik, the support of the local authority for religious services was only 24 shekels per person; in Upper Nazareth, 91 shekels; in Kiryat Gat, 154 shekels; in Hazor, 298 shekels; and in Ganei Tikva, 396 shekels. The population in the last two localities are predominantly traditional, but not Orthodox. The political significance of the institution of the religious council as one of the principle channels for allocating resources for religious needs, should be viewed in light of the competition between religious parties and the lack of an administrative formula for allocating these resources.[70]

The Arab Local Authority

In 1986 there were three Arab municipalities with city status —
Nazareth, Shfar'am and Umm al Fahm — and 51 local councils,
half large and half small. In addition, there are local authorities
with a considerable non-Jewish population, such as Jerusalem,
Ma'alot-Tarshiha and Acre. The non-Jewish local authorities in
Israel, which serve Moslem Arabs, Christian Arabs, Druze and
Circassians, are politically, economically and administratively
unique, all of which justify their treatment here as a separate category.

Historical Background

In 1947-48, a large part of the Arab municipal leadership left
the territory of the State of Israel. Among them were the council
members and employees of Arab towns such as Lod, Ramle, Jaffa,
Beersheba and Acre, that had enjoyed an urban status since the
Ottoman period, as well as of mixed cities such as Safed, Tiberias
and Haifa.[71] With the stabilization of local government in Israel
soon after the establishment of the state, the Arab municipal sector
was very small. With the exception of the two Arab cities included
within the territory of the state, Nazareth and Shfar'am, most of
the Arab population was concentrated in villages in agricultural
areas in which there was no modern local government. The
internal rule of these villages was based on clans, with a traditional patriarchal leadership.[72] During this period, in which
most of the Arab sector was under military government rule, the
internal arrangements within the Arab sector seemed convenient
to the authorities who assumed that this system was appropriate for
integrating the Arab minority into Israeli political life.

Despite this, from the first years of the state the Ministry of Interior initiated and encouraged the establishment of local councils in the Arab sector, both as a framework for political self-ex-
pression and as a tool for the advancement of local economic development. The traditional Arab leadership had many reservations about the establishment of local councils. One source of their
hesitation was probably the suspicion that the process of local elections was likely to undermine their status and authority in the
village. Another source of concern was that receiving municipal
status would increase state government involvement in their

affairs, with an increase in the tax burden as well as increased government supervision.

Despite these suspicions and reservations, over 50 local councils were established in the Arab sector. Control of these councils was still mostly in the hands of the traditional leadership. The chairman of the council was often a wealthy landowner or merchant, who continued with his business alongside his municipal position. His role as chairman of the council reinforced his overall status in the village. The members of the council often simultaneously represented a political party and a specific clan. Sometimes there was an overlap between political orientation and family ties. Commonly a political conflict in Arab local government is a result of interfamily feuds. However, local leadership has been gradually passing from clan leadership to the younger, more educated generation. The results of the 1983 elections clearly reflect this trend.

The character of the Arab municipal sector is fundamentally related to the question of the integration of the Arab minority into Israeli society. The autonomous portion of the Arab economic sector, whether agricultural or industrial, is limited, and most of the Arab sector is integrated into the lower strata of the Israeli economy, as hired workers or semi-independent contractors. In recent years there have been two basic developments, the expansion of an Arab educated class and the strengthening of a Palestinian national self-awareness with radical tendencies. These developments have affected the Arab municipal sector, which has increasingly become a framework for national self-organization.

While the Arab municipal sector participates in the Union of Local Authorities and partakes of its services, a Union of Arab Local Authorities in Israel was established in 1974. This body was established largely at the initiative of Shmuel Toledano, the advisor for Arab affairs in the office of the prime minister. The activities of the Union of Arab Local Authorities have been directed primarily toward national objectives.[73] Its demands on the state government focus both on financial issues and the ownership of land, currently designated as state land, which is in physical proximity to Arab settlements. In 1976, following land expropriations in the Galilee, a violent protest demonstration was organized and given the name "Land Day."

Since the elections to the Ninth Knesset in 1977, there has been a radicalization in Arab voting patterns in both the Knesset and local elections, and a strengthening of the Communist party at the expense of political groups which had been aligned with Jewish parties. This trend has had an impact on local government. The rise in the influence of the educated class contributed to the political radicalization of the municipal sector.

Administration, Finances and Services

The differences in revenue and expenditures in Arab local authorities as opposed to Jewish local authorities, as noted in table 6.5, reflects the fundamental differences in the level and scope of services in these two sectors. The differences in revenue and

Table 6.5

PER CAPITA EXPENDITURE IN THE ORDINARY BUDGETS
OF JEWISH AND ARAB LOCAL AUTHORITIES: 1981/82
(In Shekels and Comparatively in Percentages)

Type of Authority	Per Capita Expenditure in Ordinary Budget
Municipalities:	
Jewish	4,522
Arab	1,958
%	43.2
Large Local Councils:	
Jewish	5,727
Arab	1,381
%	24.1
Small Local Councils:	
Jewish	5,646
Arab	1,420
%	25.0

Source: Central Bureau of Statistics, *Local Authorities in Israel, Financial Data 1981/82,* Jerusalem, 1984, Tables 19 and 38.

expenditures are recognizable in all types of Arab authorities in comparison to their Jewish counterparts. In the Arab local councils, the level of expenditures is about a quarter of that of the Jewish authorities.

Allocations to state services constitute a larger share of expenditures in Arab local authorities than in Jewish local authorities. In the large Jewish authorities, the average expenditure for local services is 38 percent of the overall expenditure for services, whereas in the parallel authorities in the Arab sector, the average level is only 25 percent. In 12 Arab authorities, the expenditure for local services ranges between 8 and 15 percent, a low level unmatched in the Jewish sector. The existence of a relatively high level of expenditures for state services is to a large extent the outcome of government intervention, and specifically, of the enforcement of legislation relating to education. In the Arab municipal sector there are almost no optional municipal services such as clubs, libraries, community centers or educational frameworks beyond what is obligatory.

As described in table 6.6, the proportion of government participation in the budgets of Arab local authorities is larger than in Jewish local authorities. In absolute terms, however, the total government participation in an Arab city is only about one-half that of a Jewish city, while in the large Arab local council it is only 35 percent of its Jewish counterpart. The main reason for this disparity is that participation is often granted for services which are already being performed. If no services are provided, then no government participation will be forthcoming, and if a service is minimal, the participation will be no larger than what can be expected to help cover this minimal base. The data in table 6.7 also reflect the difference in the extent of services between Jewish and Arab local authorities.

The stance of the Ministry of Interior is that the underdeveloped infrastructure of the Arab local authority is the root cause of its narrow scope of services. The construction of this type of infrastructure is related to local demand and the attitude of the local leadership. The lack of public pressure and internal motivation to improve services in the Arab sector are the key factors in the relative backwardness of the Arab municipal sector.

There is additional evidence supporting this claim, such as the fact that in the past certain Arab local authorities have not even fully utilized the budgets at their disposal. For example, in 1975, 19

Table 6.6

PER CAPITA REVENUE IN THE ORDINARY BUDGETS
OF JEWISH AND ARAB LOCAL AUTHORITIES: 1981/82
(In Shekels and Percentages according to Sources of Income)

Type of Authority (and number)	Per Capita Revenue in Shekels	Local Revenue in %	Transferred Revenue in %	Government Participation in %
Municipalities:				
Jewish (34)	4,153	34.2	10.3	55.2
Arab (2)	1,753	26.6	7.1	66.2
Large Local Councils:				
Jewish (11)	4,640	33.7	9.8	56.4
Arab (25)	1,355	24.2	5.4	68.2
Small Local Councils:				
Old Jewish (24)	4,826	25.0	9.5	64.4
New Jewish (8)	4,824	28.0	7.4	64.4
Arab (18)	1,418	20.9	6.0	73.0

Source: Central Bureau of Statistics, *Local Authorities in Israel, Financial Data,* Jerusalem, 1984.

Arab local authorities ended the year with a surplus. Three of the authorities used no more than half of their authorized budgets.[74] Recent trends such as the increasing national consciousness have not raised awareness to the need for improvement in local services in the Arab sector. On the whole, national consciousness has actually crystallized as the antithesis of civic consciousness.

A lack of confidence that the Arab authority will put additional finances to good use, coupled with the political radicalization of the Arab municipal sector, acts to create infertile ground for radical changes in government policy toward Arab local government. The policy of the Ministry of Interior in recent years to minimize cutbacks in the Arab sector relative to the Jewish sector has contributed to narrowing the gap. However, an equalization of the

Table 6.7

EMPLOYEES OF JEWISH AND ARAB LOCAL AUTHORITIES
AS A PERCENTAGE OF LOCAL POPULATION: 1971/72-1981/82

Type of Local Authority	1971/72 %	1981/82 %
Municipalities:		
Jewish	1.8	2.1
Arab	0.6	1.0
Large Local Councils:		
Jewish	2.4	2.5
Arab	0.02	0.9

Source: Based on Central Bureau of Statistics, *Local Authorities in Israel, Physical Data 1971/72,* Jerusalem, 1973; Central Bureau of Statistics, *Local Authorities in Israel, Physical Data 1981/82,* Jerusalem, 1984.

level of services in the two sectors necessitates not only an increase in government support, but fundamental changes in the infrastructure of Arab local authorities as well.

Fundamental Characteristics of Municipal Administration

The pattern of Israeli local government was largely shaped by the state administration. However, there are several areas in municipal administration which deviate from the government pattern.

1) The level of professional specialization in the local authority, and especially in small and medium-sized authorities, is naturally lower than in the government ministries, due to the fact that every authority has a broad assortment of functions and is organized on a geographical rather than a functional basis.

2) The local authority, more than the government ministry or its extensions in the field, is integrated into community life. Its relations with the local population are multi-faceted rather than specific, both formal and informal. In the local authority there is greater flexibility in response to the needs and demands of the population. Administrative processes in the municipal sector are less institutionalized than in their state government counterparts.

3) In the municipal system, the political and administrative processes are more intertwined than in the state government.

4) In contrast to the state administration, local government has no effective central directing agencies such as the Budget Department and the Civil Service Commission.

The special status of the local authority resulting from the multitude of informal channels of contact and the lack of effective state supervision is a source of both opportunities and dangers. On the one hand, local creative initiative is made possible precisely because of the weak institutionalization. On the other hand, there is the possibility of exploitation of administrative loopholes in the municipal system. Therefore, the principal dilemma facing municipal administration is finding the proper balance between encouraging autonomous local action and guaranteeing accountability to the public and to the government bodies participating in the financing of local expenditures.

There is a great deal which differentiates local authorities from one another. The major sources of these differences are the size, location, and economic, social and political characteristics of each authority. The most important of the economic factors is the availability of local sources of revenue and the authority's ability to obtain public resources. On the political or political-economic level, the important differentiating characteristics include the extent of the integration of the authority in national politics and its ability to utilize political leverage gained through electoral strength or symbolic significance. Another dimension in which authorities differ from one another is in the degree of public awareness and involvement on the part of those who reside and work within their jurisdictions.

In the Jewish sector, several types of municipal administration can be discerned. In the local councils there are two basic archetypes: the old (pre-independence) local council and the new local council. Most old local councils are characterized in the economic dimension by a relatively high level of revenue from their own independent sources as well as a relatively high level of transferred income, and a correspondingly low level of state participation. The proportion spent for local services is high relative to that spent for state services. Municipal administration is both conservative and relatively economical. Budgetary and personnel expansion are moderate; municipal administration has a distinctively inwardly-directed orientation. The local population has considerable civic awareness and interest in municipal services and local quality of life and the municipal leadership tends to respond to their expectations. The mayors themselves tend to be leaders with a local orientation. They tend not to seek state political positions and their names are often not known beyond the boundaries of their own authorities.

The opposing archetype is the new Jewish local council, especially the large council of a development town. In this authority the level of revenue from their own sources and transferred income is relatively low, whereas the level of state government participation in the budget is high. The overall income in the budgets of these authorities exceeds that of the old authorities. There has been a relatively rapid expansion of budgets and personnel. There is considerable public participation and involvement in municipal affairs which is not necessarily confined to services provided by the authority, but rather to the totality of the authority's economic problems. The authority's leaders fill roles of economic leadership beyond the mere provision of services to local residents. They are involved in problems of employment, taxation and location of economic projects and industry. The symbolic significance of the leadership, particularly in a development area, helps the mayors to obtain resources and contributes to their advancement in state politics.

The degree of politicization in these local authorities is greater than in the older authorities. Politics often penetrates into the lower levels of administration. This politicization, coupled with a lack of local participation in the authority's expenditures, tends to decrease the motivation for effective management. This situation sets the stage for occasional administrative failures, sometimes culminating in bankruptcy, which necessitate management by a state-appointed council.

A third category is the regional council. It is similar in some aspects to the old local council, but also has several specific characteristics which differentiate it from every other category. The regional council is characterized by a high level of revenue from its own sources. The level of transferred revenue in this authority is low relative to the old local councils, whereas the revenue per capita is higher. The regional council is unique in that it is a federation of settlements included within its territory. Administration in regional councils tends to be more business-like than in other local authorities as a result of professional supervision.

In small and medium-sized cities there is considerable continuity with the two archetypes sketched above. On the one hand, there are cities which continue the administrative models of the old local council — the conservative, relatively non-political model with a focus on local services. On the other hand, there are cities which follow the pattern of the new local council with an orientation toward involvement in state politics and problematic forms of internal management.

An additional category which requires separate discussion is the satellite city — a city of medium size or above, located in a metropolitan area, which was swallowed up by suburbanization. This type of city has a particularly high level of local revenue. It benefits a great deal from the services of the central city, in which a significant portion of its residents carry on economic activities, make purchases and attend centers of culture and entertainment. There are several differences within this group of municipalities, derived mostly from their economic level as well as the motivation of the local leadership to manage them effectively and they maintain their autonomous status. Although these authorities are important electorally, their mayors do not particularly stand out on the state political scene, probably due to the fact that this position in these municipalities lacks the symbolic significance which can be used as a political asset.

Large Jewish cities comprise the last group. These cities have a high level of local revenue from property and business taxes as well as a high level of transferred income stemming from the considerable value of the property within the municipality. In these cities one frequently finds that the mayors, as well as some council members, have higher political ambitions and these ambitions influence their activities in the municipal arena. This does not necessarily lead to the total politicization of the municipal administration. As noted above, the size of the municipality and the existence of "organizational space" between the political and the executive/professional levels makes it possible for the bureaucracy to carry on professional activities without a great deal of interference from elected officials. This is in contrast to the similar situation in the smaller authorities. These cities are characterized, more than in the old local councils, by the political image of their leaders and by selective attention on the part of citizens to aspects of municipal management. The size of the authority and the distance between it and the citizen make direct and comprehensive involvement difficult.

A typology is a general framework for classification. There are of necessity cases which are difficult to classify definitively, as well as those which are borderline. For instance, Petah Tikva turned into a satellite city of Tel Aviv, but remains a semi-metropolitan center for the small settlements surrounding it.

Secondly, over the years a municipal administrative culture has been developing in Israel which tends toward uniformity. The process of the leveling of differences in the municipal culture between authorities definitely fits in with the growing share of the state government in local revenues. Unfortunately, the standardization of conditions tends to diminish qualities such as conservative and economical management. It seems that both political autonomy and administrative efficiency are largely contingent upon a greater degree of financial autonomy for local government authorities in Israel.

Notes – Chapter 6

1. See Akzin-Dror (1965), p. 37.
2. Eisenstadt and Lemarchand (1981).
3. Smith (1967).
4. For a comprehensive look at the institution of municipal federations in Israel, see Martins-Hoffman (1981).
5. Rose (1984), pp. 158-160.
6. Compare Byrne (1983), Chapters 8 and 9.
7. Ministry of Interior, Department of Local Government (1967).
8. See Weiss (1973), especially Chapter 5.
9. Byrne (1983), pp. 149-150.
10. Based on an interview on 12 August 1984 with Y. Hellerman, Ministry of Interior, Jerusalem.
11. The Local Authorities (Election and Tenure of Mayor and Deputy Mayor) Law, 5735-1975 limited the number of deputy mayors to two in a city where residents numbered up to 250,000, and three for a larger city.
12. Compare Alexander (1982), pp. 120-21.
13. See Local Authorities (Benefits to Mayors and Deputy Mayors) Law, 5719-1959.
14. This situation is different from that of England, for example, where a member of the local council devotes on the average of 79 working hours a month for his duties as a member of the council. See Byrne (1983), pp. 132-33.
15. Based on a personal inspection of 12 local authorities, Summer, 1980. See also State Comptroller (1974), pp. 886-87.
16. Brichta (1982).
17. See State Commission on Local Government (1981), pp. 86-88. See also Sanbar (1979).
18. Jenkins (1967), Chapters 4 and 5.
19. Minogue (1977), Part 3.
20. Byrne (1983), Chapters 9 and 10.
21. Ibid., Chapter 9.
22. Haynes (1980).
23. On the functions and authorities of the town clerk in Israel, see Freund (1977).
24. Figure 6.3 — Municipality of Tel Aviv (administration only), 1975. Figure 6.4 — Municipality of Petah Tikva, 1980. Figure 6.5 — Municipality of Beersheba, 1975. Figure 6.6 — Municipality of Acre, 1976.
25. The authorities studied included Tel Mond, Kfar Yonah, Ness Ziona, Rishon le-Zion, Ramat Gan and Rehovot. The survey was performed in the context of the course, "Decision-Making and Policy Formulation," given in the Department of Political Studies at Bar Ilan University under the direction of the author.

26. Torgovnik (1971), pp. 11-21; Feinstein (1971), pp. 22-27 and Kfir (1971), pp. 28-30.
27. Yardeni (1974).
28. See the discussion of questions of planning and construction in Akzin-Dror (1965), Part 3.
29. See State Comptroller (1982), pp. 907-922, which deals with the topic of administration of water in the local authorities.
30. Naor and others (1978), pp. 155-75.
31. Inspection of Schools Law, 5729-1969, *Reshumot,* 564, pp. 180-85.
32. Fruman (1972), pp. 14-18.
33. Elazar (1977), pp. 47-82.
34. Yagid (1979) and Kalchheim-Rozevitz (1980).
35. Marom and Rozevitz (1986).
36. There are difficulties in reporting the precise number of employees in the municipal system due to the lack of an agreed definition as to what constitutes a "local authority employee." There is a problem of estimation due to the different types of employment, including employment by contractors and the employment of workers from Judea, Samaria and Gaza, primarily for sanitation work. In the various reports there is sometimes reference to "employees" without differentiating between full-time and part-time positions, whereas in other cases it refers to full "positions." Since in earlier years there was no distinction made between the two categories, this chapter will deal with the number of "employees" and not "positions" and data refers to both full-time and part-time employees.
37. See at the end of this chapter, "Fundamental Characteristics of Municipal Administration in Israel" and Reuveny (1985).
38. The question of supervision of the administration of the municipal bureaucracy was raised in the first years of the state. In a proposal for the Civil Service Law, 1953, an attempt was made to deal with this issue. Paragraph 88 stated: "The third chapter of this law will apply, with appropriate changes, to the local authority." Paragraph 89 stated: "Despite what may be written in other laws, the local authority may not pay its workers a wage which exceeds the wage of a state employee in a parallel position. A committee which will be appointed by the Minister of Interior and in which the employees of the local authorities will also be represented will determine parallels between positions in the state service and positions in the local authorities for the purpose of applying this section." The proposed law was not approved. There have been other proposals concerning the organizational aspects of state supervision of local government bureaucracies. See, for example, Shari (1967), pp. 62-65. The issue was again raised in discussions of the State Commission on Local Government (1981), pp. 98-99. This issue, as well as others concerning supervision by the Minister of Interior over the local authorities are discussed in a special report by the State Comptroller. See State Comptroller (1986).

39. Supervision of local councils was established in the Local Councils (Recruitment of Employees) Ordinance, 1961, and later in the Local Councils Ordinance, 1962. See Ministry of Interior (1972).
40. According to a report of the Bank of Israel, there has been an expansion in the municipal bureaucracy in a period where there has been a shrinkage of the state government bureaucracy. See Bank of Israel (1981).
41. Taylor (1983).
42. Based on Central Bureau of Statistics.
43. Central Bureau of Statistics (1984a).
44. Weiss (1973), Chapter 3.
45. An analysis of the relation of the size of the bureaucracy relative to the population of the local authority in the Jewish sector shows that there is a positive correlation between this size and the degree of government participation in the budget.
46. Weiss, op.cit.
47. See the analysis of the method of personnel management in the Tel Aviv municipality in Halevy (1975).
48. In 1972/73, only about 2 percent of the employees of the Tel Aviv municipality retired. Compare Halevy (1975), pp. 58-59.
49. During the years 1975-80, the number of work days lost due to strikes in the local authorities was only 3.5 percent of all the work days lost to strikes in the economy. Compare Reuveny (1981), pp. 294-96. This level is below the share of municipal employees in the national workforce. It is particularly low relative to other parts of the public sector. See in particular the chapter, "Salary and Additional Benefits of Local Authority Employees," and State Comptroller (1986), pp. 3-31, 132-134. For a follow-up of previous audit findings on this subject which took place in 1984, see State Comptroller (1985), p. 890.
50. Based on an investigation by the author.
51. The Sanbar Commission referred to the subject and recommended legislation based on the Civil Service (Benefits) Law, 1955. See State Commission on Local Government, 1981, p. 99. For serious defects reported by the State Comptroller on this subject, see State Comptroller (1986), pp. 32-47.
52. Local Authorities (Discipline) Law, 5738-1978.
53. See The Committee on Rules for Prevention of Conflict of Interest of Elected Officials in the Local Authorities (1984).
54. There is a dispute in Israel over the question of whether government participation in local budgets indeed automatically leads to greater centralization, power and government control. See Kalchheim (1976). Compare also the discussion of the topic in England: Alexander (1982), Chapter 7, pp. 147-70. Representatives of local government tend to emphasize that the source of the difficulty in financing local authorities lies in government policy. One claim is that the source of the budget deficit is in the state services — education and welfare —

and that were government financing complete in these areas, or if these services were outside the field of action of the authorities, the budgets would be balanced. For a counter claim on this point, see Kalchheim (1979). There is a parallel opinion according to which the government expanded these services in light of political considerations without giving the authorities any appropriate compensation. Also the trend to increase local revenue via transferred income began with the cancellation of the municipal property tax in 1968 and ended with the cancellation of the dining and vacation tax in 1977. The institution of "transferred income," a fixed government grant in exchange for the abolition of a local property tax, is from this point of view a negative incentive for independent collection. The stance of the local authorities was presented to the author by Kalman Dinnes, the economic advisor to the Union of Local Authorities, in the summer of 1981. In the mid-1980s the Israel government instituted a new policy on this subject, see "Epilogue" at the end of Chapter 7. The lack of an incentive for local collection developed in parallel to the institution of the "transferred income." The State Comptroller pointed out that the local authorities did not exhaust the possibilities for collection. See State Comptroller (1976), p. 1125. It is also probable that the organizational mechanism of division of functions and expenses between the state and local governments in the fields of education and welfare acts in various ways to increase financial dependence.

55. Table 6.4 is based on data from 181 local authorities. It covers all local authorities with the exception of Jewish settlements in Judea, Samaria and Gaza, or settlements whose municipal status has recently been changed (settlements which recently received municipal status for the first time or which are difficult to classify in one of the categories in the table).

56. The most relevant model for purposes of comparison is England, since it is a unitary state in which the level of state government participation in the revenues of local authorities is similar to the level in Israel, and there is also a certain similarity in the criteria for computation of the level of participation. An analysis of the expenses per person in England according to the types of local authorities shows that there is less variance than in Israel. Compare data with Bennet (1982), p. 174.

57. Rozevitz (1984), pp. 475-79. Data on the gap between the authorized and the actual budget and its growth during election years was given to the author by Rozevitz.

58. Compare Ben Porat (1975), pp. 403-40.

59. The subject has been discussed in a number of articles. Compare Torgovnik (1978), pp. 211-38, and Mevorach (1981), pp. 264-69. The question arises here as to how to calculate the wealth of a local authority. Is per capita income an adequate indicator to estimate wealth or is it necessary to form an index combining many factors? In Israel there

is data on the per capita income of wage-earners from the census. Due
to the lack of any other indicator, this variable has been accepted, both
for 1971/72 and 1981/82. A census was taken in both years. In an analysis over the two periods, it was found that the revenue from local
sources is positively related to the level of per capita income of wage-
earners. A similar trend was found in relation to transferred income.
A high level of transferred income is especially frequent in
metropolitan areas and wealthy suburbs of large cities. Government
participation in the form of transferred income is by its nature regressive since it is based on the value of property and the level of economic activity within the authority. In contrast, the general grant is
progressive in character and balances the paucity of sources of local
revenue. This is more obvious in development towns than in other settlements. In recent years, the general grant was cancelled in a number of cities which had considerable sources of independent revenue.
This increased the progressive nature of the grant.

60. Sharkansky (1984), pp. 27-49.
61. For a discussion of the subject, see State Comptroller (1979), pp.
348-54.
62. Based on a list of religious councils and their budgets from the
year 1982 provided by the Ministry of Interior, August 1984.
63. See Naor et al. (1978), Chapter 5, pp. 137-54.
64. According to the estimates, the independent income of the religious councils ranged from about 3 percent of expenditures in a small
authority to about 25 percent in several of the larger cities.
65. See State Comptroller (1975), pp. 281-93.
66. The topic is discussed by the State Comptroller on several occasions. Compare State Comptroller (1983), pp. 174-81.
67. The Budget for Jewish Religious Services Law, 5709-1949;
"Regulations Concerning the Administration of the Religious Councils," *Official Regulations* 2573, (18 June 1970), sections 4-5.
68. Compare State Comptroller (1976), p. 372, which reports on the
employment of 2,600 persons in religious councils. The estimate was
based on data concerning the expansion of the work force in other parts
of the local sector.
69. Central Bureau of Statistics (1984b).
70. For a discussion of the issue, see State Comptroller (1984), pp.
236-40, as well as the earlier annual reports in the chapters on the
Ministry of Religious Affairs. Some of these problems are reflected
in the journal, *Hachever,* which is sponsored by the Union of Religious
Councils. See especially the symposium in Kislev 5731 (1971); Barzel
(1973).
71. Compare Central Bureau of Statistics (1984), p. 24, which specifies
the dates of receipt of municipal status of the cities.
72. Maoz (1962), pp. 233-40.
73. "The Koenig Document," 30 March 1976 (internal). Reches (1976).

74. See report by The Committee for the Determination of the Structure of Expenditures in the Local Councils of the Minorities (1973) (The Geraissy Committee).

PART III — BUDGET AND FINANCE

Chapter 7

THE FINANCING OF LOCAL AUTHORITIES

Arye Hecht

The Activities of the Public Sector

Local authorities are responsible for maintaining a suitable environment for the population within their jurisdictions, and for providing them with assorted environmental and communal services. Thus the local authorities comprise a part of the "public sector" which operates an extensive network of institutions for public and individual welfare. The activities of the public sector stem from the decisions of the delegated bodies, which are expressed in the various laws, regulations, precedents and formal prescriptions.

The activities of this sector can be described from several different perspectives including the economic perspective. The activities of the public sector are usually divided into three main groups:[1] *allocation functions,* which are meant to supplement the market mechanisms in the distribution of economic resources; *distribution of income functions,* intended to achieve desired changes in the distribution of income and wealth of the country; *economic stabilization functions,* which entail directing the national economy in the areas of development, employment, prices, balances of payments, etc.

Local authorities fit into this scheme primarily through the execution of the first group of functions — the allocation of resources or, in other words, the improvement of economic efficiency. Other economic efficiency functions include the provision of services which comprise "the public good," from which many different individuals simultaneously benefit, without any additional expense to each individual, and whose provision is unavoidable no matter what the cost (internal and external security are obvious examples of this type of service).

Another function is the performance of activities which are "externalities." These are activities performed by one individual who bears the burden of the expense, but which are of value to other individuals as well (such as the spraying of pesticides) or, alternatively, activities performed by one individual who does not bear the burden of the entire cost, but rather disturbs and damages the environment, which results in a social cost. This type of activity includes all of the environmental pollution created by the improper disposal of industrial wastes, spills, odors and noise.

An additional function is the provision of services which are also provided by the free market, but in insufficient quantity. These services are produced by the free market only to the extent that they can be sold at a price which covers cost. The price at which it can be sold reflects it marginal value to the individuals willing to buy the service. A society may decide that the overall utility to society of the provision of a certain service on a larger scale is considerably higher than the sum of all private utilities, and therefore that the service should be widely provided, without direct payment by the consumers. Education and health services, for instance, are of this type.

Other efficiency functions which the public sector is called upon to provide include the prevention of market distortions caused by monopolies, development of high risk projects, proper utilization of limited natural resources (water, oil, minerals) and services requiring a high investment, whose yield is not guaranteed (public transportation, mail, telephone, etc.).

The functions of the local authorities as they have developed in Western countries are included in the group of "allocation" functions mentioned briefly above. "Distribution of income" functions and "economic stabilization" functions require national policy, and generally refer to the national economy.[2] Indeed, it is possible that a certain activity required of local authorities fits in with policies for "distribution of income" or "economic stabilization," but this does not mean that a single local authority can set policy or make significant decisions in these areas.

Generally, the state government will have difficulty tolerating different levels of well-being among local authorities, whether due to a level of services far from the accepted standard, or to a level of taxes or other sources of support which vary from the norm. Similarly, the state government will be unable to sufficiently counteract the activities of local authorities if they deviate from economic policy. Therefore the local authorities are integrated into activities designed to influence the distribution of income and economic stabilization as a result of direction from national policy-makers.

The Activities of Local Authorities

Local authorities in Israel are integrated into the activities of the public sector according to the usual principles. Local authorities are not concerned with economic and social policy, but rather with the tasks of allocation of resources, including both those functions which the business sector is unable to perform at all, and those which the business sector would perform at a level and extent which would not achieve the social goals.

In the early years after the establishment of the state, Jewish local authorities carried out extensive functions in the areas of health, education and welfare, including policy-making concerning the level of services and the ways in which they should be performed. This situation was a holdover from the period of the British Mandate. The British had not bothered to properly develop public services, which were therefore established through the initiative of the local community.

Over time the Knesset, usually at government initiative, has enacted laws organizing the areas of education and welfare, clarifying both the rights of citizens and the obligations of the government and the local authorities. Over the years conceptions have developed in the fields of health, education and welfare which are similar to those accepted throughout the Western world — establishment of detailed national policy, setting up state resources to finance a major portion of the services, and even their performance by government institutions.[3] Although some of the centralization was carried out in the context of efforts to improve the financing of the local authorities, this was in accordance with accepted principles, and it is even possible to assume that, one way or another, the centralization process would have run its course in any case.

In that same period, those services which do not require national policy were developed considerably. Among these services are environmental services (local services), most of which have been prescribed by law, and among them some which were legislated entirely during the period of the state. Laws in the areas of planning and building, water and sewage, civil defense and fire protection, public beaches and licensing of businesses were established by the Knesset at government initiative, but they allow the local authorities to establish their own policies in various areas with only general restrictions. Other environmental services such as road systems, public gardening and cleaning, as well as certain social services such as community and cultural centers, are not completely fixed by law and local authorities are given extensive freedom of action.

What is the extent of the services of local authorities relative to economic activity in the country in general, and relative to the entire public sector? One way to evaluate this is by comparing the expenditures of local authorities to the Gross National Product (GNP) and to all of the expenditures of the public sector.[4] Table 7.1 presents data on the expenditures of the local authorities in comparison to the GNP and government expenditures during years chosen from the period from 1960 to 1981.

From the table it is apparent that the relationship between the GNP and expenditures of local authorities (column 7) is quite stable, varying from about 7 percent to about 9 percent over the period of more than twenty years surveyed by the data. In contrast, the proportion of municipality expenditures relative to government expenditures decreased during the late 1960s (column 8). It is easy to see (column 9) that this decrease was not due to instability in local municipality expenditures, but rather to the considerable growth in the government budget during the 1970s. This growth in the government budget stemmed largely from defense expenditures and from repayment of loans, and not necessarily from progress and development in the services. Therefore it does not reflect a relative decrease in the expenditures of the local authorities. An additional analysis of the data reveals that the expenditures of local authorities increased by a factor of 720 during the years between 1960–1981. This increase is notably higher than the combined increase in the Consumer Price Index and in the population. In other words, the expenditures of the local authorities increased in real terms, and it can be assumed that they made possible an increase in the level and extent of services. The growth of expenditures by local authorities was higher than the growth in the GNP, but considerably lower than the growth of state government expenditures. The growth of the national product and most of the increase in the government budget made possible an increase in the standard of living and with it an improvement in the level of public services.[5] Local authority expenditures grew relative to the national product in the years between 1960–1976. From that year onward, due to a decrease in resources available for activities in the public sector in the context of government policy, there was a freeze, if not a slight decrease, in expenditures.

Table 7.1

LOCAL AUTHORITY EXPENDITURES IN COMPARISON TO THE GROSS NATIONAL PRODUCT AND TO GOVERNMENT EXPENDITURES: 1960-1981

Year (1)	Authority Expenditures (in millions of shekels) (2)	Gross National Product (in millions of shekels) (3)	Government Expenditures (in millions of shekels) (4)	End-of-year Population (in thousands) (5)	Consumer Price Index on the Basis of January 1959 (6)	Authority Expenditures as a % of GNP (7)=(2):(3)	Authority Expenditures as a % of Government Expenditures (8)=(2):(5)	Government Expenditures as a % of GNP (9)=(4):(3)
1960	30	439	173	2,150	104	6.8	17.3	39
1965	89	1,025	440	2,598	148	8.6	20.2	43
1970	144	1,934	1,234	3,022	182	7.4	11.6	64
1975	701	7,889	7,303	3,943	549	8.9	9.6	93
1976	961	10,523	9,742	3,575	738	9.1	9.9	93
1977	1,386	15,239	14,602	3,653	1,019	9.1	9.5	96
1978	2,328	26,228	22,610	3,738	1,549	8.9	10.2	86
1979	4,473	51,906	47,802	3,836	3,024	8.6	9.4	92
1980	9,945	124,668	111,099	3,922	7,066	8.0	8.9	89
1981	21,592	292,261	246,306	3,978	14,842	7.4	8.8	84

Sources: Yearly and monthly reports of the Central Bureau of Statistics and yearly booklets (Central Bureau of Statistics and the Ministry of Interior).

Comments: 1) Beginning in 1970 the National Product was transferred according to the fiscal year.
2) Government expenditures include the budget with the business projects.

Without a doubt, the period between 1965–1975 was a period of considerable expansion for services provided by local authorities, based on the view that the public should be provided the services which it requests and in which society is interested. As we will see later on, government participation in financing, along with a constant increase in the independent and transferred income of the local authorities, made the expansion of local services possible. The trend toward real expansion of the local authority expenditures was halted with the beginning of the accelerated inflation of the mid-1970s.

Expenditures have not generally increased in recent years beyond the level necessary to match price increases and population growth. In this situation it is possible to see a cutback in local services and especially in investments included in development budgets. Naturally, the services continued to expand, in accordance with the decisions and habits of the past, even during a period marked by cutbacks. This trend results from the fact that when a policy is set for the advancement of social or environmental issues, it cannot be simultaneously applied in all of the local authorities in the country. This same problem applies as well on the level of each individual municipality.

During the 1970s, the structure of of the educational system developed at a rapid pace in the wake of the deployment of a network of pre-kindergarten nurseries, and the development of the reform in education which led to the establishment of middle schools, requiring new buildings and equipment. In those same years daycare centers were developed, a new style of community center (Centers for Culture, Youth and Sport) was established, and care for the aged was expanded. In the environmental field, there was progress in the building of plants for sewage purification and disposal, and garbage collection disposal. In general, the roads and their accessories (signs, lighting, safety devices) improved.

The momentum initiated with the development of infrastructure and services was not halted and could not be halted by various restrictive policies. Therefore, if it seems from the data that towards the end of the 1970s the increase in real expenditures was halted, that must mean that the increase in services and the development of new infrastructure was absorbed by the existing framework. This absorption could have been effected by improved efficiency, which made it possible to provide equal services with few inputs. In this way resources were released for the expansion of services. Of course, the absorption could also have occurred as a result of a decline in the level of some of the services. Thus, for instance, in the beginning of the 1980s the subsidized lunch program in the elementary schools which had existed since the establishment of the state was cancelled.

An additional way to explain the absorption is that it came at the expense of defective maintenance of buildings, roads, water and sewage pipes, etc. There is reason to assume that the level of maintenance of public buildings declined as a result of a lack of funds. This makes sense, since it is easier to decrease maintenance costs because the painful effects are not immediately felt. However, over and above all of the other budget cutbacks is the drastic decrease — nearly in half — of the real expenditures in "non-ordinary" budgets which made up a significant portion of local authority expenditures.

At the end of the 1970s then, the scope of the expenditures narrowed due to changes in the structure of the services and a drastic decline in the development of the environmental infrastructure and the construction of new public buildings. The above trends clearly indicate that the activities of local authorities are intertwined with the activities of the public sector, whether developing parallel to an increase in the public standard of living, or responding to an economic policy which required cut-backs.

The Structure of Local Authority Budgets

Local authorities perform several different kinds of activities. Some of their functions are not dependent on financing. These include the legislation of by-laws for influencing public behavior, activities related to land and decisions regarding physical planning, and activities within the state government organs, media and elsewhere designed to increase awareness of the authority's problems.

Most of the activities of the authority, however, do require financial expenditures. The approval of a budget detailing the authority's program of activities which require financing is the authority's central decision-making process. In order that those preparing and deciding upon the budget can make the details of the budget as clear as possible, it is necessary for the budget to be prepared systematically and according to a well-known structure. Thus an official local authority "budget structure" was introduced by way of regulations, which requires every local authority to prepare its budget for approval according to the same structure. Indeed, setting a uniform structure does pose something of a limitation on the ability of the local authority to express its decisions. Since it cannot be assumed, however, that every local authority has experts available to prepare documents to clarify the data, there is no escaping the need for uniform rules. At the same time, there is nothing preventing the administration of an authority from preparing additional explanations, material, and even an additional presentation of data, as is indeed the practice in several local authorities.

The "Regulations Concerning the Preparation of Local Authority Budgets," as most recently published in 1970, state that the ordinary budget will include an "estimate of payments whose repayment falls in that same year and allocations to funds in that same year" (section 1), while the non-ordinary budget is designated for "one-time activities" (section 15). At first glance it seems that the difference between the "ordinary budget" and the "non-ordinary budget" is in the type of expenditure. In other words, ongoing expenses — those which must be paid for during the year, including loans — are included within the ordinary budget. One-time expenses which are generally investments in future development should be included in the "non-ordinary budget." However, a more detailed analysis of the relevant definitions and directives leads to the conclusion that the central distinction is not according to the type of expense but rather according to the method of financing.

The conception established in the early years of the state was that "the ordinary budget is built on the local authority's ordinary income from municipal taxes, levies and government participation."[6] That is to say, all of the ongoing income which derives from permanent and repetitive sources belongs in the ordinary budget. The expenditure budget includes all the ongoing expenditures as well as the contribution of the local authority to the non-ordinary budget. The primary function of the ordinary budget is to finance the expense of providing regular services. It is clear that such services must be financed by permanent and repetitive income. However, it is also necessary to set aside some of this income in order to help finance the local authority's investments, which include work on the infrastructure, purchases, the construction of public buildings and the like. This setting aside can be done in two ways. First, the repayment of loans is entirely included in the ordinary budget. Loans are generally received to finance investments. Therefore, the financing of the repayment of the loans (not to be confused with the cost of financing the interest) with ongoing income in the context of the ordinary budget, is evidence of the participation of the ordinary budget in investments. Secondly, during most years there have been explicit transfers of sums from the ordinary budget to the non-ordinary budget. These come primarily from surpluses from an over-collection of taxes earmarked for development (sewage tax, road tax, and pipe-laying tax) and an improvement tax which is not earmarked for any specific project. Thus, all of the ongoing income is listed in the ordinary budget, including that which is used to finance one-time activities.

In the non-ordinary budget, non-ordinary income is listed, especially loans. Since during the last two decades loans have been made available nearly every year to balance the ordinary budget or to cover its deficits, it was necessary to list these amounts in the non-ordinary budget (since it is not ongoing income) and then transfer them to the ordinary budget.

The State Commission on Local Government (Sanbar Commission) recommended that in the future the ordinary budget be set aside for ongoing services and the cost of their maintenance, and should also include the depreciation of buildings, machinery, pipes and equipment. The non-ordinary budget should be used only for development activities and will include the entire capital account — allocations for depreciation from the ordinary budget, all of the income earmarked for the financing of infrastructure development, and loans. Therefore, every loan payment will also be in the capital account. In this way a clearer economic picture can be received of the financing of both services and investments, including the renewal of machinery and equipment.[7]

Table 7.2 presents the development of the expenditure budgets in the local authorities during the years 1960–1981 (in millions of shekels and percentages). From the data it is apparent (columns 5 and 6) that the importance of expenditures in the non-ordinary budget reached its peak in the mid-1960s and then declined drastically. This is a result of cutbacks in resources available to the local authorities. From columns 7 and 8 in table 7.2 it is apparent that the trend of increasing local authority activity accompanied an even higher increase in development expenditures (in the years 1960–1965 and 1970–1975), while during the years in which there are signs of a decline in local authority expenditures, development expenditures declined even faster than ordinary

271

Table 7.2

EXPENDITURES IN THE ORDINARY AND NON-ORDINARY BUDGETS OF LOCAL AUTHORITIES: 1960-1981

Year (1)	In Millions of Shekels			In Percentages			
	Total Expenditures (2)	Ordinary Budget (3)	Non-ordinary Budget (4)	Ordinary Budget out of Total Budget (5)	Non-Ordinary Budget out of Total Budget (6)	Growth of Ordinary Budget (7)	Growth of Non-Ordinary Budget (8)
1960	30	22	8	73	27		
1965	89	64	25	72	28	190	211
1970	144	113	31	78	22	77	24
1975	701	517	184	74	26	358	494
1976	961	734	722	76	24	42	23
1977	1,386	1,102	284	80	20	50	25
1978	2,328	1,881	447	81	19	71	96
1979	4,483	3,692	776	83	17	96	74
1980	4,945	8,618	1,327	87	13	133	71
1981	21,592	18,160	3,432	84	16	110	159

Sources of Data: Pamphlets: "Local Authorities in Israel," published by the Ministry of Interior and the Central Bureau of Statistics, from 1964/65 onward.

Comments: 1) Column "Total Expenditures" is parallel to column (2) in table 7.1.
2) The distinction between expenditures in the ordinary budget and those of the non-ordinary budget was made in accordance with the explanation in note 7.

expenditures (1965–1970 and 1976–1980). The year 1981 is an exception since increased budgets (relative to 1980) were made available to local authorities following a cutback in the development budget which even the Ministry of Finance considered too drastic.

There are many reasons for the relative flexibility in the reduction of resources for development needs during a period dominated by restrictive spending policies. When activity increases and the reins are loosened, local authorities act vigorously to take advantage of the increased availability of financing and step up the development of the municipal infrastructure and the construction of public buildings. During such periods of heightened activity, very little attention is paid to the impact on future budgets, with the resulting need to repay loans and cover maintenance and operation costs.

The distinctions between income and expenditures in the ordinary budget vis-a-vis the non-ordinary budget enables the local authority to systematically plan its activities while clarifying the different types of incomes and expenditures. The distinction also enables government ministries to follow more exactly the development of activities of local authorities and especially to integrate them into overall economic policy. As mentioned above, the State Commission on Local Government recommended that the budgetary structure be made more efficient so as to present a clearer economic picture.

The Composition of Local Authority Expenditures

Up to this point we have discussed the general structure of local authority budgets; now we will turn to their specific components. The budget is divided into chapters and sections which make it possible to identify both the designated expenditure of any budgeted sum and the way it was actually spent. Budgets are divided in the same way in all local authorities in accordance with regulations concerning accounting and budgetary preparation procedures. Thus it is possible to calculate the total expenditures and income for all local authorities and to compare expenditures and income for different local authorities and different years.

A listing of the sections of the budget makes it possible to identify every expenditure according to two criteria: 1) the purpose of the expenditure ("functional categorization,") or service given through this expenditure; 2) the type of expenditure ("economic categorization") or the type of input paid for by the budgeted sum (payment of wages or activities, etc.). A concentration of the data of all local authorities makes it possible to follow the trends in the development of activities of local authorities as they are reflected in the budgetary system.

In the ordinary budget the expenditures are divided according to the following groupings:

a. **General Administration** — Earmarked for the operation of the local authority council land administration — general administration (local authority secretary, legal advisor, personnel administration, public relations, local authority property and internal inspections); financial administration (authority treasurer, accountants, collection of taxes, account management, cash flow management and more) and the costs of financing, when they are general and not identifiable according to the various services.

b. **Local Services** — This category concentrates on expenditures for services which maintain the immediate environment of the local authority at a level prescribed by the council: sanitation services (street cleaning, garbage collection and removal, sewage collection and removal, veterinary services and the overseeing of by-laws); security and protection (civil defense services, guarding, firefighting, preparation for emergencies and the authority's part in the operation of the civil guard); planning and overseeing of construction (preparation of master plans and approval of detailed plans, granting building permits and overseeing the construction and other work of the local authority); maintenance of public property (roads, lighting, public gardens, beaches and pools); and agricultural services (in regional councils and authorities which maintain an agricultural committee).

c. **Public Services** — Services to the community and the individual, most of which are prescribed in laws and regulations, as well as those left to the discretion of the local authority — education, cultural activities, welfare, health and participation in the financing of religious services.

The Financing of Local Authorities

d. **Projects and Other Expenditures** — This group includes those services financed completely by direct income from the sale of services, thus generally comprising a "closed economy": water works; slaughterhouses; stadiums; traffic and building projects; business property (apartments, stores, markets, etc.). This group also includes a section for non-ordinary expenses, those which lack their own defined section.

The categorization of expenditures according to the structure prescribed in the regulations requires every local authority to prepare its budget and to present it for approval by the Ministry of Interior. This categorization makes possible the preparation of a "program budget" or a budget prepared in some other way. Indeed, the budget structure does not obligate the authority to a specific organizational structure and it is conceivable that a local authority will make available different parts of the approved budget to every unit manager; parts grouped from different sections or the opposite, more detailed parts from within a larger section.

The budget structure as described serves principally as the structure of the ordinary budget. With slight changes it can be adapted to suit the needs of the local authority when it must note the sections of the non-ordinary budget as well.

A change in the relative importance of different expenditures in the sections of the budget can reflect both the policies of the local authority and the influence of state government decisions in the Knesset or Cabinet. Decisions of the state government generally concern the development of a certain service, the transfer of a service from state to local authorities (or vice versa), a change in who will bear the expense (to be distinguished from performance of the service), or a global or specific cutback in services. As has been noted, in every local authority there are always development projects underway, making it inevitable that a local authority will change the components of its expenditures in the ordinary budget in some way after the work is completed. However, even during periods of budgetary cutbacks, the local authority can develop locally-generated income from one item or another in order to promote whatever it sees as essential.

Table 7.3 presents the composition of local authority expenditures according to budget chapters (designation) in 1963-1981, in millions of shekels and in percentages. From the data in the table it is apparent that the composition of expenditures has remained relatively stable in the overall expenditures for local and state

275

Table 7.3

EXPENDITURES IN THE ORDINARY BUDGETS OF LOCAL AUTHORITIES: 1963-1981

	In Millions of Shekels					In Percentages				
Year (1)	Total (2)	General Administration (3)	Local Services (4)	State Services (5)	Works and other Expenditures (6)	Total (7)	General Administration (8)	Local Services (9)	State Services (10)	Works and other Expenditures (11)
1963	41	3	13	19	56	100	7	32	46	15
1968	84	6	25	41	12	100	7	30	49	14
1973	238	20	71	121	26	100	8	30	51	11
1978	1,881	244	529	919	189	100	13	28	49	10
1981	18,159	2,550	4,645	9,184	1,780	100	14	26	50	10

Sources of Data: "Local Authorities in Israel," published by the Ministry of Interior and the Central Bureau of Statistics.
Note: In the data for 1968 the amount for repayment of loans — a fund returned from the non-ordinary budget — was divided among "local services," "state services" and "works" according to the relative repayment of debts.

services. The expenditures for "general administration" increased in importance over the years, apparently due to the stabilization of administrative arrangements during those years, such as salaries for mayors, automatic data processing and internal control systems. It is particularly noteworthy that the expense of financing increased from 1973 onward. In accordance with new directives, the interest and linkage to inflation of loans received to reduce past deficits are now listed in the sections for financial expenditures. The very existence of deficits required a certain increase in financial expenditures resulting from interest on overdrafts and delays in payment of financial obligations. A reduction in the importance of expenditures for projects and "other expenses" derives partly from a change in the way payments charged to deficits are listed, as explained above, and partly from a reduction in activities related to slaughterhouses which were closed or sold, stadiums which were taken over by sports unions or companies, and the like. The major project is the "water project" — there is a basis for the hypothesis that expenditures for this project lagged somewhat behind overall development, due to the moderate rise in the price of water to local authorities, both as purchasers of water from the national water economy and also as suppliers to residents.

The relative stability in the importance of "services" does not indicate that local authority activities were stagnant. We have already seen that the level of activity increased over the years in real terms and in certain years at a particularly rapid rate. A detailed analysis shows that there have been improvements in all of the service branches and that their levels in the 1980s are not at all similar to levels in the 1950s and 1960s. Over the years the state services have developed nurseries for three and four-year-old children, day care centers, comprehensive schools, supplementary education, centers for culture, youth and sport, libraries and welfare services. Local services have also developed at the same time. Garbage collection and removal equipment has been modernized; central sewage systems have been installed and sewage purification plants constructed; security services have been developed (civil defense, fire fighting, civil guard); master plans and detailed plans have been prepared; and public facilities have been installed at a high and efficient level (roads, lighting, public parks, playing fields, beaches, pools, etc.).

Data from the non-ordinary budget are divided up similarly according to the designation of the expenditure. Naturally, almost

Local Government in Israel

every expenditure for "public works" is included in the chapters "local services," "state services" and "projects." Only rarely will there be expenditures in the "general administration" sections (for construction of local council offices, or for purchasing storage space or data processing units). Also in the composition of expenditures in the non-ordinary budget there appears to be relative stability during the surveyed period. There was no increase or decrease in the importance of any particular type of expenditure, even though there was a large decline in the scope of expenditures at the end of the 1970s and the beginning of the 1980s.

Table 7.4 shows the composition of local authority expenditures in the ordinary budget, categorized according to the type of expenditure in selected years from 1963 to 1981, in millions of shekels and in percentages. In the budget and accounting procedures of local authorities, the section "expenditures for activities" is divided four ways, distinguishing between various types of organizational expenditures and expenditures which are directly for "activities." Due to the lack of exact definitions, it is customary to consider all of these sections as one. The sections for "wages and salaries" include expenditures for employing personnel directly by the local authorities. These sections do not include personnel hired by contractors who perform services for the local authorities. "Wages and salaries" also includes any expenditure incurred for wages from the point of view of the employer — pension payments, social welfare expenses (payments to national insurance and various funds) and taxes on wages (employer tax and loan, and value added tax).

From the table it can be seen that toward 1981, there was a significant decline in importance of the repayment of loans. This decline derives from a reduction in the scope of loans made available to local authorities, both for balancing their budgets and for investment ("development activities"). During that same year there had still not been full expression of the worsening conditions for repayment of loans from the national budget which were received after May 1979, due to linkage to the Consumer Price Index.

It is also clear from the table that in each year there was a small allocation in the ordinary budget for "one-time expenses" for small purchases or transfers from the non-ordinary budgets. As mentioned above, this is a symbolic participation in investments, while the primary allocation from the ordinary budget for this purpose goes to the repayment of loans.

Table 7.4

COMPOSITION OF LOCAL AUTHORITY EXPENDITURES IN THE ORDINARY BUDGET BY TYPE: 1963-1981

In Millions of Shekels

Year (1)	Total (2)	Wages (3)	Expenditures for Activities (4)	Participation (5)	One-time Expenditures (6)	Repayment of Loans (7)
1963	41	14	—	—19—	—	8
1968	84	35	22	8	2	17
1973	238	93	55	35	8	47
1978	1,881	684	470	248	42	437
1981	18,159	7,499	5,039	2,398	510	2,713

In Percentages

Year (8)	Total Activities (9)	Wages Expenditures (10)	Expenditures for Loans (11)	Participation (12)	One-time (13)	Repayment (14)
1963	100	34	—	—46—	—	20
1968	100	42	26	10	2	20
1973	100	39	23	15	3	20
1978	100	37	25	13	2	23
1981	100	41	28	13	3	15

Sources: 1963 — Ministry of Interior
1968 onwards — "Local Authorities in Israel," Ministry of Interior.

The section "participations" represents transfer payments to various deserving persons. There was an increase in this category in the beginning of the 1970s with the improvement of entitlement rules for those requiring welfare services. After the performance of "guaranteeing income" passed in 1982 from the domain of the local authorities to that of the National Insurance (Social Security), there was a considerable decline in local authority expenditures in this section.

Expenditures for "wages and salaries" and expenditures for activities fluctuated slightly over the years. The fluctuations reflect differences between the increase in real wages versus the increase in prices, in addition to other real changes such as a constant increase in the number of employees until 1979 and a slight decline in every following year. Only a precise analysis might identify the influence of every possible component in the changes.

The non-ordinary budget for public works can also be presented according to type of expenditure — the purchase and expropriation of property, construction planning and equipment purchase. However, the data shows that the dominant expenditure over all of the years was for "contracted projects," while the rest of the expenditures are relatively insignificant.

The Composition of Local Authority Resources

Among the characteristics of governing bodies such as local authorities is the ability to prescribe obligatory payments (taxes, levies, etc.) and to enforce their collection. It might be assumed that local authorities would finance their activities with locally-generated income, but in reality such a situation exists today neither in the state of Israel nor in any other country. The local authorities are aided by the financial participation of the state government.

As we have seen, local authority budgets are divided into two parts — the ordinary budget and the non-ordinary budget. The ordinary budget includes those incomes which repeat themselves annually and is earmarked for the financing of ongoing services, repayment of loans and, to the extent possible, participation in the development budget. The non-ordinary budget is earmarked for the financing of one-time expenses and is based on non-ordinary finances, loans which are received from time to time as well as other financing earmarked for investments or development activities. Table 7.5 presents the incomes of local authorities in various years beginning with 1953. In this table all data for loans which were received for balancing the budget or for reducing accumulated deficits has been condensed and listed as income in the ordinary budget, in addition to a listing of the expenditure for which it was earmarked. This representation deviates somewhat from accepted accounting procedures. In this way the non-ordinary budget is expressed in only those amounts designated for development activities, according to their financing.

From the data in the table we can learn that up until the 1980s, 20 to 30 percent was consistently preserved for investment budgets. As noted when discussing the composition of local authority expenditures, development budgets change at an accelerated rated in conjunction with changes in the national economy and in national economic policy, and the rate of expenditures is primarily influenced by the possibilities for mobilizing resources. Since the beginning of the 1980s, there have been several consecutive years characterized by tight fiscal policy applied in all government ministries, which has led to drastic reductions in resources available for local authority investments. As we shall see below, there has indeed been a certain expansion of locally-generated income designated for development work, but this cannot replace the amounts cut from the budgets of government ministries, resulting in a decline in the proportion of development resources in local budgets. An additional calculation shows that already in the 1970s, there were signs of a decline in the rate of expansion of resources in the ordinary budget.

The data in table 7.6 shows the composition of incomes of local authorities by source of income. Self-generated income includes all those receipts which the local authority collects itself through its workers, or in other ways directly into its treasury. This group includes the general municipal tax, water tax, sewage tax, other taxes and levies, school tuition, rental payments for use of municipal property and the like. In the past, local authorities also collected a property tax, business tax, entertainment levy and recreation tax. Transferred incomes[8] are those that the local authority receives by law from sums which the state government collects. These sums are transferred in proportion to the amount

Table 7.5

INCOME OF LOCAL AUTHORITIES: 1953-1981

Year (1)	In Millions of Shekels			In Percentages		
	Total Income (2)	Income in Ordinary Budget (3)	Income in Non-Ordinary Budget (4)	Total Income (5)	Income in Ordinary Budget (6)	Income in Non-Ordinary Budget (7)
1953	8	6	2	100	75	25
1958	21	15	6	100	71	29
1963	55	40	15	100	73	27
1968	109	86	23	100	79	21
1973	326	231	95	100	71	29
1978	2,148	1,701	447	100	79	21
1981	20,865	17,499	3,366	100	84	16

Source: 1953–1958: A. Morag: *Financing the Government in Israel*, pp. 316–21.
1963: Data of the Ministry of Interior and pamphlets "Local Authorities in Israel" (Central Bureau of Statistics and Ministry of Interior).
1969–1981: "Local Authorities in Israel," (Central Bureau of Statistics and Ministry of Interior).

Table 7.6

COMPOSITION OF LOCAL AUTHORITY INCOME IN THE ORDINARY BUDGET: 1953-1981

In Millions of Shekels

Year (1)	Total Income (2)	Locally-generated Income (3)	Transferred Income (4)	Government Participation (5)	Loans (6)
1953	6	4	—	2	—
1958	15	12	—	3	—
1963	40	32	—	6	2
1968	86	48	10	21	7
1973	231	82	44	78	27
1978	1,701	522	269	758	152
1981	17,499	6,251	1,681	8,902	665

In Percentages

Year (7)	Total Income (8)	Locally-generated Income (9)	Transferred Income (10)	Government Participation (11)	Loans (12)	Total Income (13)	Designated Income (14)	Non-designated Income (15)
1953	100	86	—	33	—	100	?	?
1958	100	80	—	25	—	100	?	?
1963	100	80	—	15	5	100	48	52
1968	100	56	12	24	8	100	42	58
1973	100	35	19	34	12	100	40	60
1978	100	31	16	45	8	100	38	62
1981	100	36	9	15	4	100	51	49

Sources: See table 7.5.
Notes: 1) In 1953 and 1958 the data for government participation do not allow for separation between the general grant and ministry participation. Therefore there is no data on designated incomes.
2) Non-designated incomes include loans.
3) Transferred incomes until 1969 were insignificant and included in locally-generated income.

283

collected within the area of the local authority or according to a formula prescribed in law or regulation. Among these are compensation for the property tax, appreciation tax, purchase tax, building permit charge and compensation for recreation levies. The transferred amounts appear in their entirety in the national budget as transferred income.

The third group is government ministry participation, which includes a general grant not earmarked to finance specific services. Such participatory financing is granted by the Ministries of Education and Culture, Labor and Social Welfare, Health and Interior. The fourth group consists of loans. These do not comprise final income for the authority and concerns sums whose source is usually not in the national budget, but in the banks and in the issuing of government bonds.

As mentioned above, the division according to these groups is primarily technical and reflects the ways in which the moneys reach the local authority. Indeed, there is also a more essential aspect reflected by this division. To the extent that a local authority has more independent resources, it is likely to have more control over allocation decisions and to be less dependent upon the state government. The same is true of transferred income; while transferred income is not directly collected by local authorities, it is guaranteed them by law. In contrast, government participation is largely dependent upon formulas which vary from time to time, uninfluenced by the wishes of individual local authorities or even their collective representatives. Thus it is apparent that part of government participation is dependent upon the discretion of ministry bureaucrats and is not assured by fixed and constant rules.

When we later take a closer look at the principal components of every group, however, we will find that this technical distinction between different types of income does not so clearly reflect local autonomy. We will find that in a significant portion of locally-generated income, the local authority does indeed collect the money from the public, but is unable to determine the levels and incidence of payment (e.g., the water tax, vehicle tax, and to a large extent, tuition in day care centers and kindergartens).

In the case of transferred income, the allocation rules can be changed by the state authorities each year. For example, the central section — exchange for property tax — is divided up according to regulations of the Ministry of Interior with the approval of the Knesset Committee for the Interior and Environmental Quality.

We will also discover that those specific sections relating to government participation such as participation in the financing of firefighting services, civil guard, preparations for emergency conditions and guard duty are all anchored in law. There are also stable arrangements for the rebate of tuition in high schools, which is supplemented by the state government, and which comes in place of the collection of graduated tuition from parents.

Therefore, we cannot estimate the degree of a local authority's control over its resources by merely calculating the proportion of locally-generated income in its overall income. There is no doubt that when this portion of income in a particular authority is high, the authority will also be more flexible in this decision-making and monetary management, even in periods of economic crisis. However, it is important to try and view the data from an additional perspective. This can be done by dividing the resources according to their belonging to one or another section of expenditures.[9] In columns (13) and (14) we have grouped those incomes which were collected in connection with the provision of certain services, with government ministry participation earmarked to finance specific services. In contrast are those incomes which reach the local authority from citizens or from the state government without being earmarked to finance any specific service.

From the data in table 7.6, it can be seen that since the end of the 1950s and until the beginning of the 1980s, there was a constant decline in the proportion of locally-generated income in the financing of local authorities. As will be seen later in the detailed description of the primary components of different types of income, some of the taxes and levies increased in real terms, at a rate which exceeded the rate of inflation during the same period. At the same time, as noted above, expenditures grew at a rate much faster than that of inflation. Sources of income needed to keep up with the level of services which developed. Locally-generated income was insufficient to meet this demand, and its proportion in the overall financing of services and loan repayments declined. Some of the changes derived from the cancellation of certain sections of income while they were replaced with other arrangements. The most conspicuous of these arrangements was the cancellation of the collection of property taxes in 1968 and their replacement by the "exchange for property tax" as a percentage of national taxes. In accordance with this, one can see the locally-generated income and the transferred income as one. However, even when joined, their proportion of overall income points to a constant decline over the years, from 80 percent in 1958 to 45 percent in 1981.

It is clear that if the proportion of locally-generated and transferred income declined, then of necessity the proportion of government participation increased. Two processes contributed to this increase in participation. One process brought significant improvements in the scope of earmarked ministry participation, primarily from the Ministry of Education and Culture and the Ministry of Labor and Social Welfare. For many years local authorities have claimed that the state government has placed responsibilities upon them without providing the appropriate funding. Without analyzing the many aspects of this claim, if there is indeed a legal or public obligation to designate full and specific funding for every "public service," and without going into the question of the efficiency of financing local authorities in this way instead of with non-designated funding, it is a fact that those government ministries which handled the matter (Ministry of Finance, Ministry of Interior and the designating ministries) brought about an increase in the level of financing for specific services. In a second process, the proportion of the general grant also increased in several of the years. In global terms, the general grant is calculated as the difference between estimated income and estimated expenditures. Naturally when the estimate of other income lags behind the increase in expenditures, this is increasingly covered by the grant. There is no evidence then of any intentional process whereby the proportion of locally-generated income was reduced and government participation increased, but rather a combination of uniform processes, some of which are detailed below.

A close look at columns (13) and (14) in table 7.6 shows that until the end of the 1970s the non-earmarked incomes, which leave local authorities with greater flexibility with regard to spending priorities, comprised over 50 percent and sometimes even more than 60 percent of income. During the 1980s, there has been a decline in the proportion of non-earmarked income and, of necessity, an increase in the proportion of earmarked income. The collection and study of additional data in the 1980s will be necessary to see whether this is a new consistent trend and, if so, to determine the factors which led to the change. Perhaps during years of budget cut-backs, those sections of the budget which are hardest hit are those expenditures which are not granted by law or fixed regulations.

In a similar way we can also look at those resources which are available to local authorities for financing development activities. Table 7.7 presents data on the types of income in the non-ordinary budgets of local authorities during selected years between 1953 and 1981.

The data reveals that in all of the periods the loans were the primary source of financing for development budgets. As noted earlier, non-ordinary budgets in this statistic are defined as those which are earmarked for investments only. According to a basic principle of finance, it makes sense to utilize loans only for purposes of investment, on the basis of knowledge that the benefit to be derived from the investment will be received over many years, with the justification that also in the future those who benefit from it (the taxpayers) will participate in financing the investment. This can be accomplished through loans which can be repaid over a number of years.

During the entire period, locally-generated income also served as an important source for financing development activities. These incomes are extremely diverse and are not dominated by any particular section. They include transfers from the ordinary budget, taxes and levies for the financing of roads, water and sewage installations, improvement levies, donations, income from accumulated funds and from the sale of property. As can be seen in column (7), this section served during the 1950s as a central source of funds. The dependency on loans developed during the 1960s and 1970s, while at the end of the 1970s and particularly since May 1979, with the beginning of increasing cut-backs in the development budget, there has been a decline in the availability of loans to the local authorities. With the worsening of loan terms from the national budget, it was decided to give some of the resources needed for development as grants rather than loans. At the same time that there was a decline in the portion of state government budgets designated for development, local authorities began again to turn increasingly to locally-generated income for development funds.

Thus we have seen that the proportion of locally-generated income in the non-ordinary budget is in constant decline and comprises no more than 30 percent of the financing of development activities. In both types of budgets the financial role of the state government has consistently increased. In the following sections we will discuss the historical development of specific sections of these budgets.

Table 7.7

LOCAL AUTHORITY INCOME IN THE NON-ORDINARY BUDGET: 1953-1981

	In Millions of Shekels				In Percentages			
Year (1)	Total Income (2)	Locally-generated Income (3)	Loans (4)	Government Participation (5)	Total Income (6)	Locally-generated Income (7)	Loans (8)	Government Participation (9)
1953	2	1	1	—	100	50	50	—
1958	6	2	4	—	100	33	67	—
1963	15	?	?	?	100	?	?	—
1968	23	5	18	—	100	22	78	—
1973	95	17	73	5	100	18	77	5
1978	447	62	329	56	100	14	74	12
1981	3,366	938	1,724	704	100	28	51	21

Sources: See table 7.5

Note: Government participation in the financing of non-ordinary budgets in the 1970s were insignificant.

Locally-Generated Income

We have seen in table 7.6 that the proportion of locally-generated income in the financing of the budget has declined significantly over the years. If in the late 1950s and the beginning of the 1960s, 80 percent of the ordinary budget was financed by locally-generated income, by 1981 this source of income comprised only 36 percent of the ordinary budget.

Before describing the primary components of locally-generated income and their development over the years, let us take a broader look at the role of "locally-generated income" in local authority financing. It is difficult to envision the existence of governmental bodies which are expected to perform the functions of maintaining the environment and providing for the welfare of their residents without their having the right to levy and collect taxes from those residents. Indeed, in Israel it is occasionally proposed to eliminate local authority taxes altogether and replace them with income from a set proportion of national taxes. However, even those who propose this do not suggest doing away completely with local collection of income. They refer only to cancellation of those taxes which are obligatory payments, have no specific designation, and are not collected in conjunction with any particular service. This does not imply the cancellation of levies, service charges or participation of property owners in the financing of public works.

It is both possible and economically and socially justifiable to collect the full or at least partial cost of service from those who benefit from that service.[10] Even those scholars who consider it essential that local authority financing be based upon user taxes recognize the need for additional sources of financing for a substantial portion of local authority activities. As long as most of the financing of local authorities came from locally-generated income, the role of non-specific taxes — obligatory payments not tied to any specific service — was more dominant. With a decline in the proportion of locally-generated income in the financing of local authorities, the section hardest hit was that of non-earmarked locally-generated income.

The central event in this process was the cancellation of the collection of the municipal property tax and its replacement by "transferred income." Over the years the tools for collection of earmarked income have improved, but their proportion has not been maintained, especially with the cancellation of the collection of high school tuition and its exchange for income from "government participation." During the 1960s and the beginning of the 1970s, there was a decline in the overall status of locally-generated income, since during most of those years local authorities were prevented from raising taxes to the levels required to finance their budgets. This trend began with the devaluation of Israeli currency in 1962 and the policy of economic stabilization which accompanied it. Until 1974, national economic policy required that the state government and those bodies subordinate to it freeze taxes nearly every year. This was in keeping with an economic policy which was based on a massive devaluation of the dollar exchange rate. Another element in this policy was a reduction in public spending which was required to reduce escalating inflation.

The year 1970 brought the additional element of "package deals" which accompanied wage agreements between the state government, the Histadrut-General Federation of Labor and the employers organizations. Thus, in the agreement on the package deals there was representation of the workers and employers as partners to the wage agreements, and of the state government as implementer of the national economic policy. The local authorities were not party to these agreements, but they were subordinate to them when it came to a freeze in tax rates and a reduction in spending.

At this time, the freeze in tax rates affected local authority financing differently than it affected state government financing. Nearly all obligatory payments which the state government collects are stated in terms of percentages of the taxable base. This is the case with the income tax, purchase tax, most customs duties, excise tax, value added tax and the like. In contrast, almost all of the obligatory payments (taxes, levies, etc.) of local authorities are stated in fixed amounts (at the time in Israeli pounds) relative to the tax base. In this situation, as economic activity, inflation and wage hikes increased, the state government collected higher amounts even though it did not raise its taxes. The local authorities, on the other hand, were stuck with the collection of a fixed rate of payment for a period of up to three years, despite a decrease in real value. Not only was it impossible to increase locally-generated income in real terms, but this income was not even linked to economic activity or to price increases.

While the package deals prevented the real growth of locally-generated income and especially affected those taxes and levies stated in fixed prices, the one section of income which was stated in percentages was affected in another way. The municipal property tax was collected as a percentage of the estimated value of real estate. The limited income from this tax during the period of economic stagnation in 1965 and 1966 resulted in its abolition and exchange for transferred income from state government taxes.

In the late 1970s and 1980s, practically no limitations were placed on local authorities with regard to their setting rates of taxes and levies. As long as there were package deals, they took place near the month of April, after the level of general municipal taxes had already been set for the coming fiscal year. It was possible, therefore, to develop the section of locally-generated income which remained by setting up mechanisms of linkage to levels of taxes and amounts of collection.

Table 7.8 presents the composition of locally-generated income according to groups of sections and in millions of shekels and percentages during the period 1953-1981. From this data it can be seen that during the surveyed period the proportion of income from services and property increased, while the proportion of general income declined. The developments described above particularly affected general income, primarily the general municipal tax and the property tax which normally were determined only once a year. Service incomes — according to by-laws and other fee schedules — can be adjusted from time to time, even when there are package deals or any type of economic policy.

During the 1980s, with the acceleration of inflation, ways were found to link general municipal tax levels and other taxes and levies to inflation, thus leading to constantly rising taxes. Therefore, the proportion of revenue from locally-generated income has increased slightly; an analysis of the data from those years should be able to determine both the proportion of each group and which types of income were most effective during the inflationary period.

General Purpose Locally-Generated Income

As mentioned earlier, it would have been proper for local authorities to finance a large portion of their income through general taxes, those taxes which are not collected in conjunction with provision of a service and which are not earmarked in advance for the financing of a specific service. Usually, authority taxes were

Table 7.8

COMPONENTS OF LOCALLY-GENERATED INCOME ACCORDING TO GROUPS OF SECTIONS: 1953-1981

Year (1)	In Millions of Shekels				In Percentages			
	Total Income (2)	General Taxes and Levies (3)	Income from Services and Properties (4)	Other Income (5)	Total (6)	General Taxes (7)	Income from Services and Properties (8)	Other Income (9)
1953	4.7	3.1	1.3	0.3	100	66	28	6
1958	13.0	7.9	4.9	0.2	100	61	38	1
1963	32.0	18.8	13.2	—	100	59	41	—
1968	48.0	24.7	22.9	0.4	100	51	48	1
1973	82.0	33.1	48.1	0.8	100	40	59	1
1978	522.0	228.6	291.4	2.0	100	44	56	—
1981	6,251.3	2,917.5	3,316.8	217.0	100	47	53	—

Sources: See table 7.5.
Comments: 1) Column (3) "General Taxes and Levies" includes the entertainment tax, welfare and recreation tax, and administrative fees. In the years 1953-1963, transferred income is also included — land transfer fees, land appreciation taxes and vehicle charges.
2) In column (2) "Total Income" is different than data in table 7.6 due to rounding.

based on the property within the jurisdiction of the authority, as well as on business and commerce, and developments in Israel initially followed this model. During the Mandate period, taxes based on property played an increasingly central role in the financing of local authorities.[11] The taxing of businesses was also largely based upon the ownership, maintenance or sale of land. Toward the end of the Mandate period a business tax was enacted and was accompanied by several other small business and commercial taxes for licensing, signs and the like. None of these played any significant part in municipal financing.

Table 7.9 presents data concerning general taxes in local authorities, in millions of shekels and in percentages, for the period 1953-1981. During this entire period the municipal property tax and the general municipal tax comprised the central components of general taxes.

Municipal Property Tax — From as far back as the period of Ottoman rule, local authorities were given the power to add to the *Vorko,* the government property tax, in order to finance their activities. During the British Mandate in the 1930s and 1940s, in accordance with the recommendations of various committees, a municipal property tax was developed and collected according to the Municipal Corporations Ordinance and the Local Council Ordinance. The definition of property according to its value, as a basis for the collection of the municipal tax, went through several incarnations. These included an adjustment to conditions which derived from the Rental Protection Law, which did not work to the advantage of property owners.

The municipal property tax was collected for four types of property: "buildings" (including the adjacent land); "agricultural land" (land actively cultivated for agriculture, livestock or forests); "occupied land" (land serving some kind of use, whether for storage, parking of cars or equipment); "building land" (any land not included in the above categories — this included non-cultivated agricultural land as well as land not designated for building in the immediate future).

The assessment of property was the responsibility of a municipal assessment committee appointed by the local council. The committee was required to include at least one person who was not a representative of the local council. At the time of the cancellation of the municipal property tax, the assessment committees were abolished and replaced by an assessment

Table 7.9

GENERAL TAXES OF LOCAL AUTHORITIES: 1953-1981

	In Millions of Shekels					In Percentages				
Year	Total	Municipal Property Tax	General Municipal Tax	Business Tax	Other Taxes	Total	Municipal Property Tax	General Municipal Tax	Business Tax	Other Taxes
(1)	(2)	(3)	(4)	(5)	(6)	(7)	(8)	(9)	(10)	(11)
1953	3.1	0.6	1.5	0.3	0.7	100	19	48	10	23
1958	7.9	2.0	3.7	0.6	1.6	100	25	47	8	20
1963	18.8	7.1	2.6	1.3	4.2	100	38	33	7	22
1968	24.7	—	12.9	2.4	9.4	100	—	52	10	38
1973	33.1	—	22.9	3.9	6.3	100	—	69	12	19
1978	228.6	—	169.9	27.4	31.3	100	—	74	12	14
1981	2,917.5	—	2,436.0	248.2	233.3	100	—	83	9	8

Sources: See table 7.5.
Comment: Column (6) "Other Taxes" includes the entertainment tax, welfare and recreation tax, and administrative fees. In the years 1953-1963, it also included all transferred income from land transfer fees, land appreciation taxes, and vehicle charges.

administrator who was appointed within the framework of the municipal administration. Decisions of the assessment committee were publicized in "assessment tables" in the office of the local authority. Appeal was possible before a local appeals board, and finally in the district court.

The assessment of building land was supposed to be based on its free market value. The value of agricultural land and occupied land were determined according to an estimate of rent which could be received for them; the assessment of buildings was calculated on the basis of estimated rental income, with due consideration for the impact of the Rental Protection Law.[12]

The municipal property tax grew at a rapid rate during the 1960s. If in the beginning of the 1950s it comprised less than half the amount collected from the general municipal tax, by 1963 the amounts collected from the property tax were higher than those collected from the general tax. In those same years and until the stagnation of 1965-66, the construction and real estate markets were booming. This enabled assessment committees to raise the assessments which served as a basis for collection, and also enabled the large local authorities to raise the percentages of the municipal property tax. At the same time, it became possible to efficiently collect the tax. Anyone who wished to sell his property was required to repay all debts to the local authority before the Office of the Land Registry would transfer title to the property. In those same years, municipal property tax collections on building land grew significantly[13] and surpassed collections from the other sources. The development of the municipal property tax was linked not only to the economic boom but also perhaps to the changing of the guard in a number of major local authorities in the 1950s, from parties of the right to parties of the left. The latter preferred to emphasize the taxation of property owners, rather than tenants of a property.

The crisis in the collection of the municipal property tax became apparent during the years of economic stagnation, which began in 1965, continued in 1966, and faded in the wake of the Six Day War in 1967. As is common in any economic crisis, the building and real estate markets were particularly hard hit. Construction projects declined, as did the transfer of land, especially that referred to as "building land." These declines brought with them a number of phenomena. It was no longer possible to raise the land assessments, since prices had gone down. The assessment committees were not quick to reduce assessments; even with a certain amount of inflation the assessments' nominal rate remained high. The scope of municipal property tax collection declined, whether because many land owners and contractors were left without enough cash, or because the sanctions for not listing transactions in the Office of Land Registry had lost its teeth now that so few transactions took place. Moreover, with the initiation of steps to increase economic activity, particularly in construction, it became clear that the debts of land owners had become a burden which prevented the effective implementation of the policy. In many cases the debts owed the municipality had reached unmanageable proportions due to the nonpayment of taxes over several years, and to the relatively high levels of taxes assessed. As a result of this combination of factors there was a decline in the collection of municipal property taxes, from 18.1 percent in 1964 to 13 percent in 1967, despite an inflation rate of about 10 percent during the same period.

Under these circumstances, and in light of the relative rigidity of expenditures, the local authorities agreed to partially accept the conclusions of the Commission for the Study of Methods of Taxation in the Local Authorities, chaired by the jurist Dr. Alfred Vitkon. One of the recommendations of the committee was to unify the assessment and collection of municipal property taxes with those of the general municipal tax and the government property tax. The local authorities agreed to concede collection of the municipal property tax and to receive in its place a fixed portion of the taxes collected by the state government. This solved a number of problems; the citizen was no longer taxed twice for his property — once by the government property tax and again by the municipal property tax. Another problem resolved was the issue of land payments by the Israel Lands Authority, which had been in constant conflict with those local authorities which had been declared "immigrant cities," in which the government undertook to pay local taxes. Local authorities sometimes determined the assessments for "building land" of the Lands Authority at a high level which was not justified by the real level of prices in that local authority. While it is true that the Lands Authority had the option of appealing before appeal boards and the courts, this was impractical for a body which administered about 90 percent of the country's land. In those years there were many attempts at compromise through arbitration between the local authorities, primarily in the development towns, and the Israel Lands Authority. However, the problem found its solution only with the cancellation of the municipal property tax.

A year before the cancellation of the tax, several changes took place in the wake of an amendment to the Municipal Corporations Ordinance which was intended to relieve the work of local authorities. The assessment committees were replace by an assessment administrator from among the municipal employees. The decisions of the council concerning levels of the municipal tax once again did not require the approval of the minister, though they were limited to a certain percentage ceiling. At the same time, the process of assessment remained a heavy burden on both the local authority and the local residents. The cancellation of the municipal property tax came as a relief to both.

General Municipal Tax — Since the cancellation of the municipal property tax, the general municipal tax has become the most important tax placed by local authorities on their residents. Today, this is the only tax whose levels are set by the local authority council, whose sums are collected by the local authority administration, and whose income is not earmarked for some predetermined use.

The power of the local authority to levy a general municipal tax derives from chapter 14 of the Municipal Corporations Ordinance and from chapter 10 of the Local Councils Ordinance. Regional councils have a somewhat more complex authority structure, as both the council and the local committee are empowered to levy similar general taxes.

In contrast to the municipal property tax, the general municipal tax is levied on those who inhabit property which is not building land. In other words, the general municipal tax applies to those who inhabit residential buildings, buildings for other purposes, agricultural land or occupied land. It is therefore possible to see the general municipal tax as a tax on residents or active inhabitants of property within the jurisdiction of the local authority; this is based on the assumption that it is they who enjoy the services of the local authority. To support this explanation it should be remembered that before 1972, empty buildings were exempt from the general municipal tax. The decision to tax owners of an empty building which remains unoccupied for more than six months stems from a desire to pressure the owners to lease or sell it in order to prevent a housing shortage.

The rates for the general municipal tax are listed in amounts per units of land for all the types of property requiring payment. Indeed the law defines "the equivalent of the building for the purposes of the general municipal tax,"[14] but it did not say how these rates should be calculated on the basis of this equivalence and no local authority has applied this section for many years. The rates are thus determined in shekels per unit of area. For residential buildings the law made it possible to relate to the number of rooms instead of units of area. However, local authorities have gradually adopted the use of precise units of measurement (square meters) instead of rooms; this criterion represents more fully the comfort of the tenants and, to a certain extent, their financial ability as well. For residential buildings different rates can be fixed for different types of buildings. The purpose of this is to charge lower rates for residents of lower quality buildings. While there is no full correlation between financial ability and level of housing, it can be assumed that there is a high correlation and each local authority can develop scales according to its own conditions.

It is also possible to set tax rates according to different neighborhoods in a local authority. A classification of neighborhoods can take into account the level of development, building and services in different areas and can also be based on more general data such as the quality of environment, prices of land, and other factors of well-being.[15] Internal political factors can also influence the exact demarkation of these neighborhoods.

For tax assessment purposes, buildings used for businesses as well as occupied land and agricultural land can be ranked according to both area and use. Classification according to use means that the same property can be charged different rates if different parts of the property are used for different purposes. Local authorities usually set different rates for offices, banks, hotels, stores, workshops or industry. This distinction can be justified as long as the higher rates are charged according to more intensive economic use, meaning that businesses can contribute more to financing municipal services. This distinction is also justified if it takes into consideration those types of businesses which place more of a burden upon public services, such as roads, garbage collection and cleaning.

General municipal tax rates are set by the local council before 1 March preceding the fiscal year for which the tax is being charged. Publication of the rates must take place by 15 March. If the council does not decide on time, the previous year's rates will continue to apply. If a local authority should see a need during the fiscal year to increase general municipal tax rates, it must receive approval from the Minister of Interior, which is given only under special circumstances. Every year there are local authorities which turn to the Minister of Interior with this request when, for various reasons, the council did not decide on time and the previous rates, not adjusted for inflation, are considered insufficient, or if some other urgent need has unexpectedly arisen which they feel necessitates an increase in the municipal tax rate.

The general municipal tax is collected directly by the local authorities. Just prior to the beginning of a new fiscal year, every obligant receives a bill for the amount owed on the property held and which details the methods of payment. Payment may be made at the cashier's window of the local authority, but is most often made at banks. This has been arranged for the citizen's convenience, so that he does not need to come to offices of the local authority in order to pay municipal taxes. This arrangement also works to the advantage of the local authorities, who are not required to open up many cashier's windows during certain periods of the year, such as the beginning of each fiscal year, a task which would cause considerable administrative difficulty.

Every local authority prefers, for reasons of cash liquidity, to receive the entire sum as early as possible. In order to encourage this, they have introduced a discount for those who pay in advance. However, even in those local authorities which work vigorously to convince their residents to pay at the beginning of the year, no more than 30 percent actually do so. The amount requested of a family or business may be too great for them to pay all at once. Therefore, the obligant can alternatively spread out his payments over the entire year, paying according to bi-monthly coupons which he received in advance in an appropriate booklet, or which are sent to his house together with the bi-monthly water bill.[16] In recent years there are also those who divide up the payments over a ten-month period by giving a standing order to their bank or to the central collection mechanism. In order to encourage obligants to enter into such arrangements with their bank, a certain discount is also given to those who pay with a standing order. This method is quite useful for a local authority, since it guarantees payment throughout the year, as well as from year to year. The amounts discounted to those paying in advance, or through a standing order in a bank or in the central collection mechanism, are listed as an expenditure in the section "financing expenses," in order to show the proper amount actually collected (as opposed to that charged) and the fact that the local authority pays a price in order to gain financial liquidity.

The general municipal tax covers a one year period; it is meant to finance local authority services in the ordinary budget for a specific year. In order to set the tax rate, it was customary for the authority to predict its budgetary requirements as well as the expected rate of inflation for the coming year. With the accelerating inflation of the 1980s, the discount for advance payment was increased to 20 percent but even this discount did not sufficiently attract obligants, since inflation made it more worthwhile to spread out payments. Inflation caused the local authority even greater hardship, since it could not withstand the declining value of the receipts which arrived during the year instead of at its beginning. If tax rates were set based on predicted inflation rates, why was there any loss? This was due to the fact that in every year of accelerating inflation, the actual inflation rate was significantly higher than the rate predicted at the time the general municipal tax rates were set.

In order to help deal with this situation, in 1980 the Knesset passed the Local Authority (Interest and Linkage on Obligatory Payments) Law, 5740–1980. According to this law, those who lag behind in payments are obligated to add the difference caused by inflation as well as interest on every obligation not paid within 60 days of the payment date. This law removed the incentive, which had increased with the increasing inflation, to be very late in making payments. The penalty is 10-20 percent, with an additional 1/2 percent for each month's delay, but altogether not more than 50 percent.[17] It is easy to see that this penalty, to the extent that it was enforced, was not enough to deter obligants from delaying their payments, and obviously was not enough to compensate the local authority for its losses. Even if the problem of late payments had been solved, there still remained the problem of the loss derived from incorrect prediction of the yearly inflation rate.

Periodically certain local authorities have had to decide on additions to the general municipal tax rates. The procedures for getting the addition approved and collecting it are complicated, entailing difficult conceptual problems in setting the correct rate or the appropriate reduction for those who have paid in advance. According to the law, the addition is levied "from the day of its approval until the end of the fiscal year" and it legally applies to all obligants. Under inflationary conditions, those residents who paid the entire sum or part of it in advance contributed greatly to the local authority treasury. A degree of relief was granted to local authorities with the passage of legislation in June 1984, which allowed that even tax payments made according to the usual arrangements would be increased to keep up with inflation.

Additional legislation is required in order to permit adequate increases in municipal tax rates during the fiscal year, or from year to year, which at least keep up with the average rate of price increases. Essentially there is nothing to prevent raising the general municipal tax rates to match the inflation rate or even surpass it. However, the decisions need to be taken every year by the full local council. Many council members hesitate to approve a very large tax increase, even if it far from matches the real increase of prices in the economy. The procedure for approving an adjustment of rates to match the economic reality turns into a complicated political event and runs into difficulties, not only from the opposition parties in the council, but even from members of the governing coalition. There is justification for increasing the general municipal tax rates automatically to match inflation, thus keeping income stable. This could be done for every traditional tax and levy used by state and local government. If this were to become accepted then the discussion in the council would focus on the real rate rather than the nominal rate.

Approximately 55 percent of the amount collected from the general municipal tax derives from buildings used as residences. The more industrial and commercial buildings a city has, the higher the portion of receipts for non-residential buildings (reaching as high as 75 percent in Tel Aviv). In cities which are primarily residential, as well as in the small settlements, most of the collection comes from residences. The collection for agricultural land and occupied land is on the average no higher than 5 percent.[18]

The general municipal tax for residences is most often levied on the family apartment. Past studies show that the general municipal tax can be regarded as a regressive tax, that is, a tax in which the proportion of payment of income of an individual or family decreases as income rises.[19] The regressiveness is particularly conspicuous among lower income wage earners, where the municipal tax reaches 3-4 percent of income. For those of higher incomes the trend is more moderate and comes to about 1 percent of the income. To understand the meaning of these statistics one must remember that these studies were undertaken using national data, and not according to the data from any particular local authority. It is possible that within each authority the picture is a bit different. In one of the studies it was pointed out that the more the analysis took into account the difference in the level of services between the local authorities, the more the regressiveness disappears and there seems to be even a certain degree of progressivism. This issue deserves to be studied again with more current data. In any case, the local authorities can counteract the regressiveness by taking advantage of the options of ranking the municipal tax according to types of housing and neighborhoods.

The local authority can also waive payment of the municipal tax, whether partially or completely, according to section 280 of the Municipal Corporations Ordinance "in consideration of the financial situation of the obligant," or for some other reason approved by the Ministry of Interior. In addition to section 280, it is customary to give various reductions to those who serve in the defense forces, the disabled and others, according to various laws. The local authorities have committees for approving these reductions according to set rules. The system of discounts and reductions can considerably dull the regressiveness of the general municipal tax as long as it is wisely applied.

Discounts and exemptions from the general municipal tax may also be applied to non-residential property, but their use in such cases is much rarer. An entire group of properties are exempt from payment of the general municipal tax according to the Municipal Taxes and Government Taxes (Exemptions) Ordinance, 1938. According to this law, properties exempt from municipal taxes include state property, based on the principle that the state does not pay taxes for its property to other bodies. As an exception, the law prescribes that within the municipality of Jerusalem and cities declared as "immigrant cities," the government ministries will pay the general municipal tax (and at the time the municipal property tax as well). About 30 local authorities were listed during the 1950s as "immigrant cities," and over the years this list has remained nearly frozen and unchanged.

Also exempt from payment of the municipal tax is all property directly utilized for education, health, welfare or religious services, as well as any property belonging to a "volunteer institution for the public good," as approved by the Minister of Interior. Over the years about 150 such non-profit organizations have been approved, all devoted to social or cultural activities. These institutions are exempt from the general municipal tax because private organizations which are providing public services should not have to pay general taxes to another body, the local authority, to finance similar services. In addition, this can be seen as a type of subsidy to assist such institutions to finance their activities.[20] According to various laws and agreements, the property of foreign embassies and consulates are also exempt from various taxes including the general municipal tax.

In addition to the general municipal tax, some local authorities levy a garbage collection tax, based on local by-laws. The state government and other institutions mentioned above are not exempt from this service tax. The garbage collection tax is sometimes based on rate schedules which take into account the amount of garbage or the size of the property, or is sometimes calculated as one-third of the general municipal tax for the same property. A significant number of local authorities do not levy the garbage collection tax on educational, health and religious institutions.

Oil installations and quarries are also exempt from the general municipal tax in accordance with legal agreements and concessions between the state of Israel and various commercial bodies. In place of the municipal tax, local authorities receive fixed amounts linked to the dollar.

The system of exemptions and discounts is extremely broad. Various pressure groups, especially retirees and those concerned with the rights of large families, are persistently working to receive automatic discounts, without consideration of the economic consequences. This system of discounts needs to be adjusted before it completely undermines the general municipal tax as a major factor in local authority financing.

The general municipal tax is usually not earmarked to finance any particular service. One exception to this is the tax charged for agricultural land. In a local authority with a minimum number of farmers or a certain proportion of agricultural land, and which therefore maintains an agricultural committee,[21] "two-thirds of the income from municipal taxes charged for agricultural land," as well as all other incomes from taxes, levies and payments regarding this land is earmarked for agricultural matters.[22] In addition, and in contrast to other types of property, the agricultural committee can appeal to the Ministry of Interior regarding any municipal tax rate set by the local council for agricultural land.[23]

The general municipal tax comprises, for all practical purposes, the only general tax charged by every local authority. The municipal tax rates are set by the local council and collection is undertaken exclusively by the authority. The original concept was "that the municipal tax should be higher for the property holder who enjoys greater benefits from the services of the local authority."[24] For example, whoever lives in the vicinity of a school, public park or other local institution or next to a paved road and sidewalk, should pay more than someone who lives distant from local institutions and has no sidewalk. Therefore "the instructions of the law do not intend to give the municipal tax a social ranking."[25] According to this concept the general municipal tax is a general service tax, levied in place of separate municipal taxes which in the distant past paid for garbage collection, firefighting, education and the like.

Many complaints have been directed against a tax based on the number of rooms in a residence as a regressive tax which should not be accepted in a modern society. We have seen that the criteria according to which municipal tax rates are set, in conjunction with the system of exemptions and deductions, make it possible to dull the regressiveness and perhaps even to create an estimated, though not precise, progressivism with reference to the incomes of the obligants. However, even without this possibility, it should be remembered that the general municipal tax comprises only a very small portion (2 percent) of the overall income of the government from taxes and obligatory payments. There is no doubt that the entire system of taxes and public services is progressive in the way expected of a modern state. Therefore, it is not such a problem if any specific tax is not progressive.

The general municipal tax is an expression of the taxation power of a local authority. It enables every authority to establish priorities in terms of tax rates and use.

Business Tax — A local authority is entitled to charge a business tax within its jurisdiction as prescribed in the Local Authority (Business Tax) Ordinance, 1945. As table 7.9 shows, income from this tax totalled about one-tenth of the overall income of the local authorities in the years surveyed. Collection of this tax ended in 1982.[26]

The tax was levied as the result of by-laws which prescribe its rates. It was collectable only from those types of businesses detailed in a supplement to the by-law. The tax was set on the basis of "the scope of the work or the business" according to characteristics such as "the number of employees, electricity consumption, the weight or capacity of machinery, the area, or other tests which can point to the dimensions of the work or the business." The tax could also be set as a percentage if the criteria for the "dimensions of the business" were the business cycle or wages. The tax could not be charged on a business's profits and so was in no way similar to an income tax.

The business tax was a supplement to the general municipal tax and to the municipal property tax. While these two taxes are tied primarily to the type and value of property, the business tax allowed the local authority to charge businesses with higher levels of taxes according to the business's capabilities or the degree if its utilization of services. The tax was relative to every type of business — number of workers, wages, area, machinery, seats in a cinema, beds in a hotel, but no principle was established for comparing rates between the different types of businesses. The rates were limited by a legal ceiling which limited the development of the tax. Only after several years was the law amended to raise the ceiling. The last amendment to the Business Tax Ordinance was in 1981 when a new ceiling was set which was linked annually to the consumer price index. The amendment also set rate limits for taxes charged according to business cycle, wages and number of employees.

The business tax was always a marginal tax and its collection was difficult. Every local authority had to approve a by-law which listed the types of businesses and the taxes charged them, according to the various criteria. The authority then had to receive data from the businesses in order to calculate the tax. Allegedly excessive tax rate assessments could be appealed to a court for business taxes, and the decision of this court could also be appealed before a district court.

The business tax was never accepted by the public. Unexplainable differences existed between rates charged similar businesses in different local authorities. It was not always possible to explain the criteria for the setting of the different rates which appeared in the supplement to the by-law. The ceiling, which was relatively low, did not leave room for appropriate ranking of rates. Many small businesses were charged high rates, thus arousing doubt as to the efficiency of the tax and its collection. There were also many appeals to the court for business taxes and to other courts, to an extent far out of proportion with the importance of the tax in local authority financing. These legal appeals were probably another expression of the poor reception of the tax on the part of the public.[27]

Several amendments to clarify the law were required over the years. In the last years of the law's implementation, some of the large local authorities set a rate based on percentages of the business cycle or of wages for a growing number of businesses. In this way, the tax became more dynamic, but at the same time some of the businesses in the commerce and service sectors were faced with a heavy economic burden, since their cycle did not reflect their net income or profit.

The business tax was limited by law and to a great extent was distorted by the measures which the local authorities enacted as a basis for the tax rates. For these reasons, and also because it was especially unacceptable to the business public, the local authorities agreed to accept a replacement for this tax and its termination.

Entertainment Tax — Section 249 (25) of the Municipal Corporations Ordinance empowers the municipalities to place a "tax on tickets sold for public entertainment." Local and regional councils are permitted to levy any tax that a municipality may charge, including this one. This tax had different names in the past, such as "admission" or "amusement tax."[28] In the first years after the establishment of the state there was a similar tax charged by the state, but in the early 1950s the government cancelled its collection. The rates for the entertainment tax have since been set by agreements anchored in legislation between local authorities, the Ministry of Finance, or the Ministry of Commerce and Industry, and organizations of cinema owners.

At its height, the entertainment tax in the large cities reached 90-100 percent of the ticket price on cinema tickets for foreign movies. Tickets to an Israeli movie or shows and concerts were charged a lower rate or were exempt altogether.

The collection of the entertainment tax was extremely efficient. The local authorities printed the tickets, on which were printed the cost of the tax as well as the price of the ticket. These tickets were given to cinema owners in exchange for the tax.

With the introduction of television in Israel in 1968, cinema attendance went into decline. Further declines occurred with the advent of color broadcasts and expanded use of videos. The situation of cinema owners became even more difficult with the introduction of the value added tax in 1975. Although it was not the burden of the entertainment tax which caused the decline in sales, the cinema owners demanded that the tax be reduced as a means of increasing ticket sales. Over the years a number of cinemas throughout the country which were no longer profitable closed.

The local authorities gradually responded to the demands of the cinema owners. Arrangements were made, for example, to return a portion of the collected tax in return for guarantees to improve the level of service in the cinemas. Beginning in 1980 there were even formal reductions in the tax rates; in the peripheral towns and suburbs it was eliminated altogether. By 1982, as a result of the pressures applied by cinema owners, who were supported by the Ministry of Commerce and Industry, the collection of the entertainment tax was halted by order of the Minister of Interior.

As part of the agreement, there was to be temporary governmental supervision of prices to assure that they would indeed decline. On the eve of its cancellation, in 1981, the amount collected from the tax totalled an estimated 80 million shekels and comprised about 3 percent of the general taxes charged by local authorities.[29]

Welfare and Recreation Tax — Until fiscal year 1978, some local authorities collected a welfare and recreation tax. Up until 1959 this tax was anchored in the Municipal Corporations and Local Council Ordinances. In that year a more detailed law was enacted, the Local Authorities (Welfare and Recreation Tax) Law, 5719–1959. The law authorized the local authority to tax the services of profitmaking guest houses and clubs. The tax was limited to 10 percent of receipts for guest houses, hotels and restaurants, and to 20 percent for clubs. The local authority is entitled to set tax rates according to types of institutions and seasons of the year. Actual assessments are determined by an assessment committee, which could rely on the accounting books of an institution which managed its accounts properly, or make an estimate for institutions which did not manage their accounts. The assessment could be appealed before an appeal committee and afterwards even in a district court. The law explicitly authorized the owners of guest houses to collect the tax from those receiving their services.

The law empowered the Ministry of Interior to grant exemptions and the ministry used this authority to exempt tourists in hotels from the tax. This exemption made it nearly impossible to use accounting books as a source for an assessment, since there was no distinction in the books between revenues from tourists and from Israelis.

The law states that "the local authority must dedicate the tax to welfare objectives in its jurisdiction." It was later determined that certain local authorities could use the money for purposes of "recreation," including the proper maintenance of the city during tourist seasons.

The collection of the welfare and recreation tax was inefficient, especially in resort cities where tourism was an important factor in the local economy. In addition, the assessment committees, composed of a member of the local council and a representative of the organizations of the guest houses within the local authority, were not always precise in their estimates. In some local authorities, various concessions and delays were granted over the years. The introduction of the value added tax, which began at a rate of 8 percent and was, therefore, similar in size to the welfare and recreation charge, resulted in the claim by guest house owners that they were becoming tax collectors.

In 1978, upon the recommendation of the Ministry of Tourism and with the agreement of the Union of Local Authorities, the collection of the welfare and recreation tax was cancelled. According to the agreement, the local authorities which had collected the tax were to receive in its place an amount equivalent to the previous year's collections. This amount would increase according to the same formula used for compensation for the property tax. In 1978, the last year of its collection, local authorities collected less than 4 million shekels from the tax, less than 1 percent of overall tax receipts.

Administrative Fees — Local authorities also collect a number of administrative fees from local citizens including: sign fee, collected at the time of approval of the placement and form of a sign; advertisement fee, for posting advertisements on city bulletin boards; and approval fee, collected with the granting of approval for the payment of taxes or other matters.

In summary, out of an entire network of locally-generated income, all that remains today is the general municipal tax and the administrative fees. The State Commission on Local Government (Sanbar Commission) recommended that even these last two be reviewed for efficiency.[30] For economic reasons, as well as the desire of local authorities to assure stable financing, a varied system of general taxes has been pared down to essentially one section. Both state and local government officials have even questioned the efficiency of this one remaining section as a source for local authority financing.[31]

The Sanbar Commission recommended that the general municipal tax be developed for residential buildings, while the general municipal tax for businesses be exchanged for a tax based on added value. This recommendation has not yet been applied. In recent years the general municipal tax has financed about 12 percent of ordinary local authority expenditures. This tax serves as a way for the local authorities to finance additional services, indicating that the potential for collecting this tax has still not been completely tapped by local government. This tax held its value even during periods of accelerating inflation, even though until 1984 it was not automatically linked to the Consumer Price Index. The general municipal tax is the last important expression of the power of the local authority as a governing body to independently levy and collect taxes from the residents and property within its jurisdiction.

Earmarked Locally-Generated Income

Local authorities supply a large variety of services to their residents. Some of these services are for the "public good," including services whose cost is impossible to collect or whose use by those who do not pay is impossible to prevent. These include the maintenance of roads and sidewalks, street lighting and traffic lights. Another type of service for the "public good" is comprehensive education from kindergarten through high school. Many local services, however, do not have such social or economic importance and the local authority may collect part or all of the cost of these services from those who benefit from them.

In addition to income from services, local authorities also receive income from property and concessions that they make available for use — apartments, stores, markets, industrial zones and other property are rented out for residences, businesses or factories. Rent is paid either directly to the local authority or to its subsidiary or organization. Local authorities grant concessions and operating rights to local businesses for beach installations, use of sidewalks, operation of swimming pools or movie halls, sports facilities and more.

Sometimes there are additional sources of one-time income, such as interest on investment of surpluses, rebates from insurance companies, or the sale of products produced in vocational schools. However, revenue from these sources is insignificant for the financing of the local authorities.[32]

Table 7.10 presents the groups of earmarked, locally-generated income according to their sources — services provided by local authority, national government or special projects — in millions of shekels and percentages in various years from 1953 to 1981. Not all local authority income is expressed in the budgets and financial reports, since some of the agreements of local authorities with other bodies are in the form of a division of function, without any expression in cash flow. The following are two examples of such agreements:

1. According to a detailed and obligatory agreement, certain local authorities have handed over the maintenance and operation of water purification installations to agricultural bodies requiring the water. In exchange for their maintenance and operation expenses, the farmers receive clean water for their use, without the local authority making an exact estimate or listing of income and expenses.

2. It is customary for local authorities to grant private companies a concession for the installation of lighted street signs, direction signs and bus shelters. Companies which erect these installations at their own expense, have the right to post advertisements on them. Here, too, the expenses for installation and the income generated from advertising rights are not listed by the local authority.

Table 7.8 shows that earmarked locally-generated income rose constantly from the 1950s to the 1980s, and that their proportion of locally-generated income rose from 28 percent to 53 percent in 1981 (and as high as 59 percent in 1973). This refers to the proportion of earmarked locally-generated income within the overall locally-generated income category, whose relative share in the financing of the ordinary budget has declined considerably over the years.

In the composition of local income, it should be noted that the proportion of locally-generated income from local services increased, while the proportion of income from national services

Table 7.10

EARMARKED LOCALLY-GENERATED INCOME OF LOCAL AUTHORITIES: 1953-1981

| Year (1) | In Millions of Shekels | | | | In Percentages | | | |
	Total (2)	Local Services (3)	State Services (4)	Works (5)	Total Local (6)	Services (7)	State Services (8)	Works (9)
1953	1.3	0.2	0.4	0.7	100	15	31	54
1958	4.9	1.7	1.3	1.9	100	35	26	39
1963	31.2	—9.0—		4.2	100	—6.8—		32
1968	22.9	8.0	6.5	8.4	100	35	28	37
1973	48.1	20.6	12.0	15.5	100	43	25	32
1978	291.4	79.5	77.3	116.6	100	33	27	40
1981	3,316.8	1,182.3	763.5	1,371.0	100	36	23	41

Sources: See table 7.5.

declined. This can be explained by the fact that charges and fees for local services have grown systematically. For national services, there have been major fluctuations in the funding of tuition in educational institutions, whose value has varied widely and at times has been totally out of date. Over the years, the local government share has declined with the introduction of graduated tuition, according to which lower amounts were to be collected from families of limited means. Indeed, the local authority did receive compensation for the discount it was obliged to give according to law, but this compensation, from the Ministry of Education and Culture, was listed as "government ministry participation" and not as locally-generated income. After the cancellation of high school tuition in 1979, all that remained was the collection of nursery school tuition for 3 and 4 year olds.

Income for Local Services

Garbage Removal Tax — This tax is collected primarily from those individuals and bodies which are exempt by various laws from the payment of the general municipal tax. In most local authorities the tax is set at one-third of the general municipal tax which would have been charged for the exempted property. In addition, the tax is collected for the removal of unconventional garbage from businesses in markets or industrial areas and hotels, in terms either of its amount or composition.

Veterinary Tax — Local authorities are required to provide veterinary services and to oversee veterinary matters in their area. It is possible to collect fees for some of these services such as for checking fish, fowl and frozen meat, vaccination and stray dog control. Usually these fees are minimal so that those requiring these services will be able to afford them.

Sewage Tax — A local authority which maintains a central system for the collection and treatment of waste water is to collect a sewage tax. The tax is calculated to cover the maintenance and operation costs of sewage installations and, if a sewage charge is not collected, even to cover the costs of investment for certain components. The tax is collected together with the water tax, under the assumption that those using water are also using the sewage system, since 80 percent of the water returns to the sewage system.

The sewage tax is likely to be as high as one-third of the water tax. It is collected only for the amounts of water which are likely to return to the sewage system, thus excluding water for agricultural and garden use. In setting the level of the tax the authority can take into account the pollution level in the sewage. Indeed, local authorities charge a higher tax for factory wastes, since the level of pollution in these wastes is usually higher than in home waste. Local authorities still do not take advantage of their option to set rates according to a pollution scale set by the Ministry of Interior. This proposal would require a periodic sampling of waste water from every factory and laboratory analysis to determine the degree of pollution. Use of this method would more justly disperse the expenses for waste water purification among those who contribute to the pollution.

There are local authorities which also collect taxes for the emptying of cesspools in areas lacking a central sewage system. There are also local authorities which receive income from the sale of treated waste water.

Sewage Charge — A local authority is empowered to collect for expenses related to the installation of sewage equipment, such as the connection of a building to the sewage system, or the installation of sewers, collectors and purification machinery. Collection is made once for each item, with the exception of building expansion, in which case an additional charge is possible. The rates can be varied according to different areas of the city, but local authorities do not take advantage of this option.

This charge is to support the financing of the entire network of sewage installations. Therefore, the calculation of rates is divided between unimproved and improved property so that the entire cost of installation is covered. The receipts from the sewage charge are listed as income in the ordinary budget for as long as the loans for financing the sewage system are being repaid. Collection may be made at the beginning of sewer or purification plant installation. Collection may also be made even before construction on a property has begun, based on the building plans, but it usually is made from existing buildings or buildings about to be built (collection is often simultaneous with the granting of a building permit).

Sewage charge collection developed with the beginning of the national sewage project, on the basis of a loan from the World Bank. Every local authority which requested a loan to finance sewage installations was required to set appropriate rates for sewage taxes and charges.

Building Permit Tax — The municipalities and some of the local councils´ comprise local planning and building commissions and are empowered under the Planning and Building Law, 5725–1965, to grant building permits. Whoever requests a building permit is obligated to pay a tax according to the regulations prescribed by the Ministry of Interior. The tax rates are ranked into three groups of local authorities on the basis of their socioeconomic situation. Tax rates are set in proportion to the size of the building and vary with its intended use — residential, commercial, industrial or agricultural.

A local authority in an area which includes several nearby authorities is represented on an area planning commission. In such cases, the commission issues the building permits and collects the taxes. The amount collected is used by the commission to partially finance its activities.

In the management of licensing and the overseeing of building, local authorities collect additional amounts such as service charges for the measurement and checking of buildings.

Participation of Owners in the Paving of Roads and Sidewalks — The local authorities collect an "owner participation" tax from property owners whose property borders public roads to finance the expense of paving the road and the sidewalk. Collection is usually done once for every property, but if the road paving is done in stages, the tax can also be collected in the same stages. The law permits different methods for determining the amount to be collected from property owners bordering the road. Recently the Municipal Corporations Ordinance was amended to allow similar methods to be used to finance the paving of sidewalks.[33]

The method accepted in the past was to charge the expense of paving a road to the owners of property bordering the road, according to such criteria as the area of the property, its frontal length, or both. This method was a considerable burden to property owners on wide streets, who enjoyed no extra benefits from this road. Therefore, in several local authorities this method covers only 75 percent of the expense. Others determined that property owner participation should apply only to the paving of a road seven meters wide. As a result, the method used leads to great differences among property owners within a local authority, since the expense of paving creates a different burden in different areas, depending on density of housing, road width, level of construction, and topography. For this reason, many local authorities charge a "road tax," collected from bordering property at the time of road paving, whose rates are equal in all areas of the local authority and reflect an average level of expenses for paving roads and sidewalks within the entire area of the local authority. These rates are calculated to include both improved and unimproved land.

In agricultural areas, property may be charged which does not directly border the paved road, but which is located within 1,000 meters and, therefore, directly benefits from the road. Yet collection from such distant properties is only partial. The income is earmarked for the paving of roads and sidewalks. Since not all of the collection is done at the time of the paving of the road, it is necessary to take out loans (as in the case of sewage and water). Thus part of what is collected is listed in the ordinary budget as income earmarked for the financing of loan repayment.

Income from Municipal Supervision — The source of this income is primarily the low penalties charged by the municipal courts and, more recently, by the courts for local affairs, which replaced them. An additional source of income comes from tickets given out by local authority inspectors for violation of local ordinances.

Income from Agricultural Services — This is usually collected when a regional council, or even an agricultural committee in a municipality or local council, provides a special service to agricultural property. Such services can include patrols, pest extermination, field services, and others in exchange for a service charge calculated to cover the cost.

Income from Educational and Cultural Services — This income comes in considerable sums through several sections. Parents of children in nurseries for the ages of three and four must pay in accordance with their economic means; for most parents this payment is set at a rate which covers the full expense of maintaining a child in a nursery. In the past there was also collection of high school tuition. Tuition collection is undertaken by local authorities by right of their position as owners of the educational institutions. The level of tuition is usually fixed by the Ministry of Education and Culture. In a number of regional institutions, primarily regional councils, there is an additional collection of funds to finance deficits in the high schools, deficits resulting from the high level of service given in these institutions which is above the standard formula. Some local authorities collect an "additional services tax" (sometimes mistakenly referred to as an "education tax") from their students. This tax is collected in accordance with regulations from the Ministry of Education and Culture, and is earmarked to finance services which supplement the educational system — dental care, psychological counselling, equipment, etc. Additional sums are directly collected in exchange for services, such as a summer camp fee, and the now abolished charge for the child nutrition program.

Income from cultural services are in the form of service charges: entrance fees to libraries, museums and clubs, as well as cultural and sporting events.

Income from Public Authorities — Income from these projects is supposed to finance their full cost. The largest and most important such project in every municipality and local council is the water works. Income from the water works derives from the water tax, initiated in December 1974 by regulations established by the Ministry of Agriculture, which are frequently updated by agreement with the Ministry of Interior. The price of water is set by the Water Commission, headed by the Minister of Agriculture, at the recommendation of the Water Commissioner. A majority on the Water Commission are representatives of farmers, who consume about 80 percent of the water used in the State of Israel. The government often finds it difficult to convince the Water Commission to set suitable prices. The general public (usually the agricultural sector) may appeal pricing decisions of the Water Commission, which are then reviewed and passed on to a sub-committee of the Knesset Finance Committee. In this committee, too, there is a respectable representation of farmers, and the committee generally leans toward protecting the consumers from the government. Following the approval of the committee, the Ministry of Agriculture, with the agreement of the Ministry of Interior, prepares the regulations governing the supply of water by local authorities.

The water tax is set at different rates, depending on the purposes of consumption. Lower rates for water are charged for watering gardens and agricultural land. One of the reasons for this is that since very large quantities of water are supplied to farmers, the fixed expenses are divided over a larger quantity than in the case of ordinary home consumption. In this area, too, the representatives of various economic interests are active. Representatives of industries and hotels often seek lower water prices similar to those in the agricultural sector.

Billing for water taxes is based on readings of water meters maintained by the local authority and installed in every apartment, or at least in every building. The measurement of water use is required by law, and is designed to charge every consumer according to actual consumption, thus hopefully leading to greater conservation (which is less likely to occur when consumers are charged jointly). For the same reason there are differential water prices for various quantities. A base-level price is charged for 8 cubic meters of water for each living unit, with an additional 2 cubic meters of water for every member of a household larger than four persons. For more water than this, a higher price is charged, while more than 10 additional cubic meters brings a penalty price. Some other types of water consumers are also given a specific quota. If they exceed their quota, they are charged a penalty price.

Due to regulations, the price of water is uniform in most local authorities. In the city of Eilat there are different prices, as there are in certain other local authorities which can demonstrate that they can balance their water economy with a different price. Yet only a few local authorities have taken advantage of this possibility.

Until 1974, water rates were set separately by every local authority. The setting of rates was performed with the aid of a joint staff of the Ministry of Interior and the Water Commission, with the goal of having every water system cover its own expenses. According to this arrangement, development towns were usually charged higher rates. In response to their complaints, uniform water prices were first established at the end of 1974. This was at the beginning of a period of accelerating inflation which corresponded with a crisis in oil prices, an important component in the production and supply of water to consumers. The old system of setting water prices according to municipal by-laws had become arduous and problematic. Thus the centralization of water rate setting significantly helped the local authorities to keep the prices current. Of additional help was the establishment of the principle that the price of water was to be 60 percent linked to increases in energy prices, reflecting the fact that the drawing and distribution of water are energy intensive processes. This linkage also helped to avoid delays in timely rate approval.

Local water ordinances also prescribe fees for services such as pipe-laying and water connection. These are set by each local authority for the purpose of financing water system development.

Other income from public authorities comes from slaughterhouses owned by a number of local authorities, parking fees in municipal parking lots and city streets as well as income from rental and leasing of property. All of these are small in scope.

In summary, earmarked locally-generated income represents revenues received in return for a specific service, whose payment is collected along with the provision of that service. This system has developed significantly and is relatively unaffected by high inflation. Their proportion in overall income has not increased since high school tuition has been cancelled. At the same time, collection methods were developed by linkage to the rate of inflation.

There still remains the classic problem of setting the level of tax rates to costs, whether according to a marginal calculation as is customary in "pricing theory," or according to an average, as is customary in the public sector. In periods of economic hardship, there is room for more organized collection from those benefitting from any service which can be sold and which does not have special social value.

Transferred Income

One of the sources for the financing of the ordinary budget is "transferred income," sums which the government collects and transfers to local authorities. The right of local authorities to receive these sums is anchored in law and regulation and is thus independent of administrative decisions within the government ministries. Thus this is basically a guaranteed source of income, although laws and regulations can be changed. Such changes are tied to public and institutional procedures which guarantee proper discussion and a hearing for representatives of local authorities, thus preventing the possibility of hasty and arbitrary decisions. Yet this advantage can also become a disadvantage. When the principles upon which an income source is based are inflexible, they are liable to be inappropriate to the special conditions in the local authorities and cause fluctuations in financing rather than the stability required for financing the ordinary budget. Moreover, in the overall allocation of resources to local authorities, unintended distortions may develop.

In tables 7.6 and 7.11, there is no separate data for transferred income prior to 1963. It is difficult to estimate their weight in overall financing, but there is no reason to assume that it was higher than in 1968, the year in which the "compensation for property rate" (now the most important component of transferred income) was added. The sources for the data in the table are the financial reports of the local authorities. Therefore, only income transferred directly to the local authorities appears in separate sections. Income transferred through a general grant by the Ministry of Interior does not appear. This income appears separately only in the national budget, but is meaningless in the separate incomes of each local authority. These amounts, therefore, are included in the tables under the heading "general grant," which will be discussed later.

Income Tax

The Local Authorities (Addition to Income Tax) Law, 5712–1951, authorized the local authority to levy an addition to the income tax at the rate of 7.75 percent of the amount of income tax collected by the tax authorities. This required that the central income tax collection system be responsible for the collection of the addition as well and then transfer the amount collected to the local authority.

This law was in existence during 1952 and 1953 and nearly every local authority decided to implement it. It was cancelled in conjunction with an agreement between the government and the local authorities that these sums would be used to finance the salaries of teachers in the public school system, and that these salaries would be paid by the state government. Thus public school teachers became state employees and the local authorities conceded their portion of the collected income tax.[34]

Other Transferred Taxes

Purchase Tax — One of the sources of the general grant that is transferred by the Interior Ministry to the local authorities is the

Table 7.11

DIRECTLY TRANSFERRED INCOME OF LOCAL AUTHORITIES: 1968-1981

Year	In Millions of Shekels					In Percentages				
	Total	Compensation for Property Rate	Land Transfer Fees	Local Appreciation Tax	Vehicle Licensing Charges	Total	Compensation for Property Rate	Land Transfer Fees	Land Appreciation Tax	Vehicle Licensing Charges
(1)	(2)	(3)	(4)	(5)	(6)	(7)	(8)	(9)	(10)	(11)
1968	41.0	9.0	0.7	0.5	0.9	100	81	6	5	8
1973	43.5	34.9	3.0	3.9	1.7	100	80	7	9	4
1978	269.4	218.5	13.0	33.8	4.1	100	81	5	12	2
1981	1,681.0	1,001.4	180.4	437.3	62.3	100	59	11	26	4

Sources: See table 7.5.

Comments: 1) In this table only directly transferred income is included. Income transferred through the grant is included in the financial reports of the local authorities in the section "general grant" as well as in the tables presented here which are concentrated from the financial reports (and not from the listing in the national budget).

2) Land transfer fees were collected in some years as an "addition to appreciation tax" and today as a "purchase tax." Due to the similarity in name to "appreciation tax" during some of the years and due to an inability to identify some of the receipts, it is possible that certain amounts were not listed exactly in some of the local authorities.

sum of 5 percent of the purchase tax. This transfer is based on a section of the Specified Goods and Luxury Tax (Amendment) Law, 5714–1954. Over time, this tax evolved into a purchase tax and as it grew, local authorities demanded a share as is customary in other countries where a "cycle tax" or "purchase tax" is levied directly by the local authorities. Since it was not feasible for each local authority to levy and collect its own purchase tax, it was agreed that part of the tax would be used to finance the local authorities in the form of a general grant. To this day an appropriate amount appears in the national budget as "transferred income," even though it is not directly transferred to the local authorities. For many years, the amount transferred from the purchase tax comprised a considerable portion of the general grant. With the introduction of the value added tax, the role of the purchase tax in financing the national budget declined, and together with the increased importance of the general grant in the financing of local authorities, the weight of the purchase tax within the general grant decreased.

Land Transfer Fee — As in other countries, land in Israel is used as a basis for local authority taxes. In 1950 the Knesset enacted the Local Authorities (Land Transfer Fee) Law, 5710–1950, which empowered local authorities to levy a tax of up to 2 percent of the market value for the purchase, donation or exchange of land. According to law, the tax would be collected by the authority in conjunction with the "land transfer fee" which it collects for the state treasury.

In 1959 this law was replaced by the general law, the Local Authorities (Land Transfer Fee) Law, 5719–1959, which stated that whoever owes the state a "land transfer fee," will also pay a tax to the local authority in whose jurisdiction the property is found. The rate of the tax to the local authority will be "half of the land transfer fee" paid to the state. In accordance with this law, the state makes available 33 percent of the amount that it collects at the time of the land transfer in the form of transferred income to each local authority in whose jurisdiction the property was transferred.

As its name implies, this tax was collected in the past in conjunction with the transfer of registration in the land registration office, which oversees the transfer of property ownership. Since in Israel there is often a considerable delay between the performance and registration of a land deal, a special section in the Land Appreciation Tax Law stated that for a deal whose registration was delayed, an "addition to appreciation tax" would be paid at a rate equal to the land transfer fee and in place of it. The local authorities also received a transfer of 33 percent of the "addition to appreciation tax." Later the law was changed once again and a "purchase tax" was placed instead of the two previous alternatives; today the government transfers 33 percent of the purchase tax collected in its jurisdiction to each local authority.

Land Appreciation Tax — In 1963 a law was enacted for the collection of a land appreciation tax, which is a tax collected as a percentage of the increase in the value of a property (land or structures) between the time of its purchase by one individual and its sale, excluding any increase in nominal value due to inflation. It can be argued that the increase in the value of a piece of property is related to urban development. The development of infrastructure in the area surrounding the property, populating of the area and the provision of services by the local authority are likely to be factors contributing to an increase in property value. Therefore, as long as a tax is collected from the increased value, the local authorities thought it only fair that they should benefit from it. The law states that 33 percent of the collected tax will be transferred to the local authority in whose jurisdiction it was collected. Under a later version of the law, the collection of the land appreciation tax was revised to exempt individual apartments which were sold for the purpose of buying a new apartment, on the condition that its price not be higher than an amount prescribed by the Finance Ministry. In order to prevent the local authorities, who were not partners to the new policy, from taking a loss, the percentage transferred from the amount collected was increased to 60 percent.

In recent years the collection of the land appreciation tax and the purchase tax has been centralized in the Income Tax and Purchase Tax Commission in the Finance Ministry, and this office transfers the sums directly to the local authorities. Since there is a delay of several months in the exact calculation of the amounts due each local authority, advance payments are transferred to the large local authorities, which receive constant sums. In 1984 a centralized transfer arrangement was established by the Ministry of Interior according to amounts listed in the national budget.

As can be seen in table 7.11, the amounts earned from the land appreciation tax and the purchase tax did not grow uniformly over the years. A more detailed study would also show that during the

1980s there were frequent policy changes concerning the status of these taxes. From time to time the Finance Ministry delayed the increase in the exemption amounts for individual apartments (that applied to the purchase tax as well), or updated the exemption by a large amount all at once. As a result of this, local authorities could make no stable estimates of income from these two taxes. The difficulties in estimating the fluctuations in collection and delays in transferring, all point to the need for renewed study of these sections of income in the ordinary budget, which requires sources of income which are more stable.

Vehicle Fees — The local authorities receive 42 percent of the amounts collected from vehicle fees according to regulations of the Transportation Ministry which are based on the Transportation Ordinance. At first it was customary to transfer 50 percent of the amounts collected.[35] In the beginning of the 1960s, a fund was established for the financing of installations to prevent traffic accidents and improve traffic safety. The fund was administered jointly by the Ministries of Transportation and Interior, the Union of Local Authorities and the Union of Regional Councils. Both the government and the local authorities contributed 8 percent of their portion of the vehicle fees. Thus the amount transferred to the local authorities from vehicle fees declined to 42 percent. During the 1970s, the fund for traffic safety became inactive and the funds allocated for it remained in the budget of the Transportation Ministry.

The local authorities receive a portion of the vehicle taxes on the assumption that they must maintain an extensive network of roads, street lights, traffic lights and traffic safety installations. It is, therefore, fitting that part of their financing should come from taxes paid by those who benefit from this service. However, the distribution of roads among the local authorities is not necessarily identical to the distribution of car owners. Even a small local authority which has few cars must properly maintain its roads, thus affording all vehicles an approach to residences and industrial and commercial areas. This was the reason for the Knesset committee decision in 1953 that the amounts received would be transferred to the authorities in two ways: half of the amount directly to each local authority in whose jurisdiction the sums were collected, according to the address of the vehicle owner and half by way of the general grant. This arrangement is anchored in regulations and amounts collected are transferred to the local authorities through the Ministry of Interior on the basis of data received from the Ministry of Transportation. The amounts are not necessarily earmarked to finance transportation and safety expenses, but national data shows that the local authorities spend similar amounts for these purposes.

Compensation for Property Rate[36] — This has been the most important section of transferred income since 1968, when the collection of a property tax by local authorities was discontinued. Prior to 1978 this section accounted for 80 percent of transferred income. Since then its portion has declined and, as can be seen in table 7.11, it has fallen below 60 percent. "Compensation for property rate" was provided to the local authorities between 1968 and 1974 under the framework of the National Budget Law, according to a calculation based on an agreement between the state government and the Union of Local Authorities. In the agreement it was determined that with the cancellation of local collection of the property tax each local authority would receive annually a percentage of state income from taxes, fees and other obligatory payments, equal to the percentage of its average yearly income from the property tax during the years 1965–1967, relative to national income from taxes during those years. On the whole, the collection of the property tax in those years reached 4.8 percent of the national tax income and this percentage was transferred each year to the local authorities. Until 1974 it was divided among them according to the original percentage of each local authority.

In 1975, legislation was prepared whose objective was to anchor the agreement and the administrative activities of the Ministry of Interior in a more permanent form. At the same time, accumulated experience had shown that the distribution of the "compensation for property rate" according to the percentages of the 1960s could not be continued indefinitely. In the ensuing years, new local authorities had been established and some of the development towns had grown significantly. There had also been a movement of population in the metropolitan areas from the central core to the surrounding cities. In addition, it became clear that certain local authorities, particularly in the Arab and Druze sector, had not charged the property tax at the appropriate level, or had not properly registered its collection and had listed the extra sums together with the general municipal tax receipts. Once the power to collect the property tax was withdrawn from the local authorities and the relative proportion of each authority remained fixed, these distortions could no longer be corrected. In 1975 the Knesset enacted the Local Authorities (Compensation for Property Rate) Law, 5737–1975, which prescribes that the state treasury will annually compensate the local authorities at the rate of 4.828 percent of the overall income of the state. State income was defined as "those amounts collected from taxes, obligatory payments and levies in the fiscal year two years preceding the fiscal year in which the compensation is distributed." The amounts are divided among the authorities in accordance with Interior Ministry regulations, which are subject to approval by the Knesset Committee on the Interior and Environmental Quality.

According to the Interior Ministry's regulations, each local authority is initially slated to receive the same amount it received in the preceding year. Additional funds are distributed according to the amount of newly-completed construction, as well as population growth. This provides more balanced compensation between local authorities which are developing and those more stable local authorities. In order to assist the smaller local authorities and those which had not succeeded in the past to collect the property tax in significant amounts, it was determined that in two of the years after 1975 every local authority would receive a sum totalling not less than 10 percent of its approved budget in the preceding year. The object of this was to guarantee a proper starting point for each local authority, and this rule also applied to new local authorities after the determination of their first budget. In 1983, after it became clear that the reduction in the share received by the large cities in the distribution of the compensation had been too drastic, an additional balancing factor was added. Ten percent of the compensation would be distributed in accordance with each authority's relative collection of the general municipal tax, thus reinstating a certain advantage to the more developed cities. This may also act as an incentive to the collection of the general municipal tax. These rules brought about a situation in which the share of compensation for those cities whose population exceeds 100,000, declined from 60 percent in 1968 to 51 percent in 1982. On the other hand, the share of compensation for the developing authorities (including the Arab sector) and the regional councils increased from 9 percent to 23 percent during those same years.

As seen in table 7.11, the share of the "compensation for property rate" within the overall amount of transferred income has declined since its beginning in 1968. The total amount grew from 10.7 million shekels in 1968 to 5,148 million shekels in 1983, which was an increase in real terms, above the rate of inflation. However, its share in the financing of the ordinary budget declined from 13 percent in 1968 and 15 percent in 1977, to 8 percent in 1982. A close look at the data and at the structure of the "compensation for property rate" shows that its decline began in the years in which inflation accelerated, and worsened as the inflation rate grew. Since the amount was calculated on the basis of state income two years prior to the year in which the compensation was to be distributed, in 1984, for example, the amount for distribution was 4.828 percent of the amount collected by the government in 1982. Thus there was a great delay in updating the amounts according to inflation. Originally this method of calculation was adopted in order to enable each local authority to know the exact amount that it would receive, prior to the beginning of the fiscal year. In order to overcome any delay, there was even an increase of 5 percent over the base amount. However, once inflation began to accelerate, the compensation could no longer keep current and its real value declined.

Transferred income is a method whose use allows every local authority to receive the monthly revenue to which it is entitled in an amount known in advance. Its evolution and formulation is an example of concerted negotiation and action by all the parties involved in local government financing.

Compensation for Welfare and Recreation Charge — In 1977, the collection of the Welfare and Recreation Charge described earlier was cancelled. According to an agreement by the Ministries of Interior and Finance and the Union of Local Authorities, those local authorities which had collected the charge prior to its cancellation are to receive compensation in accordance with revenues from the last fiscal year in which the charge was still in force. The amount grew from year to year in a way similar to the "compensation for property rate." An appropriate amount appears in the national budget and is transferred according to the agreement.

In summary, transferred income is a technique which allows local authorities to benefit from income collected by the state government from within their jurisdictions, and it relates to tax bases usually appropriate to local government. This technique is advantageous in that it saves collection expenses and allows for uniformity in the government's determination of fiscal policy. However, it is not without its disadvantages. The local authorities cannot express their own policy through the levy and collection of the transferred taxes. There is also no stability in the amounts of those taxes collected partially for the local authorities and there is no correlation with budgetary needs and ability to absorb changes. On the other hand, the "compensation for property rate" is relatively stable, since it is transferred from the overall national income, which is a base known in advance. There is room for renewed study and definition of the ways of implementing transferred income as a significant source of financing for local authorities, particularly in light of periodic efforts to replace the general municipal tax, which is levied and collected by the local authorities, with transferred income.

State Government Participation

During the 1970s and 1980s there was a considerable change in the composition of local authority financing. Locally-generated income declined, while there was an increase in income derived from the national budget, as well as in state government loans to help balance local authority budgets. Table 7.5 shows that the portion of government participation in local budgets increased from 15 percent in 1963 to 51 percent in 1981. If we consider most of the loans as coming from the state government, then the resources originating from the state government increased from 20 percent in 1963 to 55 percent in 1981. This change reflects a conscious policy, similar to changes that have taken place in all Western countries where state governments cannot afford to ignore the needs of local authorities. In the 1960s the local authorities were required to develop a range of services, particularly educational and welfare services, and the state governments in the welfare states developed ways to implement their policies through increased financial aid to local authorities. A difficult economic situation can lead to difficulties in the development of local authority financing, making it difficult for the local authorities to adapt to fluctuating situations — to cut back on budgetary expenditures for a short period or for a limited period of two or three years and afterwards to return to the previous scope of expenditures.

The need for state government participation in the financing of local authorities can also be explained without relating it to crises. There are generally recognized principles concerning the division of functions between the different levels of government, as well as for the division of the financial burden among them. When formulating these principles, the following factors are taken into account: efficiency in performance of services, efficiency in collection of taxes, the transfer of specific sums for the advancement of a specific program, and the need to finance services prescribed by national policy. An additional consideration involves making general financing available without specific directions from a dynamic, effective and just state tax system, instead of allowing local authorities to collect their own sums. A further consideration is the differing fiscal strength of different local authorities, a situation which requires aid to those which are weaker.[37]

As mentioned earlier, local authority expenditures grew over the years in real terms (at a rate higher than the increase in wages and prices) and there have been many changes in the composition of locally-generated income, whose development did not keep pace with the increased expenditures. Essentially, the locally-generated and transferred incomes both lost their primary status in the financing of local budgets, from 86 percent in 1953 to 45 percent in 1981.

Table 7.12 presents the principle data of state government participation during various years in the period 1953-1981. Detailed data exists only since the mid-1960s, at which time the government participation, particularly in the form of the general grant, began to grow rapidly.

We can see from table 7.12 that the share of the general grant increased from 41 percent of total government participation in 1968 to 55 percent in 1981. Since overall government participation increased over the years, the share of the general grant, including that part of transferred income included in the grant, increased from 10 percent of the ordinary budget in 1953 to about 28 percent in 1981. Later, in conjunction with increasing budgetary cutbacks, the share of the general grant decreased slightly. The share of government ministry participation did indeed decline vis-a-vis the general grant, but it increased in the financing of the ordinary budget from about 14 percent in 1968 to about 23 percent in 1981.

The participation of the state government in the financing of local authorities is intended to meet several objectives. A study by the International Union of Local Authorities (IULA) summarized these objectives in the following way:[38]

Table 7.12

STATE GOVERNMENT PARTICIPATION IN THE ORDINARY BUDGET
OF LOCAL AUTHORITIES: 1953-1981

Year	In Millions of Shekels			In Percentages		
	Total	General Grant	Earmarked Participation	Total	General Grant	Earmarked Participation
(1)	(2)	(3)	(4)	(5)	(6)	(7)
1953	1.6			100		
1958	2.3			100		
1963	6.0			100		
1968	20.9	8.5	12.4	100	41	59
1973	77.6	32.5	45.1	100	42	58
1978	757.8	403.7	354.1	100	53	47
1981	8,902.1	4,888.9	4,013.2	100	55	45

Sources: See table 7.5.
Comment: Government participation data, and within it the "general grant," include "income transferred through the general grant," whose source is the purchase tax, and part of the vehicle charges.

329

1. To compensate for the lack of economic equality among local authorities;
2. To particularly aid the weaker local authorities;
3. To encourage the provision of services;
4. To aid in financing expenditures which are partially local and partially national;
5. To serve as a tool in the hands of the higher authorities — to oversee;
6. To improve the local economy in order to create similar standards of living in different districts.

It is clear that state government participation in local financing is meant to serve more than one purpose. At the same time, the primary goal of the grant, particularly of the general grant, is the first goal listed above. The fifth and sixth goals are unique to those countries in which there are many natural disasters as well as those developing countries in which the local authorities are likely to be the arm for the performance of economic development.

As we will see, the general grant in Israel is intended to meet the first two objectives. Since 1982, when the National Budget Law made it possible to deduct from the grant for local authorities who had exceeded their budget, it can be said that the fifth objective is partially achieved. In Israel, the participation of government ministries is intended to achieve the third and fourth objectives and, to a certain extent, the fifth as well.

These objectives, formulated in 1969, fail to include the simple goal of balancing the budget. With the decline in locally-generated income, the role of the general grant has become more dominant. Even though it is meant to assure a minimum income for those local authorities whose potential locally-generated income is relatively low, the grant is also given to the stronger authorities as a resource for financing their budgets. In periods of budgetary crisis, the participation of government ministries has even been increased in order to compensate for the lack of other sources of financing.

The General Grant

The principle which has guided all of the formulas used for the distribution of the general grant is to make sure that even local authorities with a low income potential will have a minimum of resources. The formula used from the establishment of the state until 1954 was determined in the following ways:[39]

> The local authorities were divided into a number of categories in accordance with the economic ability of their residents, which expresses itself in the possibilities for collecting municipal taxes. The grant for each category was determined by a certain percentage of the local authority's total expenditures in the year 1950/51 for services, while deducting government participation and administrative expenses. The percentage was anywhere between 10 percent and 80 percent.

It is unclear from this formulation whether the possibilities for collection of municipal taxes would be determined by their actual collection or by some other criteria. In any case, the independent collection of the principle local taxes (the property tax and the general municipal tax) served as an indicator of the authority's economic situation and the general grant served to supplement those local authorities that could not raise enough revenue independently. In this formula there was also a link between net expenditures (after deducting what was received from participating ministries) and services (without administrative expenses), in consideration of the base year and not of each year's data. This was apparently decided upon in order to discourage local authority spending. It is less clear how the size of the grant was to fit such a formula.

Beginning in 1955 a different formula was adopted which was tied to objective factors only:[40]

1. The number of residents in each authority — one point for every resident.
2. The number of immigrants in each authority — an additional point for every resident in an authority dominated by immigrants.
3. The dispersal of residents in regional councils — an additional half point for each resident in a regional council.
4. Border settlements — an additional half point for every resident in a regional council containing border settlements.

This formula has an egalitarian base — the number of residents. In municipalities and local councils, a resident may receive an additional one or two points, and in regional councils each resident can receive anywhere from one and a half to three points. This formula was adopted during the years in which development towns, immigrant settlements and large immigrant neighborhoods within older settlements were being established. The problems of providing municipal services for immigrant absorption was central, since the proportion of immigrants in the population was quite high. Many local authorities benefitted from the addition, though the definition of "immigrant" and the number of years one remained an immigrant remained unclear. The amount of the local government grant was distributed to each authority according to the number of points it earned, while the value of each point was determined by a division of the total sum by the number of points earned by all of the local authorities. This method completely ignored the unit of services given by the local authority, the economic situation of the local residents, and their sources of earnings and income.[41]

Approximately ten years later a new formula for allocating the general grant was adopted. The locally-generated income which was collected served as a central indicator of the ability of a local authority to mobilize its own resources. In order to give expression to those factors which are a burden upon the local authority, it was decided that the level of expenditures for welfare services, which were already governed by Welfare Ministry regulations, would be taken into consideration. The comparison between local authorities would be made by "amount per person," thus paving the way for an additional distinction between authorities, according to demographic structure. Every child under 18 was assigned the value of an additional person, and children of compulsory school age received yet another point. Similarly, the elderly above 65 were given a double value. Thus an "adjusted number of residents" was calculated, which would serve as the basis for the "per person" calculations of each local authority. This statistic was translated into "points," and local authorities were divided into ten groups according to the number of points which they earned, among which were also negative points, when welfare expenditures exceeded locally-generated income. Thus rates were formed for grants per person according to ten levels, among which there was a fixed relationship. Each local authority received an amount equal to the amount of the grant per person, as determined for the category to which the authority belonged, multiplied by the number of people in its jurisdiction.

This formula, in comparison to its predecessor, took into account more of each local authority's economic and demographic situation, in addition to other factors which affect local expenditures. Its weakness stemmed from the fact that most of its data was collected and organized by each local authority, which could manipulate that data in order to receive a higher grant. As long as the grant was much smaller than the locally-generated income, there was little reason to suspect that it would affect the authority's tax collection or welfare expenditures. The potential profit was doubtful because, among other reasons, each individual local authority was absorbed into a large group of authorities in its same category. However, as the grant came to be a more prominent source of income in the 1970s, it became clear that a new approach was needed.

In 1974 the research division of the Ministry of Interior developed a new approach — the "service basket" approach.[42] This approach is inclusive and takes into account all the different parts of income, with the goal of "enabling the local authority to provide a desirable 'service basket' to its residents" — a goal which is possible to achieve only if the authority has sufficient resources. The formula defines the financing of the local authority at a rate which is the difference between the estimated expenditures (according to a certain standard calculation) and an estimate of potential income. The estimate of expenditures for the purpose of calculating the grant is neither the actual expenditures, nor even the budgetary decisions of the local authority, but rather a calculation of "efficient expenditures." The calculation of these expenditures is done on the basis of a standard basket of services, which does not include exceptional expenditures since these must be covered by special income. Beyond that, the calculation is done with the intention that the service is to be provided efficiently, with an optimal relationship between inputs and outputs.

In a parallel manner, the calculation of estimated income is not based on actual or budgetary income, but rather on the assumption that the local authority sets accepted payment rates for its residents and collects them efficiently.

According to this approach the total grant to the local authorities will be the combined sum of the calculation for each individual local authority. This is to be distinguished from all of the previous methods according to which the total grant was determined by general estimates of income and expenditures, and not according to a specific local authority.

This approach also led to ways of determining standards of expenditure based on the statistical analysis of actual expenditures. This analysis led to a proposal to establish five groups of municipalities and local councils according to population sizes, for which there were found to be similar bases for expenditure. Within each group the average expenditure was determined for each section in the service basket which could be standardized. This average would reflect the standard expenditure per person. For the purposes of calculating the service basket for a specific authority, the standard would be multiplied by the number of residents. However, since not all of the conditions in the local authorities are equal, there is also room to formulate adjustments in the calculation according to rules which express "factors of character and structure" — those factors which cause certain authorities to differ from others, such as topography, distance from business centers, climate, employment factors such as tourism or industry, location near the border, dispersal of the population, and others.

On the income side it was proposed to divide the local authorities into groups according to the level of wealth of the residents. Since no such data existed, this was to be determined using a number of measures:

1. The number of vehicles per 1,000 people.
2. The number of luxury apartments among the total of local apartments.
3. The number of large families.
4. The number of welfare-supported families.

For each group of local authorities, a standard level of locally-generated income is to be calculated, and this will be attributed to each local authority in the group according to the tax base range, whether according to the number of residents or the extent of taxable property.

Additional uses can be inferred from the formula. It can, for instance, serve as a tool for checking budgets. Indeed, not every local authority must set its budget according to the standard alone, particularly when it can mobilize resources beyond the level of the standard. However, elected officials, local authority employees, and the district commissioner will be better able to estimate the significance of the total budget and the meaning of the allocations for the various topics, as they will be able to compare these to the framework and details of the service basket which was calculated for that local authority. An additional benefit might accrue to the government ministries, who will be able to use a similar concept and integrate into this system with the determination of "service baskets" and appropriate rates of participation.

According to this concept, the application of the formula would serve as an incentive for greater efficiency, since each local authority will receive a grant which will cover only the efficient provision of services. If some service is provided wastefully, this will come in the place of other services and activities. The opposite is equally the case — the more the authority succeeds in increasing efficiency, the more it will be able to use the grant money to finance other services.

The application of this formula began at the end of the 1970s. Computer programs were developed for this purpose which would calculate the standards for each service according to the groups of local authorities. In accordance with the formula's principles, the calculation was to be based on actual past expenditures in the local authorities and not on their budgets. Since the financial reports of all the local authorities are presented only a year after the end of each fiscal year, the standards could be calculated for a specific year only according to the financial reports from three years before. It was necessary to overcome this gap by increasing the amounts according to the rules determined for increasing budgetary estimates due to wage and price increases, while deducting the budgetary reductions taking place in the same period. Prior to its application it was necessary to set the exact components of "factors of character and structure" and to determine at which levels they would influence which services. It was determined, for instance, that development towns would consistently receive an addition of five percent to their budgets. It was also decided at this beginning point that an attempt would be made to achieve a schematic standardization of the repayment of loans, by prescribing that 25 percent of the budget was to be set aside for this purpose. Exceptional sections and services were not taken into account in the service basket, while certain services were considered only for those authorities which required them, such as the internal auditor required by law for cities of over 30,000 residents, or beach services in those relevant localities. While in the process of working out the formula, it was also decided for which services there would be no standard, such as the water works built from completely earmarked income, or welfare expenditures dependent upon socioeconomic plans specific to each authority, which cannot be determined equally according to the number of residents; the amounts for these services were translated according to the authority budgets with inflationary adjustments. Similarly, it was decided to define standards in education according to the number of students at each educational level, rather than according to their overall number.

A parallel estimate of income was undertaken for each local authority. An estimate of the general municipal tax was made according to groups of local authorities which were divided by measures similar to those recommended. For each group the potential collection was calculated according to the average collection customary in that group. Income from water fees were calculated using the amount of water sold by each local authority and the projected prices. Transferred income was calculated using the obligating formulas "compensation for property rate" and "compensation for welfare charge" and according to the development of other sections of the national budget. The remaining incomes and government ministry participations were estimated according to the rules prescribed for the determination of local authority budgets in the context of deliberations concerning the national budget.

In the first year in which the grant was calculated using this formula, it became clear that it could only be applied in stages, since on the one hand there was a significant number of local authorities with a level of expenditure much higher than the service basket, while on the other hand there were other authorities, including the entire Arab and Druze sector, with levels of expenditure considerably lower than the service basket. It was therefore decided that the grant would be calculated each year in proximity to the service basket, so that every local authority which exceeded the basket would reach it within a period of 3-4 years. The increase for those authorities beneath the basket would be more gradual, since their numbers were large and there were not enough national financial resources to immediately raise the level of all services.

Already in the first year it became clear that the standardization of the repayment of loans at a level of 25 percent of expenditures would not work out well. Local authorities which did not reach this rate would enjoy additional resources for development and services, but local authorities which could not stay within this rate demanded recognition of the balance. They claimed that the loans which they had received, partly for balancing their budgets, were approved by the Ministry of Interior and they had no flexibility with regard to this expenditure since the loans were of long term. It was therefore necessary to recognize this expense, an act sometimes leading to a parallel grant. Since there were no extra resources, the standardization of the repayment of loans was cancelled, and this section was considered together with the rest of the service basket according to the specific data of each local authority in the national debt compilation.[43]

Over the years it became clear that the standards which had been calculated for the three largest cities as well as for those local authorities whose populations were below 2,000 were not adequate. The differences among them were very large and the formation of an average caused the creation of an artificial and unrealistic service basket. It was also clear that the Arab and Druze sectors were lower than the accepted basket and steps were taken to advance their services and infrastructure, even without a constant calculation of the basket.

Up until 1982 the service basket and potential incomes for each local authority were calculated, and the grant was calculated according to the rules prescribed for bringing the local authorities to the level of the service basket. In that year it became clear that nearly all of the local authorities were close to the service basket, with the exception of the development towns which provided services at a level exceeding the basket calculated for them. In that same year the rate of inflation began to get out of hand, so that the transition from the financial report to the service basket, separated by three years, required an increase of thousands of percents — a calculation which is necessarily inaccurate and cannot lead to a realistic estimate of the expenditures necessary to finance the service basket. At the same time, the government began to implement frequent and sizeable budgetary cutbacks, and budgets were not always fully or frequently updated to keep up with inflation. Under such circumstances the service basket was not calculated anew each year; instead, the amount of the grant to each local authority was calculated according to the 1982 data while keeping in mind the rules prescribed for wage and price increases, increases in tax levels, and cutbacks.

As the economic situation stabilizes it will be necessary once again to find the formulas and rules for determining the general grant on the basis of the service basket, as was recommended by

the State Commission on Local Government. In considering a
new formula, consideration should be given to such questions as:
Can the data from the Ministries of Education and Culture and
Labor and Social Welfare, which are used to calculate expenditures and financial participation for the service systems which
they direct, be better integrated? Should there be a more strict connection between earmarked income for financing certain services and the expenditures for those services? Many local authorities go to considerable trouble to prove that they are in some way
unique, and it is therefore necessary to improve the "factors of
character and structure" so that they will include the many factors
which express the special problems of local authorities. There is
also room to consider the extent of detail required to present service standards. In the original proposal it was determined that the
calculation of the basket would be in general, and that it would be
possible to analyze each budget in detail. It may be necessary to set
aside this approach for calculating the grant. For this purpose calculation of financial standards for groups of sections, without too
much detail, may be advisable, thus avoiding over-direction.

There remains the problem of explaining the system and its
outcomes. Since we are referring to a complicated, computerized
and comprehensive approach, which in some way takes into account all of the components of the budget, the grant is the result of
many formulas. Thus it is impossible to quickly grasp the justice
inherent in the allocation of specific sums to specific local authorities, and certainly not by looking at "amounts per person." It is
therefore necessary to consider how to convince the consumers of
the system's fairness.

The determination of the appropriate formula for allocation of
the general grant is a mission which has occupied the Ministry of
Interior and the local authorities for many years and it has become increasingly difficult as the share of the grant in financing
the ordinary budget increases. Government ministries and organizations of local authorities in other countries as well have
struggled with similar problems of allocating funds from the state
government.

Government Ministry Participation

The general grant was provided to the local authorities without
being tied to any specific expenditure since it is meant to be a

supplement to local taxes, particularly for those authorities with a low collection potential. In addition to this grant, several government ministries provide funding, according to various formulas, to finance certain services.

Table 7.13 shows that most government ministry participation comes from the Ministry of Education and Culture and the Ministry of Labor and Social Welfare. It is natural that in these communal areas there is a national policy with regard to the minimal level of services which must be offered to the population and that most of the financial burden is born by the state government.

The distribution of funds from among the different ministries has remained similar over the years — approximately 60 percent for Education and Culture, 30 percent for Welfare, and the rest divided among a variety of other ministries. However, this stability in the distribution of funds does not mean that the development of ministry participation has not been dynamic. Quite the contrary, over the years there have been a tremendous number of changes. The share of total ministry participation in financing the municipal budget has increased over years, though less so than the general grant. We will now take a look at the principal trends in the participation of the various ministries.

Ministry of Education and Culture — This ministry participates through about sixty sections of its budget in the financing of local authority activities.[44] The local authorities operate the formal educational system in every settlement, from kindergartens for age 5 to the end of elementary school. Many local authorities also operate nurseries for 3-4 year olds, as well as high schools. In addition, they operate the supplementary educational systems and additional services in the schools (psychological services, dental services, pedagogical centers, etc.). The local authorities also operate cultural institutions as well as youth and sport activities. The wages of teachers from kindergarten and up are paid directly by the state, as they are state employees. The large sum required for the wages of tens of thousands of teachers does not appear in the budgets of the local authorities. As mentioned earlier in our discussion of income tax as a transferred income, prior to the mid-1950s some teachers were employees of the local authorities, which had established Hebrew educational networks within their areas during the British Mandate. With the cancellation of the "addition to income tax," all teachers became state employees. Therefore the central role of local authorities today in the

Table 7.13

GOVERNMENT MINISTRY PARTICIPATION IN LOCAL AUTHORITY BUDGETS: 1968-1981

			In Millions of Shekels							In Percentages			
Year	Total	Local Services	Education	Culture	Health	Welfare	Religion	Works	Total	Education and Culture	Health, Welfare and Religion	Local Services and Works
(1)	(2)	(3)	(4)	(5)	(6)	(7)	(8)	(9)	(10)	(11)	(12)	(13)
1968	12.4	0.7	7.6	0.5	3.0	1.1	—	0.1	100	60	33	7
1973	45.1	1.6	27.3	1.4	3.2	11.3	0.2	0.1	100	63	33	4
1978	354.1	13.4	220.7	12.0	2.6	102.8	1.5	1.1	100	66	33	4
1981	4,013.2	103.3	2,474.6	132.5	67.7	1,132.9	17.4	17.4	100	65	30	5

Sources: See table 7.5.

obligatory educational system is in the construction of buildings, their maintenance, and operation of the institutions — supplying furniture and materials, secretaries and services, laboratories and libraries, and supplementary educational systems. The Ministry of Education and Culture provides financing to cover the salaries of janitors, secretaries and assistant kindergarten teachers. This arrangement was made in 1967 in order to relieve the financial burden of the local authorities and to respond to the claim that "state services" should be fully financed by the state government. In the past, local authorities also received funding for the purchase of equipment and certain maintenance items. In the earliest years the Ministry of Education and Culture itself fully supplied all equipment and services.

Prior to 1978 parents paid tuition for high school students. The tuition was graduated, allowing low income families to pay less or be exempt altogether. The burden of financing this discount was born jointly by the Ministry of Education and Culture and the local authorities. At the end of the 1960s, in order to aid the local authorities, the local authorities' share was cancelled and the entire tuition supplement was paid for by the Ministry of Education and Culture. In 1979 high school tuition was eliminated and in its place the ministry pays a certain amount for each student, with an addition for technical education.

These amounts are listed in the budgets of the local authorities as "Ministry of Education participation," since the sums reach the treasury of the local authorities from this ministry. In essence this sum represents aid to the parents, not the local authorities.

The local authorities benefit from this participation in the same way as do other operators of high schools. Perhaps it would have been more appropriate to include the sums in the "locally-generated income" or "transferred income" sections. Involved is about 25 percent of the participation of the Ministry of Education and Culture. A similar section is the participation in the graduated tuition for pre-kindergarten nurseries. The local authorities which operate such nurseries directly, finance their operation by collecting tuition. The level of tuition is set by the government ministries in cooperation with the owners. The Ministry of Education and Culture prescribes rules for reduced collection from needy families, and provides supplementary financing.

An additional major section which has developed in recent years is participation in the financing of transportation for students. Children are bussed to eliminate smaller schools which are both educationally and economically inefficient. This service is particularly widespread in the regional councils and the ministry participates in 90 percent of the expense. Ministry participation for municipalities and local councils is at 50 percent of the expense.

The remaining amounts of ministry participation are scattered over dozens of sections in education and culture, youth and sport; in some of these services and activities, participation does not exceed more than a few percentages.

After many complaints from the local authorities, there have been considerable improvements. Amounts and standards were set more efficiently for some services, the amounts were updated monthly to keep up with wage and price increases, and transfer of funds was performed in a relatively efficient manner. There are still some sections which are clumsy and in which there are considerable delays in the transfer of funds, but steps are being taken to overcome these difficulties as well. Among the new arrangements is a detailed service basket which includes pricing for high school education and psychological services. The allocations and funding transfers of many sections have also been computerized.

Ministry of Labor and Social Welfare — Several laws prescribe the obligation of the local authorities to operate agencies for social welfare and to supply social services to those who require them. In addition to these laws there is also an entire system of regulations and instructions issued by the Ministry of Labor and Social Welfare. A detailed rulebook guides social workers in the details of the various aid categories and in the administrative and financial ways in which aid can be provided for each category. Since welfare is subject to such a detailed national policy, the financing of local authority welfare activities by the ministry comes to 75 percent or more. As a rule, the performance of the services is in the hands of the local authorities. In 1982, though, a radical change took place; the key section providing "guaranteed income" for needy families was transferred by law to the jurisdiction of the National Insurance Institute, as assistance to the disabled had done a few years previously. Today the major sections of ministry participation are for the maintenance of children in boarding schools and the maintenance of mentally retarded in appropriate institutions. Additional large sections are earmarked for maintaining the children of distressed families in day care centers, maintaining of the elderly in old age homes, and social activities in the framework of Project Renewal.

Ministry participation is present in about 50 additional sections of the budget, through which the social worker can aid families in need in a wide range of areas including equipment, health care, rent, rehabilitation and more. A considerable amount is transferred to the local authorities as participation in the wages of workers in the social welfare agencies, who are employed according to ministry standards.

While the level of ministry participation in local welfare expenditures is 75 percent or more, according to standards or ceilings set by the Ministry of Labor and Social Welfare, in the sections regarding maintenance of children in boarding schools, the ministry participates at a rate of 100 percent. The entire amount is transferred directly to the institutions to cover tuition and dormitory expenses.

Until the mid-1970s there were varying levels of participation by the ministry, according to a formula which set a different rate for each local authority. The formula was supposed to determine the economic ability of the local authority and to place a greater burden on those which were stronger. As a result of the work of the Kubersky Commission in 1974–1975, it was decided that the government ministries should leave the determination of the financial ability of local authorities to the Ministry of Interior and that this should affect the general grant only.

The Ministry of Labor and Social Welfare was the first to adapt itself to this recommendation and it set a uniform level of participation of 75 percent for each local authority and for all of the budgetary sections at that time. Thus the participation allotted to the stronger local authorities increased from an average of 40 percent to 75 percent, while participation in development regions declined from 90 percent to 75 percent. The latter were outraged at this regressive act until they received appropriate compensation in the general grant. Over the years this pattern has been completely accepted, although constant accounting problems remain. The ongoing questions are: what is the budget provided to a certain municipality, how are sums updated and how will they be transferred to the municipality? The problem of transferring sums is not a difficult one, as most of the funding is transferred directly to the institutions or else serves as security for checks which the ministry prepares for those in need. The ministry claims that it often makes expenditures prior to receipt of the amounts from the local authorities.

Local Government in Israel

Ministry of Health — A number of local authorities directly operate dental care services for students, mother and child clinics, or family health clinics. The latter service is provided throughout the country, but is organized differently in different localities — sometimes funded completely by the local authorities or with a division of funding (doctors and nurses paid for by the Ministry of Health and the building and its services funded by the local authority). Some local authorities are assisted by the Kupat Holim health insurance fund for the provision of services.

The Ministries of Health and Labor and Social Welfare are jointly responsible for the financing of hospitalization of the chronically ill who require high levels of nursing and medical care. Arrangements between these ministries and the local authorities sometimes result in problems which are not easily solved.

Ministry of Interior — The Ministry of Interior participates in a number of local services. Firefighting services, under the Firefighting Services Law, receive an average of 50 percent ministry participation in their budget. The data in table 7.13 in the "local services" column includes only part of the sum, most of which is transferred to municipal unions, whose budgets are not included in the statistics presented here. The service is provided by the local authorities and supervised by the Ministry of Interior, both professionally and in the setting of personnel and equipment standards. The ministry also participates in the operating costs of the civil guard (primarily in regional councils), according to the Guarding Law to the extent that these services entail expenditures. (The guarding itself is performed without remuneration and the organizational expenses are quite minimal.) The Environmental Protection Service in the Ministry of Interior initiated the establishment of Environmental Units in 15 cities and participates in their financing at a rate of 50 percent, according to a special section in the budget. The ministry also participates in the financing of the operation and maintenance of beaches, as well as maintenance of major roads and access roads in regional councils, since all these installations serve populations beyond the residents of the specific local authority in which they are located.

Religious Services — Religious services are usually provided by the religious councils. The religious council is tightly bound to the local authority on financial matters. The participation of the

Ministry of Religious Affairs is transferred directly to the religious councils, not through the local authorities. The section "government participation in religious services" in the local authority budget primarily reflects the arrangement decided upon in the Knesset Interior Committee during the early 1970s, which was adopted by the Ministries of Finance, Religious Affairs, and Interior. The arrangement was intended to finance the wages of those providing religious services (rabbis, ritual slaughterers and the like) in the kibbutzim and moshavim, many of whom were appointed without any arrangement for their salaries. According to the arrangement, 45 percent of their wages is covered by the Ministry of Religious Affairs, 45 percent by the Ministry of Interior, and 10 percent by the regional councils. The participation of the Ministry of Interior is transferred to the regional councils from the section "government participation in religious services." In addition, sums are sometimes transferred to the local authorities to finance the religious needs of other groups, such as the Karaites and Samaritans in the Jewish local authorities, and the Moslems and Druze in the non-Jewish and mixed local authorities.

Water Works — Government participation in relatively small amounts involves the financial participation of the Water Commission in the water works in two types of local authorities. Local authorities which produce their own water earn a subsidy from the national budget similar to that which the Mekorot water company receives nationally for reducing the price of water. Local authorities which supply water to farmers and industry receive compensation for the value added tax which they pay according to the tax receipts of the water supplier, which is usually Mekorot. The farmers and industrialists demanded that they receive tax receipts from the local authorities so that they could deduct the value added tax paid on the water from the taxes they owed the government. Since the local authorities are public corporations, they do not pay the value added tax, but only taxes on wages and thus are not eligible to issue tax receipts. Therefore it was agreed that the price of water would not include the value added tax, while local authorities which pay the entire amount would receive a rebate from the Water Commission.

In summary, the participation of state government ministries in local authority budgets involves over 120 sections of the national budget. This participation is based on numerous and varied formulas for determining the levels of participation, the basis of participation, methods of transferring funds and methods of reporting. There are two overall types of participation to finance or advance certain services on the basis of national policy, and the general grant, which is not earmarked to finance any particular service, but rather to supply supplementary resources to those local authorities whose potential locally-generated income is low.

Such a large number of topics, sections and arrangements inevitable leads to complications in their implementation. Although many steps have been taken to simplify the participation formulas and reporting procedures and to set base rates according to "service baskets" and accepted pricing, there still remain sections in which the arrangements are not yet summarized, there are delays in the transfer of funds, and there are various defects in implementation. Therefore, there is a foundation for local authority claims that the rate of fund transfer from government ministries is too slow. This became increasingly problematic during the inflationary years when there were delays in updating the national budget, which resulted in delays in the transferring of funds from government ministries. Indeed, it is necessary to periodically review the entire system to improve procedures and eliminate obsolete measures.

Loans

Bank loans comprise one of the sources of financing for local government budgets. In most cases these are "directed loans" which the banking system makes available for specific uses as determined by the Finance Ministry and the Bank of Israel. Table 7.6 shows that loans began to become a significant source of financing in the early 1960s. Their share in the financing of the ordinary budget has been irregular and they have been considered "temporary" for the last twenty years. Many attempts have been made to refrain from using this type of financing and to avoid giving it any permanent status. As will be seen, a distinction must be made between loans given until 1979 and those made to local authorities during the 1980s.

Loans have been provided to local authorities to finance expenditures and obligations in the ordinary budget since 1963. It was clear to everyone concerned that it is not proper to finance the ordinary budget with loans. Their repayment returns to the budget in future years, with interest. The rationalization in the early years was that this was a case of replacing short term obligations with long term obligations and that a form of consolidation, similar to that done frequently in the business world, was taking place. Some local authorities, particularly the development towns, were in deficit. These deficits were essentially being funded by credit from suppliers. Payment of this short term credit became a burden of local budgets. The government therefore responded to the claims of the local authorities and provided loans to replace short term credit. This is what happened de jure; de facto, directed loans were provided to the local authorities and these were appropriated to the medium and large authorities as a part of the resources for financing the ordinary budget.[45]

Why did the state government chose directed loans to finance local ordinary budgets and their deficits rather than participation? The explanation for this can be found in the fact that the yearly deliberations concerning local authority budgets comes to an end only at the end of the first half of the fiscal year, in the months of August and September. By this time it is difficult to change the government budget or to transfer the appropriate amounts from reserves. Moreover, the national budget itself is financed in part from loans derived from banks, pension funds and the like. It therefore seemed natural to involve the local authorities in the same type of financing, thus relieving the national budget.

Until the mid-1970s, it was unnecessary to receive approval of the Knesset Finance Committee for the direction of credit. The loans provided were always with interest rates which were standard on the market for bond issues — 9 percent and later 7.5 percent (over and above linkage), which is the maximum interest permitted according to the Interest Law. Loan repayment terms were usually half to be repaid gradually within 7 years, with only 2 years of interest, and half to be repaid in 17-20 years, with only 5 years of interest.

Loans during the 1980s were used only to relieve deficits. The Kubersky Commission had recommended in 1976 that under no circumstances should loans be used as a resource in the ordinary budget. Indeed, at the end of the 1970s and in the 1980s no more such loans were proposed. However, when rapidly accelerating inflation began, many local authorities suffered from budget deficits. These deficits derived from their slowness in implementing required reductions, together with a delay in updating the national budget to keep up with inflation.

347

In 1980 the Finance Ministry realized that the crisis would escalate under the prevailing economic conditions and sought to help the local authorities out of their financial crisis. Every deficit would be temporarily funded by various types of credit such as bank overdrafts, debts to income tax authorities and short-term dollar loans, all of which were linked and entailed high interest or penalties. A program was arranged for more than 80 local authorities which obligated them to consolidate and reduce their debts and the government directed loans to them to reduce their accumulating deficits. Since some of these loans were intended to cover the financing costs in the ordinary budget, the loans were listed as a "transfer (from the non-ordinary budget) for the financing of the ordinary budget." The program was originally for the years 1980 and 1981, but for certain local authorities it continued for a number of years. It was even intensified with directed loans and, until 1984, open market loans, with approval of the Ministry of Interior.

Overall, the share in the ordinary budget allotted to the repayment of loans declined. This occurred despite the constant provision of new loans for balancing the budget and relieving deficits, since the share of loans for development work was not large in most years.

Although loans were not seen as a legitimate resource for financing the ordinary budget, they have played a part in local authority financing for more than twenty years. They have served, under different names, as an available source for government provided or approved financing which avoided the need for the approval of an additional grant from the national budget.

Resources for Financing the Non-Ordinary Budget

The non-ordinary budgets of local authorities are earmarked for development projects. These are seen as investments, expenditures made in the present whose benefits will be realized in the future. Financing of investments may be from a one-time source, according to the availability of this source. It also may be from loans whose repayment will take place in the years in which the investment will bring a return. As noted earlier, even loans to finance the ordinary budget are listed in the non-ordinary budget.

Table 7.2 shows that in certain years the non-ordinary budget has comprised as much as a quarter of overall local authority expenditures. The fluctuations in the size of the non-ordinary budget match the economic situation of the country and of the local authorities within it. The fluctuations in this budget are more radical than in the ordinary budget. The flexibility of this budget for one-time expenditures is naturally greater, due both to the ability to avoid expenditures in lean years and to mobilize capital in times of economic growth. Table 7.2 shows that the share of expenditures for development projects has been declining constantly since 1977. This can be explained by the decline in resources made available by government ministries for local development projects.

Table 7.14 concerns the resources allocated to local development projects in the period 1953–1981. A comparison between local authority income and expenditures for development activities (as in table 7.2) shows that in certain years there were considerable differences. In most years expenditures exceeded income. The flow of income and expenditure for any given project are naturally not in balance. Sometimes receipts arrive at the beginning of the work or even before, but usually, particularly when the funds are transferred from government ministries, most of the receipts will arrive according to an extended schedule of payment during the course of the work. Therefore, for most of the work funded by the non-ordinary budget there is an intermediate deficit on the day of the financial report. Indeed, for projects which have concluded with a deficit, the deficit is transferred to the ordinary budget. If the work concluded with a surplus, the surplus is usually transferred to a general fund or to finance a deficit in a different project.

The data in this table reflects income within a certain fiscal year for various projects, some of which may have been completed and even paid for in earlier years, especially in the year prior to the receipt of the income. A different analysis is required if we want to check the ways in which different types of development activities are financed, the extent of temporary or final deficits or surpluses, or the lag between receipts and payments.

A distinction must be made between final income and loans or credit. The amount of participation by the state government, national institutions (usually the Jewish Agency), property owners and local authority sources are final incomes which do not need to be returned in the future. Loans and credit must be returned in the future with the addition of linkage and interest. Financing investments through loans is justified because the financing burden

349

Table 7.14

LOCAL AUTHORITY RESOURCES FOR THE PERFORMANCE OF DEVELOPMENT WORK: 1953-1981

Year	In Millions of Shekels					In Percentages				
	Total	Govt. and Institutional Participation	Owner Participation	Loans and Contractor Credit	Local Authority Sources	Total	Govt. and Institutional Participation	Owner Participation	Loans and Contractor Credit	Local Authority Sources
(1)	(2)	(3)	(4)	(5)	(6)	(7)	(8)	(9)	(10)	(11)
1953	1.7	—	0.4	1.2	0.1	100	—	23	71	6
1958	5.9	0.3	1.1	3.9	0.6	100	5	19	66	10
1964*	23.1	—	3.5	16.4	3.2	100	—	15	71	14
1968	23.3	0.3	3.3	18.5	1.2	100	1	14	80	5
1973	95.3	11.5	6.2	73.1	4.5	100	12	6	77	5
1978	446.6	55.7	29.7	329.4	31.8	100	12	7	74	7
1981	3,366.2	890.1	382.2	1,723.8	370.0	100	26	11	51	11

Source of data: See table 7.5.
Comments: 1) Columns (6) and (11) include income from sale of property, funds, transfer from the ordinary budget and others.
2) * For 1963 there is no detailed data; therefore 1964 data is presented here.
3) Since 1978, "paid-for-work" is included in the column "local authority sources."

is dispersed over a number of years. The price, of course, is the interest charged on the loans. Theoretically, for public corporations which require yearly loans and thus constant repayment, one could consider doing away with the reliance on the capital market as an intermediary and, instead of repaying the loans, directly using the same funds for development. This proposal could be based upon the creation of "depreciation funds," which would be allocated for innovations.

The data shows a trend toward the decline in the use of loans to finance development and a preference for resources which do not require repayment. The government ministries decided that some of the sections supported by the national budget will be given as a full or partial grant rather than as a loan. Thus local authorities receive grants for roads, safety installations, air raid shelters, school buildings, renewal of water lines, various security activities and others. In 1981, loans comprised only 51 percent of development resources, as opposed to more than 70 percent in previous periods.

Beginning in 1977, with the introduction of the section "credit line for development" for local authorities, most of the loans derive from the state budget. Prior to that year most of the loans were received by the medium and large authorities on the open market. Thus the state government's share in financing increased to approximately 85 percent in 1978. By 1981, after reductions in the national budget, locally-generated income rose to 22 percent, while the appropriations from the government budget declined.

It was generally accepted in the past that the state government and local authorities could make investments by receiving loans on the open market. In this way they could increase the resources available for activities during the year in which they received the loans, without increasing the burden on the public. In addition to the value inherent in the possibility of spending more for public service, there is also some justice in this approach. The loans will be repaid over a number of years by those who benefit from the service in those years and not only by the investing generation. However, while the scope of government activity and its financing through loans from inside or outside of the country are significant for macro-economic and monetary policy, this does not apply to local authorities. Local authorities should see themselves as similar to businesses. Even if they do not seek to make a profit, they must adjust expenditures to income and make use of loans only when the burden of the financing costs will not be insufferable as it returns as a tax on local residents and property owners. However, it does make sense to use loans if they will bring a specific return. For example, for the financing of transportation infrastructure or water and sewage installations, taxes and fees are collected which are calculated on the basis of estimated cost, which is likely to include the cost of linkage and interest on loans. Loans may also be taken if it can be assumed that the level of local taxes will cover their repayment.

Since the government has recognized the repayment of loans as a necessary category of expenditures, the amount calculated for the general grant is intended to supplement local expenditures for the repayment of loans. The fact that this burden ultimately fell upon the government has prodded the Ministry of Finance and other ministries to provide a growing portion of development financing in the form of grants rather than loans. By doing this, the government theoretically loses a partner for securing loans on the open market and for bearing the burden of repayment, but since nearly the entire capital market is directed by the government and the Bank of Israel, this point has no real significance. In fact, it is possible that the reduction in competition between the government and the local authorities prevents increases in interest rates and commissions.

Government and Institutional Participation in the Non-Ordinary Budget

As shown in table 7.14, prior to 1974 there was very little government and institutional participation in the non-ordinary budget. During the 1970s government ministries began to gradually provide grants instead of loans for public matters or for matters involving a specific policy whose performance a government ministry was to oversee. For example, in regions which lacked adequate air raid shelters, funds were provided for the financing of public shelters as a part of civil defense. Participation was also granted for the building of other security installations, such as fire stations and civil defense headquarters and storage rooms. The Ministry of Transportation gives aid in the form of grants for major roads, improvement of urban transportation, entrances of cities and the like. For the financing of school construction, 75 percent is a grant, with the remaining portion a loan from the national lottery.

Participation of Owners

Owners of property designated for building are expected to finance the development of the necessary utility infrastructures on that property. Therefore, local authorities are empowered to collect various participation fees from property owners. For example, a local authority may place some or all of the paving costs on the owners of property which borders a road or sidewalk. At the beginning of paving advance payments may be collected and after its completion the local authority can collect in accordance with the final account. Distribution of paving costs among property owners is according to property area and/or frontage. In agricultural land or industrial regions, the local authorities may also charge owners of properties which are somewhat distant from a road if they are served by it. Because of the element of chance inherent in this method, it was recommended to local authorities that they instead collect according to a method of levies. The local authority charges a "road levy" or a "sidewalk levy" in fixed amounts which reflect the average expenditures for road and sidewalk paving within the jurisdiction of the municipality. The payment is equal in all parts of the local authority and is not dependent on the width of a specific road or the costs of its paving.

Likewise, a "sewage levy" is collected for sewage installations, which reflects the cost of the installation of a central sewage system and the average cost per square meter. At the time of the installation of sewage systems, the levy can be collected at the beginning of the work for that stage which is about to be installed — sewers, collectors or purification plants. For the establishment of a water system infrastructure, a "pipe-laying levy" may be similarly collected. Additional levies may be related to the costs of drainage, connection to the central system, and other services.

The "appreciation fee" reflects another type of ownership participation. This fee is collected according to section 196a of the third addition to the Planning and Building Law, 1965. While its collection received new legal status in 1981 and 1982, in previous years it had been collected by some local authorities as an "appreciation contribution" or "appreciation tax" according to a section of the Municipal Building Ordinance of 1934, which had remained valid until the new legislation. The "appreciation fee" is a tax set at the level of one-half of any increase in value of a property which resulted from a zoning decision of a planning commission to allow more intensive utilization of the property.

This could result from a decision to turn agricultural land into building land or a change in authorized building density. Such a change will increase an area's population density and thus require additional local services which are not covered in their budgets — the purchase of public land and compensation for expropriation, the establishment of educational, cultural and religious institutions, and the development of public parks and gardens. It is not reasonable that the property owner should profit from the entire appreciation while the general public bears all of the expenses required for the development of the area. The new law requires that local authorities earmark the entire amount received from appreciation fees for the financing of planning and development needs. The law also obligates the Israel Lands Authority to pay for property it transfers, though it did allow for an arrangement by which the precise fee could be replaced by a yearly payment of 10 percent of the Authority's income from urban land. This arrangement was temporary and was eventually to be cancelled. It had been meant to allow the Authority time to organize for payment according to the law. This arrangement existed for more than 10 years, bringing many local authorities stable incomes. It also alleviated the need for extensive deliberations with the Authority and the Ministry of Construction and Housing concerning assessments and the level of the fee, as the law requires for private property owners.

Property owners or contractors sometimes request that the local authority perform infrastructure or construction work which it is not required by law to do or which is not given priority at the time. A local authority may be willing to perform this in exchange for full payment, which may well be at a higher rate than normal.

Loans and Contractor Credit

Prior to fiscal year 1976 it was accepted for the local authorities to mobilize loans for development projects. These loans came from the development budgets of government ministries for matters that they wished to advance, particularly in the state services, and from banks and other sources, among them contractors and suppliers. The terms of the government loans were favorable, with low interest and long repayment periods. At one time loans were granted for the construction of educational institutions in development towns for a period of 45 years, which included a 10 year period with interest at a rate of only 5 percent. Loans on the open market were set according to the terms accepted at the time; during the 1970s they included linkage to the Consumer Price Index or to foreign currency.

In the mid-1960s it became clear that the local authorities needed too much credit from contractors and suppliers to finance purchases and development projects. The local authorities took such credit on the assumption that during the period of the credit they would succeed in collecting owner participation for the final financing of the projects. However, contractor and supplier credit is by its very nature short-term. When the local authorities were not completely successful in collecting owner participation, the credit became a burden on the authorities. This credit is not listed in the section for repayment of loans and is not recognized as an expenditure in the ordinary budgets; it was therefore not covered. With the provision of loans to replace this credit in the years 1966 and 1967, the Ministries of Interior and Finance decided to prevent receipt of credit from contractors and suppliers as a source of financing development projects and the purchase of heavy equipment. Since then they do not usually approve short term credit from suppliers as a source of financing in the non-ordinary budget.

In the 1970s a different phenomena came to light. With the growth of inflation, loans which could be obtained on the open market were linked and carried high interest. Indeed, according to the Interest Law the linked loans were limited to an interest rate of 9 percent, and afterwards even to 7.5 percent, but the effective interest paid was higher and reached as high as 11 or 12 percent. This was the result of commissions, calculation of value days, making the loan available on the 14th of the month (one day before publication of the consumer price index), interest calculations in different periods, and other reasons.

In those same years the government and the local authorities were nearly alone in taking out linked loans. Thus there was competition between these bodies and, according to the Bank of Israel, this competition caused the increases in effective interest. Clearly it is senseless for public bodies to compete among themselves for the few sources of credit, which can only lead to an additional burden of interest on the public budget. Moreover, the more that reliance on loans from the open market grew, the higher was the role of chance in the attainment of resources by local authorities. Only the requests of the larger local authorities were heeded by the banks. Entire sectors including development towns, small settlements and the Arab sector were forced into complete dependence on diminishing state government sources. In addition, the receipt of each loan was random and depended more on the ability and will of the banks than on the organized budget planning of each local authority. Therefore, when a loan was offered to a local authority, it required municipal acceptance and Ministry of Interior approval within a period as short as a few days, not enough time to check how it integrated into a firmly based budgetary program. Furthermore, the entire loan would be received from a bank or some other body all at once, not necessarily according to the stages of performance in a project or the immediate need for cash. Sometimes this situation would bring temporary relief to local authorities, but linkage and interest would immediately be charged, sometimes without justification.

During those same years a number of incidents were revealed in which the local authorities were involved in loan deals with private intermediaries who were ultimately unable to provide the financing in exchange for the notes they received, whether due to managerial complications or a lack of integrity. The Ministry of Finance and the Bank of Israel wished to prevent over-encouragement of the private market, and particularly of private investors and intermediaries, from this "easy living" to be made by making available unplanned amounts of financing to local authorities. In the context of the deliberations of the Commission for the Improvement of Financing of Local Authorities (the Kubersky Commission), it was proposed that the authorities not make use of financing from the open market and that in its place the Ministry of Interior would offer a "credit line for development" which would not be earmarked in advance for any specific purpose. Each local authority could earmark it in accordance with its own decisions. This amount together with the loans of the government ministries would meet budgeting conditions without linkage.

The conclusions of the Kubersky Commission were accepted by the government in fiscal year 1976. The credit line to local authorities was put in a section of the state budget beginning in the 1977 fiscal year. The local authorities decided to refrain from obtaining loans on the open market for development projects and purchases. Indeed, since then the financing of development projects by such loans has nearly disappeared and there are no longer instances of loans from non-bank sources.

The credit line was set in 1977 at 600 million Israeli pounds, an amount nominally equivalent to those loans approved by the Ministry of Interior which had been obtained by the local authorities in fiscal year 1976. In the years 1977 and 1978 an amount was allocated to the credit line which correlated to the patterns of receipt of past loans, but which also covered those local authorities that previously had not succeeded in obtaining loans on the open market. In 1979, an allocation formula developed for the Ministry of Interior under the guidance of a joint steering committee which included representatives of local government was introduced.[46] The computerized formula is based on population in the local authorities, but also takes into consideration the level of development of the local authority as expressed by the spread of the population, distance from a large city, topography, age of the settlement since 1930, number of private cars, average income of wage earners, locally-generated income from taxes, number of needy families and expenditures for welfare services. Also considered are such indicators of the future as the average yearly rate of growth in the previous ten years and the average predicted growth according to official plans for population spread and development policy (granting more weight to local authorities in development areas and to those which have specific functions like the metropolitan local authorities).

A slightly different formula was determined for the regional councils, which takes into consideration the number of settlements. In the credit line the Arab and Druze sectors receive their share according to their populations, while in some years they have even received, in real terms, a special addition. According to the formulas about 90 percent of the credit line is distributed in the budget, while the remaining portion serves to solve special problems of certain local authorities, or a number of local authorities together, which cannot be solved within the local quota.

The introduction of the credit line in the national budget ushered in a new era in the financing of development projects. The amounts were given each year to each local authority according to a known formula, to be allocated in accordance with local preferences. However, despite its advantages, the status of the credit line has diminished. Beginning in May 1979 there was a worsening of the terms of government development loans and they were linked to the Consumer Price Index. In order to distinguish between them and the loans on the private market, an interest rate of only 1 percent was set. As the national budget was reduced, the portion of the

357

credit line decreased as well and its real value in 1984 was only about 40 percent of its value during its first year of existence. Thus the local authorities actually receive small amounts which enable them to do no more than supplement the financing of projects which are financed from a different source, or to make some improvements and repairs in public institutions and infrastructure when the ordinary budget is not enough to cover these.

Thus the sections for loans in local authority budgets are primarily from the credit line which is set aside for them in the national budget, loans from government ministries (primarily Education and Culture, Interior, Construction and Housing, and Transportation), and a small amount from other sources, led by the national lottery, which offers loans for the construction of education, health and welfare facilities in cooperation with the relevant government ministries.

Other Sources for Development Financing

Other sources for the financing of development activities include the occasional sale of land. Such a sale may be undertaken only in exchange for the purchase of other land or for some other development purpose approved by the Ministry of Interior, according to section 188 of the Municipal Corporations Ordinance. Some local authorities have succeeded in accumulating special funds such as for depreciation or innovations. One fund common to many authorities is designated for the replacement of water lines. This was established at the initiative of the Water Commission, the Ministry of Interior and the Ministry of Finance and is financed by funds set aside by the local authorities in accordance with the amount of water which they sell, as well as by direct state government participation. The fund is administered jointly by the Union of Local Authorities, government ministries and the local government treasury. An additional source of development funds in the past was a transfer from the ordinary budget. This is generally no longer possible, even when significant sums are collected as "owner participation" within the framework of this budget.

In summary, resources available for development activities have declined during the 1980s, primarily as a result of the state government policy to reduce public sector activity. This policy has brought about a drastic reduction in budgets earmarked for development activities. These budgets are more flexible in the short term and are easier to cut without causing any obvious damage to the welfare of local residents. This also serves to limit future expenditures, in that what was not constructed does not require operation and maintenance. This is true only for new installations, however, and not when old installations which are expensive to operate and maintain must be replaced by new ones. With the reduction of government resources, there was a corresponding increase in the share of other sources of income which the local authorities could obtain, such as from property owners, although these sources are by nature quite limited. During these years it was generally decided that new settlements and neighborhoods built at public initiative receive full development funding from the Ministry of Construction and Housing or from the Jewish Agency, thereby relieving the burden on the local authorities. However, new neighborhoods and even settlements are still being built privately, thus maintaining pressure on local authority resources. This is in addition to the need to renew installations, to fill gaps left over from the past, and even to improve services. Thus the reduction in funds for municipal development cannot continue for too long.

Summary

The financing of local authorities appears to be an issue in constant crisis. Once every few months public attention is directed toward a discussion between the state government and local authorities concerning a predicted crisis in the treasury of the local authorities, or concerning the need to update their budgets or to consolidate and reduce their accumulated budget deficits. It is likely that the problems of specific local authorities will be raised, where there has been a breakdown of the provision of services. This can happen as the result of a strike by municipal workers who have failed to receive their wages, disruption of water or electricity supplies due to lack of payment, or seizure of funds or equipment by income tax authorities and the like.

Studies have shown that after all of the discussions, solutions were found to most of the problems, and local authorities were not left with exceptional deficits. In the period from 1969 to 1978 there were five years which concluded without any ongoing deficit, eight years with a deficit no higher than 4 percent of expenditures, and only two years with a deficit of 7 percent.[47] In the years from 1979 onward, the situation got slightly worse, but at the same time there was a more massive program of loans for reducing the deficit, after the government ministries recognized that resources had worn too thin. A deficit of a few percentages is of minor significance and can be explained by differences in accounting procedures. While expenditures are listed according to an accumulating method (that is, every account which is approved is listed as a budgetary expense even if it will actually be paid at a later date), receipts are listed according to the cash method (that is, the receipt is listed only when the amount is received and not when it is charged).

The situation in the many local authorities varies greatly. This has always been the case, regardless of the current state of the economy. This means that a difficult budgetary situation in a specific local authority is not necessarily due to external economic circumstances. In many cases local budget management is below standard. This can result from a number of factors such as incorrect decisions concerning the scope of the budget relative to resources, lack of implementation of the budget within its agreed-upon framework, or low rates for obligatory payments and/or slackness in their collection. There may also be factors which are beyond the control of the local council and its administration.

Since from time to time local authorities claim that their budget management tools are insufficient, much attention has been given to improving these tools, including improvements in the mobilization of resources and the transfer of resources from the government. Some of this attention has occurred in the context of public commissions which were appointed to discuss the financial situation of the local authorities, as well as other issues, at whose center is the relationship between the state and local governments. These commissions have brought together a high level of professional and systematic effort at formulating new proposals. In the last twenty-five years there have been three such commissions, known popularly after their chairmen — the Vitkon Commission, the Kubersky Commission, and the Sanbar Commission.

The Vitkon Commission

In 1961 the Minister of Interior appointed the Commission for the Study of Methods of Taxation in the Local Authorities, headed by Supreme Court Justice, Dr. Alfred Vitkon. The commission was requested to make proposals concerning the proper methods of taxation for local authorities and to express its opinion regarding their overall financing. Participating in the commission were three members of the Knesset, high ranking officials of the Ministries of Interior and Finance and the Bank of Israel, and two economists who were public figures. At its outset the deputy mayor of Tel Aviv also participated on the commission as a representative of local government. He resigned, however, when it became clear that the commission would not recommend empowering the local authorities to collect an income tax or allow them to have some part in this tax. The recommendations of the commission were completed in May 1964.

The principle recommendations of the Vitkon Commission were: to unify the assessment and collection of the municipal property tax, general municipal tax, and government property tax (the assessment would be made according to the capital value of each property when it was empty, without taking into consideration the Renter Protection Law); to divide the tax burden more justly among the residents; and to uphold the power of individual local authorities to set municipal tax rates. The commission also recommended changes in the principles behind the business tax, the welfare and recreation tax, and the entertainment tax, a phasing out of the charges for licences and signs, and the cancellation of education charges.

In the matter of the budget and expenditures, the commission recommended that the authorities be helped to get out from under the burden of heavy debts and that standards be set as a basis for a "government policy in the area of state services whose financing will be divided between the government and the local authorities." The commission also recommended programs, rules and limitations for the arrangement of the sections of the development budget, receipt of loans and the terms of their repayment. Finally, the commission recommended that the Ministry of Interior assure that the local authorities act in accordance with all of these recommendations. The recommendations of the Vitkon Commission were not fully implemented, but they served as the basis for many of the steps taken during the 1960s, such as the attempt to limit the repayment of loans to 20 percent of the budget; improvements in the business tax, entertainment tax, and welfare and recreation tax; cancellation of the municipal property tax in 1968; and the offering of loans for the relief of the municipal debt burden from 1965 onward.

The Kubersky Commission

In 1975 the Ministries of Interior and Finance agreed on the need for a renewed look at local authority financing since accelerating inflation had led to reports of increased instability and inability to function properly. The Commission for the Improvement of Local Financing was established, chaired by Haim Kubersky, the director-general of the Ministry of Interior, with the participation of Arnon Gafni, director-general of the Ministry of Finance and Pinchas Eilon, chairman of the Union of Local Authorities. The commission was asked to explore the current situation and to recommend whatever reforms it deemed necessary.

After months of intensive activity, the commission submitted its proposals in November 1975. Its recommendations dealt with the determination of principles and rules for the functioning of the budgetary system and the mobilization of resources in the local authorities. According to these recommendations, a meeting was to be held every year at a date prior to the beginning of the fiscal year between the Ministries of Interior and Finance and the Union of Local Authorities for the purpose of formulating the principles for balanced budgets in the coming year.

It was also determined that a detailed forecast of income and expenditure sections would be supplied on time to each of the local authorities, to the extent that this depended on the state government. This consultation and provision of information would also take place if the need for changes were revealed during the fiscal year. The financing of the ordinary budget would include the participation of government ministries for state services, at a rate of 75 percent for obligatory services and 50 percent for optional services, on the basis of standards which would be accompanied by "calculations of reasonable real cost of each service provided according to the standard." Additional resources would come from the general grant and transferred income.

Transfer of sums to the local authorities would be regular throughout the year and the required reporting would be reduced to once a year. The local authorities would also continue to collect locally-generated income in the form of taxes, charges and service fees. The commission left open the question of the collection of the general municipal tax, since opinions were divided as to the value of its continued collection.

Concerning the development budget, it was determined that every local authority would put together a general, multi-year development plan from which it would derive yearly development plans according to local capabilities. Government ministries would make available participations and non-linked loans for projects for which they were responsible at a rate which would cover the full cost. There would also be resources of locally-generated income. The commission proposed that "the local authorities not undertake financing in the open market." Instead, the government would put a credit line for municipal development in the national budget. Its allocation would be handled by the Ministry of Interior on the basis of certain fixed principles.

It was recommended generally that the local authorities take steps toward efficient management and economizing. Other recommendations dealt with the establishment of a Committee of Directors-General for dealing with issues of local government (to include representatives of the Union of Local Authorities), as well as other joint forums. It was also recommended that a "commission of experts for the study of issues of local government" be set up.

The recommendations of the Kubersky Commission were validated in the government decision of November 1976 and were even partially implemented. From fiscal year 1977 onward a credit line was set up for local authority development. Work was begun on the determination of a "service basket" for state services, primarily by the Ministry of Education and Culture. The Ministry of Labor and Social Welfare made the transition to unified financing at a rate of 75 percent of expenditures, and various divisions of the Ministry of Education and Culture changed over to financing on the basis of the commission's recommendations. The Ministries of Interior and Finance established an "experts committee" in 1978, in which the two ministries and the Union of Local Authorities participated, and in which the financial issues between the state government and the local authorities were clarified.

The Sanbar Commission

At the recommendation of the Kubersky Commission, the government established a commission to undertake an in-depth study of the issues of local government — the State Commission on Local Government. The activities and recommendations of this commission, headed by Moshe Sanbar, are detailed elsewhere in this book. In matters of budget and finance, the commission prescribed principles for four components of the financing of the ordinary budget — locally-generated income, transfers from government ministries, transferred income, and the general grant of the Ministry of Interior. It also proposed the formalization of government participation according to clear and well-known rules and the basing of the general grant on a basket of services. The commission recommended that locally-generated income be changed by making changes in the general municipal tax from residential buildings, by replacing the general municipal tax for businesses by a local tax on the basis of added value, and by establishing local, rather than state, collection of a property tax on land.

The commission also recommended that the budgets be structured differently — the ordinary budget would be for services, the development budget would be for purchases and development projects, and a "capital budget" would be set up as a bridge between the two budgets and to handle problems such as repayment of loans, deficit financing and the like. These recommendations are only a small part of a wider set of recommendations concerning state-local government relations, made on the background of a new and different general approach to the status of local authorities in Israel.

These recommendations were not fully accepted until the summer of 1984, which marked the end of the term of the government which acted on behalf of the Tenth Knesset, and only a small portion of the recommendations in the financial area were implemented. At the same time, during those years there was a severe acceleration in inflation, to the extent that the standard budget and accounting tools were becoming obsolete. In fiscal years 1984 and 1985 the budget was updated every three months, and even this was often late and overtaken by developments. Together with repeated reductions in resources and budgets and the wearing away of the participation of government ministries, all of these factors placed the local authorities in a grave situation marked by uncertainty and difficulty in functioning. If this situation continues, it will require different tools than those in use at present. If the economic situation stabilizes it will be possible to try once again to implement the recommendations of the various commissions and even to take additional steps to improve local financing and budgeting with the goal of once again placing the responsibility for local management upon the local authority council and its administration, with minimal involvement of the state government in the details of local activities.

Epilogue

The outline and analysis presented in this chapter is based on data covering the period up until 1981. A further investigation of the principle developments in the financing of local authorities in Israel from 1982 to 1986 is of interest as this period saw substantial change.

The years 1982–1986 represented the peak of an economic crisis in Israel and the introduction of a drastic stabilization program. The economic crisis continued until the middle of 1985 and was characterized by rampant inflation running into hundreds of percent per year, an economic freeze, lack of growth, an increase in unemployment, and one of the worst periods for the balance of payments. The crisis also included shocks in the money markets and on the stock market and a national budget deficit which caused inflation to spiral. Beginning in 1979, anti-inflation and other economic measures were undertaken at the state level.

Local authorities were among the first to be affected by the policy of cutbacks which affected the entire public sector. They were forced to reduce activities each year according to the rate set by the state budget. Nevertheless, methods were developed which guaranteed the real value of general taxes, fees and levies. Thus the real value of local authority budgets was reduced while the real value of internal revenue was maintained, to the extent that it even gained in value against general revenues. Some local authorities raised their potential revenues beyond the budget framework worked out by the Interior Ministry. As a result, these local authorities no longer required a general grant, as set forth in the relevant regulations.

In 1986, with Knesset approval, the state government allowed local authorities to raise their general tax rates by 170 percent (based upon the January-December 1985 consumer price index), while the financial year (April-March) budget rose only 100 percent. In this manner local authorities enjoyed greater value from the general rates within their budgets. Since the state government decreased the general grant according to the difference between the assessment of expenditures and general local authority revenues, it became necessary to estimate the returns forthcoming to those local authorities, which through various methods had developed a theoretical surplus, and to pass these on to the other local authorities. This was done by varying the distribution of property and other taxes. This resulted in a situation in which most of these taxes were passed on to the above-mentioned local authorities (195 local authorities out of 230, representing 52 percent of the population and budget of local authorities). This situation is likely to continue into 1987, and accordingly, more fundamental changes are planned for the transfer of income.

In the years 1985–1986, arrangements were also made to reduce the accumulated deficit of several dozen local authorities. One of the results of the years of high inflation had been a substantial deficit among a large number of local authorities. The same conditions had necessitated updating budgets several times a year, careful project management of contracts with linked prices, a real cutback in manpower and in budgets, and strict linkage in general tax payment plans and in rates for fees and levies. Nonetheless, guidance and budget update schedules were slow in coming and even those government offices dealing with updates of assessments were, at times, in arrears. Furthermore, the consumer price index rose excessively and irregularly, leaving many local authorities with substantial deficits.

In July 1985, a number of new economic steps were undertaken to reduce inflation which established the conditions for greater economic stability for the local authorities. It is true that for several months interest rates remained high, causing a substantial increase in the deficit of those local authorities already suffering from a deficit. However it was expected that the local authorities would reduce surplus positions by about 4,000 and this was actually effected through the dismissal of 5,500 workers from public service. This enabled local authorities to raise general tax rates according to the consumer price index, while freezing other tax rates, prices and rent. Some local authorities managed to reduce their deficit independently. As noted, others were assisted by state government aid and deficit reduction programs. Each local authority entering into these arrangements was obliged to work within a framework which provided that it raised the level of internal revenue collection, avoided unprofitable credit schemes and undertook further steps.

In 1986, ordinary budgets reached 2 billion new shekels. (The new shekel inaugurated on 1 January 1986 was the equivalent of 1,000 old shekels). Non-ordinary budgets reached 400 million new shekels in the same year. Consequently, approximate expenditures amounted to 2.4 billion new shekels or $1.6 billion.[48] The local authorities employed 10,000 fewer workers than were employed in 1979. Presently, manpower cutbacks average 15 percent. Funds for the ordinary budget for 1986 are comprised of 35 percent from general taxes and 20 percent from other locally-generated income. This means that the state's budget role has dropped to only 45 percent. Two categories of local authority now exist: those which do not require the Interior Ministry's general grant and whose financial state is generally sound, and those which require the general grant and therefore are obliged to operate strictly within their budget in order to avoid running a deficit.

As noted, developments have occurred in ordinary budget funding which require more fundamental change, towards stabilizing funding for all local authorities and preventing greater gaps between different groups of local authorities.

Table 7.15—APPENDIX
COMPARISON OF GROWTH IN LOCAL AUTHORITY EXPENDITURES, THE GROSS NATIONAL PRODUCT, GOVERNMENT EXPENDITURES, THE POPULATION, AND THE CONSUMER PRICE INDEX: 1960-1981

Year	Local Authority Expenditures		Gross National Product		Government Expenditures	
	On the basis 1960=100	Growth from Year to Year in Percentages	On the basis 1960=100	Growth from Year to Year in Percentages	On the basis 1960=100	Growth from Year to Year in Percentages
1960	100	—	100	—	100	—
1965	297	197	233	133	254	154
1970	480	62	441	89	713	180
1975	2,337	387	1,797	308	4,221	492
1976	3,203	37	2,397	33	5,631	33
1977	4,620	44	3,471	45	8,440	50
1978	7,760	68	5,974	72	13,069	55
1979	14,910	92	11,824	98	27,631	111
1980	33,150	122	28,403	140	64,219	132
1981	71,973	117	66,574	134	142,373	122

Year	Population at the End of the Year		Consumer Price Index	
	On the Basis 1960=100	Growth from Year to Year in Percentages	On the Basis 1960=100	Growth from Year to Year in Percentages
1960	100	—	100	—
1965	121	20.8	142	42
1970	141	16.3	175	23
1975	162	15.6	528	202
1976	166	2.3	710	34
1977	170	2.2	980	38
1978	174	2.3	1,489	52
1979	178	2.6	2,908	95
1980	182	2.2	6,794	134
1981	185	1.4	14,272	110

Comment: In studying the data note that until 1975 the gaps between years are five years long, and the indices and percentages are calculated accordingly.

Notes – Chapter 7

1. The description in this section is based upon Musgrove (1959), Ch. 1 and Due (1963), pp. 13-18.
2. For a discussion of this topic, see Hirsch (1970); Due (1963), p. 27 and Richardson (1971), pp. 146-148.
3. There have been outstanding events in the transfer of functions or financing resources from local authorities to the state government. 1) Since 1953 the salaries of teachers in the elementary schools have been paid by the Ministry of Education and Culture; teachers became state employees in exchange for cancellation of local authority rights to a 7.5 percent addition to the income tax. 2) Since 1967 the burden of financing and maintaining municipal hospitals has fallen upon the state government. 3) Since 1968 the participation of local authorities in the financing of graduated tuition for high school students has been cancelled. 4) Since 1975 there is a fixed participation of 75 percent in the financing of the expenditures of local authority agencies for social welfare. 5) In 1982 implementation of guaranteed income to the needy was transferred to the National Insurance Institute.
4. See the comparison made by the International Union of Local Authorities (IULA) in: Marshal (1963) and Caulcott (1981), pp. 69-85 and Morg (1967), Ch. 9. A distinction must be made between the comparison of the overall expenditures of local authorities to the national product and a measure of the part of the local authorities in the national product itself; that is, the creation of new activities by their activities, excluding the purchase of products and services in the private market and purely financial activities. In addition, the comparison is not completely similar to an analysis of the share of the local authorities in public consumption and investment. The latter are in national accounting concepts and present economic phenomena.
5. For an additional analysis of the development of the budgets of the local authorities and an attempt to estimate the extent of real growth in activities (excluding wage and price increases, repayment of loans and population growth) in the 1970s, see Hecht (1985).
6. Rotenberg (1956), p.14.
7. See State Commission on Local Government (1981), pp. 22-32. In the data included in this chapter all of the ordinary transfers were listed in the ordinary budget, while in the non-ordinary budget only the development projects, in the broad sense of the term, were listed. Therefore, loans for balancing the budget were listed as income in the ordinary budget and not as a transfer from the non-ordinary budget.
8. As "transferred income," only "directly transferred incomes" are listed in the local authority budgets and in the tables in this chapter. The "transferred income" from the purchase tax and part of the vehicle charge, transferred through the general grant, are listed in the financial reports of the local authorities, as well as in these tables, as

a "general grant." There is no way to differentiate this data and this would also have no significance from the point of view of the individual local authority.

9. See the conclusions of Davey (1971).

10. For discussions of this question, see Kalchheim (1979), pp. 101-10; Steinman (1975), pp. 41-46 and Yizraeli (1980), pp. 335-48.

11. For a short description of the development of local authority taxes in Israel, see The Tax Museum (1968), pp. 289-91. More detailed descriptions are found in Gurion (1957).

12. For examples, see the Commission for the Study of Ways of Integrating Assessment and Collection of Property Taxes and the General Municipal Tax of the Government and of the Local Authorities (1963), p. 39.

13. Examples from the data of the municipality of Tel Aviv-Jaffa in the years 1960 to 1963 can be found in ibid., p. 36.

14. Section 273 of the Municipal Corporations Ordinance.

15. See Bone and Lu-Yon (1980).

16. This is the most widespread method. There are also other arrangements, such as collection in six consecutive monthly payments in the first half of the year, as in Jerusalem.

17. Section 301 of the Municipal Corporations Ordinance, which was cancelled according to section 9 of the new law.

18. See Harvestman (1979).

19. Morag (1967), pp. 232-325 and Barlev-Levy (1975), pp. 16-40.

20. Shafat (1979), pp. 225-30.

21. The Municipal Corporations Ordinance, sections 150-161; the Local Councils Ordinance, Section 121 and the second supplement.

22. Section 161 of the Municipal Corporations Ordinance. In local councils only one-half of the municipal tax.

23. Section 160 of the Municipal Corporations Ordinance.

24. Rotenberg (1956), pp. 7-36.

25. Further on, Rotenberg, who was the financial advisor to the Ministry of Interior and afterwards ministry director-general for local government, explains that: "For this purpose (social ranking) the addition to income tax is placed on residents, for it is a tax whose rate is determined in accordance with the social situation of the obligant. These two types of taxes — the general municipal tax and the addition to income tax — together form a single tax system which attempts to be as fair and socially just as possible."

26. According to the agreement among the Ministry of Interior, the Ministry of Finance, Union of Local Authorities and the Union of Regional Councils, it was determined on the basis of the assurance of the Ministry of Finance that beginning in 1982, in this way or another, a value added tax would be made available to the local authorities.

27. For a detailed description of a large part of these claims, see Vitkon Commission (1964), pp. 40-45.

28. See the formulation of section 98 (21) to the formulation of the Municipal Corporations Ordinance with the establishment of the state.

29. Ministry of Interior (1981), p. 23.

30. State Commission on Local Government (1981), pp. 37-39.

31. Expression of this is found in The Commission for the Financing of Local Authorities (1975), p. 6.

32. Categorization according to the source of income and its character can be found in the booklets "Local Authorities in Israel" published every year by the Central Bureau of Statistics and the Ministry of Interior. Additional details in national terms can be found in the booklets summarizing the "ordinary budgets of the local authorities" published by the Department of Finances and Budgets in the Administration for Local Government, Ministry of Interior.

33. The concept of the Municipal Corporations Ordinance in the past was that the paving of sidewalks is the responsibility of the owners bordering them, according to the request of the municipality. Authority was granted the municipality to pave the sidewalk at the expense of the owners, if they did not do so themselves. At the initiative of members of the Knesset the law was amended to state that the paving of sidewalks is a function of the local authorities and they can divide the expense among owners in ways similar to methods used for roads.

34. The description is in accordance with the wording of the law and also according to Rotenberg (1956), p. 40.

35. Ibid., p. 49.

36. For more complete description of the Compensation for Property Rate, the rules and formulas, see Hecht-Gair (1984).

37. Among the many books and articles, see Buchanan (1950); Reagan-Sonzone (1981); and the works of the U.S. Advisory Commission on Intergovernmental Relations.

38. Marshal (1963), pp. 23-24.

39. Rotenberg (1956), pp. 64-65.

40. Ibid.

41. Ibid.

42. See Barzel (1976), pp. 425-46 and the State Commission on Local Government (1981), appendix.

43. In those same years (1977 onward) a credit line for local authority development was introduced, and thus the standardization of grants passed to the operation of the credit line, which replaced the loans from the private market in accordance with the abilities of each local authority.

44. See the list of sections and amounts for 1984 in Finance-Interior (1984), pp. 103-10.

45. Indeed the ordinary budget is financed in accordance with the principles only by the final incomes. Every loan is received in the

manner of the non-ordinary budget. In certain years, therefore, sections of repayment of loans to the non-ordinary budget which were financed by loans were removed. Afterwards it was decided not to disturb the sections whose place was in the ordinary budget, and therefore the loans were transferred from the non-ordinary budget as a "transfer to the ordinary budget." In financial data of the local authorities all of the expenditures whose place is in the ordinary budget are listed without transfers, as are loans which served to finance the repayment of loans, deficits and for relief of the treasury situation, as income of the ordinary budget.

46. For a full description of the formula, see M.R.B. Company (1978).

47. See the Central Bureau of Statistics — Ministry of Interior (1982), p. 10, Table b.

48. When reading the data, one should remember that from 1 July 1985 until January, 1987, the exchange rate of the Israeli shekel remained steady vis-a-vis the dollar and therefore the adjustment to the dollar lagged behind the increase in prices. In comparison to the increase in the consumer price index, there was a decrease in the budgets during the years surveyed.

Appendix I

NEXT STEPS IN LOCAL GOVERNMENT REFORM: THE RECOMMENDATIONS OF THE STATE COMMISSION ON LOCAL GOVERNMENT

Daniel J. Elazar

The Commission and Its Task

In the previous chapters we have described the present system of local government in Israel as it now exists. On one hand it reflects the great strides made in the development of a comprehensive system of local government in Israel after 1948. On the other it also reflects any deficiencies of that system.

In 1976, the government of Israel, under the leadership of Prime Minister Yitzhak Rabin and Interior Minister Yosef Burg, voted to establish a State Commission on Local Government to view the existing system and recommend changes for its improvement. Moshe Sanbar, the former governor of the Bank of Israel, was appointed chairman of the Commission and its members were drawn from those involved in local government affairs, public affairs and academic communities. The Commission was comprised as follows:

Public Figures:
Chairman, Mr. Moshe Sanbar
(Former Governor of the Bank of Israel; former head of State Budget Division, Ministry of Finance and Chairman, Interministerial Committee for Efficiency)
Mr. Mordechai Ish-Shalom
(Former Mayor of Jerusalem)
Mr. Yaakov Salman
(Former head of Property Tax Division, Ministry of Finance and coordinator of Interministerial Committee for Efficiency)

Representatives from Local Government:
Mr. Pinchas Elon
Chairman, Union of Local Authorities; Mayor of Holon
Mr. Dov Barzelai, Esq.
Deputy Chairman, Union of Local Authorities; Mayor of
Hadera
Mr. Yosef Schein
Chairman, Union of Regional Councils

Representatives from the State Government:
Mr. Meir Gabbai, Esq.
Director-General, Ministry of Justice
Mr. Amiram Sivan
Director-General, Ministry of Finance
Mr. Haim Kubersky
Director-General, Ministry of Interior

Academics:
Dr. Subhi Abu-Gosh
Political Science (Resigned from the Commission before it
completed its work.)
Professor Daniel J. Elazar
Local Government
Professor Eitan Bragles
Economist (Resigned from the Commission after a short
time.)
Professor Yehezkiel Dror
Public Administration
Professor Yitzhak Zamir
Constitutional Law (Resigned from the Commission before
it completed its work when he was appointed as legal advisor
to the government.)
Professor Yaakov Ne'eman
Fiscal and Civil Law (During the period of the Commission
he was appointed Director-General, Ministry of Finance.)
Professor Arye Shahar
Geography and Urban Planning

After the 1977 Knesset elections, the new government under
Prime Minister Begin reaffirmed the Commission's mandate.
The Commission worked for three years, issuing its final report
in 1980. That report offers a basis for a comprehensive but realistic

program in local government reform. What follows are summaries of its recommendations. The full report is available as *Local Government in Israel, Report* (Jerusalem: June 1981).

Introduction: Theoretical Framework, Principles and Goals

The charge given to the Commission by the government of Israel was to examine local government, inter-local, and state-local relations with regard to the appropriateness of their structures and functions and to recommend needed improvements. The Commission understood this mandate to include the strengthening of both the civic and service capacities of local government to enable it to provide the services entrusted to it and to provide the citizenry with means of expressing their local interests.

The Commission approached its task by first clarifying its own position as to what the role of local government should be within a modern state, most particularly in the State of Israel, and how to move toward that goal within the Israeli context. While clarifying their own sense of what was desirable, the Commission members abjured any effort to propose radical changes on the grounds that insistence on what is perceived to be best is frequently the enemy of decent improvement because, for whatever reason, the best cannot be implemented all at once. Thus the Commission attempted to walk the narrow line between simply accepting what is and suggesting what ought to be but cannot be realized. At the same time, the Commission members well understood that a recognition of realistic limits did not and should not mean an abjuration of basic values and larger goals.

Basic Principles

The Commission's recommendations were derived from three sources:

1) Its understanding of the optimal situation.
2) The experience acquired by Israel up to the present with regard to local government relations, relations among local authorities, and relations between state authorities and local authorities.

3) The experience of reforms in other states since World War II.

In addition, the Commission tried to understand Israel's political culture, specifically as it has developed out of the Jewish political tradition, in order to adapt its recommendations to orientations and behavioral patterns which are well rooted in this political culture and which derive from it. We will examine these three sources in reverse order.

The Experience of Other Countries

The Commission's effort to improve local government in Israel parallels the numerous efforts to achieve local government reform initiated in Europe and North America over the past three decades. Therefore, it was natural and proper for the Commission to study these reforms. Without going into detail, it can be said that virtually all recent reform efforts have been based upon the managerial perspective which views effective local government as essentially a problem of organization for better management and starts with a hierarchical view of state-local relations. The two views are closely related and reflect the conventional wisdom of our times.

The modern conceptions of the nature of the sovereign state which were developed in Europe are based on the notion that power should be centralized within one governing authority. The democratic revolutions of the modern epoch in Europe attempted to gain control of the process of governance as well as the state bureaucracy for the benefit of the citizens. However, for the revolutionaries themselves, the state remained essentially a centralized, hierarchical entity.

According to this theory, a single center and authority should hold all power in order to enable the state to function properly. The local authorities constituted the periphery, whose authority derived solely from the center. The center defined the proper nature of state-local relations. The local authorities were simply tools of the state government while the state determined to what extent it was willing to entrust them with responsibility and authority. According to this theory, the motive for reforms was to provide for the needs of the state government.

This historical approach is supplemented by, and intimately related to, the managerial understanding of the role of government in general and local government in particular. The idea of the reified state emerged in the 16th and 17th centuries to introduce the modern era. Managerial theories emerged in the 19th and 20th centuries as a response to the industrial revolution. Managerial theories understand government activity as another form of management, essentially a problem of organization and administration.

The managerial idea emerged in two ways — as part of the process of the consolidation of the state in countries like France and Prussia where strong leaders such as Napoleon and Frederick the Great reorganized their respective state structures so as to better be able to control them from the top. In countries where democratic or republican institutions prevented the development of such strong leaders, managerialism emerged as a result of the emergence of great industrial empires, whereby great entrepreneurs built large enterprises and then needed to find ways to organize them for better management and control.

In either case, the underlying principle of managerialism is clear. To be managed well, organizations must be managed by bureaucracies structured according to the principles of an authoritative administrative hierarchy. They must be built around such principles as a proper span of control, economies of scale, and lower levels reporting to higher — all considered necessary for good management. Managerial theories had a natural affinity to the underlying conceptions of the reified state in an era of expanding government. As the state took on more responsibilities, the center sought to increase its control over the periphery and adopted management tools to do so, adding a pyramid-like structure to the original model.

The introduction of managerial ideas and techniques brought with it a number of benefits and management as a tool has become very important in the administration of any modern state. At the same time, to the extent that management ceased to be a tool and was presented as a substitute for governing — which involves not only the application of managerial principles but considerations of politics and policy which must take precedence even over considerations of administration, especially in a democracy — the virtues of a managerial approach are much less apparent.

In the modern centralized state, the local authorities became, *ipso facto*, subject to the state bureaucracy. Indeed, one of the major struggles in revolutionary Europe concerned local freedom and the existence of original local rights vis-a-vis state control, in light of the new ideas of "freedom, equality and fraternity." The tendencies to subject local governments to greater state control were strengthened by the managerial view which justified local government as existing for administrative purposes only.

The first stage, therefore, was to change the earlier community structure into that of a local authority and then, using the managerial view, to change the local authority into a local administration. Most contemporary attempts to reform local government adopted this view without criticism.

However, the Commission did not adopt this approach for two reasons. The first was its understanding that it should not apply the European definition of sovereignty. There is another approach which received its modern expression in the New World, in countries settled by Europeans who sought another way to organize political life. According to this approach, whose earlier roots are found in the Bible, the status of local government is no less important in an orderly democratic state. In this view the local authorities are an integral part of the political system and not merely administrative extensions of the state government for dealing with local affairs.

The Commission had available to it the results of reform efforts elsewhere, particularly the grand European consolidations of the 1960's and 1970's which reduced the number of local governments in Germany, Belgium, Great Britain, and the Scandinavian countries by reorganizing them on "rational lines," that is to say, following doctrines that were developed as a result of the managerial approach. Follow-up reports on the results of those changes prepared on those countries clearly indicated widespread disappointment with the results even on the part of those who had been the greatest devotees of the changes, including those most committed to managerial principles.

Not only did the reforms not bring the kinds of savings presumed to be derived from streamlining the governmental structure and division of functions, but they sacrificed those elements of civic community, including citizen concern for the public life of the community, which make local government desirable in the first place. In short, actual costs of administration rose while civic concern and responsibility declined.

Surveys of the field reveal that in only two countries is local government thriving — Switzerland and the United States, both of which had rejected comprehensive reforms of this character. In both countries decisions on such matters are in local hands. In both, the citizenry themselves perceived what leaders in other countries did not, namely what was truly of the essence in local government and what was peripheral. Responding as citizens, they remained concerned first and foremost with the civic tasks of local government as the proper measure of local organization.

The empirical evidence was impressive enough, but in addition there is now serious research investigating and disproving the claims of the conventional local government reform advocates, particularly the work of the Workshop in Political Theory and Public Policy Analysis at Indiana University, which has examined the claims of the managerial school from a variety of perspectives through meticulous field study and has found most of them to be severely wanting. Similar evidence came to the Commission from the Jerusalem Center for Public Affairs, the Joint Center for Federal and Regional Studies in Basel, and the Center for the Study of Federalism at Temple University in Philadelphia.

Researchers from these institutes made their contribution to the Commission by providing background materials and by meeting with Commission members and staff to discuss various aspects of their studies. Hence, the observations and responses received from those who were involved in reforms elsewhere and the scientific evidence from empirical studies all helped to convince the Commission that the European approach to local government reform was incomplete and would not help the Commission to achieve its goals.

In light of this, the Commission sought to maximize local autonomy in ways appropriate to the Israeli situation, improve state-local relations within a cooperative framework, and strengthen inter-local relations on a regional and federal rather than a consolidated basis.

The Israeli Experience

What the Commission learned from the experience of other nations complements what was known of the Israeli experience and what characterizes the culture of the Jewish state. The State of Israel is composed of a cross-section of communities gathered in various localities. The basis of the founding of the State of Israel, through the Zionist movement, was comprised of many local groups which founded settlements which, only at a later date, united into a national community which, still later, became a state.

This applies to the first settlements, founded through agreements between the first settlers during the final years of the 19th century; to the kibbutzim and moshavim founded in the years preceding World War I; to the separate neighborhoods which would unite to become cities; and to local councils, which comprised federations of agricultural settlements.

Israel is a country, like the United States or Switzerland, which evolved upwards from its local communities and was not founded in order to maintain control of these communities. Furthermore, as a new society, local independence was not the result of fortified feudal rights which impeded the process of development in republican democracies, as was the case in most European states. On the contrary, from the outset local communities were employed as the principle basis for a republican authority at its most democratic. It is difficult to name a local authority in Israel, rural or municipal, which did not establish the public assembly, organized as a cooperative union in which all were generally recognized as members, as the highest authority for the formation of policy in the first stages of its existence. In fact, most Israeli dialectics, whether oriented towards centralization or decentralization, strongly uphold the local authorities and only the societal requirements of modern statehood, especially in a besieged developing state, demand the existence of the aspect of centralization.

This element can be traced along the scale of the political culture of the Jewish people, from the dawn of their history, in the success of the Jewish capability for living a Jewish life. There has never existed a legitimate Jewish hierarchical state in which sovereignty emanates from only one source. The concept of sovereignty being only in the hands of God and human power existing only through divine providence is founded in ancient Judaism.

Thus flows the clearly pronounced principle from the written word: that power is divided according to different factors and among different power bases — the ancient judges, the kings, the priests and the prophets, the people, the congregation — all of which function flexibly within the received law, known to us as Moses' revelation.

This application has ingrained itself into Jewish political tradition, continuing to influence Jewish behavior even if, in the most recent centuries, it was not its sole political influence. The State of Israel, while in many respects modelled on those European states which developed in the direction of the establishment of a centralized state, exists in a reality in which it is difficult for government institutions serving the Israeli public to exist in a framework which goes against the grain of the fundamental public political culture. Consequently, different methods have been developed to formalize the process of government, establishing and instituting relationships which comfortably ensconce themselves in the corresponding political culture. Therefore while formal centralization is not altogether unfamiliar to the Israeli experience, it is indeed a stranger to Israeli destiny.

All this means that the State of Israel is in reality far less centralized than it would seem at first glance. Local powerbrokers could, through informal procedures, achieve a great measure of maneuverability and independent capability on behalf of their authorities. However, this has not solved structural determinative and power-dispensing problems which have needed to be addressed, not only to allow greater independence, but greater cooperation between the authorities, considering the security and strength felt by their leaders.

Today a confrontation exists between formal structure and the reality of hobbled administration. The Commission's task was to repair and bridge that gap as far as possible.

The Commission sought a way out of the centralized tendencies inherent in the existing structure in order to improve relations between the state and local authorities. Insofar as the current system is largely supported by formal machinery, it becomes difficult to alter the current system due to resistance from both sides: state authority unwilling to cede formal power and local powerbrokers having arrived at their posts through great personal effort. The Commission believed that only once the local authorities sensed greater security would greater cooperation exist between local and state authorities on a level allowing a modern state to function on a sound basis.

Conclusions of the Commission

In light of these characteristics of Israeli society, the Commission worked on the basis that the legal model defining state/local authority relations in Israel is not hierarchic in the sense of local authorities acting as administrative arms of the state government. Nor is it centralized as opposed to a periphery, in the sense of the local authorities occupying the periphery surrounding the machinery of the central power. The Commission viewed the whole of the State of Israel as a mosaic in which the state and local authorities function together, each according to its specific talents, powers, usefulness and functions, and each receiving its authority through public acclamation. Whether elected to local or state office, authority is granted by the public in an identical manner, while the position within the general structure is stipulated by the size of the electorate.

This mosaic framework is accomodated by the state and the state machinery is responsible for its operation. However, working within the limits set by that framework, the local authorities and their responsible machineries, according to the definition of their function, bear an identical responsiblity to the state authority. This does not mean that the state does not exercise its power over local authorities, within the law and relating to a wide variety of fields, including its exclusive and implicit legal power to set the lines of local authority conduct. This essentially means that the rights of the local authority are natural and granted according to Israel's legal tradition, anchored in ancient Hebrew justice and enjoyed once again through the actuality of the State of Israel which was realized through the Zionist revolution. This right exists as an inseparable part of the unifying covenant joining the public with the state community framework.

The Commission arrived at the following consensus defining the basic lines of the status of the local authority:

1) Both local and centralized authority are included in the apparatus of statehood.
2) Local authorities are the elected local voices of their constituents.
3) Local authorities represent their residents' physical and cultural welfare in line with the aims of the state.

4) Local authorities shall exist at the same level as the state government in the context of actions affecting both. In supplying services and development programs, all national considerations, including the wider aspects of society and the economy, and the specific considerations of local residents' needs and wants, shall take precedence.

5) Nothing will be enacted effecting local authorities without the cooperation of or prior consultation with local residents.

6) A wide field of local authority power shall be defined implying the power to enact any activity included within this field.

7) In dividing the functions and areas of action between local and state authorities, the greatest consideration shall be given to the benefit of the citizen/voter/taxpayer and will therefore be determined according to the principles guaranteeing public involvement, diligently and speedily improving service on the one hand, and keeping costs down on the other.

8) Local authorities shall be guaranteed the basic funding required to fulfill their roles.

9) Economic arrangements which will be finalized between the local authorities and the state government must be along the following lines: that proper management of local authorities will guarantee that past and present financial difficulties will gradually be solved, and further difficulties will be prevented in the future.

10) Local authority management shall be based on the principle of granting wide powers of action to the local authority head in order to strengthen the local authority in all matters concerning budgeting, personnel, legislation, aid, auditing, etc.

The Scope of the Recommendations

If local self-government is to have any meaning, it must be accompanied by appropriate fiscal resources. This is not only to provide localities with greater autonomy but also to force them to accept greater responsibility. To be free to act when someone else is paying the bills represents only half of what autonomy is about.

Autonomy must also mean the necessity to weigh one's actions in light of their costs. The fiscal recommendations are directed to that end on the principle that the local authorities should have greater fiscal resources at their disposal so that they may make the choices and assume responsibility for them.

With regard to functions and services, the conventional wisdom is to assign different functions to different governmental arenas. Upon closer inspection, however, it becomes clear that this kind of separation is not possible within the context of the modern state. Rather, the issue is how functional responsibilties should be shared and how can successful state-local partnerships, as well as public-private partnerships, be developed. The Commission's recommendations are directed toward that end, taking each function for itself and examining it in light of its particular character, environment, and past experience.

A perennial issue in the area of state-local relations is that of state oversight in relation to local autonomy. Any sensible check and balance system must provide for sufficient state assessment of the quality, efficiency, and honesty of local activities so that effective repairs may be instituted where local breakdowns occur without damaging the fundaments of local self-government. In the past, there has been a tendency to rely upon two basic approaches: on one hand, to allow the local authorities very little formal discretion, requiring them to get permission or clearance for almost every step they take, and on the other hand, to provide very drastic penalties if they do not. The end result has been to encourage the local authorities to find ways to circumvent these stringent formal requirements which they have often been able to do, while denying state officials any recourse other than the most Draconian measures which they are naturally reluctant to invoke.

The Commission's recommendations have sought to break this vicious circle, to eliminate the idea that local authorities must conform to rulings that touch upon minutiae, while at the same time providing a scale of sanctions which the state realistically can invoke when the more limited standards and regulations are violated. This position represents a compromise between those members of the Commission who sought to abolish *ultra vires* and to reduce state administrative direction of the localities, and those members who felt the necessity for close state direction, even in fields in which the local authorities were to be given substantial administrative responsibilities.

With regard to the consolidation of local authorities and the question of inter-local relations, it is clear that there is no optimal size of cities in the general sense. While it is true that there are economies or diseconomies of scale which influence the performance of particular functions in cities of different sizes, and size questions can and do influence the possibilities for public participation in local civic and political life, looking at the larger picture, even these depend upon other factors such as a city's location, the character of its residents, its fiscal resources, and the like. Consequently, except in a few marginal cases, there are few virtues in outright consolidation of existing cities, given the amount of effort necessary to achieve such consolidations and the risks run at disturbing existing civic commitments for dubious and highly uncertain economic and administrative gains.

The Commission's approach was to avoid consolidation or merging of cities. Rather, it sought to achieve greater inter-local collaboration or linkage on broadly construed federal principles. The Commission devoted considerable effort to explore the variety of possibilities and arrangements which can be derived from those principles and to develop ways to apply them to the local scene. It recommended a wide range of options for restructuring inter-local cooperation on federal lines including coordinating committees to deal with technical issues; inter-local contracting for services; strengthening the system of voluntary inter-local agreements; encouraging formal contributions of cities, whether for specific functions or as comprehensive bodies; the mandatory federation of small cities for certain limited purposes; and regional federations of cities for comprehensive purposes.

With regard to local structures and functions, the approach of the Commission was two-fold. First was its strong commitment to strengthening the possibilities of citizen involvement in local government affairs and the corresponding increase in local government responsiveness to the citizenry. Secondly, it was concerned with strengthening the ability of local governments to carry out the added functions which they should be given.

In response to the Knesset legislation providing for the direct election of mayors, the Commission recommended appropriate changes in existing legislation to enable the local authorities to function within the new system. This led to the introduction of a separation-of-powers form of government on the local plane which should clarify lines of accountability and strengthen both the mayors and the local councils within their respective spheres of authority. The new arrangement provides more clear-cut lines of responsibility for each body as well as for the appointed members of the executive branch in city government. The Commission's goal in doing this was to provide more appropriate checks and balances than existed under the old system, while enabling the mayor to administer the city more effectively.

The Commission also tried to introduce flexibility in local government organization in a number of ways, to offer local authorities greater opportunities for choosing options appropriate for them. It recommended that cities be allowed to appoint a professional manager to assist the elected mayor or head the local authority's administrative structure. One major purpose in doing this was to encourage citizens to seek office without committing themselves to full-time service and thereby widen the possibilities for participation in local government, one of the major justifications for decentralization.

The Commission also undertook to clarify lines of authority and powers of local government in a variety of fields. It did so on the grounds that clarification of such lines of authority would permit greater citizen access to government and would assist local authorities in their relations with state ministries and authorities.

Appendix 2

List of Laws Pertaining to Local Government *

Municipalities Ordinance (new version)
Local Councils Ordinance (new version)
Local Councils Ordinance (a), 5711-1950
Local Councils Ordinance (b), 5713-1953
Local Councils Ordinance (Regional Councils), 5718-1958
Elections Law (Campaigning), 5719-1959
Local Authorities (Elections) Law, 5725-1965
Local Authorities (Election and Tenure of Mayor and Deputy
    Mayors) Law, 5735-1975
Local Authorities (Land Transfer Fee) Law, 5719-1959
Local Authorities (Sewage) Law, 5722-1962
Local Authorities (Benefits to Mayor and Deputy Mayors) Law,
    5737-1977
Local Authorities (Restriction on Right to be Elected) Law, 5724-
    1964
Local Authorities (Regulation of Guard Service) Law, 5721-1961
Local Authorities (Vesting of Public Property) Law, 5718-1958
Local Authorities (Legal Advice) Law, 5736-1976
Local Authorities (Joint Public Tenders) Law, 5732-1972
Local Authorities (Discipline) Law, 5738-1978
Local Authorities (Objection to Determination of General Rate)
    Law, 5736-1976
Local Authorities (Exemption of Soldiers, War Sufferers and Po-
    lice Officers from Rate) Law, 5713-1953
Local Authorities (Interest and Linkage on Obligatory Payments)
    Law, 5740-1980
Local Authorities (Compensation for Property Rate) Law, 5735-
    1975

---

* 1) This list does not include some of the Regulations and Ordi-
    nances that were enacted under the authority that was given in the
    relevant laws.
  2) Source: State Comptroller, *Report on Auditing of Local Govern-
    ment*, Jerusalem, 5747-1986, pp. 325-29 (Hebrew).

Local Authorities (Television and Radio Antennas) Law, 5736-1976

Local Authorities Regulations (Budget Preparation), 5731-1971

Local Authorities Regulations (Bookkeeping), 5715-1955

Local Authorities Regulations (Land Registry), 5727-1967

Local Authorities Regulations (Registry of Personal Bonds), 5727-1967

Municipalities Regulations (Report of Municipality Comptroller), 5734-1974

Municipalities Regulations (Purchasing and Managing Storerooms), 5719-1958

Municipalities Regulations (Signature on Certain Documents), 5720-1959

Municipalities Regulations (Tenders), 5738-1977

Municipalities Regulations (Tenders for Personnel), 5740-1979

Municipalities Regulations (Assignment of Street Names and House Numbers), 5720-1959

Municipalities Regulations (Safekeeping of Forms of Financial Value), 5721-1961

Municipalities Ordinance (Transferring Between Budget Items), 5720-1959

Municipalities Ordinance (Establishment of Corporations), 5740-1980

Municipalities Ordinance (Finable Offenses), 5722-1962

Local Councils Ordinance (Assignment of Street Names and House Numbers), 5731-1971

Local Councils Ordinance (Finable Offenses), 5733-1973

Local Councils Ordinance (Service of Employees), 5722-1962

Local Councils Ordinance (Safekeeping of Forms of Financial Value), 5721-1961

* *

Municipal Corporations Law, 5715-1955

* *

Planning and Construction Law, 5725-1965

City Construction Ordinance, 1936

Planning and Construction Regulations (Requests for Permission, Conditions, and Fees), 5730-1970

Planning and Construction Regulations (Licensing for Electricity, Water and Telephone Services), 5741-1981

Planning and Construction Regulations (Delegation of Authority from Regional Authority to Subcommittee), 5735-1974

Planning and Construction Regulations (Delegation of Authority from Local Council to Subcommittee), 5726-1966

Planning and Construction Regulations (Consideration of Suits for Compensation), 5731-1971

Planning and Construction Regulations (Appeals of Licensing Decisions), 5726-1966

Planning and Construction Regulations (Special Instructions Regarding Licensing Security Installations), 5727-1966

Planning and Construction Regulations (Improvement Fee Debts and Substitutes for Transferring Property Debts), 5741-1981

Planning and Construction Regulations (Licensing Limited Work), 5729-1968

Planning and Construction Ordinance (Licensing by Chairman of Local Committee and Engineer), 5735-1974

Planning and Construction Regulations (Procedures for Considering Planning Objections), 5726-1966

Planning and Construction Regulations (Procedures before Appeals Committee for Agricultural Land), 5729-1968

Planning and Construction Regulations (Procedures before Appeals Committee for Beaches), 5730-1969

Planning and Construction Regulations (Procedures for Appeal on Improvement Appraisal), 5741-1981

Planning and Construction Regulations (Significant Deviations from a Plan), 5727-1967

Planning and Construction Regulations (Special Arrangements in Public Buildings for Handicapped), 5741-1981

Planning and Construction Regulations (Work and Usages which Require Licensing), 5727-1967

Planning and Construction Regulations (Guarantees for Insuring the Payment of Improvement Tax and Postponement of Payments), 5741-1981

Planning and Construction Regulations (Appeal before State Council), 5732-1972

Planning and Construction Regulations (Appeal of Decision of Special Committee before Ministers), 5730-1970

Planning and Construction Regulations (Appeal on Decision Regarding Detailed Plan of Special Committee before State Council), 5730-1970

Planning and Construction Regulations (Environmental Impact Statements), 5742-1982

Planning and Construction Regulations (Documents Regarding Tax Payment), 5741-1981

Planning and Construction Regulations (Easing of Improvement Tax Payment on Residential Housing), 5741-1981

Planning and Construction Ordinance (Determination of Public and Professional Bodies Regarding Planning Objections), 5734-1974

* *

Business Licensing Law, 5728-1968

Business Licensing Regulations

Business Licensing Regulations (Period of Validity of Licenses, Renewal and Fees), 5735-1974

Business Licensing Ordinance (Business Which Require Licenses According to Other Legislation), 5734-1974

Business Licensing Ordinance (Determination of Businesses Which Require Licensing), 5733-1973

Business Licensing Regulations (Oil Storage), 5737-1976

Business Licensing Regulations (Licensing Forms), 5735-1974

Business Licensing Regulations (Extermination of Pests), 5735-1975

Crafts and Industries Regulations (Manufacturing Gunpowder), 5710-1940

Ordinance of 17 November 1940 Concerning Special Conditions for the Manufacture of Gunpowder

Crafts and Industries Regulations (Manufacturing Potassium Chlorate), 5711-1941

Regulations for Wood Storage, 5706-1936

Business Licensing Regulations (Medical Laboratories), 5737-1977

Business Licensing Regulations (Sanitary Conditions for Swimming Pools), 5733-1973

Business Licensing Regulations (Sanitary Conditions for Food Vending), 5734-1973

Business Licensing Regulations (Sanitary Conditions for Restaurants), 5743-1983

Business Licensing Regulations (Conditions for Licensing Poultry Raising), 5741-1981

Business Licensing Regulations (Sanitary Conditions for Gas Stations), 5730-1969
Business Licensing Regulations (Sanitary Conditions for Transportation of Meat, Fish, Poultry and their Products), 5732-1972
Business Licensing Regulations (Sanitary Conditions for Food Manufacturers), 5732-1972
Business Licensing Regulations (Sanitary Conditions for Camps and Recreation Areas), 5736-1975

* *

Beach Facilities Standards Law, 5724-1964

* *

Water Law, 5719-1959
Water Metering Law, 5716-1955
Water Metering Regulations (Water Meters), 5736-1976
Water Regulations (Water Tariffs in Local Authorities), 5745-1985

* *

Education Ordinance (new version), 5738-1978
Education Regulations
Compulsory Education Law, 5709-1949
State Education Law, 5713-1953
Public Health Ordinance, 5710-1940
Public Health Regulations (Quality of Drinking Water), 5734-1974
Animal Health Ordinance, 5715-1945
Public Nuisance Prevention Law, 5721-1961
Prevention of Nuisances Regulations (Air Quality), 5732-1971
Prevention of Nuisances Regulations (Air Pollution from Yards), 5722-1962
Prevention of Nuisances Regulations (Air Pollution from Vehicles), 5723-1963
Prevention of Nuisances Regulations (Air Pollution from Vehicles) (Hertridge Test Standard), 5724-1963
Prevention of Nuisances Regulations (Air Pollution from Home Heating Oil Furnaces), 5733-1972

Local Government in Israel

Prevention of Nuisances Regulations (Noise Prevention), 5726-1966
Prevention of Nuisances Regulations (Small Particle Emission), 5733-1972
Prevention of Nuisances Regulations (Unreasonable Noise), 5737-1977
Prevention of Nuisances Regulations (Unreasonable Noise from Building Equipment), 5739-1979
Preservation of Cleanliness Law, 5744-1984
Renovation and Maintenance of Houses Law, 5740-1980

* *

Jewish Religious Services Law (new version), 5731-1971

* *

Welfare Services Law, 5718-1958

* *

Firefighting Services Law, 5719-1959
Firefighting Services Regulations (Fire Hydrants and Water Supply), 5731-1971
Firefighting Services Regulations (Ranks and Positions of Firefighters), 5736-1976
Firefighting Services Regulations (Arrangements and Conditions for Mutual Help), 5722-1962
Firefighting Services Regulations (Firefighters' Employment in Shifts), 5741-1981
Firefighting Services Regulations (Appointment and Employment of Firefighters), 5729-1969
Firefighting Services Regulations (Discipline), 5740-1980
Firefighting Services Regulations (Authority of Fire Chiefs), 5739-1978
Firefighting Services Regulations (Authority of Fire Chief Supervisor), 5732-1972
Firefighting Services Regulations (Joint Activities), 5721-1960
Firefighting Services Regulations (Firefighting Equipment), 5725-1964
Firefighting Services Regulations (Firefighting Equipment in Commercial Buildings), 5732-1971

Firefighting Services Regulations (Firefighting Equipment in Hospitals), 5732-1972

Firefighting Services Regulations (Firefighting Equipment in Residences), 5732-1972

Firefighting Services Regulations (Firefighting Equipment in Hotels), 5732-1972

Firefighting Services Regulations (Firefighting Equipment in Schools), 5732-1972

Firefighting Services Regulations (Firefighting Equipment in Entertainment Halls), 5730-1969

Firefighting Services Regulations (Firefighting Equipment in Houses of Worship), 5732-1972

Firefighting Services Regulations (Firefighting Equipment in Storerooms), 5732-1972

Firefighting Services Regulations (Firefighting Equipment in Factories and Workshops), 5732-1972

Firefighting Services Regulations (Payments for Services), 5735-1975

Firefighting Services Instructions (Discipline), 5741-1980

BIBLIOGRAPHY

ENGLISH

Adler, M. (1960). "Local Government in Israel," *Public Administration in Israel and Abroad.*

Adler, S. and Hecht, A. (1970). "Local Autonomy in Israel," *Public Administration in Israel and Abroad.*

Akzin, B. and Dror, Y. (1966). *Israel: High-Pressure Planning* (Syracuse, N.Y.: Syracuse University Press).

Alderfer, H.F. (1964). *Local Government in Developing Countries* (New York, McGraw-Hill).

Alexander, A. (1982). *Local Government in Great Britain Since Reorganization* (London, Allen & Unwin).

Althusius, J. (1614). *Politica Methodice Digesta* (translated by F.S. Coney).

Arian, A. (ed.) (1972). *The Elections in Israel — 1969* (Jerusalem, Jerusalem Academic Press).

— (1975). *The Elections in Israel — 1973* (Jerusalem, Jerusalem Academic Press).

Aronoff, M.J. (1973a). *Frontierstown: The Politics of Community Building in Israel* (Manchester, Manchester University Press).

— (1973b). "Development Towns in Israel" in Curtis and Chertoff (eds.) (1973).

Av-Razi, J. (1962). "History of Israel's Local Government," *International Seminar for Local Government Administration*, vol. 1. (Jerusalem, Ministry of Foreign Affairs; Ministry of Interior; Israel Union of Local Authorities).

Baker, H.E. (1968). *The Legal System of Israel* (Jerusalem, Israel Universities Press).

Baldwin, E. (1972). *Differentiation and Cooperation in an Israeli Veteran Moshav* (Manchester, Manchester University Press).

Ben Porat, Y. (1975). "The Years of Plenty and the Years of Famine — a Political Business Cycle," *Kyklos*, 28.

Bennet, R.J. (1982). *Central Grants to Local Government* (Cambridge, Cambridge University Press).

Berler, A. (1970). *Absorption in New Towns and Rural Hinterland* (Rehovot, Settlement Research Center).

Bernstein, M.H. (1957). *The Politics of Israel: The First Decade of Statehood* (Princeton, Princeton University Press).

Blair, J.P. and Nachmias, D. (1979). *Fiscal Retrenchment and Urban Policy* (Beverly Hills, Sage).

Brown, D.W. (1974). *Ideology and Political Relations in Israeli Immigrant Cooperatives (Moshavei Olim)* (Manchester, Manchester University Press).

Brownson, O. (1866). *The American Republic.*

Buber, M. (1950). *Paths in Utopia* (New York, Macmillan).

Buchanan, J. (1950). "Federalism and Fiscal Equity," *American Economic Review*, vol. XL, September.

Byrne, T. (1983). *Local Government in Britain* (London, Penguin).

Caulcott, T. (1981). "Responding to the Challenge – The Public Sector," *Local Government Studies*, vol. 9.

Central Bureau of Statistics (1952). *Statistical Abstract of Israel 1951/52)* (Jerusalem).

— (1977). *Statistical Abstract of Israel 1977* (Jerusalem).

— (1978). *Statistical Abstract of Israel 1978* (Jerusalem).

— (1979). *Statistical Abstract of Israel 1979* (Jerusalem).

— (1980). *Statistical Abstract of Israel 1980* (Jerusalem).

— (1981). *Statistical Abstract of Israel 1981* (Jerusalem).

— (1982). *Statistical Abstract of Israel 1982* (Jerusalem).

Bibliography

— (1983). *Statistical Abstract of Israel 1983* (Jerusalem).

— (1984). *Statistical Abstract of Israel 1984* (Jerusalem).

— (1985). *Statistical Abstract of Israel 1985* (Jerusalem).

— (1986). *Statistical Abstract of Israel 1986* (Jerusalem).

Central Bureau of Statistics/Ministry of Interior (1972). *Local Authorities in Israel, 1969/70, Physical Data* (Jerusalem).

— (1973). *Local Authorities in Israel 1971/72, Physical Data* (Jerusalem).

— (1980). *Local Authorities in Israel 1978/79, Physical Data* (Jerusalem).

— (1982). *Local Authorities in Israel 1979/80, Financial Data* (Jerusalem).

— (1984a). *Local Authorities in Israel 1981/82, Physical Data* (Jerusalem).

— (1984b). *Local Authorities in Israel 1981/82, Financial Data* (Jerusalem).

Clark, T.N. (ed.) (1974). *Comparative Community Politics* (New York, Sage).

Cohen, E. (1970a). "Development Towns — The Social Dynamics of 'Planted' Urban Communities in Israel," in Eisenstadt *et al.* (eds.) (1970).

— (1970b). "The City in the Zionist Ideology," (Jerusalem, Eliezer Kaplan School of Economics and Social Sciences, The Hebrew University).

Commissioner for Complaints from the Public (Ombudsman) (1973). *Annual Report 2* (Jerusalem).

Criden, Y. and Gelb, S. (1976). "How a Kibbutz is Governed" in *The Kibbutz Experience — Dialogue in Kfar Blum* (New York, Schocken Books).

397

Curtis, M. and Chertoff, M.S. (eds.) (1973). *Israel: Social Structure and Change* (New Brunswick, Transaction Books).

Davey, K.J. (1971). "Local Autonomy and Independent Revenues," *Public Administration*, vol. 49, Spring.

Dearlove, J. (1973). *The Politics of Policy in Local Government: The Making and Maintenance of Public Policy in the Royal Borough of Kensington and Chelsea* (London, Cambridge University Press).

Deshen, S. (1970). *Immigrant Voters in Israel* (Manchester, Manchester University Press).

Dois, J.W. and Danielson, M.N. (1980). "Government's Impact on Urban Development," *Policy Studies Journal*, 8, Summer.

Due, J.F. (1963). *Government Finance* (Homewood, Ill., Richard D. Irwin).

Dunshire, A. (1981). "Central Control Over Local Authorities: A Cybernetic Approach," *Public Administration*, Journal of the Royal Institute of Public Administration, vol. 59.

Dye, J. (1978). *Understanding Public Policy* (Englewood Cliffs, N.J., Prentice Hall).

Eisenstadt, S.N. (1967). *Israeli Society* (London, Weidenfeld and Nicholson).

Eisenstadt, S.N. *et al.* (eds.) (1970). *Integration and Development in Israel* (Jerusalem, Israel Universities Press).

Eisenstadt, S.N. and Lemarchand, R. (eds.) (1981). *Political Clientelism, Patronage and Development* (London, Sage).

Elazar, D.J. (1962). *The American Partnership: Inter-Governmental Cooperation in Nineteenth-Century United States* (Chicago, University of Chicago Press).

— (1968). *Federalism and the Community* (Pittsburgh, University of Pittsburgh).

— (1970). *Cities of the Prairie* (New York, Basic Books).

— (1973). "Local Government as an Integrating Factor in Israeli Society" in Curtis and Chertoff (eds.) (1973).

Bibliography

— (1975). "The Local Elections: Sharpening the Trend Toward Territorial Democracy" in Arian (1975).

— (1977). "The Compound Structure of Public Service Delivery Systems in Israel," in Ostrom and Bish, (eds.), 1977.

Elazar, D.J. *et al.* (1979). *Project Renewal: The View from the Neighborhoods* (Jerusalem, Center for Jewish Community Studies).

— (1980). "Project Renewal: An Introduction to the Issues and Actors" (Jerusalem, Center for Jewish Community Studies).

— (1983). *The Extent, Focus and Impact of Diaspora Involvement in Project Renewal* (Jerusalem, Jerusalem Center for Public Affairs).

Elston, R.D. (1963). *Israel: The Making of a Nation* (London, Oxford University Press).

Freudenheim, Y. (1967). *Government in Israel* (Dobbs Ferry, N.Y., Oceana Publications).

Galbraith, J.K. (1969). *The Affluent Society*, 2nd ed. Rev., (Boston, Houghton Miflin).

Gaziel, H.H. (1982). "Urban Policy Outputs — A Proposed Framework for Assessment and Some Empirical Evidence," *Urban Education*, vol. 17, No. 2, July.

Gevirtz, Y. (1962). (1) "Rural Local Government in Israel," (2) "Agricultural Cooperatives in Regional Councils," (3) Elections to Regional Councils," *International Seminar for Local Government Administration*, vol. I (Jerusalem, Ministry for Foreign Affairs; Ministry of Interior; Israel Union of Local Authorities).

Goldberg, G. (1984). "The Local Elections in Israel – 1983," *Electoral Studies*, vol. 3, No. 2, August, pp. 204-205.

Goldwin, R.A. (ed.) (1972). *A Nation of States*, 2nd rev. ed. (Chicago, Rand McNally).

Gradus, Y. (1983). "The Role of Politics in Regional Inequality: The Israeli Case," *Annals of Association of American Geospheres*, 73.

Gremion, C. (1987). "Decentralization in France: The Political Debate" (Paper delivered in the Franco-Israeli Workshop on Centralization-Decentralization, Jerusalem, February 1987).

Grodzins, M. (1960). "The Federal System," in *The American Assembly, Goals for Americans* (Englewood Cliffs, N.J., Prentice-Hall).

Gutmann, E. (1958). *The Development of Local Government in Palestine* (Microfilm of Ph.D. thesis, Columbia University, 1957) (Ann Arbor, University of Michigan).

— (1963). *The Politics of Israel Local Government* (Milan, Ediziani di Communita).

Hansen, H.E. (1973). *Location Preferences, Migration and Regional Growth* (New York, Praeger).

Harris, J.S. (1955). *British Government Inspection* (London, Stevens & Sons).

Hartley, O.A. (1972). "Inspectorates in British Central Government," *Public Administration: Journal of the Royal Institute of Public Administration*, vol 50.

Haynes, R.J. (1980). *Organisation Theory and Local Government* (London, Allen & Unwin).

Hirsch, W.Z. (1970). *The Economics of State and Local Government* (New York, McGraw-Hill).

Hoven, W. and Van der Elshout, A. (1963). *Local Government in Selected Countries: Ceylon, Israel, Japan* (New York, United Nations).

IULA (1955). *Local Government and its Importance for Local Autonomy* (Reports prepared for the Rome Congress, The Hague, IULA).

Jenkins, J. (1967). *Local Government in Britain* (Wheaton of Exeter).

Kalchheim, Ch. (1980). "The Limited Effectiveness of Central Government Control over Local Government," *Planning and Administration*, vol. 7, No. 1, Spring.

Kasarada, J.D. (1980). "The Implications of Contemporary Redistribution Trends for National Urban Policy," *Social Science Quarterly*, 6, December.

Kesselman, M. (1974). "Political Parties and Local Government in France: Differentiation and Opposition," in T.N. Clark (ed.). *Comparative Community Politics* (New York, Sage).

Bibliography

King, P. *et al.* (1987). *Project Renewal in Israel: Urban Revitalization Through Partnership* (Lanham, Md., University Press of America, co-published with the Jerusalem Center for Public Affairs).

Kirk, R. (1972). "The Prospects for Territorial Democracy in America" in R.A. Goldwin (ed.) (1972).

Kirschenbaum, A. (1972). *Selective Migration and Population Redistribution — A Study of New Towns in Jerusalem* (Haifa, Technion).

Kraines, O. (1961). *Government and Politics in Israel* (Boston, Houghton-Mifflin Company).

Kramer, R.M. (1970). *Community Development in Israel and the Netherlands* (Berkeley, University of California Press).

Landau, M. (1969). "Redundancy, Rationality and the Problem of Duplication and Overlap," *Public Administration Review*, 20.

Lantzman, A. (1983). "The 1983 Israeli Municipal Elections: Mixed Trends and Minor Upsets," *Jerusalem Letter*, 68.

Lazin, F. (1979). *Welfare Policy Formation in Israel: The Policy Role of the Local Agency* (Washington, D.C., American Political Science Association).

Maas, A. (ed.) (1959). *Area and Power*, (Glencoe, Ill., The Free Press).

Marshal, A.H. (1963). *Local Government Finance* The Hague, IULA).

Meljon, Z. (1962). "Union of Local Authorities," *International Seminar for Local Government Administration*, vol. III (Jerusalem, Ministry for Foreign Affairs; Ministry of Interior; Israel Union of Local Authorities).

— (ed.) (1966a). "Local Government in Israel" (Tel Aviv, Israel Union of Local Authorities).

— (1966b). "Towns and Villages" (Tel Aviv, Israel Union of Local Authorities).

Minogue, M. (ed.) (1977). *Documents on Contemporary British Government: Local Government in Britain* (Cambridge, Cambridge University Press).

Musgrave, R.A. (1959). *The Theory of Public Finance* (New York, McGraw-Hill).

Ostrom, V. and Bish, F.P. (eds.) (1977). *Comparating Urban Public Service Delivery Systems*, (Beverly Hills, Sage Publications).

Reagan, M.D. and Sonzone, J.G. (1981). *The New Federalism* (New York, Oxford University Press).

Richardson, H.W. (1971). *Urban Economics* (Middlesex, Penguin Books).

— (1980). "Polarization Reversal in Developing Countries," *Papers of the Regional Science Association*, 45.

— (1981). "National Urban Development Strategies in Developing Countries," *Urban Studies*, 18.

Rose, R. (1984). *Understanding Big Government* (London, Sage).

Rosen, D. (1962). "The Amalgamation of Small Local Authorities in Israel," *Public Administration in Israel and Abroad 1962*, vol. 3.

Rosenbloom, R.A. (1979). "The Politics of the Neighborhood Movement," *South Atlantic Urban Studies*, 4.

Samuel, E. (1953). "Local Government in Israel," *Israel Youth Horizon*, 11, November-December.

— (1957). *British Traditions in the Administration of Israel* (London, Valentine Mitchell).

Shari, R. (1967). "A Civil Service Commission for Local Government in Israel," *Public Administration in Israel and Abroad*.

Sharkansky, I. (1979). *Whither the State* (Chatam, N.J., Chatam House).

Silverstone, M. (1973). "The Israel Ministry of Religious Affairs and the Chief Rabbinate of Israel", *Public Administration in Israel and Abroad 1973*.

Smith, B.C. (1967). *Field Administration* (London, Routledge and Kegan Paul).

Bibliography

Soen, D. (1983). "Migration Balance and Socio-Economic Image: The Case of Israel's New Town," *Planning Outlook*, 26.

Spiegel, E. (1966). *Neue Staedte in Israel* (Stuttgart and Bern, Karl Kramer Verlag).

Stendel, O. (1967). *Arab Villages in Israel and Judea-Samaria* (Jerusalem, Israel Economist).

Stock, E. (1968). *From Conflict to Understanding: Relations Between Jews and Arabs in Israel Since 1948* (New York, Institute of Human Relations Press).

Taylor, Ch.l. (ed.) (1983). *Why Governments Grow* (London, Sage).

Thrasher, M. (1981). "The Concept of a Central-Local Government Partnership: Issues Obscured by Ideas," *Policy and Politics*, vol. 9. No. 9, October.

Torgovnik, E. (1972). "A Perspective on Central Metropolitan Relations," *Journal of Comparative Administration*, 3.

— (1978). "Central Aid and Local Policy," *Public Finance Quarterly*, 6, April.

— (Forthcoming). *Urban Policy and Politics in Israel*.

Torgovnik, E. and Barzel, Y. (1979). "Block Grant Allocation: Relationship Between Self-Government and Redistribution," *Public Administration*, 57, Spring.

Torgovnik, E. and Weiss, S. (1972). "Local Non-Party Political Organizations," *Western Political Quarterly*, 25.

United Nations (1966). *Local Government Personnel Systems* (New York, U.N. Department of Economic and Social Affairs).

Walsh, A. (1969). *The Urban Challenge to Government* (New York, Praeger).

Walsh, G. (1982). "Is Renewal Renewing?" *The Israel Economist*, June.

Weingrod, A. (1966). *Reluctant Pioneers — Village Development in Israel* (Princeton, Princeton University Press).

Local Government in Israel

Wilner, D. (1969). *Nation Building and Community in Israel* (Princeton, Princeton University Press).

HEBREW

Adler, M. (1956). "Shilton Merkazi O Shilton Meqomi Atzmi" [Central Government or Local Self-Government], *HaMinhal*, 26, Summer.

Alexander, A. (1980). *Shiqum Shekhunot Metzuqa BeIsrael — HaHebet HaMinhali Mossadi — Duah Benaiim* [Rehabilitation of Distressed Neighborhoods in Israel — Administrative and Institutional Aspects — Interim Report] (Haifa, The Technion).

Almogi, Y. (1980). *B'ovi Haqora* [The Heart of the Matter] (Jerusalem, Idunim).

Amiaz, M. (1971). "Igudei HaRashuyot HaMeqomiyot VehaSherutim HaTechniim" [The Unions of Local Authorities and the Technical Services] *Devar haShilton HaMeqomi*, June-July.

Amiran, D. and Shahar, A. (1969). *Arei Pituah BeIsrael* [Development Towns in Israel] (Jerusalem, The Hebrew University).

Bank of Israel (1981). *Din VeHeshbon LiShnat 1980* [Report for the Year 1980] (Jerusalem, The Bank of Israel).

Barlev, B.Z. and Levi, Ch. (1974). "HaMivne Hafinansi Shel Hakhnasot HaRashuyot HaMeqomiyot — Tahaziyot LeAtid" [The Financial Structure of Local Authority Income — Projections for the Future], in Steinman (ed.) (1974).

— (1975). "Regresiviyut HaArnona HaKelalit" [Regressiveness of the General (Municipal) Property Tax] *Ir VeAizor*, February.

Bar-Sela Committee (1983). (See the Committee for the Examination of Representativeness in the Regional Councils).

Baruch, N. (1971). *HaTikhnun HaFissi BeIsrael – Irgun HaMa'arachot* [Physical Planning in Israel – Organizing the Systems] (Jerusalem).

Barzel, Y. (1973). "Ma'anak Memshalti VeRamat Sherutim" [Government Grant and Level of Services] *HaHever* 8-10, Elul.

Bibliography

— (1976). "Yahasei Shilton Meqomi-Merkazi: Aspektim Finan-siim" [Relationships between Local and Central Governments: Financial Aspects], in Yardeni, et al. (eds.) (1976).

— (1982). "Ma'aglei HaHitdainut BeHaktza'at Kesafim Shel HaShilton HaMerkazi LaShilton HaMeqomi — Ha'im Hem Drushim?" [Negotiation Cycles in State Government Allocation of Funds to Local Government — Are They Necessary?] (Ramat Gan, Institute for Local Government, Bar-Ilan University).

Ben-Arieh, Y. (1965). *Emek HaYarden Hatikhon* [The Middle Jordan Valley] (Merhavia, Hakibbutz HaMe'uhad).

Ben-Shahar Committee (1973). (See Israel Institute for Urban Research and Information, Ltd.).

Biltzky, A. (1981). *BaYetzira UvaMa'avak: Moetzet Po'alei Haifa, 1921-1981* [In Deeds and in Struggle: The Workers' Council in Haifa, 1921-1981] (Tel Aviv, Am Oved).

Bone, A. and Lu-Yon, H. (1980). "Eqronot LeHaluqat Azorei HeMegurim Umatrot Shumot Arnonot BeHaifa" [Principles for Zoning Residence Areas and the Aims of Municipal Tax in Haifa] (The Municipality of Haifa, Internal Document).

Borochov, A. and Werczberger, E. (1980). "Gormim Mashpiim Al Hitpathut Arei Pituah BeIsrael" [Influencing Factors on the Development of Development Towns in Israel] (Working Paper no. 2) (Tel Aviv, Sapir Center, Tel Aviv University).

Borochov, B. (1944). *Ketavim Nivharim* [Selected Writings, arranged by Z. Rubashov] (Tel Aviv, Am Oved).

Brutzkus, E. (1964). "Tikhnun Pizur HaOchlosia BeIsrael" [The Plan for Spatial Distribution of Population in Israel] *Riv'on LeKhalkala*, 11, December.

— (1973). "Tokhnit LaTifroset HaGeografit Shel Medinat Israel Bat 5 Milionim" [The Plan for Spatial Distribution of 5 Million Population in Israel] *Ir VeAizor* April.

Brichta, A. (1982). "Rashei Rashuyot Meqomiyot BeIsrael — He'arot VeShinui Shitat HaBehirot" [Mayors in Israel — Comments and the Change of the Elections System] (Jerusalem, Ministry of Interior).

405

Central Bureau of Statistics – Supervisor of Elections, Ministry of Interior (1955). "Totz'ot HaBehirot KaKnesset HaShlishit Ve-laRashuyot HaMekomiyot" [Results of Elections to the Third Knesset and to Local Authorities — July 7, 1955] (Jerusalem).

— (1961). [Results of Elections to the Fourth Knesset and to Local Authorities — November 3, 1959] (Jerusalem).

— (1967). [Results of Elections to the Sixth Knesset and to Local Authorities — November 2, 1965] (Jerusalem).

— (1970). [Results of Elections to the Seventh Knesset and to Local Authorities — October 28, 1969] (Jerusalem).

— (1974). [Results of Elections to the Eighth Knesset and to Local Authorities — December 31, 1973] (Jerusalem).

Cohen, E. (1966). "Va'adot Munitzipaliyot BeAyarot HaPituah" [Municipal Committees in Development Towns] (Jerusalem, The Hebrew University, Department of Sociology and the Public Council for Community Service).

— (1966). "Be'ayot Shel Ayarot Pituah VeShikunim Ironiim" [Problems of Development Towns and Urban Housing] *Riv'on LeKhalkala* 49-50, June.

Commission for the Examination of the Tax System in the Local Authorities (1964). *Report* (Jerusalem, Ministry of Interior) ("The Vitkon Commission").

Commission to Improve the Financing of Local Authorities (1975). *Report* (Jerusalem, Ministry of Interior) ("Kubersky Committee").

Committee for the Examination of the Merging of Assessment and Collection of Property Taxes (Municipal and State) and General Municipal Tax (Subcommittee of the Vitkon Commission), (1963). *Report* (Jerusalem, Ministry of Interior).

Committee for the Examination of the Representativeness in the Regional Councils (1983). *Report* (Jerusalem, Ministry of Justice) (The "Bar-Sela Committee").

Committee to Determine the Structure of Expenditures in Arab Local Authorities (1984) *Report* (Jerusalem, Ministry of Interior) ("Jeraisi Committee").

Bibliography

Committee to Suggest Rules for Preventing Conflicts of Interest By the Elected Representatives in Local Authorities (1984). *Report* (Jerusalem, Ministry of Justice) ("Shpanitz Committee").

Degani, A. (1980). "Shechunat HaTikva 1979: Misgeret Metodologit LeTikhnun Shiqum Hevrati U'Fizi Shel Shekhunat Metzuqa" (The HaTikva Neighborhood 1979: Methodological Framework for Planning Social and Physical Renewal of Distressed Neighborhoods] (Tel Aviv, Tel Aviv University).

Development Towns Advisory Bureau (1984a). "Reshimat Tamritzim LaOvrim LeAyarot Pituah" [List of Incentives to Those Who Move to Development Towns] (Tel Aviv, Ministry of Labor and Social Welfare).

— (1984b). "Hatza'a Shel HaMerkaz LeMediniyut Memshaltit Be-Arey Pituah" [A Suggestion by the Center for Government Policy in Development Towns] (Jerusalem, Ministry of Labor and Social Welfare).

Don-Yehiya, E. (1987) *Sherutim Datiim U'Politika: Haqamatan VeIrgunam Shel HaMo'atzot HaDatiyot BeIsrael* [Religious Services and Politics: The Establishment and Organization of the Religious Councils in Israel] (Ramat Gan, Jerusalem, Bar-Ilan University and the Jerusalem Center for Public Affairs).

Doron, G. and Mevorach, B. (1982a). "Otonomia BeQabalat Hahlatot Tziburiyot BaRashuyot HaMeqomiyot BeIsrael — Tahalich o Totza'a" [Autonomy in Public Decision-Making in Local Authorities in Israel — Process or Outcome?] *Netivei Irgun U'Minhal*, 137-138, Winter.

— (1982b). "HaMa'anaq HaKelali VeHakhnasot HaRashuyot HaMe-qomiyot BeIsrael" [The General Grant and the Income of Local Authorities in Israel] *Riv'on LeKhalkala*, 114, September.

Dror, Y. and Gutmann, E. (eds.) (1961). *Mishtar Medinat Israel* (Osef Meqorot) [The Government of Israel] (Jerusalem, Hebrew University, Kaplan School for Economic and Social Sciences).

Efrat, E. (1976). *Arim VeIur BeIsrael* [Cities and Urbanization in Israel] (Tel Aviv, Ahiasaf).

— (1983). *Geografya Upolitiqa BeIsrael* [Geography and Politics in Israel] (Tel Aviv, Ahiasaf).

Elazar, D.J. (1981). "Ma'arekhet HaYehsim Bein HaRashuyot HaMeqomiyot VeHaShilton HaMerkazi BeIsrael" [The Interrelations between the Local Authorities and the State Government in Israel] *Seqira Hodshit*, 28, July.

Feinstein, R. (1971). "Menahel Ir BiMedinat Israel" [City Manager in Israel] *Netivei Irgun U'Minhal* 5(III), October.

Freund, Tz. (1977). "Mazkir HaRashut HaMeqomit" [The Town Clerk] (Ramat Gan, Bar-Ilan University, Institute for Local Government).

Fruman, D. (1972). "HaProblematika Shel Lishkat HaSa'ad" [The Problems of the Welfare Bureau] *Sa'ad* 2, March.

Gat, M. (1976). "Netunei Yesod LeMivneh HaRashuyot HaMeqomiyot" [Basic Data Regarding the Structure of Local Authorities] (Ramat Gan, Institute for Local Government, Bar-Ilan University).

Gaziel, H. and Bravi, M. (1981), "Otonomia Beqabalat Hahlatot Tziburiyot BaRashuyot HaMeqomiyot BeIsrael" [Autonomous Public Decision-Making in Israeli Local Authorities] *Netivei Irgun U'Minhal*, 136, Winter.

Giladi, D. (1973). *HaYishuv BeTequfat HaAliya HaRevi'it* [The Yishuv During the Fourth Aliya] (Tel Aviv, Am Oved).

Gol, S. (1979). "Hebetim Hevratiim BeTikhnun HaTifrosset Ha-Geografit Shel Okhlosyat Israel" [Social Aspects in Planning the Geographical Distribution of Population in Israel] *Tikhnun Sevivati* December.

Goldman, M.D. (1973). "Hoq HaTikhnun VeHaBeni'ya BeMivhan HaMetziut" [The Law of Planning and Building in Practice] *Ir VeAizor*, January.

Goreni, Y. (1973). *Ahdut HaAvoda 1919-1930: HaYesodot HaRa'ayoniim VeHaShita HaMedinit* [Ahdut HaAvoda 1919-1930: The Ideological Foundations and the Political System] (Ramat Gan, Tel Aviv University and HaKibbutz HaMeuhad).

Gradus, Y. and Krakover, S. (1977). "Sivug HaYishuvim HaIroni'im BeIsrael Al Basis HaTa'asuka" [The Identification of City Groups in Israel on an Occupational Basis] *Ir VeAizor*, January.

Green, D. (1984). in *Kesafim*, March 12, 1984.

Bibliography

Gurevitz, D. and Gratz, A. (1940). *HaYishuv HaYehudi BeEretz Israel* [Jewish Settlement in the Land of Israel] (Jerusalem, HaMahlaqa LeStatistica, The Jewish Agency for Palestine).

Gurion (Wager), M. (1957). *Mavo LeToldot HaShilton HeMeqomi BeIsrael* [An Introduction to the History of Local Government in Israel] (Jerusalem, Beit HaSefer LeMishpat U'LeKhalkala).

Halevy, Y. (1975). "Minhal Ko'ah Adam BeIriyat Tel Aviv-Yafo" [Personnel Administration in the Tel Aviv-Yafo Municipality] (Ramat Gan, Bar-Ilan University, Department of Political Studies).

Hecht, A. (1972). "Mashber BaMeshek HaKaspi Shel HaRashuyot HaMeqomiyot" [Crisis in the Financial Management of Local Authorities], *Ir VeAizor*, October.

— (1985). "Hitpathut Taqtzivei HaRashuyot HaMeqomiyot BiShnot HaShiv'im" [The Development of Local Authorities in the 1970s] *Ir VeAizor*, December.

Hecht, A. and Gager, R. (eds.) (1984). "Tmurat Arnonat HaRekhush — Seqira Kelalit Ve'Hitpathut HaNusha LeHaluqata Bein HaRashuyot HaMeqomiyot" [Substitute Allocation for Municipal Property Tax — A General Review and the Development of the Formula of its Distribution Among Local Authorities] (Jerusalem, Ministry of Interior).

Herbstman, M. (1979). "Arnona Kelalit — Nituah Netunim" [General Municipal Taxes — Data Analysis] (Jerusalem, Ministry of Interior).

Herut Movement (1966). *HaVe'ida HaArtzit HaShminit Shel Tenuat HaHerut, Din VeHeshbon* [The 8th National Convention of the Herut Movement, A Report] (Tel Aviv).

— (1975). *HaVe'ida HaArtzit Ha-12, Din VeHeshbon* [The 12th National Convention, A Report] (Tel Aviv).

Horowitz, D. and Lisak, M. (1977). *MiYishuv LiMedinah* [From Yishuv to State] (Tel Aviv, Am Oved).

Israel Institute for Urban Research and Information, Ltd. (1973). *Reforma Munitzipalit BeArei Gush Dan* [Municipal Reform in the Dan Metropolitan Area] (Commissioned by the Ministry of Interior, Tel Aviv).

Jeraisi Committee (1973). (See Committee to Determine the Structure of Expenditures in Arab Local Authorities).

Kalchheim, Ch. (1976). *Iriyat Yerushalaim U'Misredei HaMemshala: Pereq BeYahasei Gomlin Bein HaShilton HaMerkazi LeVein HaShilton HaMeqomi* [The Municipality of Jerusalem and the Government Ministries" A Case Study in Central and Local Government Relations] (Ph.D. Thesis, submitted to the Senate of the Hebrew University, Jerusalem).

— (1979). "HaMeqorot Hakaspi'ym Shel HaRashuyot HaMeqomiyot VeHaTelut Bamemshala Be'enei Anshei Hashilton HaMeqomi BeIsrael" [The Financial Resources of the Local Authorities and the View of Local Government Leaders in Israel of their Dependence on the Government] *Medina, Mimshal VeYahasim BeinLeumiym*, 13, Winter.

— (ed.) (1980). *Biqoret U'Piquah Heshbonai BaRashuyot HaMeqomiyot* [Control and Supervision in the Local Authorities] (The 7th Conference on Local Government and Administration, Ministry of Interior, Jerusalem).

Kalchheim, Ch. and Rozevitz, Sh. (1980). "Mosdot HaBiqoret BaRashuyot HaMeqomiyot" [Control Institutions in the Local Authorities] in Kalchheim (ed.) (1980).

Karmon, N. and Hill, M. (1979). "Shiqum Shekhunot Metzuqa BeIsrael" [Renewal of Distressed Neighborhoods in Israel — First Report] (Haifa, The Technion, Shmuel Ne'eman Institute for Advanced Research in Science and Technology).

Katz, M., et al. (1982). "Irgun Azori U'Minhal HaPituah — Israel VeHaGalil" [Regional Organization and the Development Administration — Israel and the Galilee] (Publications on Problems of Regional Development) (Rehovot, Settlement Study Center).

Katzav, M. (1983). "Hevra VeKhalkala BeShiqum Shekhunut" [Society and Economy in Neighborhood Renewal] (Ramat Gan, Bar-Ilan University, Institute for Local Government).

Kfir, A. (1971). "LeShe'elat Menahel Ir" [On the Issue of City Manager] *Netivei Irgun U'Minhal*, 5 (111) October.

King, P. and HaCohen, O. (1986). "Va'adei Shekhunut BeIsrael" [Neighborhood Committees in Israel] (Jerusalem Center for Public Affairs).

Bibliography

Kokhav, D. (1969). "HaVa'ada HaBein-Misradit LeMediniyut Pizur Ochlosia" [Inter-Ministerial Committee for Population Dispersion Policy] (Jerusalem).

Kubersky Commission (1975). (See the Commission to Improve the Financing of Local Authorities).

Kubersky, H. (1965). "Yahasei HaShilton HaMerkazi VehShilton HaMeqomi BiTehum HaHinukh," *Yahasei HaGomlin Bein HaShilton HaMerkazi U'Bein HaShilton HaMeqomi* ["The Relationships Between the Central and Local Government in the Field of Education," in *Yahasei HaGomlin*, etc. (Tel Aviv, Israel Center for Management).

Lanir, Y. (1978). "HaKibbutz KeMa'arekhet Medinit VehaMoked HaRa'ayoni Shelo — Hebetim Hitnahagutiim Ve Tifkudiim Shel HaKibbutz BeTahalikh Qabalat Hahlatot Hamedhaivot et Haverav" [The Kibbutz as a Political System and its Ideological Focus — Behavioral and Functional Aspects of the Decision-Making Process] (M.A. Thesis, Ramat Gan, Bar-Ilan University).

Levy, Y. (1980). "Hoq HaTikhnun VeHaBeniya, 5725-1965" [The Law of Planning and Building] *Da Et HaHoq* (Jerusalem, Information Center in cooperation with the Ministry of Justice and the Ministry of Interior).

Lichfield, N. (1971). *Arim Hadashot BeIsrael: Estrategiat Pituah* [New Towns in Israel: Development Strategy) (Jerusalem, Ministry of Housing, Vols. 1-3).

M.R.B. Company (1978). "Tahshiv LeHaktza'at Taktziv HaPituah LaRashuyot HaMekomiot" [Calculation to the Allocation of the Development Budget to Local Authorities] (Submitted to the Ministry of Interior, Jerusalem).

Ma'oz, M. (1962). "HaMimshal HaMeqomi BaYishuvim HaArviim BeIsrael" [Local Government in Arab Settlements in Israel] *HaMizrah HeHadash* vol. 12.

Marom, Z.R. and Rozevitz, S. (1986). "HaMinhal HaTziburi BeRe'i Tlunut HaTzibur" [Public Administration as Reflected in Citizen Complaints] (Jerusalem, Jerusalem Center for Public Affairs).

Martines, L. and Hofman, H. (1981). *Igudei Arim BeIsrael* [City Associations in Israel] (Jerusalem, Ministry of Interior).

Menuhin, N. and Ludmir, H. (1982). "HaNidbakh HaSheni Shel HaShilton BeIsrael, HaShilton HaMehozi" [The Second Layer of the Government in Israel, The Regional Government] (Jerusalem, Ministry of Energy and Infrastructure, National Council for Research and Development and the Center for the Study of Rural and Urban Settlement).

Mevorach, M. (1981). "Hanhenim Mehagera'on BeTaqtzivei Ha-Rashuyot HaMeqomiyot" [The Beneficieries from the Deficit in the Budgets of Local Authorities] *Quarterly for Economics*, 10-111, November.

Ministry of Construction and Housing (1984). "Tamritzim Ve-Halva'ot" [Incentives and Loans] (Jerusalem).

Ministry of Interior (1967). "Va'adot HaRashuyot HaMeqomiyot, Samkhuyoteihen, Defusei Avodatan" [The Committees of Local Authorities, Their Authorities and Working Patterns] (Jerusalem).

— (1972a). "Hora'ot Bidvar Qabalat Ovdim LaRashuyot HaMekomiot" [Instructions Regarding Acceptance of Employees to the Local Authorities] (3rd edition) (Jerusalem).

— (1972b). *Tokhnit LaTifroset HaGeografit Shel Ochlosyat Israel Bat 5 Milyonim* [The Plan for Spatial Distribution of 5 Million Population in Israel] (2 vols.) (Jerusalem).

— (1973). "Pe'ulut Misrad HaPnim — Sqira Liqrat HaDiyun al Taqtziv Misrad HaPnim Lishnat Hakesafim 1973/74" [The Activities of the Ministry of Interior — A Review for the Budget Year 1973/74] (Jerusalem).

— (1978). "Totz'ot HaBehirot LaRashuyot HaMeqomiyot — 1978" [Results of Elections to the Local Authorities — 1978] (Jerusalem).

— (1982). "HaTaqtzivim HaRegilim Shel HaRashuyot HaMeqomiyot LiShnat HaKesafim 1981" [The Regular Budgets of Local Authorities for the Fiscal Year 1981] (Jerusalem).

Morag, A. (1967). *Mimun HaMemshala BeIsrael — Hitpathut U'Veayot* [The Financing of the Government in Israel — Development and Problems] (Jerusalem, Magnes).

Naor, G. (1972a) *Din VeHeshbon LeSivug Arei Pituah* [A Report for Classification of Development Towns] (Jerusalem, The Inter-

Bibliography

Ministerial Commission for the Classification of Development Towns).

— (1972b). "Hamlatzot Mitokh Din VeHeshbon Va'adat HaMumhim LeInyan Sivug Ayarot HaPituah" [Recommendations from the Report of the Specialists' Commission on the Classification of Development Towns] *Tiknun Sevivati*, 21-22, July-December.

Naor G., et al. (1978). "HaShilton HaMeqomi BeIsrael, Ma'amado VeTafkidav" [The Status and Roles of Local Government in Israel] (Rehovot, Center for the Study of Rural and Urban Settlement).

Petah Tikva Municipality (1964). *Petah Tikva — MiToldot HaMoshava VehaIr* [Petah Tikva — From the History of the Moshava and the City] (Petah Tikva).

Reches, A. (1967). "Arvi'yei Israel LeAhar 1967 — Hahrafata Shel Be'ayat HaOrientatzia" [The Arabs of Israel After 1967 — The Exacerbation of the Orientation Problem] (Tel Aviv, Shiloah Institute).

Reichman, Sh. (1973). "Al Teqefut HaTochni'yot LaTifroset Ha-Geografit Shel Ochlosyat Medinat Israel" [On the Validity of the Spatial Distribution Plans of Israel's Population] *Ir VeAizor*, April.

Reuveni, Y. (1981). "Shvitot BeIsrael: HaHebet HaSektoriali" [Strikes in Israel: the Sectorial Aspect] *Riv'on LeKhalkala*, 110-111, November.

— (1985). "Minhal Mangenon Munitzipali VeZiqato LaMa'arekhet HaMemshaltit" [Municipal Personnel Administration and its Tie to the Governmental System] (Ramat Gan, Bar-Ilan University, Institute for Local Government).

Revital, Sh. (1984). *Dinei HaTikhnun VehaBeni'ya* [The Laws of Planning and Building] (Tel Aviv, Sadan).

Rosen, D. (1973). "Seqer Munitzipali" [Municipal Review] (Jerusalem, Ministry of Interior).

— (1978). "Shesh Ma'archot Behirot LeIriyot VeleMoetzot Meqomiyot Ivriyot BeShloshim Shnot HaMedina" [Six Election Campaigns in Jewish Municipalities and Local Councils] (Jerusalem, Ministry of Interior).

413

Rotenberg, S.S. (1956). *HaMesheq Hakaspi Shel HaRashut HaMeqomit* [The Financial Administration of the Local Authorities] (Jerusalem, Hotza'at Sefarim Munitzipaliim).

Rozevitz, Sh. (1984). "Mahzor Asaqim Munitzipali BeIsrael" [The Political Business Cycle in Israel: Local Government] *Riv'on LeKhalkala*, 123, December.

Rupin, A. (1925). "HaHityashvut HaHaqlait Shel HaHistadrut HaTzi'yonit BeEretz Israel, 1904-1924" [The Agricultural Settlement of the Zionist Organization in Palestine, 1904-1924] (Tel Aviv, Dvir).

Sanbar Commission (1981). (See the State Commission on Local Government).

Sanbar, M. (1979). "Tfissot Hadashot Bemivneh HaShilton HaMeqomi BeIsrael" [New Concepts in the Structure of Local Government in Israel] (Ramat Gan, Bar-Ilan University, Institute for Local Government).

Segev, T. (1984). *1949 — HaYisraelim HaRishonim* [1949 — The First Israelis] (Jerusalem, Domino).

Shafat, A.Y. (1979). "Rashuyot Meqomiyot V'Mosdot Tzadaqa Vahesed" [Local Authorities and Welfare Institutions] *Sefer Zikaron LeAvraham Shpigelman* (Tel Aviv, Moreshet).

— (1984). "Bhira Yeshira Shel Rashei Rashuyot Meqomiyot — Sikumei Beinaim" [Direct Election of Mayors — Interim Report] (Jerusalem, Ministry of Interior).

Shahar, A., et al. (eds.) *Arim BeIsrael, Miqra'a* [Cities in Israel, A Reader] (Jerusalem, Akademon).

Shapira, Y. (1975). "Ahdut HaAvoda HaHistorit" [The Historic Ahdut HaAvoda] (Tel Aviv, Yad Tabenkin).

Sharon, D. (1968). "Igud Kolelani LeShituf Azori" [Comprehensive Union for Regional Cooperation] *Devar HaShilton HaMeqomi*, August-September.

Sharkansky, I. (1984). "Taktziv BiTnaei Inflatzia T'lat Sifratit: Israel" [Budget in a Situation of Three-Digit Inflation: Israel] *Iyunim BeVikoret HaMedina*, 37 (Jerusalem, The State Comptroller's Office).

Bibliography

Shechter, Y. (1975). "Mishnato Shel A.D. Gordon" [The Ideas of A.D. Gordon] (Tel Aviv, Dvir).

Shereshevsky, R., et al. (1968). "Me'ah Shana VeOd Esrim" [One Hundred Years and Twenty More] (Jerusalem, Ma'ariv).

Shpanitz Committee (1984). (See the Committee to Suggest Rules for Preventing Conflicts of Interest By Elected Representatives in Local Authorities).

Sicron, M. and Lassman, B. (1976). "HaTmurut BeOchlosyat Mehozot HaAretz BaShanim 1961-1972" [Changes in the Geographical Distribution of the Israeli Population in 1961-1972] *Ir VeAizor* January.

Silverstone, M. (1965). "Hitpathut HaYahsim Bein HaShilton HaMerkazi U'Vein HaShilton HaMeqomi BiMedinat Israel Minequdat Re'uto Shel HaShilton HaMerkazi," *Yahasei HaGomlin Bein Hashilton HaMerkazi U'Vein HaShilton HaMekomi* [The Development of Relationships Between Central and Local Governments in Israel from the Central Government's Point of View," in *The Relationship Between the Central Government and the Local Governmentt* (Tel Aviv, HaMerkaz HaYisraeli LeNihul).

Slutzky, Y. (1973). *Mavo LeToldot Tenu'at HaAvoda HaYisraelit* [An Introduction to the History of the Israeli Labor Movement] (Tel Aviv, Am Oved).

State Comptroller (1969). *Annual Report 19* (Jerusalem).
— (1974). *Annual Report 24* (Jerusalem).
— (1975). *Annual Report 25* (Jerusalem).
— (1976). *Annual Report 26* (Jerusalem).
— (1979). *Annual Report 29* (Jerusalem).
— (1980). *Annual Report 30* (Jerusalem).
— (1981). *Annual Report 31* (Jerusalem).
— (1982). *Annual Report 32* (Jerusalem).
— (1983). *Annual Report 33* (Jerusalem).
— (1984). *Annual Report 34* (Jerusalem).
— (1985). *Annual Report 35* (Jerusalem).
— (1986). *Report on Local Government* (Jerusalem).

Steinman, Y. (ed.) (1974). *Herkev Hachnasot HaRashuyot HaMeqomiyot* [The Composition of Local Authority Income] (Jerusalem, The 6th Conference on Local Government and Administration, Ministry of Interior).

— (1975). "Meqomam Shel HaMisim HaIroniim BeMa'arekhet Shituf HaHachnasot" [Municipal Taxes in the Participating Revenue System] *Ir VeAizor*, February.

Swirsky, Sh. (1981). *Lo Nehshalim Velo Menuhshalim: Mizrahiim VeAshkenazim BeIsrael — Nituah Sotziology VeSihot Im Pe'ilim U'Peilot* [Not Distressed and Not Deprived: Oriental and European Jews in Israel — A Sociological Analysis and Discussions with Activists] (Haifa, Mhebarot LeMehqar U'LeViqoret).

Tax Museum (1968). *Hitpathut HaMisim BeEretz Israel* [The Development of Taxes in the Land of Israel] (Jerusalem).

Tel Aviv Municipality (1945). *Sefer HaShana Shel Iriyat Tel Aviv, 1945* [The Tel Aviv Municipality Yearbook, 1945] (Tel Aviv).

Torgovnik, E. (1971). "Menahalei Arim VeNeyetraliyut BeMinhal" [City Managers and Administrative Neutrality] *Netivei Irgun U'Minhal*, 5(111) October.

Treasury-Interior (1982) [Budget Proposal for Fiscal Year 1982 — Ministry of Interior] (Jerusalem).

— (1984). [Budget Proposal for Fiscal Year 1984 — Ministry of Interior] (Jerusalem).

— (1986). [Budget Proposal for Fiscal Year 1986 — Ministry of Interior] (Jerusalem).

Treasury-Israel Lands Authority (1973). [Budget Proposal for Fiscal Year 1973 – Israel Lands Authority] (Jerusalem).

— (1982). [Budget Proposal for Fiscal Year 1982 — Israel Lands Authority] (Jerusalem).

Vilnai, Z. (1960). *Yerushalaim Birat Israel* [Jerusalem — the Capital of Israel] (Jerusalem, Ahiever).

Vitkon Commission (1964). (See the Commission for the Examination of the Tax System in the Local Authorities).

Yagid, B.Z. (1979). "Toldot Biqoret HaMedina BeRashuyot Meqomiot" [The History of State Control in Local Authorities] *Iyunim BeVikoret HaMedina*, 30 (Jerusalem).

Bibliography

Yardeni, Tz. (1974). "HaMivne HaIrguni HaFormali Shel Iriyot BeIsrael — Hatza'a Lediyun" [The Formal Organizational Structure of Municipalities in Israel — A Suggestion for Deliberation] (Jerusalem, Association of Town Clerks in Israel).

Yardeni, Tz. et al., (eds.) (1976). *Sefer HaKeness HaShishi LeShilton U'leMinhal Meqomi* [The Proceedings of the 6th Conference on Local Government and Administration] (Jerusalem, Ministry of Interior).

Yzre'el, A. (1980). "HaMissui HaIroni BeIsrael — Alut U'Yeilut" [Municipal Taxation in Israel — Cost and Efficiency] *HaRiv'on Ha Yisrael: LeMissim*, 44.

Weiss, Sh. (1973). *Haifa — Metziut Medina VeEtgar* [Haifa — Reality, State and Challenge] (Haifa, Renaissance).

— (1973). *HaShilton HaMekqomi BeIsrael* [Local Government in Israel] (Tel Aviv, Am Oved).

Zuckerman-Bar'eli, H. (1978). "Gormim LeAzivat Ir Pituah" [Causes for Leaving Development Town] *Riv'on LeKhalkala* 98, September.

Index

Acre, 154, 245
Administration for Employees of Local Councils, 229
Afridar Housing Company, 68
Afula, 14
Agudat Israel (party), 136, 137, 138, 154
Ahdut Ha'avoda (party), 135, 136
Allon Plan, 114
Amidar, 68
Arab local councils, 149, 152, 153, 205, 245-250, 324, 336, 337, 345, 357
Arab villages, 9, 15, 16, 32, 191, 192
Arad, 87
Ariel, 115
Ashdod, 140, 157
Association of Local Treasurers, 49
Association of Town Clerks, 49
Bank of Israel, 346, 352, 255, 356, 361
Bank of Local Government, 204
Bat Yam, 14, 98, 183, 227
Beersheba, 96, 105, 157, 160, 245
Beit Dagan, 153
Beit She'an, 154
Beit Shemesh, 156, 232
Bnei Brak, 14, 29, 154, 157, 244
Book of Statutes, 165
British rule (see also Mandatory government), 6, 8, 10, 11, 12, 13, 131, 165, 166, 167, 192, 201, 265, 339
Carmiel, 154
Citizens' Rights Movement (party), 137
Civil Service Commission, 235
Commission for the Improvement of Financing of Local Authorities (Kubersky Commission), 343, 347, 356, 360, 362-363
Commission for the Study of Methods of Taxation in the Local Authorities (Vitkon Commission), 296, 360, 361-362
Commissioner for Complaints from the Public (see also State Comptroller), 47
Committee for the Preservation of Agricultural Land (CPAL), 115-117
Communist (party), 246
Company for Automation, 204
Compilation of Regulations, 165
Dan region, 18, 23, 194, 195
Degania, 6, 7, 91
Democratic Movement (party), 153
Dimona, 153, 154, 232
Eilat, 168, 317
Environmental Protection Service, 344
Even Yehuda, 153, 158
Free Center (party), 137
Gahal (party), 136, 137, 140, 157
Ganei Tikva, 244
General Zionist (party), 7, 9, 131, 132, 133, 134, 135, 144, 145, 146, 157
Givat Shmuel, 187
Givatayim, 29, 154, 218, 232
Government Tourist Corporation, 68
Gush Emunim, 114
Hadera, 14
Haifa, 12, 21, 22, 29, 48, 97, 101, 140, 141, 143, 144, 151, 154, 158, 170, 194, 244, 245
Hapoel Hamizrachi (party), 133
Hazor, 153, 244

Index of Laws

ABOUT THE AUTHORS

Professor Daniel J. Elazar is President of the Jerusalem Center for Public Affairs, Director of the Institute for Local Government at Bar-Ilan University, and Senator N.M. Paterson Professor of Political Studies at Bar-Ilan University. He was Chairman of the Subcommittee on the Structure of Local Authorities of the State Commission on Local Government (Sanbar Commission). He has published widely on local government and the government of Israel.

Dr. Giora Goldberg is Senior Lecturer in the Department of Political Studies at Bar-Ilan University and also teaches at the Department of Political Science at Tel Aviv University. He has published tens of papers in periodicals and collections in Israel, the United States and Europe on topics relating to Israeli politics.

Arye Hecht is the Director of the Local Government Section and Accountant for Municipalities in the Ministry of Interior. He teaches "Local Authority Financing" at the Sapir College in Shaar HaNegev and is a doctoral candidate in the Department of Political Studies at Bar-Ilan University.

Dr. Chaim Kalchheim is Senior Lecturer at the Institute for Local Government and the Department of Political Studies at Bar-Ilan University. He is the Deputy Director of the office of the Commissioner for Public Complaints in the office of the State Comptroller. He has published articles on local government in Israel in various publications in Israel and abroad.

Dr. Israel Peled has been a member of the Zionist Executive and the Board of Governors of the Jewish Agency since 1973. He was the Mayor of Ramat Gan from 1969 to 1983 and Chairman of the World Maccabi movement from 1973 to 1987. He has taught "Legal Aspects of Local Authorities" at the Institute for Local Government at Bar-Ilan University.

Dr. Jacob Reuveny is Senior Lecturer at the Department of Political Studies and the Institute for Local Government at Bar-Ilan University. He has published books and research articles on contemporary public administration in Israel and managerial history and is currently writing a book on the Mandate government.

Professor Ephraim Torgovnik is Professor of Political Science at Tel Aviv University. He has published numerous articles on public policy in Israel. He has served on the council of the Tel Aviv Municipality since 1985 and became deputy mayor in 1987.